The Sustainable Society

edited by
Dennis Clark Pirages

The Praeger Special Studies program—utilizing the most modern and efficient book production techniques and a selective worldwide distribution network—makes available to the academic, government, and business communities significant, timely research in U.S. and international economic, social, and political development.

The Sustainable Society

Implications for Limited Growth

PRAEGER SPECIAL STUDIES IN U.S. ECONOMIC, SOCIAL, AND POLITICAL ISSUES

Praeger Publishers   New York   London

Library of Congress Cataloging in Publication Data

Main entry under title:

The Sustainable Society.

   (Praeger special studies in U.S. economic, social,
and political issues)
   Includes bibliographies.
   1. Economic development—Addresses, essays, lectures.
2. Environmental policy—Addresses, essays, lectures.
3. Energy policy—Addresses, essays, lectures.
I. Pirages, Dennis.
HD82.S875 1977   301.24   76-24365
ISBN 0-275-23890-3
ISBN 0-275-64760-9 student ed.

PRAEGER PUBLISHERS
200 Park Avenue, New York, N.Y. 10017, U.S.A.

Published in the United States of America in 1977
by Praeger Publishers, Inc.

789   038   987654321

Printed in the United States of America

ACKNOWLEDGMENTS

Every book that is written is in many respects a team effort. Among the members of the team that produced this book I owe special thanks to The Institute for World Order for funding the conference that initially brought together the authors of these selections, Michael Washburn for his continued support, ideas, and enthusiasm, Herbert York for his help in arranging the initial conference, and to William Greene, Sue Ritchie-Aguirne, Marjorie Cox, and Leesa Weiss for their specialized help at various stages in working with the authors and the manuscript.

CONTENTS

LIST OF TABLES

LIST OF FIGURES

1

INTRODUCTION: A SOCIAL DESIGN FOR SUSTAINABLE GROWTH

Dennis Clark Pirages

In the last quarter of the twentieth century the rapid economic growth that has been taken for granted during the course of the Industrial Revolution seems to be dramatically slowing or even coming to an end. The rate of economic expansion in most industrial economies over the last ten years has been significantly lower than it was during the previous decade. In 1974-75 the industrial world actually experienced an economic decline from which many countries have not fully recovered. Simultaneous high unemployment and double-digit inflation have added to economic worries. These events have given rise to new arguments of a semi-Malthusian nature purporting to explain the persisting economic malaise. While the validity of some of these arguments is questionable, others seem to make a great deal of sense, particularly in light of recent economic performance.

For the last 300 years industrial societies have been experiencing a cornucopian revolution of plenty. This revolution has been based on new technologies and the more effective utilization of fossil fuels in doing work previously done by human beings and draft animals. Discovery of these fossil fuel benefits and new technologies caused a "great transformation" in the norms, values, morals, and growth expectations within newly industrializing societies. Pre-industrial societies characterized by stability and resistance to change were rapidly transformed into dynamic and rapidly growing industrial economies by these discoveries. The increased abundance accompanying this transformation permitted many institutions that are now taken for granted to come into existence in industrial societies. The free market, the 40-hour work week, social security, mass democracy, and so on, have all been fostered by industrial abundance.

There is now increasing evidence that industrial societies are entering a postindustrial period in which this rapid industrial expansion is drawing to a close. Fossil fuels are no longer easily discovered and there are serious questions about the size of current reserves. The energy problem lies at the center of many other related concerns. Food produced in industrial societies requires a substantial fossil fuel input in the form of fertilizers, pesticides, mechanized equipment, and fuels. It is estimated that only about three calories of food energy are now produced for every calorie of fossil fuel going into the production of the U.S. corn crop. Preservation of a clean environment also requires additional energy. Mining and processing less rich grades of nonfuel mineral ores place additional burdens on the energy supply.

The intricacies of the many varieties of limits to growth arguments have been explicated elsewhere and are not repeated here. The subject matter of this volume is the nature of the "transition" from societies of rapid growth to postindustrial "sustainable societies" in which rapid growth may well be the exception rather than the rule. Although there is still much uncertainty about the rate of future industrial growth, a plausible case that this more frugal economic future is likely has been made. It seems prudent to begin to consider the social, economic, and political implications of slowed economic growth of a traditional nature, whether such growth slows because of its own internal dynamics or through political and economic actions or preferences of human beings.

The rapid economic growth characteristic of the industrial revolution has at least partially been built upon a generous fossil fuel subsidy. Coal and petroleum were in use long before the burst of industrialization that took place in the seventeenth and eighteenth centuries, but only in very modest amounts and not usually for large-scale industrial purposes. It was during the early stages of the Industrial Revolution that fossil fuel-based technologies made possible a large-scale substitution of fossil fuel energy for that previously produced by human beings and draft animals. These new technologies permitted human beings to tap solar energy stored in the form of fossil fuels in a systematic and significant manner. A symbiotic relationship developed between new industrial technologies and fossil fuels. New technologies led to a greater use of fossil fuels which, in turn, dramatically increased the efficiency of labor. This created greater incentives to harness ever more of what seemed to be an infinite supply of fossil fuels.

The history of industrial growth is written around fossil fuel innovations. In 1619 coke was first used to replace charcoal in blast furnaces; in 1640 an oil well was completed in Italy; the steam engine was invented in the 1760s; in 1829 a successful oil well was drilled in

Kentucky; in 1838 a steam-driven ship crossed the Atlantic Ocean; in 1860 the first internal combustion engine was built; the first large-scale application of natural gas occurred in the United States in 1884; in the early 1900s the expansion of oil production into Texas and California occurred; and in 1959 liquified natural gas was first shipped via cryogenic tanker. Each new industrial application of fossil fuels led to greater demand for them and sparked additional innovations in mining, drilling, transporting, and refining of fossil fuels.

It is impossible to estimate accurately the total impact of the fossil fuel subsidy on economic growth. Frederick Dewhurst in his book America's Needs and Resources, published in 1955, estimated that in 1850 in the United States work animals contributed 52 percent of total work energy, human beings contributed 12 percent, wind, water, and wood contributed 28 percent, and fossil fuels contributed only 7 percent.[1] By 1950, however, work animals and human beings each contributed less than 1 percent of total work energy and wind, water, and wood contributed 8 percent. Fossil fuels contributed over 91 percent of total work energy and this percentage has further increased since then. But this is only a rough estimate of the many changes that have taken place over the last 100 years as each farmer and factory worker became more productive by harnessing more "energy slaves." It has been this fossil fuel subsidy that has permitted worker productivity to rise above the level required for subsistence, which, in turn, has led to capital accumulation and economic growth. The fossil fuel subsidy has also had an unmeasured multiplier effect as it has freed large segments of society from day-to-day subsistence farming and indirectly financed scientific research and development which has permitted additional economic growth.

Economic growth based on fossil fuels is an ephemeral type of growth. The geologic processes by which solar income has been transformed into fossil fuel capital have not been widespread and have taken place over millions of years. An industrial world is now using fossil fuels at a pace that makes their geologic production rate infinitesimal by comparison. And the reserves of fossil fuels that appeared infinite related to early industrial needs now appear to be very finite indeed. While there is no real consensus among experts, most seem to agree that petroleum and natural gas will become scarce shortly after the year 2010, given optimistic assumptions about industrial growth. A more pessimistic growth scenario would stretch available supplies only by a few years. While coal will be available for perhaps two more centuries, there are many practical problems associated with using it as a substitute for petroleum and natural gas.

The absolute depletion factor is not necessarily most important when analyzing prospects for sustainable growth. Over the last decade the actual amount of the fossil fuel subsidy has been steadily diminishing. In the heyday of fossil fuel discovery it cost almost nothing in energy or economic terms to find and recover fuels. Even today in some parts of the Middle East it is still possible to drill a shallow and relatively cheap well and be certain of its productivity. But in most parts of the world, and particularly in the United States, this type of exploration and recovery is the exception rather than the rule. New reserves of petroleum and natural gas are now found in remote locations such as the Alaskan North Slope or in Soviet Siberia. The economic and energetic costs of transporting petroleum and natural gas from such remote locations are considerable. Drilling in more remote and inhospitable locations increases costs. The cost of drilling to greater depths to get petroleum and natural gas increases exponentially rather than in a linear manner along with depth. All of these added economic and energetic costs combine to shrink the amount of the current fossil fuel subsidy and restrict potential for future growth based upon it. Sometime within the next two or three decades a point will be reached where the subsidy will disappear entirely and one of the main sources of economic growth will disappear.

There are alternative sources of energy that may close the energy gap when petroleum and natural gas are no longer practical sources of energy. None of them promise a subsidy of the same magnitude; both capital and energy costs for alternatives are very high. Nuclear power is proving to be much more costly than its early proponents had hoped because of high construction costs, repairs, downtime, and deterioration. Even power from fusion, if and when it is ever brought "on-line," may not produce a great margin between energetic and economic costs and benefits. Alternative energy sources may meet the world's energy needs, but they will not likely provide a relatively cost-free subsidy of the magnitude of the original fossil fuel bonanza.

Edward Renshaw in his book The End of Progress has documented many other reasons why growth in industrial societies is slowly coming to an end.[2] Among these are environmental constraints, diminishing returns from economies of scale, and limits to the applications of automation. When the likely contribution of all the sources of past growth to future growth are analyzed and after the horizon has been scanned for potential new sources of abundance, it seems likely that the cornucopian growth of the Industrial Revolution is coming to an end. While no one can be certain that fantastic new discoveries do not lie just over the horizon, prudence dictates that planning be done within the bounds of realistic growth expectations.

SOCIAL DESIGN

Given the projected loss of a fossil fuel subsidy and numerous socioeconomic factors that indicate much slower economic growth in the future, there are two ways that industrial countries can respond. The first response is a lack of response. It is a response that has been characteristic of industrial problem solving. Advocates of the do-nothing philosophy caution against too much planning and social experimentation. They argue that a "free market" can optimally allocate resources during the coming period of less robust growth. The assumption is that economic and political "muddling through" that has supposedly served industrial societies well in the past will continue to do so in the future. What these advocates of "hands off" policies ignore is that muddling through can work during periods of rapid economic expansion when there is a large margin for waste and error. It will not work as well under conditions of slowed growth when resources must be reallocated to insure maximum social satisfaction with minimal real growth. There can be little doubt but that industrial societies can painfully adjust to limited growth by doing nothing and letting the unfettered market continue to allocate resources. But the consequences of such inaction would be severe, particularly to the poor who would be left with little purchasing power in a stagnant marketplace.

A second and preferred response to limited growth opportunities is to develop anticipatory institutions to use social design processes to plan rationally for a less affluent future. This requires a deeper understanding of the sources and consequences of economic growth and calls attention to a long agenda of unresolved social issues. Social design in anticipation of limited growth means establishing collective goals other than growth for the sake of growth. But this is difficult in societies in which goals previously have been deliberately kept implicit rather than explicit so as to avoid unnecessary political conflict.

Social design refers to a creative social change process by which preferred and viable social futures can be envisioned, collectively debated, and eventually implemented through mutually agreed upon transition strategies. At present, experience with social design and anticipatory institutions is minimal in capitalist societies and there are few precedents to rely upon. Social design requires two separate, but related, sets of skills. The skills of physical scientists and technologists are required to develop new sources of energy, to assess adequately the costs and benefits associated with these technologies, and to design new ways of more efficiently utilizing natural resources. But social design also requires the talents of social and behavioral scientists who must understand better the complex linkage between industrial growth syndrome and the norms, habits, and values that now define social reality.

Human beings are born into, develop within, interact with, modify, and are shaped by both the physical and social components of their environment. The physical component consists of natural systems and stocks of resources that human beings have manipulated and been manipulated by in seeking their ends. The social environment is composed of institutions and networks of social relationships that have created social processes that have shaped human beliefs and behavior. The industrial revolution has been financed by an abundant physical environment. This abundance has, in turn, shaped a social environment in which patterns of behavior dependent upon rapid growth are now highly rewarded. The present dilemma facing industrial societies is that past conditions of fossil fuel and natural resource abundance have created growth expectations that cannot be met from presently known stocks of natural resources or presently conceivable new technologies.

Thomas Kuhn in his The Structure of Scientific Revolutions has used the term "dominant paradigm" as a way of describing the lenses through which social groups--in his case groups of scientists--give meaning to social and physical phenomena.[3] In scientific research individuals concentrate on "normal science," as defined by the wisdom of a dominant paradigm, in choosing their research topics and in interpreting their findings. Dominant scientific paradigms become entrenched in the social system of science because of reward structures and vested interests that develop among those working within them. Few individuals have strong and innovative minds and nonconformity exacts a heavy psychological toll among those who deviate from established norms.

The dominant paradigm concept can be broadened easily to include entire social systems. A dominant social paradigm consisting of common values, beliefs, and shared wisdom about the physical and social environments is essential to any stable society. When a dominant social paradigm is shared by most members of a society, social and political stability is easily maintained. When fundamentally different social paradigms are encompassed within the same society, separatist pressures are certain to increase. Social paradigms are passed from one generation to the next through socialization processes. When the information, values, habits, and so on, passed on in a dominant social paradigm do not give value guidance in dealing with the social and physical environments, over time pressures for change are likely to grow. The present differences between the norms, values, beliefs, and so on, that have been nurtured by hundreds of years of industrial growth and the reality of physical and social limits to future growth represent an impetus for either rapid, perhaps revolutionary, social change in advanced societies or for the rational redesigning of these societies within sustainable growth constraints.

Human beings are affected by two types of evolution in response to changing environmental conditions. Biological evolution takes place within the pool of genetic information that is passed from generation to generation through reproduction. This "natural selection" is the product of human genetic endowment-environment interactions. Those individuals possessing genetic endowments more suited to environmental conditions have reproduced more successfully than those not so well suited. Natural selection is a process that is not amenable to human intervention despite the claims of optimistic geneticists. Natural selection takes place across many generations and it is a difficult process to map and understand.

A parallel type of social evolution also takes place. This "cultural" evolution occurs in the information that is verbally or symbolically passed from one generation to the next. This information has survival value similar to the information that is passed on through natural selection. The major difference in the two types of evolution is that social or cultural evolution is more amenable to human understanding and human control. Although the dominant social paradigm-- the matrix of norms, values, beliefs, and habits--may be very complex, the processes by which it is passed from one generation to the next are now well understood. Cultural evolution is a process that can be controlled by human efforts and this gives Homo sapiens an important survival weapon. Just as geneticists have been learning more about biological evolution and genetic codes, social scientists are developing a more sophisticated understanding of social evolution. Socialization processes are well understood and methods by which attitudes can be changed are known and employed every day by Madison Avenue. It is now possible to begin to design a sustainable society that can persist through the period of economic transition that will soon be upon us.

The design task is one of better understanding the growth limitations of both the physical and social environments, the habits and values that are now accepted parts of the dominant industrial paradigm, and devising both institutions and strategies to aid in a transition to a period of less robust economic growth. Designing a sustainable society requires moving beyond detached academic analysis to a confrontation of real-world value and behavior problems. Thanks to the innovative work of those whose efforts are included here and others, the nature of physical limits to growth is now much better understood and the agenda of future growth-related social problems has been outlined.

Designing a sustainable society consists of five closely related tasks:

To continue to increase collective understanding of the many types of limits on future economic growth. This includes not only its physical aspects, but also an analysis of the social dimensions of the problem which have heretofore been much neglected.

To analyze further the present industrial dominant social paradigm in order to understand the internal growth dynamics that make it both appealing and resistant to change. This includes calling attention to social issues that have been covered over by growth and that are only now beginning to emerge.

To outline a variety of sustainable preferred futures for both the industrial nations and the planet as a whole. Just as increasing anomalies within the growth syndrome now create discontent, a positive vision of a sustainable planetary future can provide incentives for stability during a transition to a more sustainable society.

To develop a transition strategy for reaching preferred futures. Utopias are useless in the absence of action rules for creating them. Such a transition strategy must be well-grounded in social theory as well as relevant to real world problems and decisions.

To implement transition strategies once they are developed. Social design for sustainable growth requires action as well as study and talk. Without willingness to get involved in social, economic, and political processes, alternate futures and transition theories are meaningless.

The task of designing a transition to sustainable growth is one of uprooting a firmly entrenched dominant social paradigm and replacing it with one that fosters sustainable expectations in the long run. The magnitude of this task is tremendous and should not be underestimated. It means taking the institutional "glasses" through which most people see industrial society and substituting "contact lenses." It means moving from a world in which bigger is better to one in which small is beautiful. The transition process requires an empirical understanding of the social and economic roots of the habits, values, and institutions of industrial society. It also involves designing social strategies to change those that are leading to future security-related social conflict.

This type of approach to designing a sustainable society is now much maligned in industrial societies. The main obstacle to its acceptance is a very narrow definition of freedom, one that stresses freedom of the individual without examining the diminution of collective freedom or good that can result from self-interest behavior. Garrett Hardin has exposed this basic flaw in social thinking in his classic essay "The Tragedy of the Commons."[4] He points out that supposedly rational individuals acting in situations where individual freedom and self-interest are maximized often unwittingly behave in a manner that not only harms the general welfare, but their own welfare as well. His example is the traditional English commons where villagers were once permitted collectively to graze their animals. Given a very high degree of individual freedom, untempered by concern for the common good, each herdsman attempts to put as many animals as possible on the commons. The inevitable result is collective self-destruction as the commons becomes overgrazed and livestock die. Apparently rational self-interest strategies on the part of each individual in a situation of maximum individual freedom and limited growth inexorably lead to a loss of freedom for the collective and even to self-destruction.

During the Industrial Revolution it appeared that maximizing individual freedom was the best way to maximize gain for the collective. Only a minimal amount of mutual coercion mutually agreed upon was essential to progress, given the open frontiers and rapid economic growth of the early industrial period. Given the present lack of open frontiers, the declining fossil fuel subsidy, disappearing economies of scale, and constricted growth of opportunities, collective growth is no longer enhanced by a laissez-faire approach.

But designing sustainable growth raises very delicate questions about who controls a transition to a sustainable society. The identity and powers of future social designers cause a great deal of concern among those who envision an Orwellian 1984 situation developing. Others see design and democracy to be antithetical. A meaningful answer to this question requires a realistic appraisal of political leadership and followership. There has never been a mass democracy in which the masses have actually ruled. Ruling oligarchies, elected elites in a mass democracy, have performed differently in representing a variety of interests, but in no case has there been a perfect congruence between mass desires and public policy. In fact, the extent to which an elected representative in a democracy should lead or follow is still a topic of debate among political philosophers. Social design is compatible with mass democracy as it has historically developed, but emphasis is placed on expert leadership rather than on followership.

Mass democracy has certain authority and legitimacy advantages during periods of transition, but it is certainly not the only form of political authority conducive to the social design process. In fact, only a small minority of contemporary political systems are presently democratically governed. Participants in social design can represent a variety of political experiences and philosophies. Social design presupposes no specific political ideologies, but it

requires a future orientation, a degree of altruism and human com-
passion, and a realistic assessment of the problems of making a
transition to limited growth on the part of all participants. It is a
process that can be carried out within present authority structures
whether they be democratic or dictatorial. It is not necessary, although it might be preferable, that authority relationships be changed.
It is the vision of authorities that must be transformed.

SUSTAINABLE GROWTH--THE AGENDA

There has been much recent discussion of limits to planetary
economic growth. The initial shock wave following publication of
The Limits to Growth in 1972[5] was accompanied by a sometimes
acrimonious debate between growth advocates and those whom they
accused of wanting no growth at all. In reality there have been few,
if any, proponents of no growth. Many have advocated carefully
planned economic growth with an aim of conserving energy and other
natural resources. Some have advocated variants of a steady-state
economy as does Herman Daly in a chapter that follows (see Chapter
5). But even advocates of a steady-state economy have foreseen significant growth in the quality of life taking place within the constraints
of limited resource consumption.

While there is still considerable debate about the economic
future of industrial countries, all but the "hard-core" technological
optimists have been sobered by economic performance in the 1970s.
A substantial period of economic collapse in 1974-75, simultaneous
unemployment and inflation, and new demands from proponents of
the emerging new international economic order have all had an impact on this optimistic economic thinking. But on the other hand
there are few remaining prophets of doom who see the industrial
world collapsing in a cloud of pollution or grinding to a halt because
petroleum and natural gas are no longer available.

Slow growth does not mean no growth, but it does create an
agenda of growth-related social and economic issues that must be
confronted. This agenda represents the substance of the social design task and the subject of the chapters that follow. Social design
raises matters of equity, social mobility, political stability, intergenerational ethics, and distribution of wealth that have been carefully covered over during the period of rapid economic expansion.

Sustainable growth is a difficult concept with which to deal,
but it seems to be the best guide to the future that we have at present.
It means economic growth that can be supported by physical and social
environments for the foreseeable future. An ideal sustainable society
would be one in which all energy would be derived from current solar

income and all nonrenewable resources would be recycled. In this respect a sustainable society would be akin to a steady state. In the real world it is difficult to approach such an "ideal" and we must instead deal with what is "practical." Sustainable growth is limited by abundance of natural resources as well as technologies that are on-line at any particular point in time. Growth dependent upon fossil fuels cannot be considered to be sustainable growth. Particularly in the less developed countries it makes little sense to predicate development efforts that will have an impact 20 to 30 years from now on an abundant supply of petroleum or natural gas. Nor does it make sense to make growth plans assuming that the promise of fusion power will be fulfilled in the very near future.

A sustainable society can only be created by confronting the agenda of problems caused by loss of a fossil fuel subsidy and the end of rapid industrial growth. The key element in future sustainable growth is an adequate energy supply. But alternatives to the fossil fuels are costly and each alternative has significant implications for society's future. The social costs and benefits of energy alternatives are described in the selections in Part I of this book.

A change in economic priorities is an essential part of sustainable growth. A more efficient economy that gets more production out of each unit of natural resources has more sustainable growth potential than does its less-efficient counterparts. Eventually all industrial economies will be forced to adjust to a world in which small is beautiful. Some will do it in a planned and orderly manner while others will undoubtedly experience pains of unexpected economic collapse. These economic concerns are described in Part II.

Slowed economic growth, whether by design or by neglect, raises additional social and political questions that are addressed in the rest of the book. Growth limitations have important implications for existing social hierarchies in industrial societies. One of the issues on the agenda of social design is the matter of equitable wealth distribution. Current compensation for work performed in industrial societies has been determined through protracted economic combat. Powerful labor unions have been able to extract large wage increases while the poor and unorganized have lost out in an economic struggle that took place in an atmosphere of increasing abundance. Differential wage increases didn't mean that much as long as all were getting more. Given likely limitations on future economic growth, combat over limited increments of real growth can be expected to become more intense. Prolonged and bitter labor disputes even in an era of growth have resulted in major worker-government confrontations in Great Britain, Japan, India, Italy, and even the United States during the past decade.

A new rationale for determining and distributing economic rewards is a priority item on the agenda of social design. The types of empirical information needed include clarification of criteria used in determining rewards and some conception of what people consider to be acceptable differences in incomes. Lee Rainwater has done much work in this area and has found that most people tend to be more egalitarian than common wisdom would have us believe (see Chapter 12).

There is also a set of political questions that is of very high priority. Critics of pluralist liberal democracy have pointed to a number of flaws that presently lead to less-than-optimal sustainable growth decision making. These include the role played by vested interests in opposing change, the lack of resolve in carrying out programs, difficulties in getting political leaders to extend planning horizons beyond the next election, and the problem of getting relevant information into the policy-making process. Add to these the threat to mass democracy as rapid economic growth comes to an end.

Designing new political institutions capable of coping with problems of limited growth represents an especially great challenge. Most large-scale changes in political institutions have taken place only as a result of revolutionary activity. Political scientists now possess a fairly accurate map of the existing political terrain although little in terms of a design perspective now exists in the discipline. The political implications of limited growth have been considered by very few political scientists and practicing politicians but they are certainly high on the agenda of sustainable growth concerns.

Finally, slowed economic growth in the industrial world has important implications for less developed countries dependent upon industrial markets. Sustainable growth policies in the developed world must be forged in cooperation with less developed countries if the gaps between rich and poor countries are to be kept from widening. A social design for sustainable growth requires cooperation between rich and poor countries and must provide for higher growth rates in the less developed countries which have not yet experienced the benefits of the Industrial Revolution.

NOTES

1. Frederick Dewhurst, America's Needs and Resources (New York: Twentieth Century Fund, 1955).

2. Edward Renshaw, The End of Progress (North Scituate, Mass.: Duxbury Press, 1976).

3. Thomas Kuhn, The Structure of Scientific Revolutions (Chicago: The University of Chicago Press, 1962).

4. Garrett Hardin, "The Tragedy of the Commons," in Toward a Steady-State Society, ed. Herman E. Daly (San Francisco: W. H. Freeman, 1973).

5. Donella Meadows et al., The Limits to Growth (New York: Universe Books, 1972).

ENERGY CHOICES AND
SUSTAINABLE GROWTH

The debate over growth prospects has gone through several phases. Publication of <u>The Limits to Growth</u> in 1972 first brought these new scarcity issues forcefully to public attention. The Malthusian curves printed by the MIT computer indicated a world in which population would continue to grow exponentially, per capita demands would rapidly increase, food production would fail to keep up with human needs, and fuel and nonfuel mineral reserves would rapidly dwindle. As the growth debate progressed to a new phase, however, the concept of generalized scarcity was replaced by a view that took account of significant differences among minerals, recognized that substitutions were possible in many cases, that new technologies would make ores and fuels that are presently not considered resources economically recoverable, and that rising prices would foster a more frugal society. More recently, the growth debate has focused on the steady-state economy concept. The steady-state economy is noted by resource conservation and recycling. Steady-state institutions would be responsible for stretching out reserves of natural resources and negating many of the Malthusian arguments.

At present the scarcity problem is not perceived as one of "running out" of any particular fuel or nonfuel mineral. It is recognized as a much more complex collection of problems. This complex "macroproblem" is much more difficult to deal with than are its component parts. It is possible, for example, to imagine continued improvements in agricultural technology, additional applications of fertilizers, and greater use of pesticides and herbicides overcoming projected world food shortages. It is also reasonable to assume that shortages of nonfuel minerals can be overcome by mining and processing less-rich grades of ore or by "harvesting" manganese nodules from the world's oceans. But these answers and suggested solutions to other scarcity-related problems assume an abundant future supply of energy.

An abundant future supply of energy, thus, lies at the core of the scarcity problem. The Industrial Revolution has been facilitated by an abundance of fossil fuels. These sources of energy, however, have been produced by very slow geological processes that have taken place over millions of years. At present, consumption of these fuels is taking place at an infinitely greater rate than is the formation of new supplies. While experts disagree on precisely how much petroleum and natural gas remains in the ground, estimates center on about 35 more years' consumption given current expectations of future increases in demand. Without adequate energy supplies, industrial growth would come to an end and the Malthusian-Meadows growth problems would remain unsolvable.

Just as a fossil fuel subsidy gave rise to a "great transformation" that created powerful industrial nations out of their preindustrial counterparts, the search for alternative sources of energy is likely to lead to a "great transition" as postindustrial nations adjust to the exigencies of the energy alternatives chosen. The current crop of suggested alternatives offers no panaceas, only difficult choices. There are advantages and drawbacks to each course of action. Abundance and sources of energy determine much about the nature of a society. For example, the United States consumes nearly three times as much energy on a per capita basis than does Switzerland because fossil fuels have been historically abundant in the former and not in the latter. Transportation networks, building design, and industrial processes are very much different in these two countries, the differences largely due to differing energy supplies.

A sustainable society is one in which future growth can be indefinitely sustained by available sources of energy. But each alternative source of energy has social and economic costs that will have a serious impact on the society that chooses it. Solar energy is obviously one preferred alternative because it is a renewable energy source and there need be no concern about depletion. Nuclear energy, on the other hand, is costly in both an economic and social sense given the danger of accident and sabotage and the need for strict security and perhaps a garrison state. In a sense we are designing a new society through the energy choices that we make. It is for this reason that the three chapters in Part I concentrate on the energy problem and the costs of energy alternatives.

In Chapter 2 Earl Cook examines the factors that shape the future of the fossil fuels. He points out that a fossil fuel subsidy has been essential to the Industrial Revolution. The subsidy results from the fact that more energy can be derived from fossil fuels taken out of the ground than go into obtaining them. The replacement of labor formerly done by man and beast by fossil fuel-driven machines lies at the core of industrial progress and has been accompanied by large increases in population and per capita energy demands. Unfortunately, the world's supply of fossil fuels, particularly petroleum and natural gas, is limited. The rapid switch from current solar income to fossil fuel capital that has been part of the Industrial Revolution has created a serious dilemma for energy-dependent complex societies. It is difficult to conceive of supporting so many people at such high standards of living by retreating to the limits imposed by current solar income. On the other hand, new energy alternatives are both costly and unproven.

Cook points out that the amount of the fossil fuel subsidy available is diminishing. It now costs more energy to get each barrel of petroleum out of the ground. An exponential imperative is operative in the energy industry. The cost of drilling new oil and gas wells doubles with every 3,600 feet of depth. While common sense indicates that a 30,000-foot well should cost only about six times as much as a 5,000-foot well, the actual cost is 130 times as great. Thus, going further and digging deeper to find petroleum and natural gas is an increasingly costly venture, one that continually chips away at the subsidy offered by each barrel of petroleum. Cook concludes his chapter, as does John Holdren in Chapter 3, by calling for renewed attention to energy conservation as a way of making present supplies of fossil fuels stretch further into the future.

In Chapter 3 John Holdren offers a systematic overview of the different types of costs that are attached to a variety of commonly suggested alternative sources of energy. He points out that the direct capital costs of alternatives represent only part of the bewildering array of other costs that must be considered in making future energy choices. When attempts are made to compare the aggregate costs of various energy alternatives some facts can be measured and compared, others can be quantified but are difficult to compare, and a significant number are impossible to quantify. Cost calculations for major energy alternatives are very complex, but Holdren concludes that each of them will exact much higher socioeconomic costs than society now pays.

Holdren injects another sobering note into his chapter when he estimates how soon each of these alternatives can be brought on-line. He uses 10 percent of 1975 energy consumption as a criterion for each alternative "making a significant contribution" and finds that most suggested alternatives could not provide this much energy before the year 2010. He also contends that it is very unlikely that more than one alternative source of energy could meet this criterion because of the all-out effort that would be required to bring each on-line. He concludes that when incremental costs of developing alternatives begin to exceed incremental benefits the gains of increasing energy consumption vanish. He echoes Cook's argument and contends that the United States is very near this point at the present time.

Nazli Choucri concludes this section by examining some international political implications of future energy choices. While some developing countries have recently gained new leverage in the international economy by their control of fossil fuel reserves, the industrial countries will be able to counter this in the future by virtue of their control over new energy technologies. The choice of new energy alternatives is obviously as much a political decision as it is an economic one.

Some countries will be big winners and others will be big losers depending upon the energy alternatives that are chosen. It is clear that the United States is becoming more dependent on external sources of virtually all fuels ranging from petroleum to uranium. The Soviet Union, by contrast, has extensive reserves of petroleum, natural gas, and coal. The United States will be a major source of new energy technologies in the future, but this will create foreign policy dilemmas. Development and export of nuclear technology is accompanied by the risk of nuclear weapons proliferation and even nuclear terrorism. The only certainty in the future energy international market is that it will be much more complex and decentralized than the present one that is centered on petroleum.

All three of these solutions stress the very high costs of opting for various alternatives to fossil fuels. But there is also a consensus that fossil fuels, particularly petroleum and natural gas, can remain a major source of energy for only a limited time. One obvious conclusion is that energy conservation combined with a greater emphasis on renewable and therefore sustainable energy sources is critical to the evolution of a sustainable society.

2

FOSSIL FUELS:
BENEFITS, COSTS,
AND FUTURE SUPPLIES
Earl Cook

Fossil fuels have provided mankind with an enormous natural subsidy. Far more energy can be gotten out of them than needs to be expended in their getting. This energy surplus represents work we have had neither to do nor to pay for. In nature work has been done in the conversion of solar energy into the chemical energy of plant food; in the concentration, preservation, and transformation of tiny organic packets of chemical energy into deposits of the fossil fuels; and in the differential movements of the earth's crust that created the proper depositional environments for all the fuels as well as geologic traps for the fugitive ones.

In 1900 an American coal miner produced in a six-day work-week energy equivalent to that consumed by 300 of his compatriots in a seven-day week. Much of the energy in the coal was wasted in the thermodynamic and mechanical inefficiencies of engines, power plants, and heating systems, but the net energy surplus was suffi-cient--with a great boost from petroleum--to transform an advanced agricultural society quickly into an advanced industrial society.

Today cheap energy from fossil fuels subsidizes mechanized, chemically assisted agriculture in the industrialized countries and makes it possible for 600 or more units of plant-food energy to be valued the same as one unit of human work (see Figure 2.1; human muscle energy cannot be shown on this scale, because at $3 per hour it costs about $6,000 per million BTUs). In the most efficient hand-agriculture societies, less than 20 units of plant-food energy are

An expanded and more detailed presentation of the ideas in this chapter is found in Earl Cook, Man, Energy, Society (San Francisco: W. H. Freeman, 1976).

FIGURE 2.1

Comparison of Price of Energy Derived from Fossil Fuels with Those Derived from Feed and Food

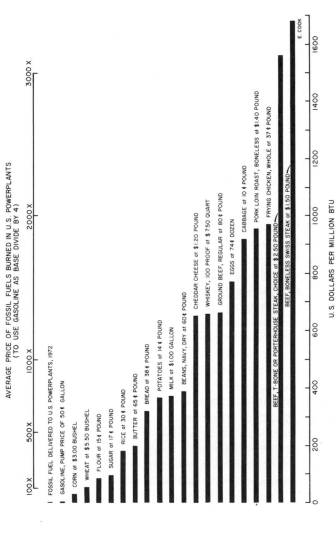

Except where otherwise indicated, prices are wholesale as of early February 1974.
<u>Source:</u> Compiled by the author.

obtained for each unit of human energy expended. Thus we have a
direct measure of the fossil-fuel subsidy. The subsidized units of
plant-food energy cannot be eaten directly, for there would be an
enormous surplus above the ingestive capacity of the population; in
the main they are diverted to animal feed which, in the United States,
at present is converted to edible animal products at an average energy
efficiency of about 5 percent for meat, 7 percent for poultry, and 15
percent for milk.

THE ROLE OF TECHNOLOGY

The natural subsidy, or net energy surplus, realized from any
natural energy stock or flux is a function of exploitation efficiency.
Technologic advances have greatly increased the energy profits from
coal and petroleum. Early coal-burning steam locomotives could
convert only 1 percent of the energy in the coal into propulsion of
themselves and their trains; later oil-burning locomotives achieved
better than 10 percent efficiency, an experimental coal-fired gas-
turbine locomotive about 16 percent, and modern diesel-electric
locomotives approach 30 percent efficiency. In the early years of
this century, thermal electric power plants had overall conversion
efficiencies of about 3.5 percent, whereas a large modern coal-fired
generating plant is 40 percent efficient. Such triumphs of economic
technology have increased greatly the amount of useful heat and work
available to those nations which have implemented the technologic advances through the construction and use of energy converters. Those
who could get a higher energy surplus from a ton of coal or petroleum
could afford to pay more for the raw fuel, and thus the world's fossil-
fuel resources have flowed toward the industrialized minority of the
world's nations.

Exploitative efficiency, however, is not a direct function of
technologic progress. Automotive technology, for example, has
made many advances in the past 75 years, yet the modern American
automobile is less efficient as a machine than it was 50 years ago.
The reason is that the automobile has been a source of rapture as
well as transport; the inefficiencies entailed in supplying rapture have
overwhelmed the efficiencies applied to transport.

DEPENDENCE ON FOSSIL FUELS

The high-energy nations, accounting for perhaps 30 percent of
world population, have grown utterly dependent on a continually increasing inflow of fossil energy. In the United States, 98 percent of

the gross energy consumption comes from natural gas, crude oil, and coal (see Figure 2.2). A high-energy nation or society, at the present time, may be defined as one in which per capita energy consumption is above 50,000 kilocalories (kcal) (200,000 BTUs) a day. No nation achieves that level without relying heavily on the fossil fuels; even Switzerland and Sweden, with their abundant hydroelectric power, import 80-90 percent of their energy needs in fossil form (see Table 2.1). The world average in 1971 was about 38,000 kcal per person per day. These numbers do not account for energy consumed as food, fuelwood, or dung; the latter two are the largest sources of energy in much of the world. The full range of daily per capita energy consumption by humans today is from less than 5,000 to 250,000 kilocalories.

World population appears to have increased, not steadily, but in surges related to abrupt increases in energy availability (see Figure 2.3). The most recent surge, which began in Western Europe in the Middle Ages, at first was sustained by waterpower, windpower, musclepower, and fuelwood--in other words, by renewable resources; but it is now sustained by fossil fuels--in other words, by nonrenewable resources.

COSTS AND BENEFITS OF FOSSIL ENERGY USE

The social costs of high fossil energy consumption are the subject of much concern, research, and legislation. The health costs of polluted air, the ecologic costs of oil spills and power-plant discharges, the esthetic costs of strip mining and oil drilling are in the front rank of a host of perceived adverse impacts of high energy use; in our minds and on the lips of our conscience are the urban sprawl, the rot of the inner city, the dreadful retreat from urbanity, the spread of dirt and fear that characterize many high-energy human communities; a stubborn pattern of debilitating diseases--cardiovascular, respiratory, malignant, mental, degenerative--confronts those who, like Japan in recent years, enter the high-energy world. Perhaps worst of all, friends multiply into strangers, children achieve their escape velocities and drift away into space before we have a chance to know them, and the rocks of church and state turn into weightless toys.

Thus we began feeling the costs of what Alvin Weinberg has called the Faustian bargain, which was made when we started using fossil fuels. Better to say when we started using up the fossil fuels, for that simple adverb reminds us that a nonrenewable resource, although inert, has a life history similar to that of a man. Like each of us, who starts to die when he is born, a nonrenewable resource starts down the path of depletion toward exhaustion as soon as it is utilized.

FIGURE 2.2

Approximate Flow of Energy through the U.S. Economy, 1971

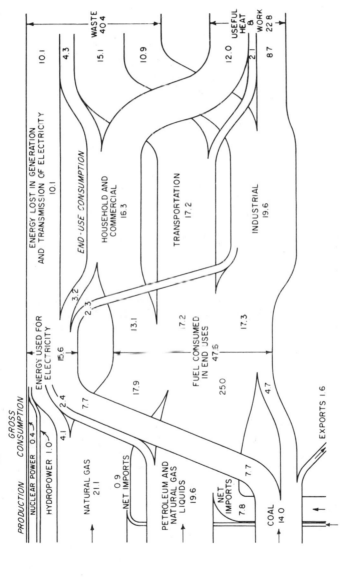

Note: Units are in 10^{12} Btu.
Source: Compiled by the author.

TABLE 2.1

1971 Per Capita Energy Consumption*

Country	capita daily energy consumption (kcal)	Percent (net) Imported
USA	222,400	10.6
Kuwait	201,900	NE
Canada	184,600	NE
Czechoslovakia	131,000	18.6
Bahrein	127,600	NE
East Germany	124,900	21.5
Belgium	121,000	94.6
Sweden	120,500	89.5
Developed Countries----	118,900----	
United Kingdom	109,000	46.8
Australia	107,800	NE
Denmark	105,500	100.0
West Germany	103,400	50.4
Norway	103,200	60.9
Netherlands	101,400	36.9
USSR	89,800	NE
Poland	86,500	NE
France	77,700	78.1
Switzerland	70,800	80.0
Japan	64,600	98.1
South Africa	57,300	27.0
New Zealand	55,800	58.0
Israel	52,600	0.1
Italy	52,600	91.1
World Average----	38,200----	
Argentina	34,900	11.7
Spain	33,000	82.9
Greece	29,100	69.8
Mexico	25,100	3.3
Iran	20,300	NE
Portugal	16,100	100.0
Peru	12,200	29.6
China	11,100	1.5
Brazil	10,200	53.7
Undeveloped Countries----	6,900----	
Egypt	5,600	NE
India	3,700	18.1
Indonesia	2,500	NE
Pakistan	1,600	51.5

NE = net exporter

*Fossil and nuclear energy and hydroelectricity; food, fuelwood, animal, and human power not included.

Source: Compiled by the author.

FIGURE 2.3

Population and per capita Daily Energy Consumption, 1,000,000 B.C. – 2000 A.D.

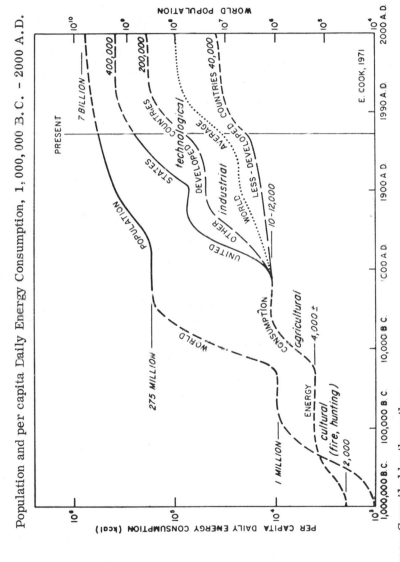

Source: Compiled by the author.

The benefits of high-energy use are not talked about these days as much as the costs. But we have received a great deal from the bargain. You and I may be afflicted with allergies, gout, and high blood pressure, but we have chemicals that control the symptoms and keep us going; we do not live in constant fear of epidemic contagion as our recent forebears did. We may complain about dirty rivers, but we do not turn aside the proffered glass of water because of the danger of typhoid or dysentery as our grandparents did and as we still must do in most of the low-energy places of the earth. We grow testy when we feel crowded, yet we don't have to pass the winter waking hours stifled in the one heated room of the house as most Americans did until the present century, and even the least Medicared-for among us is not forced to share a hospital bed with a stranger--a common practice in Europe and the United States until well into the nineteenth century. The average person in a high-energy, fossil fueled, society enjoys comforts, health care, and recreational and educational opportunities unobtainable by the Great Khan or the Sun King.

Had I been born 100 years before I was, but still in the United States, the chances are that my father would have been a farmer and I would have had no easy time escaping the toils of agriculture. The evolution of high-energy society is marked by a striking reduction in the farm portion of the work force, by a marked but later growth in the service portion, by an increase in the ratio of women workers to men, by the emergence of a large middle class, by a great decline in infant mortality and a lengthening of the average life span, by a later and more irregular decline in the birth rate, by an increase in the weight and height of its members, and by a decrease in the age of menarche. This pattern represents a more equitable distribution of the material benefits of energy use, a great rise in per capita income, much improved health conditions, and a striking increase in occupational and social mobility--all of which I think most of us would classify as substantial benefits. It does not, however, represent greater average leisure, compared either to primitive societies or to the advanced agricultural society of the High Middle Ages in Western Europe.

HOW MUCH LONGER?

A question of considerable interest to the industrial world is how much longer we can rely on the fossil fuels as our primary energy base. The question is of interest as well to the low-energy countries which have been trying to increase food supplies through mechanized and chemically fertilized agriculture and to move from an agricultural to an industrial economy. Unfortunately for those who seek information on this question, there is a considerable lack of agreement among the professed experts.

If one attempts to assemble relevant information, the hard facts appear to be as follows:

Energy consumed in a high-energy society is overwhelmingly of fossil fuel origin, and probably will continue to be for several decades. We can hope for the ultimate substitution of renewable energy resources such as solar radiation or of very abundant nonrenewable resources such as the deuterium in sea water for our present energy sources, but such salvation--if it proves possible--is a considerable distance off, and our energy problems for the rest of this century will be related mainly to utilization of fossil and, secondarily, nuclear fuels.

Although the geologic environments of the fossil fuels offer a high degree of order and predictability, their geographic distribution is very uneven. The world's known fossil fuel reserves are concentrated in the Persian Gulf area, the Soviet Union, and North America (see Figure 2.4).

By far the most used fossil fuel is crude oil; coal is second, natural gas third, shale oil and oil from tar sands make a negligible contribution. World consumption of crude oil has been increasing at a rate greater than 5 percent per year in times of economic growth.

Among the industrialized nations there is the maximum range of energy self-sufficiency (see Table 2.1), from those such as Mexico and the Soviet Union which are net exporters of energy and thus completely self-sufficient, to Denmark which imports 100 percent of its energy.

World crude oil reserves still are increasing faster than consumption and at the moment there is excess producing capacity. World coal reserves are sufficient for several hundred years at present rates of consumption. World natural gas reserves are large, but they are distant from and largely unconnected with the major demand centers. Striking features of the world picture are the dependence of the high-energy nations on fossil fuels, the highly uneven distribution of reserves, and the consequent fact that some nations are completely or largely dependent for their energy on foreign sources they do not control.

In the United States both production and known reserves of crude oil and natural gas are falling despite rising prices; imports of petroleum and its products are nearing the level of domestic production of crude oil. Figures for one week in March 1976 showed imports exceeding domestic production for the first time in U.S. history. Coal, of which the United States has large reserves, presents

FIGURE 2.4

Fossil Fuel Reserves of Selected Nations and Groups of Nations in 1969

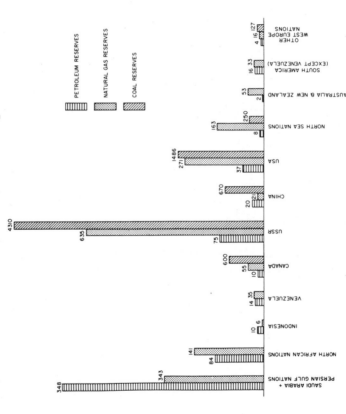

Sources: Petroleum and natural gas reserve estimates as of January 1, 1973, from Oil & Gas Journal, December 25, 1972. Coal reserve estimates based on Paul Averitt, 1969.

troublesome barriers to rapid increases in production: opposition to strip mining, a shortage of underground miners, a shortage of equipment (it now takes about seven years from the time of order to get delivery on a large dragline), the high sulfur content of much Midwest and Appalachian coal. Recent sharp increases in energy prices within the United States result from an effective cartel of foreign crude-oil-producing countries, from declining production of domestic oil and gas in the face of strongly rising demand, and from difficulties encountered in implementing the Clean Air Act of 1969.

Deposits of fossil fuels have sharp boundaries; they do not grade from rich core to lean penumbra. Consequently, the reserves in a single oil pool or coal seam are more a function of the cost of extraction than the price of the product.

THE EXPONENTIAL IMPERATIVE

The exponential imperative, the barrier in work cost that we invariably encounter when we challenge scarcity, pursue speed, or seek perfection, is well illustrated by curves of drilling cost against depth of oil and gas wells drilled in Texas. In 1971 the drilling cost doubled with each 3,600 feet of depth (see Figure 2.5). A hole drilled to 30,000 feet costs not six times more than one drilled to 5,000 feet, but 130 times more. Similar cost curves apply to enhanced recovery techniques in known oil fields. In the United States we have left behind more than two barrels of oil for each barrel of crude oil extracted, but we probably shall not see any substantial increase (to 40 percent or more) over the present 31 percent cumulative recovery ratio because of the cost barrier. We won't go far up the steepening slope of the cost curve before an alternative energy source or system becomes economically preferable. The moment it costs more to find and produce a barrel of "new" crude than it does to manufacture a barrel of substitute crude from coal, oil shale, or tar sands, there will be no more "undiscovered" crude-oil reserves or resources and the question of how much oil remains in the ground will be of no further importance, as long as a cheaper alternative is available.

There are at least three kinds of costs that tend to follow exponential curves: the costs of speed, the costs of scarcity, and the costs of perfection. To a large degree the economic efficiency of production has been the result of speed. Industrial historians tell us that U.S. industry caught up with and surpassed the maternal British industry by running cheaper machines faster. As long as speed had a low cost in human terms, as long as cheap fuel and iron ore were available, it was an attractive way to increase the material

produce of the natural subsidy. But inevitably we have come to the
steep part of that curve: the cost per seat-mile in the Concorde is
more than three times that of a seat-mile in the 747, and as the cost
of fuel increases, the gap widens.

FIGURE 2.5

Cost of Drilling and Equipping Oil and Gas Wells,*
United States, 1971

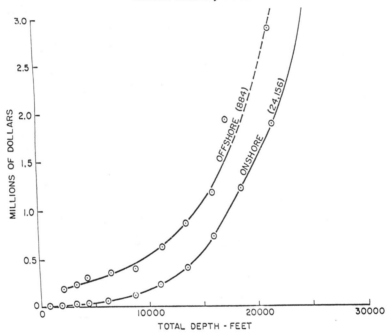

*Including dry holes.
Source: Based on Joint Association Survey.

FOSSIL FUELS, ENVIRONMENTAL QUALITY,
AND LIVING LEVEL

A high-energy economy based on the fossil fuels conflicts with
ideals of clean air, clean water, undisturbed scenery, and maintenance of fragile or complex supporting ecosystems. Energy use
and environmental quality are interdependent variables which cannot
be maximized simultaneously. But there is a third variable in the
system: the material level of living. Environmental quality can be

paid for in three ways: by increased energy costs in the prices of
goods and services; by decreased energy consumption; and by increased taxes to pay those environmental costs that are not internalized in the prices of goods and services. All three charges decrease
disposable income and thereby lower the material level of living.

As we look for deeper deposits of the fossil fuels farther away
from the centers of use and in hostile environments or recalcitrant
reservoirs, as we are forced to share the natural subsidy represented
by foreign fuels with the producing nations, and as we try to increase
agricultural production by using more fertilizer and machinery, our
costs increase. If we at the same time try to prevent oil spills, to
restore strip-mined land to its original contour, to eliminate the
noxious effluents of refineries, power plants, and automobiles, to protect "fragile ecologies" from invasion by pipelines and draglines, and
to ban the use of effective pesticides, we face increases in costs, some
of which, because they represent the pursuit of perfection, follow exponential (or almost) curves: for example, the cost of reducing sulfur
oxide discharges from petroleum refineries (see Figure 2.6) and the
cost of exhaust-emission controls on automobiles (see Figure 2.7).
Some environmental protection costs are not small, especially if we
try to approach perfect cleanliness and ecologic tranquillity while continuing to convert fossil energy into heat and work at a high rate.

FIGURE 2.6

Costs of Reducing Discharge of SO_2 from a Typical
U.S. Petroleum Refinery

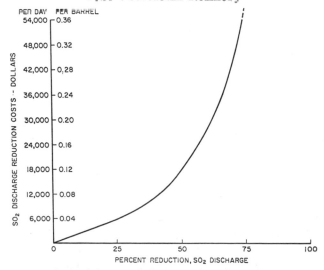

Source: Adapted from 1972 Annual Report of Resources for
the Future, Inc., p. 42.

FIGURE 2.7

Extra Cost of Cars with Emission Controls

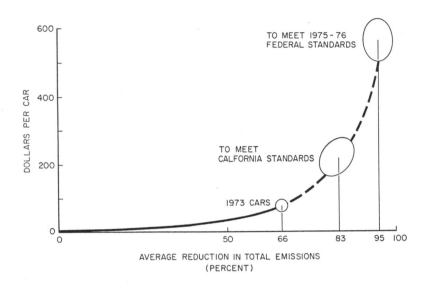

Source: Mobil Oil Corporation, 1973.

DEPLETION HISTORIES

The complete depletion histories of geologic resources which occur in relatively small, relatively shallow, sharply bounded deposits and which have a high utility or commodity value (based on the natural subsidy inherent in the resource) appear to be similar. Three such resources are mercury, silver, and crude oil.

On the scale of a single-vein system or oil field, there is no doubt that exhaustion takes place and that production and depletion are essentially synonymous, although production may be extended and depletion retarded by new discoveries, by new extraction or processing technology, by reduced transport costs, and by higher product prices. The production history of a mine or an oil field is a unique event, one that cannot be repeated.

When we move to the national or continental scale, the record is less clear, but far from contradictory. The more accessible and richer deposits are exhausted first. Increasing depth, leanness, and distance from centers of use impose rising costs as production increases. Let us look closely at the U.S. production histories of mercury and silver. The United States has accounted for about 10 percent of the world's mercury production but has only 2.4 percent of the remaining reserves. U.S. mine production of mercury peaked in 1877, although it has not yet ceased (see Figure 2.8). The relation of price to production suggests three main phases of exploitation: a waxing phase, during which price was a decreasing function of production; a mature phase, in which price and production were more or less in equilibrium; and a waning phase, during which production has been a decreasing function of price. In the waning phase successive surges in price have evoked progressively weaker responses in production. The global production curve, however, has not yet reached the waning phase. The pattern in silver (see Figure 2.8) is similar, with the flagging production responses to sharp price surges in the waning phase even more pronounced.

The waxing phase of such a history represents a period of falling real cost of the desired material because of new discoveries, cheaper transport, and technologic improvements in the exploitation system. The falling cost stimulates demand which in turn encourages production. Increased production hastens the discovery and exhaustion of high-grade, easily exploited deposits and puts more pressure on technology to counter increasingly adverse geologic and geographic conditions. When technology begins to lose the battle, real costs rise; if low-cost and low-priced foreign reserves continue to exist, domestic production will drop precipitously unless protected by import barriers. If low-cost and low-priced foreign reserves do not exist, prices will rise with the marginal costs of production and demand will fall with the marginal utility of the product. Sharply rising prices will stimulate the search for a substitute; if found, the production of the primary resource will cease at the point where the cost of an additional increment produced exceeds the cost of an equally useful increment of the substitute.

Passage from the waxing to the waning phase of the U.S. crude-oil production history was abrupt (see Figure 2.9), mainly because of a large cost differential between domestic and foreign crude oil at a time of strongly rising consumption, which forced a rapid shift from domestic production to imports.

U.S. FOSSIL FUEL ALTERNATIVES

The United States, despite its casual and voracious consumption, still has great fossil fuel resources. Natural gas, a clean and highly useful substance, is running out (see Figure 2.10). Recent corporate decisions to invest large amounts of capital in systems to import liquefied natural gas and to manufacture substitute gas from

FIGURE 2.8

U.S. Mercury Production and Prices, 1850-1971

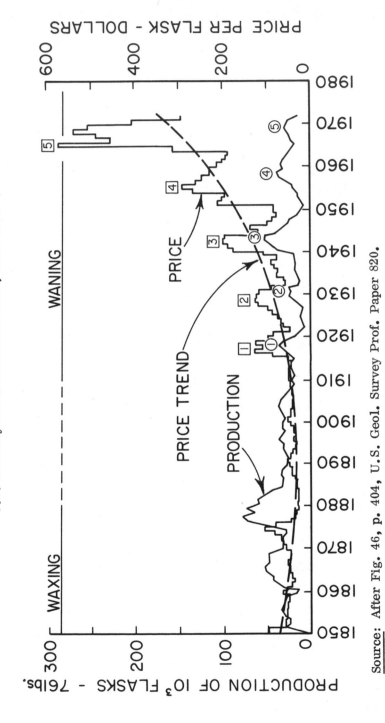

Source: After Fig. 46, p. 404, U.S. Geol. Survey Prof. Paper 820.

FIGURE 2.9

Depletion History of Crude Oil in the United States Including Alaska, 1900-2015, and Establishment of a New Depletion Curve for Synthetic Crude

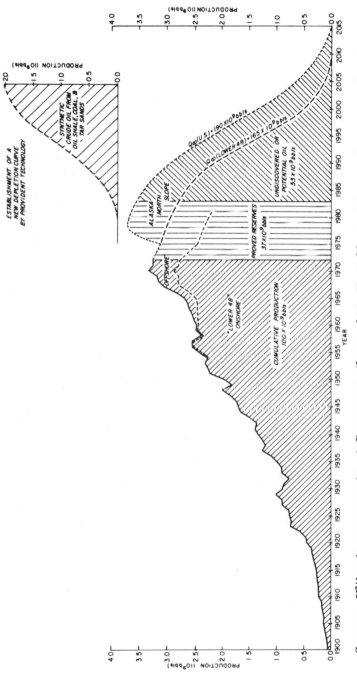

Source: Ultimate recovery (Q_∞) figures are those of M. K. Hubbert, "Energy Resources," in Resources and Man, Committee on Resources and Man (San Francisco: W. H. Freeman, 1969), pp. 183-84.

37

FIGURE 2.10

U.S. Natural Gas Supply, 1960-90

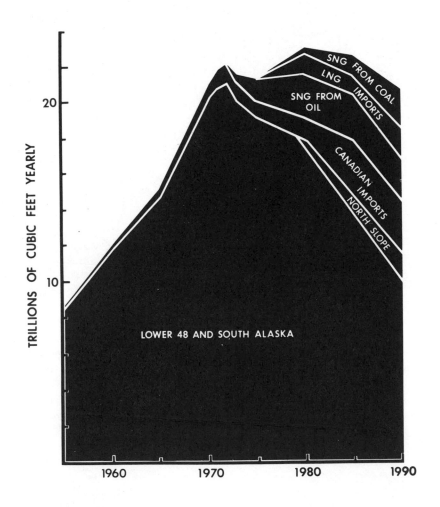

Source: Compiled by the author using Shell Oil Company's 1973 projections.

coal at costs five to six times the present average wellhead price
for interstate gas underline that conclusion. The cost of natural-gas
exhaustion will be felt not only in municipal and industrial conversion
to other fuels but in the cost of food, because nitrogen fertilizer is
now made almost entirely from natural-gas feedstock.

The amount of U.S. crude oil remaining to be produced may
turn out to be somewhat more than all prior domestic production
(experts disagree widely on this point), but the amount of time remaining during which domestic crude oil will be a major part of our
energy base almost surely does not exceed 25 years, and the time
remaining on the world scale probably is about 50 years (see Figure
2.11). These figures set the time scale for the development and
economic emplacement of substitute energy systems.

It is naive to expect countries which have oil to export, including Canada, to relax their attempts to capture a large share of the
commodity value (the economists' measure of the natural subsidy)
of that oil and to protect the future of their own peoples. Consequently, we probably shall continue to pay high prices for foreign oil (and
gas) and be forced sooner or later either to the economic expense of
substitute systems based on domestic resources or to the social expense of not having those substitutes.

Unlike many nations, we do have the capacity to develop substitutes. The United States has great coal and oil shale deposits,
and in addition, large, low-grade uranium deposits. The economic
costs of developing these deposits on a large scale are rather well
known. Coal is the cheapest of these resources; low-sulfur Rocky
Mountain coal is being delivered to the Midwest for $50 ¢/10^6$ BTUs
and can be delivered to Texas or Pittsburgh for $75 ¢/10^6$ BTUs (crude
oil in the United States now costs about $1.40 per million BTUs, and
on the world market $2.00 or more; natural gas, interstate, aver-
ages almost $0.50 per million BTUs, but on the uncontrolled intra-
state markets of Texas and Louisiana goes for as much as $2.00).
Coal offers the greatest range of conversion alternatives: it can be
converted to a gas, a liquid, or to electricity at the mine mouth or
elsewhere. The gas can be low, medium, or high quality. The
liquid can be methanol, ethanol, or a fluid resembling crude oil.
The cost of the product probably will be in the range of $1.50-$2.50
per million BTUs, about the same as imported liquefied natural gas.

The cost of shale oil is now anticipated to be about $2.00 per
million BTUs. Oil from the tar sands of Alberta is being produced
at less than this amount. The physical problem of developing a large
shale-oil industry is largely environmental, although scarce surface
water may impose a limit on the production rate if the problem of
disposing of more than a ton of fine spent shale for each barrel of
retorted oil does not. Estimates of potential reserves of shale oil

FIGURE 2.11

Complete Cycle of World Crude Oil Production, 1900–2100

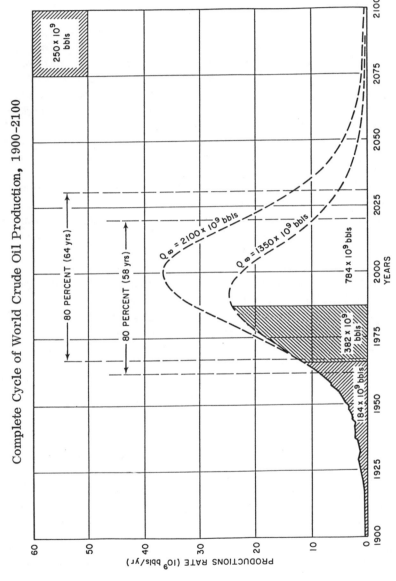

Source: Compiled by the author using Shell Oil Company's 1973 projections.

in the United States range upward from 80 billion barrels (the cumulative crude-oil production of the nation is just over 100 billion barrels), while as many as 300 billion barrels may be recovered from the Canadian tar sands.

HOW MUCH U.S. OIL REMAINS?

In forecasting the U.S. energy future or in attempting to design a national energy policy, one of the key elements is an estimate of the amount of crude oil that remains to be discovered and recovered economically. On this point the experts differ. Estimates of ultimately recoverable crude oil in the United States published within the past ten years (see Table 2.2) state or imply a range of recoverable oil remaining to be discovered of 15 times, from the lowest to the highest estimate. Such a range is almost useless for formulating national energy policy, because strategies based on the lowest estimate would be quite different from those based on the highest estimate.

There are two ways by which estimates of crude oil remaining to be added to reserves are calculated. One is by geologic analogy and geographic extrapolation of finding and recovery rates, the other is by a statistical study and projection of the exploitation history. The former is the only practicable method for estimating the quantitative production potential of geologic terrains in which there has been little or no production; the latter method requires that the production history of the area of concern have passed its youthful phase.

From the viewpoint of national policy and strategies, the exploitation-history method offers a major advantage over the geologic-analogy method, in that the former method expresses its conclusions, or can readily be made to do so, in years as well as in barrels. To the nation it is more important to know how much time there may be to prepare for the massive effort of replacing crude oil as a primary energy source, and how many years the national depletion curve is ahead of the global depletion curve, than to know how many barrels remain to be added to reserves.

Economists of Resources for the Future and geologists of the U.S. Geological Survey have promoted the use of what is known as the resource-base concept in estimating mineral reserves, including those of the fossil fuels. The resource base includes "the sum total of a mineral raw material present in the earth's crust within a given geographical area,"[1] while "resources" are "the natural stock of the mineral raw material from which will come the supply of the metal [or mineral fuel] within the period considered."[2] The audacity of such notions, in the face of geologic complexities and the inability to see through rock that have plagued economic geologists from

TABLE 2.2

Estimates of U.S. Crude Oil Recoverable beyond Known Reserves, 1965-74
(10^9 barrels)

Authors	Year	Method	Oil in Place		Ultimately Recoverable[a]	Recoverable beyond Known Reserves[a]
			Initially	Initially Discoverable		
McKelvey and Duncan	1965	Geologic analogy	--	--	320/660[b]	184/524[b]
Hendricks	1965	Geologic analogy	1,600	1,000	400[c]	264
Weeks	1965	Geologic analogy	--	--	270	134
Hendricks and Schweinfurth	1966	Geologic analogy	2,000	1,250	500	364
Hubbert	1967	Exploitation history	--	--	170	34
Elliott and Linden	1968	Exploitation history	--	--	450	314
Hubbert	1969	Modified exploitation history	--	--	190[d]	54
Arps, Mortada, and Smith	1970	Exploitation history	--	--	165[e]	29[e]
Moore	1971	Exploitation history	727	727	587[f]	451
National Petroleum Council	1971	Geologic analogy	720	720	242[g]	106
American Association Petroleum Geologists	1971	Geologic analogy	--	--	432[f]	296
U.S. Department of Interior	1972	Geologic analogy	2,830	--	549	413
Theobald, Schweinfurth, and Duncan	1972	Geologic analogy	--	1,895	596[h]	439[h]
Berg, Calhoun, and Whiting	1974	Modified geologic analogy	--	--	400	264
Ford Foundation	1974	Geologic analogy?	3,680	--	682[i]	520
Mobil Oil Corporation	1974	Geologic analogy	--	--	--	88
Hubbert	1974	Modified exploitation history	--	--	213[j]	77

[a]On January 1, 1973; cumulative production (100) and proved reserves (36) not included.
[b]Higher figure includes "resources" considered uneconomic in 1965.
[c]Based on 40 percent cumulative recovery.
[d]Includes 25 for Alaska.
[e]Does not include Alaska.
[f]Based on 60 percent cumulative recovery.
[g]Based on 33.3 percent cumulative recovery.
[h]Includes NGL.
[i]Sources, method not given; figures are converted from heat-content equivalents of report.
[j]Includes 43 for Alaska.
Sources: See Bibliography at the end of this chapter.

42

Agricola to now, and in view of the difficulties of forecasting technology and prices in a market of increasing scarcity, is exceeded only by their potential for misleading those who will suffer when the ultimate recovery falls far short of the resource base.

The pernicious impact of the resource-base concept injudiciously presented can be illustrated from two publications of the U.S. Department of the Interior. On the first page of the lead section entitled "Summary and Conclusions" of a 1968 report clearly aimed at the interested layperson are estimates of crude oil, natural gas liquids, and natural gas originally in place within the exploitable jurisdiction of the United States compared to cumulative domestic production of oil and gas through 1967 (see Figure 2.12). The first sentence below the table hammers home the point: "The remaining petroleum resources of the United States are obviously adequate to support consumption for many years into the future."

FIGURE 2.12

The Resource Base in <u>Non Sequitur Flagrans</u>

SUMMARY AND CONCLUSIONS

The Resource Base

Total original oil and gas in place in the United States and its Continental Shelf to a water depth of 600 feet is estimated to be:

	Originally in Place	Withdrawn to 1/1/68
Crude Oil (bill.bbl.)	2,000	84
Natural Gas Liquids (bill.bbl.)	150	n.a.
Natural Gas (trill.cu.ft.)	5,000	332

The remaining petroleum resources of the United States are obviously adequate to support consumption for many years into the future. The real question is whether they can be located and produced at costs which permit them to compete with other energy sources.

Source: U.S. Department of the Interior, <u>United States Petroleum through 1980</u> (Washington, D.C.: Office of Oil and Gas, 1968), p. vii.

The contradiction in the next sentence, which states that the "real" question is whether these resources will ever become resources, is not obvious to the nonprofessional reader and he may never reach the passage on page 12 of the same report which might have jerked him up short, for it reads: "The fact that we have X billion barrels of oil and Y trillion cubic feet of gas in the ground, however, says nothing at all about how much of these same quantities will eventually be found and put to use."

In 1972 the Department published in histogram form (see Figure 2.13) estimates of the U.S. crude-oil resource base which added together, both graphically and numerically, past oil production, undiscoverable and unrecoverable oil, and everything between.

FIGURE 2.13

A Visual Aid to Error

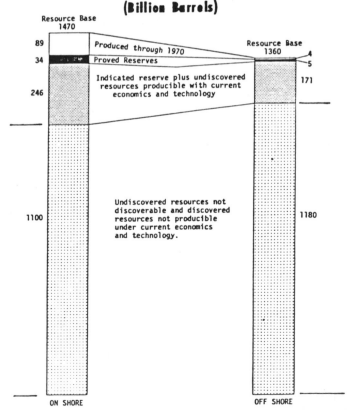

U.S. CRUDE OIL RESOURCES
(Billion Barrels)

Source: U.S. Department of the Interior, United States Energy--
A Summary Review (Washington, D.C.: U.S. Government Printing
Office, 1972), p. 27.

Early in 1974 the Energy Policy Project of the Ford Foundation published its first report. The project, whose staff and advisory board were liberally larded with economists, contracted with Resources for the Future (RFF) for its analysis of future national energy supply. The table of U.S. energy resources in the project's first report is in resource-base format (see Figure 2.14); when converted to barrels from the heat equivalents given, the figures for petroleum represent new highs in estimates of oil originally in place ($3,680 \times 10^9$ barrels) and in "recoverable resources" (520×10^9 barrels). Not surprisingly, the report states (p. 44): "The work done for the Project by RFF suggests that energy resources are at least sufficient to meet the year 2000 requirements with major reliance on oil and gas supply."

The use of the term "resource" in the ways documented above can mislead the uninformed into unjustified complacency about the future availability of nonrenewable geologic commodities. They encourage a picture of an inevitable continuity from potential resource to proved reserve to usable commodity.

The statistical basis for rejecting the resource-base model as a guide to estimation of future recovery has been thoroughly presented by King Hubbert, who points out the "leverage" on estimates of remaining recoverable supplies represented by relatively small changes in estimates of the base or of the ultimate recovery ratio.[3] The recovery ratio, as a manipulable factor in projection based on oil-in-place estimates, unbridles the technocopian enthusiast and allows estimates that put extreme demands on the technological cavalry or Providence.

The resource-base model fits the fiction of the "endlessly retreating line" that is supposed to divide the profitably minable from submarginal materials.[4] This cornucopian thesis has been epitomized by economist Carl Kaysen, who writes: "The fact that some limits exist, that the earth is in principal finite, is hard to deny, but does not in itself lead to any very interesting conclusions. . . . Resources are properly measured in economic, not physical terms."[5]

Some deposits of some mineral resources seem to fit the "endlessly retreating line" hypothesis; most do not. Among those whose deposits do not seem to fit at all are silver, mercury, and crude oil. As already shown, once the peaks of U.S. silver and mercury production were passed, rises in price excited weaker and weaker responses in production. This same relation is about to be demonstrated for crude oil and natural gas.

FIGURE 2.14

A New High in "Recoverable Resources" of Petroleum

Major Energy Resources, U.S.	1973 Consumption (Quadrillion Btu)	Cumulative Production (Q Btu)	Reserves (Q Btu)	Recoverable Resources (Q Btu)	Remaining Resource Base (Q Btu)
Petroleum	34.7	605	302	2,910*	16,790
Shale oil	--	--	(465)	n.a.	975,000
Tar sands	--	--	--	n.a.	168
Natural gas	23.6	405	300	2,470	6,800
Coal	13.5	810	4,110	14,600	64,000
Strippable coal	n.a.	n.a.	925	2,600	2,600
Low-sulfur coal	n.a.	n.a.	2,390	n.a.	38,200
Uranium					
Used in light-water reactors	.85	2	228	600	3,200
Used in breeders	--	--	17,700	47,000	200,000,000
Thorium used in breeders	--	--	4,200	17,500	570,000
Hydropower	2.9	--	--	5.8†	

Note: The terms "Reserves," "Recoverable Resources," and "Remaining Resource Base" are geological estimates. "Reserve" estimates are based on detailed geologic evidence, usually obtained through drilling, while the other estimates reflect less detailed knowledge and more geologic inference. All of these estimates are based on assumptions about technology and economics. They may increase over time as technology improves or prices increase.

*520 x 10⁹ barrels at 5.6 x 10⁶ Btu per barrel.

†Ultimate capability.

n.a. = data not available.

Source: Ford Foundation Energy Policy Project, Exploring Energy Choices (Washington, D.C., 1974), Table 3.

RELATION OF ESTIMATES TO NATIONAL POLICY

That large "resource" estimates may dwindle to small additions to reserves is only one reason large estimates are a poor guide to national policy. Even if such an estimate should be verified by production, the amount of additional time the resource will be available may be advanced relatively little. A resource that is available will be used. If availability increases, consumption will increase; when consumption increases, depletion is increased. Hubbert's logistic curves (see Figure 2.9) illustrate this point as do calculations by Elliott and Turner, made by several different methods, for all the world's fossil fuels.[6]

A large estimate of the domestic quantity available (which may be translated as a long time by national decision makers) may lead to a set of national strategies featuring incentives for domestic exploration and production, relaxation of environmental constraints on such activities, and restrictions on imports in order to encourage domestic exploration. On the other hand, a small estimate of the quantity available from domestic sources--or of the time remaining for emplacement of an adequate substitute system--may lead to a different mix of national strategies, highlighted by subsidized development of coal conversion, nuclear technology, and shale-oil production; strong conservation incentives; creation of a strategic economic reserve or stockpile; continued efforts to secure foreign resources at costs which are less than the costs of domestic energy resources; and, possibly, disincentives to domestic exploration and production, in order to save crude oil for a higher use or a greater need. The two sets of strategies, and the policies they would be designed to implement, would differ substantially, as would their potential benefits and costs to the nation.

THE BENEFITS OF ENERGY CONSERVATION

We might be able to decrease energy costs and at the same time improve the environment if we could increase the efficiency of its use. At first glance there seems little hope. The efficiency of the U.S. energy system almost quintupled in 100 years (see Figure 2.15), but has by now reached a plateau. Indeed, the aggregate efficiency of the U.S. energy system probably declined between 1970 and 1977, owing to the increasing inefficiency and continued proliferation of the automobile, a steep increase in air conditioning, increased energy consumption in the home, especially in frost-free refrigerators and color television sets, and the increased energy costs of maintaining or improving environmental quality.

FIGURE 2.15

Efficiencies in the Energy System of the United States, 1800–1973

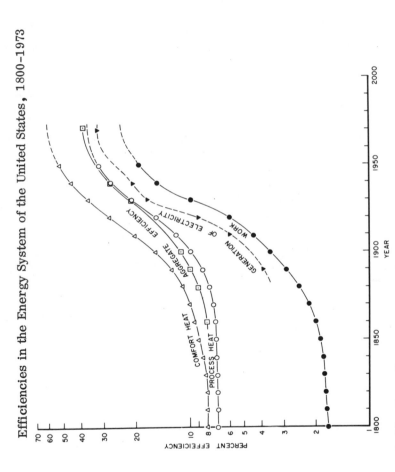

Source: Compiled by the author.

Although it would be difficult to increase the efficiency with which fossil fuels are used in large electric power plants and loco-motives, it would be relatively easy to make substantial cuts in con-sumption if we'd be content with automobiles of the same size the rest of the world gets by with, and if we would accept a hard ride. If we'd design our buildings and their thermal systems properly, use heat pumps wherever advantageous, and go back to using cloth-ing instead of fossil energy to keep our bodies warm, we'd save much irreplaceable fuel. If we'd eat good grade of beef instead of choice, which is as much as 20 percent fatter and requires a heavy grain in-put, there'd be less need to hit our soils with massive injections of nitrogen fertilizer made from a rare and clean fuel, natural gas. In thus stretching out national reserves of crude oil and natural gas, we'd relax some of the pressure on our environment and be healthier.

SUMMARY

The day of cheap energy for the United States appears to be over. It could return only if the cartel of the Organization of Petro-leum Exporting Countries (OPEC) were to collapse, and then only briefly, for there are many nations now eager to consume petroleum at low prices.

On the other hand, the price increases in energy that appear probable over the next few decades are not so great as to cause a collapse of our high-energy, industrialized society. There will be some dislocations of energy-intensive industry, there will be some sacrifices in comforts and pleasures, but the potential for energy saving is so great that remaining domestic reserves of oil and gas could be stretched out, and substitute systems based on coal could be emplaced without serious degradation of the material level of living.

The greatest problem will be to achieve and maintain political consensus on what needs to be done. With experts disagreeing over how much oil remains to be found, over the durability of the OPEC cartel, over the proper role of the private sector in energy decisions, over the environmental impacts of new or expanded energy systems, and over the technological promise of fusion, solar, and geothermal power, the outlook for consensus appears poor.

NOTES

1. S. H. Schurr and B. C. Netschert, Energy in the American Economy, 1850-1975 (Baltimore: Johns Hopkins University Press, 1969), p. 297.

2. H. H. Landsberg, L. L. Fischman, and J. L. Fisher, Resources in America's Future (Baltimore: Johns Hopkins University Press, 1963), p. 425.

3. M. K. Hubbert, U.S. Energy Resources, a Review as of 1972, U.S. Senate Committee on Interior and Insular Affairs, 93d Cong., 2d Sess., 1974, Committee Print Serial No. 93-40.

4. C. W. Merrill, "The Significance of the Mineral Industries in the Economy," in Economics of the Mineral Industries (New York: American Institute of Mining, Metallurgical, and Petroleum Engineers, 1959), p. 36.

5. Carl Kaysen, "The Computer That Printed out W*O*L*F," Foreign Affairs 50 (1972): 661, 663.

6. M. A. Elliott and N. C. Turner, "Estimating the Future Rate of Production of the World's Fossil Fuels," paper presented at the American Chemical Society meeting, Boston, April 9-14, 1972.

BIBLIOGRAPHY

Arps, J. J., M. Mortada, and A. E. Smith. "Relationship between Proved Reserves and Exploratory Effort." Journal of Petroleum Technology, June 1971, pp. 671-75.

Berg, R. R., J. C. Calhoun, Jr., and R. L. Whiting. "Prognosis for Expanded U.S. Production of Crude Oil." Science 184 (1974): 331-36.

Elliott, M. A., and H. R. Linden. "A New Analysis of U.S. Natural Gas Supplies." Journal of Petroleum Technology, February 1968, pp. 135-41.

_____, and N. C. Turner. "Estimating the Future Rate of Production of the World's Fossil Fuels." Paper presented at the American Chemical Society meeting, Boston, April 9-14, 1972.

Ford Foundation, Energy Policy Project. Exploring Energy Choices. Washington, D.C., 1974.

Hendricks, T. A. "Resources of Oil, Gas, and Natural-Gas Liquids in the United States and the World." U.S. Geological Survey Circ. 522, 1965.

_____ and S. P. Schweinfurth. Unpublished memorandum cited in United States Petroleum through 1980, U.S. Department of the Interior. Washington, D.C.: Office of Oil and Gas, 1968, p. 11.

Hubbert, M. K. "Degree of Advancement of Petroleum Exploration in the United States." American Association of Petroleum Geologists Bulletin 51 (1967): 2207-27.

_____. "Energy Resources." In Resources and Man. San Francisco: W. H. Freeman, 1969, pp. 157-242.

_____. U.S. Energy Resources, a Review as of 1972. U.S. Senate Committee on Interior and Insular Affairs, 93d Cong., 2d Sess., 1974, Committee Print Serial No. 93-40.

Kaysen, Carl. "The Computer That Printed out W*O*L*F*." Foreign Affairs 50 (1972): 661, 663.

Landsberg, H. H., L. L. Fischman, and J. L. Fisher. Resources in America's Future. Baltimore: Johns Hopkins University Press, 1963.

McKelvey, V. E., and D. C. Duncan. "United States and World Resources of Energy." In Symposium on Fuel and Energy Economics. 149th National Meeting, American Chemical Society, Division of Fuel Chemistry 9, no. 2 (1965): 1-17.

Merrill, C. W. "The Significance of the Mineral Industries in the Economy." In Economics of the Mineral Industries. New York: American Institute of Mining, Metallurgical, and Petroleum Engineers, 1959.

Moore, C. L. "Analysis and Projection of Historic Patterns of U.S. Crude Oil and Natural Gas." In Future Petroleum Provinces of the United States--Their Geology and Potential, American Association of Petroleum Geologists Memoir 15, 1971, pp. 50-54.

National Petroleum Council. U.S. Energy Outlook--An Initial Appraisal, 1971-1985, Vol. 2. Washington, D.C., 1971.

Schurr, S. H., and B. C. Netschert. Energy in the American Economy, 1850-1975. Baltimore: Johns Hopkins University Press, 1969.

Theobald, P. K., S. P. Schweinfurth, and D. C. Duncan. "Energy Resources of the United States." U.S. Geological Survey Circular 650, 1972.

U.S. Department of the Interior. United States Energy--a Summary
    Review. Washington, D.C.: U.S. Government Printing Of-
    fice, 1972.

Weeks, L. G. "World Offshore Petroleum Resources." American
    Association of Petroleum Geologists Bulletin 49 (1965): 1680-
    93.

3

ENERGY COSTS AS
POTENTIAL LIMITS
TO GROWTH
John P. Holdren

The basic material ingredients essential to existence and prosperity are air, water, food, fiber, energy, physical space, and nonfuel minerals. The most obvious question concerning natural limits to growth of human populations and economies is the adequacy of supply of these basic ingredients. The question is uninstructive, however, if posed strictly in terms of how much material exists (in the case of air, water, space, and minerals) or in terms of how much could theoretically be produced (in the case of food and energy) if economic and social costs could be ignored. In these terms, adequacy invariably seems assured for any population and level of per capita consumption that can reasonably be envisioned for the next 50 to 100 years. This is true both for the United States and for the world.

There are, however, meaningful questions involving possible limits to growth on a more easily visualized time scale of a few decades. These questions concern not absolute potential supply but rather economic costs, achievable rates of deployment of new or existing technologies, and social costs. With respect to economic costs, for example, it is questionable whether potential resources can be converted into available supplies at economic costs society can pay. Oil shales provide an example of a vast resource the existence of which is assured, but for which the economics of exploitation is uncertain. With respect to rates there are constraints of logistics, economics, and social and technological inertia that might not permit the rate of mobilization of resources to keep pace with the anticipated growth of needs. Limitations on capital for new power plants or shipyards for tankers could constrain the rate of growth of U.S. energy supply quite apart from fundamental constraints on the ultimate level of consumption. With respect to social costs more must be known about the direct effects on human health of pollution

53

associated with high levels of resource use or high rates of increase, and about the effects on human well-being of disruption of social systems and of geophysical processes that influence food production, recycle wastes, and otherwise maintain a hospitable environment for humans.

As an indispensable ingredient of prosperity and a major source of social costs, energy is a particularly fitting focus for the study of such questions. Let us therefore look more closely at the technological choices for energy supply and at the questions that must be asked concerning their economic and social costs. Many answers are missing, but trying to ask the right questions in a systematic way seems a useful beginning.

TECHNOLOGIC OPTIONS FOR ENERGY SUPPLY

The principal choices for energy supply during the next several decades, together with my personal estimates of the earliest date at which each one could contribute energy equal to a 10 percent share of the total annual energy use of the United States in 1975, are listed in Table 3.1. These estimates are "optimistic" in the sense that they assume in each case that a major national commitment is made to develop and deploy the source in question as rapidly as possible. It is most unlikely, of course, that the country would make such a commitment for all the sources at once.[1]

Oil and gas (domestic plus imported) contributed almost 75 percent of U.S. energy supply in 1975, but most experts agree that the contribution of domestic resources of oil and gas will continue the decline entered in the early 1970s owing to diminished discoveries.[2] Imported oil was 17 percent of U.S. energy supply in 1975 and could be increased, at least temporarily, if the country cared to pay the economic and political costs. Imported gas in 1975 made up just over 1 percent of U.S. energy supply and probably could not reach 10 percent before 1985, owing to the need to construct offloading, conversion, and storage facilities for liquified natural gas to be imported.

Use of coal in conventional facilities--electric-utility boilers and steel making, for example--accounted for 19 percent of U.S. energy in 1975. The greatest potential for expansion is thought to be in advanced applications such as liquefication and gasification and combined-cycle power plants. These technologies require further development to make them commercially attractive. Even if the commitment were to be made, which at this time is uncertain, the large and expensive facilities involved could not be built rapidly enough to reach the 10 percent criterion before the mid-1990s.

TABLE 3.1

Options for Energy Supply

Energy Source	Date	Energy Source	Date
Fossil fuels		Solar	
Petroleum/gas		Direct	
Domestic	now	Thermal collectors	2010
Imported	now	Photovoltaics	2015
Coal		Direct fuel produc-	
Conventional	now	tion	2015
Advanced (gasifica-		Indirect	
tion, liquefaction,		Wind	2030
combined cycle)	1995	Hydrological cycle	never
Oil shales/tar sands	2000	Waves/ocean	
Nuclear		thermal gradients	2030
Fission		Geophysical	
Light water reactors,		Geothermal steam	never
high temperature		Hot rock	2015
gas reactors, heavy		Tides	never
water reactors	1990	Technologies of	
Breeders	2000	conservation	
Fusion		Transportation ⎤	
Magnetic confinement ⎤ 2015		Industrial processes ⎟ 1980	
Laser ⎦		Residential/commer- ⎦	
Hybrids	2010	cial	

Note: Dates are estimates for earliest contribution of an
amount of energy equal to 10 percent of total energy use in the
United States.
Source: Compiled by the author.

More uncertain still is whether oil shale will be developed on
a large scale. The technology is less developed than that for advanced coal conversion, and industry seems at the moment to lack
enthusiasm for pushing ahead. Possibly oil shale and tar sands combined (the latter deposits mostly in Canada) could achieve the 10 percent figure in 2000 if incentives materialize.

The rather late dates given in Table 3.1 for fission become
understandable when it is recognized that nuclear reactors at present
contribute only to the electrical portion of the energy budget, and

that electricity as a whole makes up only 25 percent of our annual drain on primary energy sources. Fission reactors in 1975 generated about 8 percent of the nation's electricity, hence accounting for 2 percent of total energy supply. These reactors were all of the "converter" type--relatively inefficient users of uranium. The pace of construction has fallen far below the enthusiastic nuclear-industry estimates of a few years ago, and it seems unlikely that this energy source could quintuple its 1975 contribution before 1990. The more efficient but even more controversial breeder reactors cannot be developed, tested, and deployed quickly enough to meet my 10 percent criterion before 2000, despite massive federal investment in this enterprise.

Controlled fusion may achieve a laboratory demonstration of scientific feasibility around 1980, but the obstacles between laboratory and commercial power plants should not be underestimated. The engineering problems of fusion are so severe that the first commercial plant can hardly be expected before the year 2000, and many experts find that estimate (which is the U.S. Energy Research and Development Administration's target) overly optimistic. If the target were met and if the plant worked well, it would still be difficult to build the hundred or so large plants needed to meet by 10 percent criterion by 2015. This is true for laser fusion as well as for magnetic confinement, although less is known today about the newer and still partly classified laser approach.

Fusion-fission hybrid reactors--a fusion core surrounded by a blanket where fusion neutrons either induce fission or produce fissile fuel for fusion reactors located elsewhere--conceivably could prove feasible before pure fusion does. Whether such devices would be attractive enough economically to justify a major program is doubtful, but even if they do they are at least ten years behind the fission breeder reactor.

The speed with which solar energy could make a major contribution if a national commitment were made has been widely underrated. Among "direct" approaches to harnessing the sun's energy, the easiest to implement quickly is collection of the energy as heat on flat-plate or focusing collectors. The main applications are heating and cooling of buildings, industrial process heat, and thermal generation of electricity. These thermal approaches in combination could meet the 10 percent figure by 2010, possibly sooner. Photovoltaic cells have a chance of making the 10 percent level by 2015 to 2020 if progress in lowering their production costs continues. Production of fuel by photosynthesis, chemical mimics of photosynthesis, and catalytic dissociation of sea water could probably meet the 10 percent criterion between 2015 and 2025, depending on the degree of success with these more esoteric approaches.

Sunlight is already harnessed indirectly for electricity generation in the form of hydropower (the hydrologic cycle is driven by the
sun). It provided 15 percent of U.S. electricity in 1975. There
probably are not enough suitable dam sites for its contribution ever
to reach 10 percent of total 1975 energy use. Wind power might be
able to reach the 10 percent level by 2030 to 2040, depending on
technological developments now very hard to predict. Ocean waves
and thermal gradients together perhaps belong on the same timetable. Of the nonsolar "geophysical" energy sources, probably only
hot dry rock has the potential to reach the 10 percent criterion at all.
With great effort and good luck, this might be achieved by 2015.

The most rapidly accessible "new" energy technology is the
technology of energy conservation. By conservation I mean more
efficient use of energy. Strictly speaking, energy is always con-
served--so says the first Law of Thermodynamics--but the term
"energy conservation" is useful shorthand for getting more well-
being per unit of energy used. Most people are unaccustomed to
thinking of increased efficiency as an energy "source," but a barrel
of oil saved by better insulation is every bit as real a contribution to
national energy supply as a barrel of oil imported or pumped from a
domestic field. Like other energy technologies, raising efficiency
has economic and social costs, but there is reason to believe these
are often smaller than those of alternative technologies. And there
is so much "fat" in the U.S. energy budget--energy use that can be
trimmed by the most modest and innocuous conservation measures--
that there would be no difficulty in making a 10 percent contribution
to energy supply in this way by 1980. The contribution by the year
2000 could easily be 35 percent of the total U.S. energy use in 1975.[3]

A TAXONOMY OF ECONOMIC AND SOCIAL COSTS

One of the greatest pitfalls in cost-benefit comparisons of all
kinds is leaving something important out of the accounting. A useful
precaution is to develop a logical framework for ordering the subject
to help assure at least that the right questions are asked. I concentrate here on the costs, inasmuch as the benefits of energy supply
have been amply and enthusiastically described elsewhere. It is useful in this connection to distinguish among:

The origins of the costs; namely, the specific activities that gener-
    ate them. For a given energy technology, what is important here
    is not to leave out of the accounting any of the steps undertaken in
    the discovery and delivery of the energy, or any of the phases
    associated with each step (see Table 3.2).

The character of the impacts produced by these activities, meaning
   what is taken from, added to, or done to the economic, social,
   and physical environments (see Table 3.3, column 1).
The costs themselves, meaning the nature of the damage to human
   well-being produced by the impacts (see Table 3.3, column 2).

TABLE 3.2

Origins of Costs of Energy Supply

Steps in Energy's Path through Society	Phases Associated with Each Step[a]
Exploration	Research
Harvesting	Commercial construction
Concentration	Commercial operation
Refining	Eventual dismantling
Transportation[b]	Management of any long-lived
Conversion[b]	wastes
Storage[b]	Regulation and monitoring[c]
Marketing	
End-use	

[a]Not every phase is associated with every step.
[b]May occur more than once.
[c]Occurs in parallel with all other phases.
Source: Compiled by the author.

   In Table 3.4 the list of impacts from Table 3.3, column 1 is
made more concrete with examples from the major energy technologies. (The list is illustrative, not comprehensive.) One theme that
begins to emerge from Table 3.4 is that few categories of impact
are unique (in a qualitative sense) to a single energy option. Equity
effects and military ramifications attend both fossil fuels and nuclear
power, for example. In the same vein, the possibility of devastating
accidents accompanies not only nuclear reactors but also hydroelectric dams upstream from population centers and liquefied natural gas
(LNG) tankers in big-city ports; long half-life radioactive effluents
come from geothermal power and coal-burning facilities as well as
from the nuclear fuel cycle; and mutagens, manifesting themselves
as genetic diseases and deaths in future generations, come from

TABLE 3.3

Impacts and Costs of Energy Supply

Impacts	Costs
Initial investment	Opportunity costs (goods and ser-
Operating expenses (wages,	vices foregone because the money
taxes, insurance, fuel	to pay for them was spent on en-
costs, maintenance)	ergy instead, or because other re-
Resource consumption (land,	sources needed to produce them
water, energy,[a] other raw	were used to produce energy in-
materials)	stead)
Material effluents[b] (solid,	Death and disease (among energy
liquid, gaseous, including	workers, members of the public
radioactive materials)	now living, future generations)
Electromagnetic radiation[b]	Damage to economic goods and ser-
(ionizing, microwave, and	vices (for example, property,
other)	tourism)
Heat[b]	Damage to environmental goods and
Noise[b]	services (for example, climate,
Physical transformation of	nutrient cycles)
environment[b] (structures,	Aesthetic loss and nuisance (for ex-
land-forms, vegetation,	ample, impaired visibility, ugly
fluid dynamics)	structures, loss of environmental
Aggravation of inequity	diversity)
Redistribution of population	Uneasiness and other psychological
Facilitation of military	distress (for example, among per-
developments	sons displaced by energy technol-
Other altered vulnerabilities	ogy, or fearful of other costs be-
(of the energy sector or	fore they materialize)
society as a whole, to geo-	Undesirable social or political
physical, biological, or	change (for example, loss of civil
sociotechnical disruptions)	liberties as a part of government's
	response to technology-induced
	vulnerability)

[a]Investing energy to get energy does not seem such a remarkable phenomenon, but a field of investigation called net-energy analysis has emerged to deal with its ramifications.

[b]These may occur as a foreseen consequence of routine operations or as results of accidents, malicious intervention (sabotage,
terrorism), or natural disasters.

Source: Compiled by the author.

TABLE 3.4

Examples of Impacts of Energy Technologies

Resource consumption
    Solar: land, metals for collectors, energy for fabrication
    Oil shale: water for extraction and processing
    Fission: water for evaporative cooling, energy for fuel enrichment
    Hydropower: evaporative water losses from reservoir
Material effluents
    Fossil fuels: sulphur oxide, nitrogen oxide, carbon monoxide particles (including heavy metals)
    Fission: tailings from uranium mills, tritium and krypton-85 from reprocessing
    Geothermal: hydrogen sulfide, mineral salts
    Conservation: asbestos from manufacture and installation of insulation
Electromagnetic radiation
    Fission: neutrons in reactors, gamma rays from spent fuel in shipment
    Fusion: neutrons, stray magnetic fields
    Electric transmission: stray fields near lines
Heat
    All energy conversion: discharge, as heat, of part of energy handled
    All energy end-use: conversion of all energy used to heat, mostly immediately and at point of use
Physical transformation of environment
    Geothermal: subsidence
    Imported oil: dredging and filling for port facilities
    Strip-mining coal: altering landforms and vegetation
    Ocean geothermal: altering local circulation pattern
    Windmills: bird traps
    Oil/gas pipelines: barriers to wildlife migration
Aggravation of inequity
    Fossil fuels: create worst air pollution in central cities where poor cannot escape
    Fission: steers rich-country research and development into channels unlikely to benefit most poor countries
    Conservation: energy-saving investments in insulation, better appliances, and so on, out of reach of poor
    End-use: energy-intensive mechanization and automation may eliminate unskilled jobs
Redistribution of population
    Hydropower: displacement of valley residents
    Offshore oil: coastal urbanization around support facilities
    Western coal: development on the High Plains
    Solar: development in the Southwest desert
Facilitation of military developments
    Fission: international proliferation of nuclear weapons
    Imported oil: oil revenues fund armaments for exporting nations
    Laser fusion: possible links to military lasers and design of fusion bombs
Other altered vulnerabilities
    Hydropower: dam failure from earthquake or sabotage
    Fission: reactor failure from earthquake, terrorist A-bombs
    Imported oil: political blackmail
    All-electric economy: regional blackout from central-system accident or sabotage, dependence on central authority

---

Source: Compiled by the author.

virtually all combustion as well as in the form of ionizing radiation.
This is not to suggest that choices as to "better" and "worse" among
the various energy options cannot be made, but only that the criteria
are not quite so clear-cut as sometimes is assumed.

EVALUATING SEVERITY OF IMPACTS AND COSTS

To proceed beyond a mere listing of the impacts and costs of
various energy options, three tasks must be undertaken: identifying
the most appropriate criteria by which to evaluate the severity of
the impacts and/or costs; acquiring the information needed to quantify
the performance of various energy options against these criteria,
where quantification is possible; comparing the results from different energy options in a way that can enlighten decision making.[4]
(The tasks are listed here in increasing order of difficulty.)

These considerations suggest the classification of criteria for
evaluating severity into three broad categories: those that are quantifiable (at least in principle) and amenable to comparisons among different technologies; those that are quantifiable but difficult or impossible to compare from one technology to another; and those that are
difficult or impossible to quantify even for a single technology.
Table 3.5 provides a listing of some of the most important criteria,
arranged according to this scheme.

Comparability is greatest, of course, for direct economic
costs. Some capital costs for various energy facilities as of about
1974, in 1974 dollars, appear in Table 3.6.[5] It is important to note
that costs of energy technology have been escalating considerably
faster than the rate of inflation for the economy as a whole. A company planning to construct any of the facilities listed in Table 3.6
starting in 1976 might expect to pay, in current dollars, between 50
percent and 100 percent more than the figure given. What is most
significant about the numbers in Table 3.6, then, is not so much the
absolute values but the relative values among the various technologies; the clear message is that the trends in energy development--
toward more remote deposits of oil, toward more abundant but lower-
grade resources such as coal and oil shale, toward sophisticated
technologies of fission and fusion, toward the inexhaustible but dilute
solar resource--are all trends toward more expensive energy. The
era of cheap energy is over.

Beyond this broad assertion, drawing detailed conclusions from
numbers such as those in Table 3.6 can be dangerous. Information
on economic costs is quantitative, but that is not to say it is always
accurate. Costs of present technologies may be distorted by subsidies of various kinds and by other imperfections in the market,

TABLE 3.5

Indexes and Criteria for Evaluating Impacts and Costs:
Some Examples

Criteria quantifiable in principle and amenable to comparison among
energy options
    Initial investment: dollars per unit of deliverable energy flow, for
        example, per kilowatt or per barrel per day (must be adjusted
        in comparisons to account for different load factors and equip-
        ment lifetimes)
    Operating costs: dollars per unit of energy, for example, per
        kilowatt hour or per barrel or per million BTU (initial invest-
        ment may be factored in to give total dollar cost per unit of
        energy)
    Resource consumption: joules of energy, cubic meters of water,
        square kilometers of land
    Material effluents: kilograms of the same substance emitted by
        different options (for example, sulfur dioxide from coal and oil)
    Deaths: number, or number of days of life lost
    Disease: number of cases, or number of days of activity lost
    Damage to economic goods and services: dollars
    Damage to environmental goods and services: dollars
    Damage to environmental goods and services: dollar cost of re-
        placing services with technological equivalents (quantification
        very difficult in practice)
Criteria quantifiable in principle but difficult to compare
    Risk to environmental goods and services: magnitude of interven-
        tion in a natural process as a fraction of characteristic scale of
        that process (for example, cumulative human CO_2 input to at-
        mosphere $\div$ natural inventory = 0.10)
    Resource consumption: kilograms of different materials (for exam-
        ple, niobium for fusion versus cadmium for solar photovoltaics)
    Material effluents: kilograms of different substances, curies of
        radioactive ones
    Spatial and temporal distribution of harm: quantitative distribu-
        tion functions in space and time
Criteria difficult or impossible to quantify
    Degree of irreversibility of harm
    Degree of voluntarism in risk (for example, occupational versus
        public risk)
    Degree of coincidence of risks and benefits (for example, are bene-
        fits widespread and risks concentrated or vice versa?)
    Extent of sociopolitical implications (not only almost impossible to
        quantify but usually controversial even qualitatively)
    Quality of evidence of harm (speculation, theory, extensive ex-
        perimental evidence)

Source: Compiled by the author.

and they are further clouded by inconsistent use of accounting schemes by different estimators.[6] Costs of future technologies are uncertain because no one knows what a highly complex facility will cost to build until it has been done. (It can be argued, in fact, that one doesn't really know the cost accurately until not one but dozens of examples have been built.)

TABLE 3.6

Capital Costs for Energy Technologies
(1974 dollars)

Fuel and Heat	Dollars per Thermal Kilowatt of Flow (24-hour average)
Oil well, Persian Gulf	4
Oil well, U.S. onshore	100
Oil well, U.S. offshore	200
Oil pipeline (1,500 km)	12
Tanker from Persian Gulf	20
Oil refinery	30
Coal strip mine	20
Coal underground mine	40
Coal train (1,500 km)	4
Coal slurry pipeline (1,500 km)	25
Coal liquefaction or gasification	180
Oil shale extraction and processing	200
Solar home heating	600

Electricity	Dollars per Electrical Kilowatt
Geothermal dry-steam plant	200
Hydro dam and power plant	300
Coal-fired plant	450
Fission reactor (light-water cooled)	600
Uranium mining and milling[a]	3
Uranium enrichment[a]	23
Solar thermal electric plant[b]	1,200??
Fusion reactor	1,200??
Transmission and distribution of electricity	200

[a]Cost normalized to peak electrical kilowatts of reactor capacity.

[b]Cost not based on peak power but on yearly production in kilowatt hours divided by 6,100 hours. This puts capital cost on a comparable basis with nuclear or fossil-fueled plant with annual load factor of 70 percent.

Source: Compiled by the author.

    The uncertainties inherent in comparisons of dollar costs are
illustrated by the results of a study conducted by the author and two
colleagues in 1975. [7] Total electricity generating costs for 1990 in
mid-1974 mills per kilowatt hour were estimated for eight fossil fuel
and nuclear generation alternatives, letting capital costs, fuel costs,
load factors, and plant efficiencies vary over the range of recent estimates for these parameters by competent analysts. The results
are summarized in Table 3.7. The clear conclusion is that the uncertainties are far bigger than the intersource differences in the
"base-case" or "best" estimates.

TABLE 3.7

Electricity Generation Costs in 1990--
Result of a Sensitivity Analysis
(mills/kWhe, 1974 money)

Generating System	Low Estimate	Base Case	High Estimate
Coal with stack-gas scrubber	27	32	62
Coal, fluidized bed boiler	22	27	52
Gasified coal, combined cycle	26	31	61
Imported residual fuel oil	32	43	57
Light-water reactor, no plutonium cycle	19	23	69
Light-water reactor, plutonium cycle	18	21	67
Liquid metal fast breeder reactor	18	22	71
High temperature gas reactor	18	21	66

    Source: Kirk Smith, John Weyant, and John P. Holdren,
Evaluation of Conventional Power Systems (Berkeley: University of
California, Energy and Resources Group Report ERG 75-5, July
1975).

    Like direct economic costs, consumption of resources such as
land, water, and energy can be quantified and readily compared
among alternative energy options. Some economists argue that there
is no need for such separate tabulation and comparison, since the
dollar cost of the resources used is already included in the overall
dollar costs of the various options. A major weakness in this position is the distortion introduced by subsidies and other market

imperfections, as noted above. Since land or water may well be subsidized or underpriced for one energy option and not for another, it is instructive to disaggregate from deceptive dollar totals the physical quantities used, in hectares, liters, joules, and so on.

Still, there are ambiguities in quantifying resource use. Does one distinguish between water that is evaporated and water that is polluted but returned to the surface? In fuel cycles for electricity generation, evaporative cooling towers (if used) invariably dominate the water use, whether water polluted and returned is counted or not (Table 3.8). [8] Concerning land use, accounting problems arise in discriminating between temporary and permanent commitments of land. It is probably useful to distinguish inventory commitments (km^2 per megawatt [MWe] installed, committed for the duration of the facility's operation; for example, the land on which the plant sits), temporary commitments (km^2 years per MWe years of delivered electricity; for example, km^2 strip-mined per MWe year, multiplied by the mean number of years required to restore the land to other uses), and permanent commitments (km^2 years per MWe year; for example, repositories for radioactive wastes). Very few land-use data are available disaggregated in this detail; some figures are collected in Table 3.9. Another question related to resource use is how far one traces these impacts. In net-energy accounting, for example, one would usually ascribe to the energy costs of coal-fired electricity generation the fuel burned by trains hauling the coal. Should one also count the energy used to manufacture the trains? Or the gasoline used by workers commuting to work to manufacture the trains?

Difficulties in comparing different technologies arise even with easily quantified impacts such as use of nonfuel minerals. If construction of a solar power plant were to require 100 kg of aluminum per electrical kilowatt, for example, and a nuclear power plant required 10 kg of stainless steel per electrical kilowatt, how would one decide which is the more serious impact (aside from price, which as noted above may not accurately reflect the real costs)? Measurement of the material demands against known reserves, annual consumption for other purposes, and estimates of eventually recoverable resources provides indices that are a step toward comparability, but are still imperfect. (Resource estimates are flawed, and consumption for other purposes may change.)

The same problem arises with respect to material effluents. A kilogram of carbon monoxide is not equivalent in social costs to a kilogram of sulfur dioxide. A curie of tritium is not equivalent to a curie of plutonium. An increasingly popular index that supplies some measure of comparability in these instances is the number (in units of volume) obtained by dividing the quantity of the material by the

TABLE 3.8

Use of Water in Fuel Cycles for Electricity Generation
(10^6 m^3/plant-year)

Fuel	Evaporated in Wet Towers at Power Plant	Blowdown Water in Plant Cooling Towers[a]	Fuel-Processing Water Use[b]	Waste Management Water Use[b]
Standard coal[c]	11.	6.6	0.3	1.7
Coal gasification/combined cycle[d]	6.6	4.0	0.5	--
Oil	10.	6.0	1.5	--
Uranium (LWR)	17.	10.	0.5	0.01

[a]Returned to surface polluted.
[b]Some evaporated, some returned.
[c]Wet-lime scrubbing for SO_2 removal.
[d]Combined-cycle power plant efficiency equals 47 percent; fuel-cycle thermal efficiency equals 37 percent.

Source: Robert J. Budnitz and John P. Holdren, "Social and Environmental Costs of Energy Systems," in Annual Review of Energy, ed. J. Hollander (Palo Alto, Calif.: Annual Reviews, Inc., 1976).

TABLE 3.9

Land Use in Fuel Cycles for Electricity Generation

Fuel	Inventory (km^2 per plant)[a]	Temporary Commitment (km^2 year per plant year)[b]	Permanent Commitment (km^2 per plant year)
Deep-mined coal	12-15	10-29	--
Surface-mined coal	12-15	20-240	--
Oil	3-14	--	--
Surface-mined uranium for LWR	1	1-2	0.001
Solar-thermal	56	--	--

[a]Includes facilities for processing and transportation, but not transmission.
[b]A 10-year mean time for restoration to other use.
[c]Plant capable of delivering 1,000 MWe-year per year at 100 percent load factor (18 MWe average per km^2).

Source: Robert J. Budnitz and John P. Holdren, "Social and Environmental Costs of Energy Systems," in Annual Review of Energy, ed. J. Hollander (Palo Alto, Calif.: Annual Reviews, Inc., 1976).

maximum concentration permitted by applicable regulations. In this way, the impact of discharges is represented in terms of the volume of air or water needed to dilute the effluent to the permissible concentration. Thus a kilogram of SO_2, divided by the primary federal (U.S.) standard of $80 \mu g$ per cubic meter of air, corresponds to a "dilution volume" of 12.5 million cubic meters of air. A curie of tritium (about a tenth of a milligram), for which the Recommended Concentration Guideline (RCG, formerly Maximum Permissible Concentration, or MPC) for public exposure is $0.2 \mu Ci$ per cubic meter of air, has a "dilution volume" of 5 million cubic meters of air. Dilution volumes for several fuel cycles are shown in Table 3.10. This approach has the defects that standards for different effluents do not contain equal margins of safety (or nonmargins) with respect to the level at which adverse effects on health appear, and that the different physical properties of different effluents lead to vastly different rates of dilution and/or detoxification.

When one is concerned with ecological disruptions, it is generally useful to compare the scale of the technological disturbance against the yardstick of the relevant natural process. For example, one can compare additions of CO_2 to the atmosphere with the "natural" concentration of CO_2 or with natural flows into and out of the atmosphere; one can compare technological energy flows in a specified area with the natural energy flows that govern climate; and so on. Some comparisons of this kind are presented in Table 3.11. It is sometimes hard to know, however, which of several candidate natural yardsticks is most meaningful, and the comparison between completely different kinds of impacts is not straightforward in any case. [9]

Counting deaths and injuries is straightforward only for occupational accidents (Table 3.12) or dramatic disasters such as dam failures. Deaths and illnesses due to pollution are obscured by multiple causative factors (some energy-related and some not) and by other epidemiological difficulties: synergistic effects, data inadequate because of small sample size or short period of observation, preexisting conditions, lack of a good control group. Estimating death and disease that might result from eventual accidents involving technologies with which we have little experience to date (such as nuclear fission) is even more difficult because no reliable estimates of the probability of such events are available. Some of the uncertainties are reflected in Table 3.13, which shows the ranges of competent opinion concerning impact on public health of the routine operation of some alternative electricity-generating schemes. [10] For rough comparison, the range of conceivable values of the contribution of major fission-reactor accidents to public risk (computed as 6,000 person-days lost per death, including delayed cancers but ignoring nonfatal illnesses and genetic effects) spans not less than 5 orders of magnitude--from 0.005 person-days lost per megawatt year to 50 person-days lost per

TABLE 3.10

Dilution Volumes in Air for Routine Effluents of Fuel Cycles for Electricity Generation
(10^3 km^3/plant year)

Fuel	Effluents	Dilution Volume (power plant only)[a]	Dilution Volume (all other steps)
Coal with lime scrubbing	NO$_2$, SO$_2$, HC,	200-550	7-8
	particles, heavy metals	23-48	29-370[b]
Coal-gas/combined cycle	NO$_2$, SO$_2$, HC	8-77	7-8
	particles, heavy metals	5-48	29-370[b]
Oil (RFO)	NO$_2$, SO$_2$, HC	66-450	21-58
	particles, heavy metals	12-120	1-4
Uranium	^{3}H, ^{85}Kr, ^{222}Rn	0.0003-0.027	0.013-1.9
	trans-U	--	0.5-1.6

[a] Standards used, per m^3: NO$_2$ = 100 μg, SO$_2$ = 80 μg, HC = 160 μg, particles = 75 μg, heavy metal = 1.5 μg, ^{3}H = 0.2 μCi, ^{85}Kr = 0.3 μCi, ^{222}Rn = 0.003 μCi, transuranium nuclides = 5 x 10^{-8} μCi.

[b] High figure includes coal losses in transport, probably not comparable to other particulate emissions.

Source: Robert J. Budnitz and John P. Holdren, "Social and Environmental Costs of Energy Systems," in Annual Review of Energy, ed. J. Hollander (Palo Alto, Calif.: Annual Reviews, Inc., 1976).

TABLE 3.11

Environmental Inputs from Energy Cycles as Fractions[a] of Natural Yardsticks

Energy-Related Input	Natural Yardstick	Input/Yardstick
Petroleum in oceans	Natural seepage	6-20
CO$_2$ in atmosphere	Atmospheric CO$_2$ reservoir	0.1[b]
Particles in atmosphere	Volcanoes, sea salt, dust	0.05-0.5
Sulfur in atmosphere	Sea salt, biological processes	0.5
Nitrogen fixation (N → NO$_x$)	Biological processes, lightning	0.7
Heat dissipation at surface	Sunlight absorbed at surface	0.0001 (global) 0.01 (large urban regions)

[a] Ratio of annual flows on a global basis, unless otherwise noted.
[b] Cumulative perturbation in inventory.

Source: Robert J. Budnitz and John P. Holdren, "Social and Environmental Costs of Energy Systems," in Annual Review of Energy, ed. J. Hollander (Palo Alto, Calif.: Annual Reviews, Inc., 1976).

megawatt year--even if the potential contribution of sabotage to the probability of disaster is not considered.

TABLE 3.12

Occupational Accidental Deaths and Injuries in Fuel
Cycles for Electricity Generation
(one significant figure)

Fuel	Deaths per Plant Year	Injuries per Plant Year	10^3 Man-Days Lost per Plant Year[a]
Deep-mined coal	2-6	30-100	10-40
Surface-mined coal	1-4	10-60	7-30
Oil	0.1-0.2	4-10	1-2
Uranium (LWR)[b]	0.1-0.3	5-10	1-2

[a]Evaluated at 6,000 man-days/death and 50-100 man-days/injury, depending on fuel cycle and stage.

[b]Range encompasses surface and underground uranium mines.

Source: Robert J. Budnitz and John P. Holdren, "Social and Environmental Costs of Energy Systems," in Annual Review of Energy, ed. J. Hollander (Palo Alto, Calif.: Annual Reviews, Inc., 1976).

TABLE 3.13

Public Health Impacts of Routine Operations of Alternative
Electricity Generation Schemes: Person-Days
Lost per Megawatt Year*

	Low Estimate	High Estimate
Coal plant with stack-gas scrubber	5	1,500
Coal plant, fluidized bed combustion	4	800
Coal gasification plus combined cycle	0.3	200
Residual fuel oil	2	1,500
Fission reactor (light-water cooled)	0.01	0.1

*Person-days lost computed at 6,000 per death, 50 per illness other than cancer, 100 per cancer.

Source: Kirk Smith, John Weyant, and John P. Holdren, Evaluation of Conventional Power Systems (Berkeley: University of California, Energy and Resources Group Report ERG 75-5, July 1975).

It is important, of course, to specify the way in which social and environmental costs are distributed in space and time. One distinguishes among local, regional, and global effects, and among effects that are borne essentially at the time of the causative event (for example, accidental deaths), later in the life of the exposed person (for example, cancer), or in future generations (for example, genetic disease). In practice, people seem more impressed by costs that are concentrated in space and time and society is usually willing to pay more to avoid them. As an ethical problem, however, perhaps more attention should be given to those cases in which the bearers of the costs are far removed in space and time from those who reap the benefits of the activity in question. How assessments that compare different technologies should weigh differences in the spatial and temporal distribution of impact is not at all clear.

The boundary between quantifiable and nonquantifiable criteria is a fuzzy one, as the foregoing paragraph illustrates. Areas and times affected can be specified quantitatively, at least in principle, but the associated issues of the degree of voluntarism in imposed risks and the degree of coincidence of risks and benefits lend themselves to no tidy index.

Two other criteria that are clearly important but, at the same time, quite resistant to quantification are degree of irreversibility of harm and quality of evidence of potential harm. These aspects are not unrelated. The greater the degree of irreversibility potentially associated with a particular course of action, the heavier should be the burden of proof upon those advocating this action to show that the irreversible harm will not in fact materialize--or, in other words, the less conclusive the evidence against proceeding should have to be in order to stop the action. Some semblance of a quantitative index for irreversibility can in principle be supplied in the form of the time required to repair the damage, but this is enormously uncertain in many cases of greatest interest (for example, nuclear war or climatic change). Quality of evidence can be characterized (for example, as speculation, hypothesis based on limited data, theory with extensive empirical support, and so on), but hardly quantified.

CONCLUDING OBSERVATIONS

The foregoing observations on the uses and liabilities of various approaches to evaluating the economic and social costs of energy technologies have been intended to be illustrative of the sorts of problems encountered in technology assessment in the energy field, certainly they are not comprehensive. The interested reader should consult the references for more detail.

While acknowledging that space has not permitted developing many of the points that are relevant to this very broad topic, and that lack of knowledge would in any case preclude developing others, I will venture some broad observations on the connection of energy costs and limits to growth.

First, in the short term, the main problems will arise from dynamics of growth more than from absolute limits on scale of operations. Attempts to maintain a high growth rate on an already large base, and to increase national self-sufficiency rapidly, will lead to economic gambles on untried technologies that will fail expensively, strains on investment capital, and bigger social costs than would be incurred if there were time to weigh alternatives carefully (particularly troublesome is high risk of irreversible environmental errors).

Second, the data needed to evaluate with confidence the magnitude of the social costs of present energy technologies (to say nothing about future ones) are in many cases not available, and much further research is needed. Nevertheless, the information that is available suggests the possibility in the next few decades of significant interference in critical environmental processes and of a significantly increased chance of the aggressive use of nuclear weapons, to name two important problem areas. That we have come to the point where such disruptions are plausible, without having developed the capability to understand--let alone control--the possibilities in detail, gives reason to slow greatly the growth of energy consumption while more knowledge of the threats, and more benign technologies, are sought.

Third, energy technologies for the longer term are not likely to be cheap, even excluding social costs. For solar energy, hot-rock geothermal, controlled fusion, and fission breeder reactors, raw fuel is free or nearly so, but capital costs are likely to be more than high enough to erase these savings. These capital costs include heavy requirements for nonfuel raw materials, possibly exotic ones.

Fourth, there is no energy technology presently known or imagined (solar energy not excepted) with negligible environmental impact. Among the most fundamental problems are environmental damages associated with materials requirements of energy technologies, and potential disruption of climate by perturbing regional and global energy flow patterns. (The principal climatic threat is not global warming and melting of ice caps, which is slow and far away, but altering circulation and rainfall patterns with disastrous consequences for agriculture, which may be happening already.[11])

Fifth, technological therapy for social costs of existing and future energy technologies is often worthwhile, indeed essential, but laced with pitfalls: logistic constraints on achievable rate of implementation; high economic costs; limitations on level of impact reduction, with diminishing returns to investment at high levels of reduction;

and the difficulty that many fixes only shift the impact, creating new problems to replace old ones.[12]

In the end, then, there will remain a deep-rooted dilemma in energy's two-sided role in human affairs--its contributions to well-being through material prosperity on the one hand, and its undermining of well-being through environmental and other social costs on the other. It is inevitable that a point will be reached where the incremental gains in well-being from applying more energy do not compensate for the incremental losses due to the social costs of making more energy available. This point represents a "rational" limit to growth, although a physical limit enforced by unmistakable disaster might be some distance beyond it. There is some reason to suppose that the United States (although not the world as a whole) is already near or beyond this "rational" limit to energy growth.

NOTES

1. A more complete discussion of the status of various energy technologies than can be given here is to be found in Paul R. Ehrlich, Anne H. Ehrlich, and John P. Holdren, Ecoscience: Population, Resources, Environment (San Francisco: W. H. Freeman, 1977), Chapter 8.

2. Statistics on U.S. production and use of energy are from U.S. Department of Commerce, Statistical Abstract of the United States (Washington, D.C.: U.S. Government Printing Office, 1976).

3. Lee Schipper, "Raising the Productivity of Energy Utilization, in Annual Review of Energy, Vol. 1, ed. J. Hollander (Palo Alto, Calif.: Annual Reviews, Inc., 1976).

4. Some of the discussion in this section is condensed from a more comprehensive treatment in Robert J. Budnitz and John P. Holdren, "Social and Environmental Costs of Energy Systems," in ibid.

5. The principal source of these cost figures is Carl J. Anderson and others, An Assessment of U.S. Energy Options for Project Independence, University of California Lawrence Livermore Laboratory Report UCRL-51638, September 1974. Estimates for fusion and central-station solar are the author's.

6. An excellent discussion of these problems is I. C. Bupp et al., "The Economics of Power," Technology Review 77, no. 4 (February 1975): 14-25.

7. Kirk Smith, John Weyant, and John P. Holdren, Evaluation of Conventional Power Systems (Berkeley: University of California, Energy and Resources Group Report ERG 75-5, July 1975).

8.   Tables 3.8 through 3.12 appeared previously in Budnitz and Holdren, op. cit. and are based on the compilation by Smith, Weyant, and Holdren, op. cit.   The extensive primary literature from which these data were collected is referenced there.

9.   The view that disruption of natural biogeochemical systems on a large scale may represent a greater threat to human well-being than the direct toxic effects of civilization's effluents on people is developed in detail in John P. Holdren and Paul R. Ehrlich, "Human Population and the Global Environment," American Scientist 62, no. 3 (May-June 1974): 282-92, and in Ehrlich, Ehrlich, and Holdren, op. cit., Chapter 11.

10.   The fission reactor accident estimates in this paragraph are based on Smith, Weyant, and Holdren, op. cit.

11.   See Holdren and Ehrlich, op. cit. and S. Schneider and L. Mesirow, The Genesis Strategy (New York: Plenum, 1976).

12.   These points are developed at length in John P. Holdren, "Technology, Environment, and Well-being: Some Critical Choices," in Growth in America, ed. Chester L. Cooper (Westport, Conn.: Greenwood Press, 1976).

4

INTERNATIONAL EXCHANGES OF ALTERNATIVE ENERGY SOURCES: TECHNOLOGY, PRICE, AND MANAGEMENT
Nazli Choucri

The events of October 1973 triggered major changes in international economic and political relations, calling into question established assumptions about power politics, the use of economic power for political purposes, and the simple division of the world into rich and poor. Three trends have crystallized, each with potentially far-reaching implications. First, a growing realization by rich and poor states alike of the emerging interdependencies that bind them in a common quest for valued goods in an environment of potential scarcity; second, the development of a resource "crisis" stemming initially from impending shortages in petroleum supplies and maturing into a generalized concern over the possibilities of induced shortages, higher prices, or manipulated supplies of other resources critical to industrial processes; and third, the convergence of these two developments in an anxious concern for the international implications of investments in alternatives to petroleum and the possibility of greater reliance upon other sources of energy.

The effectiveness of the Organization of Petroleum Exporting Countries in raising petroleum prices did more than simply signal impeded access to oil resources and effective interference in the functioning of the world petroleum market. These interventions in the oil market led to the politicization of resource questions in international politics, and this politicization created a growing awareness by all states of the potential for serious malfunctioning of international economic exchanges.

The mobilization of countries of Asia, Africa, and Latin America in common opposition to the advanced industrial states placed new pressures on existing international institutions and confronted the advanced states with new constraints in the conduct of foreign policy. The very foundations of established global transactions prior to the crisis have been challenged and international institutions are facing an unprecedented demand for effective representation of the interests of the developing world. The General Assembly of the United Nations has become a forum for debates on a new international economic order. The discussions so far have been both rhetorical and pragmatic. The rhetoric reflects the ideological concerns of both rich and poor states--the former, in preserving their pre-eminence in international politics, and the latter, in seeking a more favorable economic condition vis-a-vis the industrial societies. The pragmatism indicates a shared appreciation of exchange problems and an awareness of the necessity of facilitating international trans actions to the joint satisfaction of both rich and poor.

This chapter describes some political consequences of a future global energy system based on alternatives to petroleum. We assume that the higher the price of crude petroleum, the more likely it will be that consumer countries will make greater investments toward the development of alternative sources of energy. Different sources of energy will invariably generate patterns of global interactions sub-stantially different from those created by petroleum exchanges. So too, different energy sources will highlight different types of in-equalities among nations, defining resource-rich and resource-poor differently, and giving rise to divergent sets of national options and priorities.

Our purpose is to delineate the characteristic features of in-ternational exchanges of alternative energy sources. We seek to identify some structural imperatives of the exchanges that might generate international political challenges for all states and con-tribute to the need for new organizational responses to these chal-lenges.

CHALLENGES TO WORLD ORDER

The resolutions calling for a new international economic order provided the impetus for the Sixth and Seventh Special Sessions of the UN General Assembly.[1] Throughout the Sixth Special Session, a spirit of confrontation between rich and poor states prevailed, pro-ducing stiff reactions on all sides by the end of 1974. The ameliora-tion of the oil crisis and plans for restructuring UN activities in social and economic affairs contributed to a perhaps only temporary lessening of tensions between advanced and less developed states.

Control over access and diffusion of advanced technology to de-veloping countries provides advanced states with marked leverage over international transactions. Similarly, control over raw ma-terials may provide the poorer producing countries leverage in their relations with advanced states. The focus on international exchanges of alternative sources of energy is designed to highlight different structures of interdependencies, economic and political potential conflicts associated with alternatives to petroleum, and the role of technological advances in international energy exchanges--all with respect to their implications for the development of world order.

The global institutional arrangements governing transactions in energy have yet to be developed to any significant degree. It is clear that national governments will assume a primary role in such arrangements. Whatever agreements importers and exporters of crude petroleum might develop in the immediate future, it is unlikely that such arrangements could be readily transferable to other sources of energy. Thus, the question of competing conceptions of world order for energy transactions will emerge increasingly as an important international political problem. A fundamental aspect of this problem will be devising institutionalized means by which the costs and benefits of global exchanges of energy will be regarded as equitable to both importers and exporters. The nature of the exchange will become one of the most fundamental issues in debates between producers and consumers, importers and exporters, and rich and poor states.

PROFILES OF ENERGY EXCHANGES

The major alternatives to petroleum are coal, natural gas, nuclear fission, solar energy, geothermal energy, and tar sands and shale oil.[2] Different cost factors, time perspectives, and technological imperatives are attached to each. Although petroleum will remain the dominant energy source at least until the end of the century, its importance may recede in the economies of the major industrial states.[3] In the years to come, we are likely to be confronted with a situation in which different countries will utilize different "mixes" of alternative energy sources.

Consumption of different energy sources by the developed nations is presented in Figure 4.1. Several trends stand out:

The volume of petroleum consumption increased sharply between 1949 and 1976, and the percentage of oil of total energy consumed nearly doubled during this period.

Although the total amount of coal consumed remained fairly stable, the share of coal in relation to other sources of energy declined appreciably.

The volume of natural gas consumed increased markedly over the 27 years, but its share as a percentage of total energy utilized remained fairly stable.

FIGURE 4.1

Consumption of Major Energy Sources by the Developed Nations,[a] 1950–75
(in million metric tons of coal equivalent)

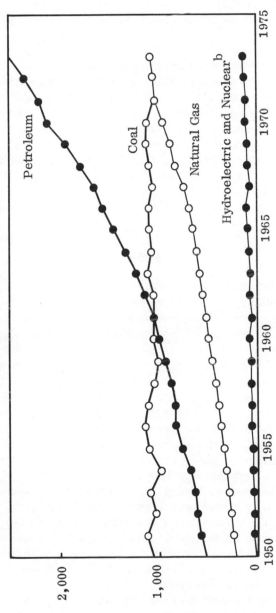

[a]The developed market economies of Australia, Canada, Israel, Japan, New Zealand, South Africa, United States, and Western Europe (including Yugoslavia).
[b]Includes imported electricity.
Source: United Nations, World Energy Supplies, 1970–1973, ST/ESA/STAT/Ser.J/18 (New York: United Nations, 1975).

While these figures do not disaggregate hydroelectric and nuclear power, we can assume that the amount of hydroelectric power
consumed has remained fairly stationary over time, whereas the
percentage of total energy utilized has declined somewhat. With respect to nuclear energy, however, both the amount utilized and the
percentage of total energy consumed have increased dramatically
over time.

There are clearly shared interests among non-oil-exporting
countries in the development of any source of energy in that such activity would expand the amount of energy available, decrease pressures for the utilization of petroleum, diversify the sources of potential political and economic power associated with the control of energy, and give the advanced states in particular a more important
role in energy-related transactions. Beyond these general communal-
ities, there are specific characteristics of each alternative to petroleum that highlight possibilities for the development of shared interests among nations, but also signal potential conflicts and cleavages.

Coal

The major consumers of coal also produce the most and control
the greatest volume of known reserves.[4] The United States and the
USSR together make the greatest use of coal, in about equal amounts.
The Soviet Union has the largest known reserves of coal, 56.5 percent of the world total in contrast to 17.5 percent for the United
States. Together they control 74 percent of world reserves. The
United States produced 21.49 percent of world coal in 1973 and the
Soviet Union 20.03 percent; they consumed 20.45 percent and 18.94
percent, respectively. The other major producers and consumers
are China, Poland, West Germany, and the United Kingdom. They
have comparatively small potential in that their individual reserves
are quite small, in no case greater than 5 percent of known world
reserves. The People's Republic of China has been a fairly large
producer in the past, providing 16.39 percent of the world's output
in 1973. The other three countries produced less than 8 percent
each. During the same year, China consumed 16.08 percent of recorded world consumption, the United Kingdom 5.29 percent, Poland
5.16 percent, and West Germany 4.90 percent. With few exceptions,
the major consumers are self-sufficient and the major producers
have extensive known reserves.
The major importers of coal are Japan (28 percent of world
imports in 1973), France (7.9 percent), Canada (7.5 percent), and
Italy (5.7 percent). Other West European countries also imported

coal but in relatively negligible amounts. The United States is the major exporter (about 24.5 percent of total world exports in 1973), followed by Poland (19.46 percent), the USSR (14 percent), Australia (13.9 percent), and West Germany (11.74 percent). Only Japan is clearly dependent on external sources for its coal consumption, but only to a fraction of the degree of its dependence for petroleum.

In the event that the United States becomes a major supplier of coal, it will find itself in a pivotal position in the world economy, not an implausible possibility given the magnitude of the country's reserves. Such a position would present none of the security-related problems associated with access to petroleum. Since the world's largest reserves of coal are found in the Soviet Union, potential competition between the United States and the USSR for security of access will also not be at issue. Greater utilization of U.S. coal resources may also have a positive effect upon U.S. relations with Western Europe and Japan by reducing competition for Middle Eastern oil. But such an eventuality might also broaden the gap between U.S. interests and those of its allies in terms of coordinating their energy policies and devising acceptable means of interaction with the Middle Eastern countries.

Because of the relative abundance of high-grade deposits, every nation has an interest in the development of coal. Although technological processes of liquification and gasification have been known for some time, there continues to be the need for considerable refinement in these techniques. But there are many petroleum uses for which coal would simply be an inefficient substitute.

Some difficulties pertaining to coal extraction and processing are readily identifiable. First, coal can be cheaply extracted only by large-scale surface mining. The technology of site restoration is still at a relatively primitive stage.[5] Some types of land, most notably those that are steep or arid, cannot be restored. The social costs of such activities are deemed in many cases to be too high. Second, coal production, regardless of mining method or geographical location, generates extensive wastes that may ignite and often contaminate nearby streams.[6] So far it has not been common practice to return these wastes to the mines. Third, gasification processes require large amounts of water. In areas where water is scarce, there is a built-in disincentive for investments of coal gasification projects.[7]

In short, given these considerations, in the absence of marked technological developments, it is unlikely that a substantial part of the increase in global energy requirements could be met by coal in the foreseeable future. Indeed, it is even questionable whether coal could even make a significantly larger contribution to world consumption of energy than presently made. At best, the international incentives for expanding both the availability and utilization of coal deposits remain highly constrained.

Natural Gas

    The international situation regarding natural gas is somewhat similar to that of coal. The United States and the USSR are the major producers and consumers.[8] The USSR controls the largest reserves, accounting for 31. 9 percent of the world's known deposits. The second largest deposits of natural gas reserves are in the Middle East, which accounted for 20. 8 percent of the world total in 1974. The United States has only 12. 6 percent, an estimate which is sometimes considered rather high since proven reserves have been steadily dropping for the last four years and reserves are at their lowest since 1956.[9]
    The United States consumes slightly more natural gas than it produces domestically. In 1973 the country accounted for 51. 85 percent of world consumption, while producing 50. 01 percent of world production. The same is generally true of the USSR, but the volume processed is considerably lower; in 1973 the USSR produced 19. 20 percent of world production and consumed 19. 83 percent.[10]
    The other major producers are Canada (6. 10 percent of total world production in 1973), the Netherlands (5. 75 percent), the United Kingdom (2. 34 percent), Rumania (2. 24 percent), and Iran (1. 5 percent). The consumption patterns for that year are somewhat different, in that all of Western Europe consumed 12. 46 percent of world consumption, Canada 3. 68 percent, Latin America 3. 28 percent, and Eastern Europe 3. 89 percent.
    Natural gas is becoming a more heavily traded source of energy, a consideration not entirely appreciated in current assessments of the world energy situation. In 1969 only 4 percent of world marketed natural gas production moved across national boundaries. In 1973 this figure increased to 7. 6 percent, hardly a dramatic rise, but it may well signify an emerging trend.[11] The potential strength of OPEC members in influencing the price, production, and distribution of natural gas might become an important factor in international exchanges of this source of energy. But their influence will continue to be marginal unless they coordinate their policies with those of other major producers, an eventuality that appears unlikely at the present time. However, some mutual overtures have been made between Russia and some OPEC members. For example, the USSR has agreed to allow the Iranians to build a pipeline from Iran to West Germany over Russian soil. The project should transport 13 billion cubic meters of gas annually over the 900-mile pipeline by 1981.[12]

It might be premature to anticipate a major role for the USSR in international exchanges of natural gas, but there are some indications that the USSR appreciates its international position and is seeking to expand attendant gains. It is expected, for example, that exports to France will reach an annual rate of 2.5 billion cubic meters in 1976.[13] So, too, the USSR has been exporting natural gas to Italy, Austria, West Germany, and Finland. In sum, it is generally believed that although the USSR is likely to remain a relatively small trader in oil and gas, it has considerable potential for becoming a major energy supplier in the 1980s. Present exports to Western Europe are viewed as a prelude to more extensive exchanges and as indications of potential expansion of Soviet influence.

Against this background it is important to recall that only a small fraction of total energy consumed will draw upon natural gas in the near future and there are presently few incentives for expanding the exploration of available fields in the West. The extension of OPEC and Soviet influence over natural gas exchanges may well provide potential importers with new problems and everyone with new challenges to any evolving conceptions of world order.

Nuclear Fission

The world nuclear capacity grew from an ability to generate 8,356 megawatts of nuclear-produced electricity in 1960 to 39,864 megawatts in 1972.[14] Of this capacity, 41 percent is controlled by the United States. Other major producers are the United Kingdom, the USSR, and France. Projected use of nuclear power in the world is noted in Table 4.1; Figure 4.2 presents nuclear production of electricity for five industrial states.

Reserves of uranium are estimated to pose no immediate problem. The United States has by far the largest known reserves of less costly uranium and also the world's largest reserves even under assumptions of high prices. Estimates on production of uranium indicate that the United States generated 51.57 percent of total non-communist production of the world in 1973, Canada 18.76 percent, South Africa 13.67 percent, France 7.81 percent, and Niger 4.8 percent.[15] Despite a favored U.S. position, it is expected that after 1975 from 15 to 25 percent of U.S. uranium needs will be supplied from external sources.[16] This situation may well increase the country's concern for assuring "safe" sources of supplies and possibly for its autonomy in the nuclear area.

The breeder reactor is the next immediate phase in the development of energy technology. A reactor is a "breeder" when it creates more than one fertile atom for every fissile atom it burns.[17]

This will make the use of uranium more efficient by enabling an increase in the utilization of energy content of natural uranium from between 1-2 percent to about 60-70 percent. These estimates are speculative, yet appear increasingly plausible.[18] The Soviet nuclear program to develop large, economical, fast breeder reactors is moving
more rapidly than programs in the United States or Western Europe.
The emphasis and the technological base are different, however: the
Soviets preferring the use of graphite, not pressurized water reactors,
as cheaper and safer than conventional reactors of similar size.[19]
In addition, the Soviet nuclear program is motivated by anticipated
large-scale expansion of domestic demands.[20]

TABLE 4.1

Projected Use of Nuclear Power, 1970-85
(Gigawatts--10^3 megawatts)

Country	1970	1975	1980	1985
Australia	--	--	1.0	3.0
Austria	--	--	1.4	3.0
Belgium	--	1.7	3.0	5.5
Canada	0.2	2.5	6.5	15.0
Denmark	--	--	0.7	1.5
Finland	--	--	1.5	3.0
France	1.7	3.8	13.4	32.5
Great Britain	4.2	8.8	16.4	35.0
Greece	--	--	--	1.8
Italy	0.6	1.4	6.0	16.0
Japan	1.3	8.6	32.0	60.0
Netherlands	--	0.5	2.5	5.0
Norway	--	--	0.8	2.0
Portugal	--	--	0.6	2.0
Spain	0.1	1.1	8.5	12.0
Sweden	--	3.2	8.6	16.5
Switzerland	0.4	1.0	5.5	8.0
Turkey	--	--	0.4	1.0
United States	7.5	57	132.0	280.0
West Germany	0.9	5.2	21.0	45.0

Source: Commissariat a l'Energie Atomique, Rapport Annuel
1972 (Paris: Synelog, 1973), p. 14.

FIGURE 4.2

Nuclear Production of Electricity, 1960–75
(million kilowatt hours)

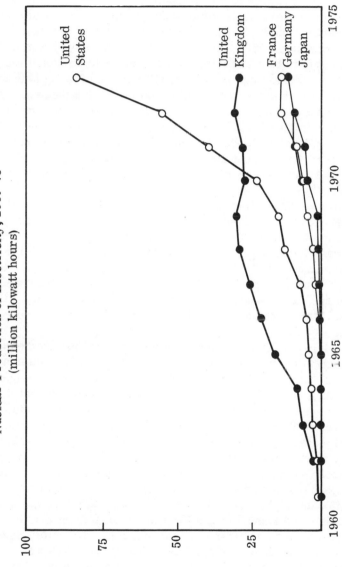

Source: United Nations, World Energy Supplies, ST/STAT/Ser.J (New York: United Nations, 1960 to 1973).

At this time the technology for enrichment of uranium (presently limited to gaseous diffusion) is expensive, complex, and closely guarded. Three gaseous diffusion plants owned and operated by the U.S. government have to this point supplied most of the noncommunist world's requirements for enriched uranium.[21] In addition, the United States clearly dominated international trade in the nuclear reactor industry. Only Canada with its heavy-water reactor (CANDU), has been able to break into the export market to any significant degree. This process has the decided advantage of being able to employ natural rather than enriched uranium.[22] But there are other developments. South Africa, for example, claims to have brought on-line a centrifuge method of enrichment which is 40 percent cheaper than conventional methods.[23] And the Israelis claim to have developed a laser-enrichment method which is both cheap and efficient.[24] But the full implications of these technological developments remain unclear.

Greater use of nuclear power could at least have two destabilizing effects from the perspective of national or global security. These are, first, increased proliferation possibilities with inadequate safeguards; and second, possibilities of terrorist potential in the use of plutonium itself, in the manufacture of nuclear weapons, or in the sabotage of nuclear plants. Clearly, the industrial countries are more vulnerable to such eventualities. For the developing states, however, there are added problems inherent in a nuclear energy system.

At least seven countries have the potential for producing nuclear explosives in the near future:[25] Argentina, Brazil, Pakistan, South Africa, Taiwan, and Israel.[26] These countries are seeking development guidelines for the transfer of nuclear technology, but so far little has been concluded.[27] Despite frequent disagreements, the development of shared nuclear interests exists among the advanced industrial states, but also the greatest differences between them and the rest of the world. In addition, there are further cleavages between those states that possess nuclear weapons and those that do not.

Against this background, five types of countries emerge, each with different interests and priorities, and with different conceptions of problems and requirements for resolution. First are the advanced states that possess nuclear weapons, namely, the United States, the Soviet Union, France, and the United Kingdom. They are concerned primarily with maintaining close control over the expansion and dissemination of this source of energy. Then there are the advanced countries with no nuclear weapons capacity, such as Japan and West Germany. These countries regard the availability of nuclear power primarily as a source of energy and so far are not willing to accept the costs of utilizing nuclear energy for military purposes. Third are the developing states that possess nuclear technology and seek to employ it for military purposes. India and China are the major representatives. They regard the possession of nuclear technology as one indicator of power in international politics and are willing to draw upon this source of energy for military purposes. Fourth there are the countries that are less developed but growing and as of now do not possess nuclear weapons. They consider the safeguards proposed by the developed states as an attempt to deny them an opportunity to demonstrate their capability in international politics. Finally there are countries of the "fourth world." They are the poorest of the states, with no ready prospects for rapid development and no possibilities for the acquisition of advanced nuclear technology. They are essentially peripheral to global efforts to regulate exchanges in nuclear technology but will invariably be affected whatever rules and regulations are established.

There are few common interests uniting all five groups beyond those of devising safe means of transportation, controlling terrorism, and minimizing the possibilities of accident. Clearly, international cleavages with respect to the issues pertaining to the development and expansion of nuclear energy are likely to persist along these lines for some time to come.

Solar Energy

The major advantages of solar energy are derived from its virtually unlimited availability, with little of the environmental contamination associated with the alternatives. It is estimated that with present technology, its maximum contribution to total energy requirements will not be greater than 20 percent of expected consumption.[28]

Those nations controlling the technology involved would essentially control access to solar energy. Thus, the major cleavages to be expected will be along technological lines and the resulting interdependencies will be technological. As in the case of any alternative to petroleum, solar energy would free the United States from potential demands upon Middle East oil, thus making greater petroleum supplies available to its allies.

Possibilities for shaping solar technology might increase the prospects for world order, providing acceptable means of transferring, sharing, or regulating such technology are developed. Inevitably, the poorer nations will not have access to this source of energy, unless it is made available to them by the advanced industrial societies. Solar technology might well be employed as a political instrument in the years to come, by threatening to withhold access unless certain political (or other) demands are met. Thus, the uses of control over sources of energy as a political instrument will persist. From a global perspective, the most critical problem still involves the development of regularized means of interactions and transactions related to access and transmission of solar energy.

Geothermal Heat

Geothermal heat is essentially a form of heat created by internal pressure. It is estimated that by 1985 a level of proved recoverable heat reserves could be established in the range of 29-290 quadrillion BTUs. The more important geothermal targets are deep sedimentary basins and shallow magma chambers.[29] But insufficient investments in research and development have placed strong constraints upon any rapid technological developments. Indeed, there exists no exploratory tool for locating geothermal deposits and existing methods have had limited success. Another major obstacle lies in the ability to drill holes of greater depth than is presently possible.[30]

In addition, there are major unresolved questions pertaining to air pollution resulting from the high sulfur content of steam, or other form of heat, that would be brought to the surface. Furthermore, the time required to develop environmental impact statements, assess overall environmental implications, and handle legal problems would significantly reduce the pace of geothermal exploration and development. Even under the optimistic assumption that geothermal sources of energy could be developed on a competitive economic basis in the near future, they would supply no more than 1 percent of anticipated U.S. energy requirements in 1985. On a worldwide basis the percentage would be considerably lower, rendering geothermal heat an improbable energy option.

Tar Sands and Shale Oil

Tar sands are hydrocarbon-bearing deposits distinguished from more conventional oil and gas reservoirs by the high degree of viscosity of the hydrocarbon which cannot be recovered by the same means of production. Reservoir energy is minimal, so some outside form of energy is needed to produce energy from tar sands.[31] Large tar sand deposits exist in Canada, Venezuela, and possibly Colombia as well. Deposits in the United States are much smaller and are not expected to yield considerable amounts of energy given present technology or levels of recovery. Given additional techno-

logical advances to process usable oil from such deposits, it is likely
that both Canada and Venezuela will continue their policies of exportation to the United States.

Oil shale is an oil-bearing rock which may be burned directly
and distilled to obtain oil products.[32] World production of shale oil
is about 25 million tons per year exclusive of production in mainland
China. The Soviet Union is a main producer of shale oil.[33] The
United States has extensive reserves of oil shale which could be marshalled as a viable source of energy. Oil shale deposits in the U.S.
western areas are estimated to yield a possible 1.8 trillion barrels
of crude shale oil. But less than 6 billion barrels of recoverable reserves could be recovered given limitations imposed by construction
time and environmental and legal constraints.[34] In the absence of
marked technological developments, it is highly unlikely that this
energy source will be utilized to any great extent in the near future.

Extensive technological developments in producing shale oil
may occur as the industry develops and as national priorities are
reoriented to take into account the extensive U.S. reserves. Present
bottlenecks in mine and plant organization, in processing, and in the
establishment of increased automation must be removed before any
significant cost reductions will be possible.[35] There are also considerable ambiguities regarding the formal status of shale lands.
Mining claims are yet to be accorded a clear legal position. Federal
leasing policies will invariably influence the level and rate of production, largely because over 80 percent of oil shale resources are located on federal lands.[36] Again, as national energy priorities are
reassessed and appropriate measures taken, such problems might
be resolved to enhance the potential contribution of shale oil to U.S.
energy needs. On a worldwide basis, however, this source of energy
will continue to have only marginal impact (if any) toward the meeting of energy requirements.

DIMENSIONS OF CONTROL

The control of alternative sources of energy will undoubtedly
pose the greatest global challenges in the decades to come. There
are three aspects to the problem, each reflecting a different perspective on the predicament of control. First is the question of price:
Who sets the price of energy; who are the major participants in debates regarding price; and what are the determinants of the pricing
algorithm? Second is the question of distribution: Who controls,
manages, and manipulates flows of energy across national boundaries;
who sets the conditions of exchange; and who determines the codes to
be employed? Finally is the question of regulation: What aspects of

energy transactions are to be regulated; who determines the nature
of the regulatory mechanisms; what policing methods are applied;
and what authoritative or legal basis is devised?

Control of price, distribution, and regulation of alternative
sources of energy are thus the most important legacies of the
petroleum crisis of October 1973. That crisis has politicized the
issue of control, drawing worldwide attention to the political implications of economic exchanges and to the leverage that producers of
energy may exert over the international system. This leverage
might well involve imposing the producers' own conception of world
order upon the global community. Indeed, the aftermaths of the 1973
events can best be described as a struggle around control, reflecting
differing conceptions of world order and of the appropriate rules and
regulations for the management of this order. Conflict over the control of price, distribution, and regulation of energy thus represents
the generic predicament of world order posed by the events of October 1973.

Price

The petroleum crisis initially involved the issue of embargo,
but, increasingly, difficulties over price and the unilateral increase
imposed by the oil-producing countries made it clear that the more
durable aspects of this crisis will invariably revolve around price.
At the present time the major international debates pertain to a definition of equitable price--a price that both producers and consumers
regard as acceptable to them. The definition of what is equitable is
itself dependent upon three related factors: the varying relationship
between cost and price; the extent to which the gap between cost and
price differs in relation to the costs of different sources of energy;
and the realization that price reflects a variety of preferences, both
private and public, that are aggregated and manifested in a statement
of economic value.

In the case of petroleum, the cost of extracting one barrel of
oil constitutes only a marginal component of the price per barrel.
The government tax of the oil-producing countries and the markup
factor of the international oil companies determine price. That the
cost of production is minimal in no way influences the final determination of price. Prior to October 1973 the preferences of the multinational companies determined price. Following the embargo and the
subsequent price increases, the national objectives of the oil-producing countries assumed a greater impact upon price. The shift
from a price dominated by the oil companies to one dominated by the
governments of oil-producing states indicates most sharply the recent

outcome of a conflict over the control of the price of petroleum.
The disagreements within OPEC reflect further this struggle for
control. Any resolution will invariably reflect the preferences of
all oil-producing states, some degree of compromise by everyone,
and some willingness to bear marginal social, economic, or political costs for the compromise.

Both producers and consumers of petroleum agree that the
higher the price of oil, the greater will be the incentives for investments in alternative sources of energy and, by extension, for reducing the cost of production. These incentives are, however, partly determined by the present price of alternatives to petroleum.

The price of coal has been steadily increasing because of rises
in the price of oil. In addition, safety regulations in U.S. mines,
environmental regulations, and transportation costs all influence the
price of coal. The cost component of price differs according to the
grade of ore. On balance, however, most of the variables influencing
price in the United States are tractable and potentially amenable to
government regulation or, alternatively, to being shaped by market
forces. Other than the power exerted by the coal lobby, there are
no clear systematic influences that might distort market mechanisms
to the degree exhibited in the case of petroleum.

Price calculations with respect to nuclear energy are considerably more complex. Price is most generally determined by the high
capital costs. "Cumulative capital expenditures in the non-Communist
world for nuclear power plants and equipment could exceed $250 bil-
lion by 1985, with approximately 50 percent of that sum expended in
the United States, 30 percent in Western Europe, 12 percent in Japan,
and the remainder in various other countries."[37] The price of uranium is a small fraction of the cost of nuclear energy. Thus, any
distortions imposed upon the price of uranium by joint action on the
part of the major uranium producers would affect the overall price
of nuclear energy only marginally.

The difficulties inherent in economic calculations of the costs
of alternatives to petroleum are overshadowed by far by those involved in calculating environmental, political, and social costs. To
date we have only the most rudimentary understanding of the com-
posite cost calculus associated with alternative sources of energy.
We have only begun to appreciate the overall costs of reliance on
petroleum. Only the vaguest glimpse of the overall costs of alternative energies is available, and almost no visions of the costs of different "mixes" of energy alternatives have yet been made. Even the
most sketchy observations may not be warranted given the state of
knowledge of overall cost assessments. It is clear, however, that
for any alternative to petroleum, cost will be the major determinant
of price. It is trite, but important, to stress that the gap between

cost and price, so large in the case of petroleum, will not be repli-
cated for any other alternative for the foreseeable future. This is a
fundamental reality that shapes all decisions regarding investments
in alternatives to petroleum and provides the basic parameters of
the potential price structure.

The debates between producers and consumers of petroleum
over the past several years have reflected varying assumptions of
equitable price and different conceptions of what each ought to accept
from the other. But it is the debates among the oil-producing countries themselves that highlighted most dramatically the fact that a
price preference reflects national priorities and represents an aggregated index of government demands for resources. Development
plans, national objectives, and political priorities together shape and
translate into a set of economic preferences for a specific price or a
range of prices. We do not yet fully know how national preferences
are expressed into a preferred price, nor the type of mapping function that states one in terms of the other. So, too, there is little
understanding in both policy-making and academic circles of the appropriate algorithm for this mapping. Yet everyone agrees that the
price of petroleum as stipulated by the oil-exporting governments
represents a social welfare function and not simply that of profit
maximization. Equally important is the realization that the objectives that are pursued may not even be conceived in terms of a
maximization algorithm (however implicit, vague, or inarticulate it
might be), but that some form of satisfying occurs, whereby at
times minimalist rather than maximalist strategies dominate.

How national preferences are shaped, who is instrumental in
defining these preferences, and how national goals are reflected in
a price preference thus remain a mystery. Some clues are available in comparing the price preferences of countries with high petroleum reserves and those with low known reserves, particularly when
their respective population sizes and level of economic development
are also taken into account. But once these comparisons are made,
there are few ready means of attributing (or predicting) a particular
price preference to particular national attributes and characteristics.
Therein lies one of the major uncertainties regarding national preferences for price structures. The few efforts currently undertaken
to clarify this relationship are tentative at best.[38]

At the international level, the most critical debates over price
now pertain to the criteria of equity: By what measuring rod ought
nations determine the appropriate price for an international exchange
of resources? The Seventh Special Session of the UN General Assembly reflected the range of arguments and preferences. The various proposals by the producing as well as consuming countries indicate the differences in priorities. Despite the ambiguities, this

much is clear: Any evolving conception of world order will inevitably take into account the conflicting criteria for the determination of equitable price.

Distribution

Economic and political factors tend to determine the flow and distribution patterns of energy as a basic resource. The petroleum "crisis" of 1973 indicated changes in the distribution of petroleum. The multinational corporations have exercised control over the flows of petroleum and the ways by which the product is distributed. Increasingly, the producing countries are seeking to obtain greater control over the process, although it is not yet clear precisely what form this control will take. Political considerations are coming to the fore in the distribution of petroleum, and the ability to evoke the oil "weapon" as a policy instrument is testimony to this development. These changes signal analogous possibilities for alternative sources of energy.

A combination of economic and political factors will serve to shape the distribution of nuclear energy in the years to come. The availability of uranium is geographically determined. Moreover, technological developments, notably in the form of breeder reactors, will play an increasing role in the distribution and diffusion of nuclear energy. So, too, control over the transfer of technology can be exercised as a political "weapon" to be accorded to nations whose policies are consistent with those of major donors.

The distribution of nuclear reactors on a worldwide basis is still subject to political constraints, as most of the nonnuclear powers are ready to argue. But the full potential for employing such transactions as instruments of foreign policy is yet to be explored. So far, there have been only discrete cases, too few to draw broader generalizations. Even more severe ambiguities persist with respect to needs for and trends in regulation of alternative sources of energy.

The distribution (and diffusion) of the technology for solar power, energy from oil shale and tar sands, and geothermal energy is likely to be shaped primarily by economic factors. The extent to which technological developments enable the advanced industrial societies to make use of these alternative sources of energy will determine their ability to make them available to other nations. The possibilities appear more remote than for nuclear energy. Yet they are plausible enough to warrant assessment as to the international implications of their development.

Regulation

Control over the regulation of energy exchanges is perhaps most central to the question of world order.[39] At the present time the regulation of petroleum exchanges is undertaken largely through the conjunction of the policies of the oil-producing countries, the services of the international oil companies, and the legacies of a world petroleum market that has produced a situation of considerable stability of exchanges over the past 25 years. The oil-consuming nations have attempted, and continue to attempt, to influence existing patterns of regulation. But, so far, control remains with the producers.

There are no formal mechanisms for the regulation of coal, nationally or internationally, nor are there any institutions for the worldwide regulation of natural gas transactions. In the United States, government control of price is an important regulatory factor with potential international implications insofar as low domestic prices create high demand which may then affect the international market. The International Energy Agency may itself become involved in the regulation of natural gas in the event of another oil embargo. OPEC is also trying to develop mechanisms for regulating transactions among its natural gas exporters. Algeria and Iran are likely to take a major role in the event of an official OPEC posture on this issue.

By contrast, there are a number of ways in which the dissemination of nuclear technology is regulated and, by extension, the availability of nuclear energy. First, there are bilateral controls. When Canada made nuclear technology available to India, it insisted on fairly stringent controls.[40] U.S. sales to Egypt, Iran, and Israel are also predicated on strong bilateral controls. Such constraints are not necessarily effective in limiting the expansion of nuclear technology. The Indian nuclear explosion, for example, indicates that diversion of fissionable materials is entirely possible under a system of bilateral controls.[41] Adequate safeguards cannot be developed unless both nations are in agreement about the content, processes, outcome, and intents of the safeguards. Clearly, there are fundamental differences among the nuclear and nonnuclear powers on this issue, just as there are between the developed and developing states.

Two perplexing problems continue to confront the international community in this regard. First, the question of the "rights" nations have to develop nuclear weapons capabilities; second, the question of equal rights to access and distribution of such capabilities. The dual problem has been posed as follows: "No matter what the rhetoric, a world in which five or six nations control the weapons technology is by

definition discriminatory; a system which leaves all the decision
making in their hands is by definition paternalistic. Clearly there
is an unfilled need for a more attractive option than either accepting
the monopolistic position of the 'nuclear OPEC,' or going it alone."[42]
Clearly, too, the need for such options is viewed differently by different nations.

The prospect for development of an active uranium cartel of
national governments appears increasingly implausible. The major
producer countries--the United States, South Africa, Canada, Australia, and Niger--seem too diffuse in their political orientations or
economic objectives as to preclude any ready agreement among them.
More important, however, is the fact that the uranium market is controlled by private interests. The Uranium Producer's Forum, a
group comprised of Britain's Rio Tinto Zinc, Canada's Rio Algom
and Denison Mines, Australia's Western Mining, France's Uranex,
and an organization of South African Mines called Nuclear Fuel
Corporation control most of the world's production. But within this
group the strength of the individual members is unequal. The
Rothschilds of France and England have an interest in nearly every
major uranium mine in the world, with controlling interests in the
Rio Algom Mines of Canada, which owns the largest uranium reserves in North America, as well as major interests in Rio Tinto
Zinc, Anglo-American Corporation, Mohta and Pennarya Companies.[43]
However, demand is predicted to be sufficiently high to preclude any
disagreements about market shares. Risks and costs are ambiguous
but do not seem to be very different for different producers. In addition, the market will probably bear prices above cost because of the
projected structure of demand. Available estimates for demand are
calculated prior to the oil embargo of 1973, thus probably under-
estimating what actual demand will be. In sum, while the prospects
of a national cartel of uranium producers might be unlikely in the
foreseeable future, one of private producers appears increasingly
possible.

The symbolic importance of the International Atomic Energy
Agency (IAEA) as an international regulatory mechanism should not
overshadow two important facts: It performs basically a bookkeep-
ing function; and it has no effective control over the producers' policies. The IAEA determines how much nuclear fuel is processed
within a country and expects to be informed by individual nations exactly where nuclear fuels are being utilized. In the event that some
nuclear fuel is unaccounted for, the IAEA "operates on the principle
that if there is an international system which will give the proper
alarm whenever a state is suspected on reasonable grounds of intentional diversion, this in itself should provide sufficient deterrence."[44]

The weakness of the IAEA is perhaps best revealed by the fact
that the most severe sanction it can impose is to expel a member
and call its violations to the attention of the international community
and to the UN Security Council. In the final analysis there are no
international arrangements that can prevent nations from demonstrat-
ing their ability to build their own nuclear weapons.[45] The raw
materials and the technology both exist and the intent to develop
nuclear weapons can always be justified in the name of national sovereignty, punctuated by arguments of national defense.

TECHNOLOGICAL IMPERATIVES IN ENERGY EXCHANGES

Undoubtedly the most critical considerations in international
exchanges of alternative sources of energy are technological. The
costs of alternatives to petroleum--and the attendant price of imports
and exports--will continue to be determined by technological constraints. Therein lies the major difference in energy exchanges:
For petroleum, physical control over the underlying resource has
come to dominate control over extractive and processing technologies
in shaping prices and influencing availability. For alternatives to
petroleum, control over technology will continue to be the major determinant of price and, by extension, of distribution and regulation.
Since the advanced industrial states control the development
and diffusion of advanced technology, they are both the producers
and the consumers for any source of energy other than petroleum.
They will inevitably become the rule makers as well as the managers
of international exchanges of alternative sources of energy. The advantages enjoyed by the oil-producing countries in this regard will
not extend to coal, natural gas, nuclear power, or other energy
sources. It is partly in recognition of their unfavorable position in
international exchanges that the poor countries have sought to tie debates regarding equitable prices of petroleum and other raw material
to exchanges in, and availability of, advanced technology. Indeed,
the transfer of technology from richer to poorer states has dominated
international debates leading to the Sixth and Seventh Sessions of the
UN General Assembly in 1974 and 1975. These arguments revolved
around the question of a global reorientation of international exchanges
in resources, technology, financial flows and trade relations.
Specifically, the Seventh Special Session centered around eight
issues: (1) establishment of a new international economic order,
(2) problems of international trade, (3) transfer of real resources
for financing the development of poorer countries and international
monetary reforms, (4) problems of science and technology, (5) industrialization problems, (6) food and agriculture, (7) problems and

prospects of cooperation among developed and developing countries, and (8) the restructuring of the economic and social sectors of the UN system.

Different positions crystallized around each of these issues, with the major cleavages between the less developed countries and the United States, Western Europe, and Japan, and sometimes major differences arose among the less developed countries themselves. Generally the Western world took positions at variance with those adopted by poor states, but there were notable exceptions and it was not uncommon for the United States to find itself in disagreement with the European Community or its allies in general. The final U.S. position on many of these issues differed markedly from its initial stiff reaction and a modicum of reconciliation appeared to emerge. The positions and preferences of the developing countries are still being clarified and there is, as yet, no commonly agreed upon stance and no single perspective that represents poorer states.

Undoubtedly the most pervasive corollary of the Seventh Special Session was the increased awareness in both national and international circles of the growing interdependence among states and of the international constraints on national behavior. Concern of the advanced states over the possibility of impeded access to supplies of raw material from poorer states has been accompanied by a growing concern by the producers of raw materials for greater access to advanced technology.

In sum, the events following the petroleum crisis of October 1973 leading to a greater concern for the development of alternative sources of energy have contributed to a deeper appreciation of the role of technology in international energy exchanges and to the criticality of control over access and diffusion of advanced technology. By seeking to press their advantage in this regard, the industrial states have contributed to the mobilization and politicization of technological transfers to developing countries. Exchanges in alternative sources of energy are now closely coupled to debates on technological exchanges. More important, the issue of access to advanced energy technology is now closely related to debates over the access of poorer countries to advanced technologies for development. In each case the transfer of technology across national borders raises important questions of management and of the appropriate criteria of exchange.

INTERNATIONAL TRANSFER OF ENERGY TECHNOLOGY

The importance of technological change in rendering alternative sources of energy commercially viable is well recognized in both national and international circles. Less clear, however, are the magnitudes of investments required for effective technological development, the precise technical requirements for each source of energy, and the appropriate criteria for technological decisions. Despite these uncertainties everyone recognizes the importance of technological exchanges among nations and the fact that such exchanges are becoming an important medium for exerting political influence. Indeed, the transfer of technology has become a clear form of political leverage.

Technology transfer is a diplomatic term that fails to convey the fact that technology is bought and sold in international markets, and that commercial considerations dominate such exchanges. Even more compelling is the fact that such transfers are largely in the hands of multinational corporations rather than national governments. Although nation-states are assuming an increasingly important role in global exchanges, the transnational firm is still the major conveyor for the movement of technology between states. Private firms seek to maximize profits and national governments seek to maximize social objectives. The conflict between the two types of goals is often manifested in the attempt of governments to control and the multinational corporations' activities in their own countries, and in the efforts of the international organizations to develop viable codes of conduct both for the multinationals and for national governments. These efforts have to a large extent been unsuccessful. Yet a momentum has set in, and the international community is seeking greater authority and responsibility for the management of technology transfers.

The view from the developing countries is that the technological decisions need to be made within a developmental context, that energy-related decisions need to be evaluated on their social and political merits rather than on their economic merits exclusively, and that poorer countries should share in the global management of technology transfers. Although everyone agrees that the "right" technical decisions for the development of energy resources in an advanced country need not necessarily be "right" for a developing state, fundamental disagreements persist regarding what might be viewed as "right" in each context. The debates are over appropriate criteria for investment in energy-related technology and for the transfer of technology across national boundaries. For example, what might be considered an appropriate technical decision on the grounds of productive efficiency may not be desirable or acceptable in terms of potential for generating employment, contributing to political stability, or enhancing the international position of a nation.

These differences become all the more compelling in the nuclear energy field where the five types of countries described earlier are

likely to have diverse technical priorities and differing conceptions
of appropriate criteria for technical investments or technology transfers. Advanced states with nuclear capacity will seek to control the
diffusion of technology and to dominate the decisions for technical
investments. Advanced states with no nuclear capacity are likely to
value technological investments on scientific grounds rather than in
terms of their immediate power or military potential and to view
technological investments in this light. Less developed states that
possess nuclear capacity will be concerned with the foreign policy
implications and the military value of their capabilities and will employ criteria of national power and prestige as major determinants
of technological investments and technical exchanges. Less developed countries that do not possess nuclear technology may seek to
influence the evolution of international codes for the management of
energy exchanges in a way that might preserve for them open options
for the future such that they might be able to influence the nature of
technological exchanges in the years to come. Finally, the "fourth
world" countries that have minimal influence, if any, on such debates, will attempt to align energy-related decisions to development
decisions in such a way as to assure there be participation in international debates pertaining to the transfer of technology for development. In sum, states with differing nuclear status employ different
criteria for what is "appropriate" for technical investments and
technological transfers. These differences constitute the essence
of alternative views of world order as they pertain to different conceptions of the management of energy exchanges.

MANAGEMENT OF INTERNATIONAL EXCHANGES

    The problem of establishing international patterns of collabora-
tive behavior in the energy field is undoubtedly one of the most critical of our times.[46] The absence of agreements among nations regarding control of the price, distribution, and regulation of energy
exchanges accentuates the need for the development of collaborative
behavior. Four alternative modes of regulating international energy
transactions illustrate some differences among alternative conceptions of world order: market mechanisms, joint exchanges, multilateral coordination, and international agreements; they all differ in
their accommodation to the requirements of collaborative behavior.
    International energy exchanges based on market principles
would also predicate control of energy products upon resource, capital, and technological considerations and the distribution of energy
upon market structures. But specific national interests would be
taken into account, allowing national governments to exercise direct

control over the structure of emerging arrangements. A joint exchange (in terms of bilateral agreement, for instance) would take the national interests of the participants into account while basically relying on the price mechanism to regulate energy transactions. Thus, the role of government would be more direct than in a free market situation.

By contrast, multilateral and international energy exchanges would differ substantially in their underlying premises and in their approach to the issues of price, distribution, and regulation of energy forms. A multilateral exchange involving government-to-government regulative mechanisms would predicate the control of energy products upon community values and upon the maximization of benefits to the group as a whole. An international system of energy exchange would develop institutionalized means of assessing the energy needs of its members and develop means of apportioning available resources accordingly. In such a situation, conventional principles would be superseded by institutionalized means of regulating energy flows based on procedures agreed upon by the participant states.

The distribution of energy in a multilateral coordination system would differ from that in an international arrangement. In the first case, community interests as well as the market mechanism would shape the nature of energy transactions; in the other, social welfare considerations would predominate. So, too, the price system in a multilateral energy exchange is likely to be predicated upon principles of community equity as well as supply and demand factors; but in an international arrangement a broader view of price would predominate, based on equity and encompassing the interests of all participant states. Similarly, the underlying regulatory mechanisms would also differ. Thus, a multilateral arrangement would develop means of regulating energy transactions according to community-oriented rules and regulations, whereas an international exchange will be public-regarding in that the organizational framework would be based on explicit rules and regulations, to be applied to all participants on rational-legal principles. Regulatory mechanisms for international or multilateral energy systems exchanges would be fundamentally different from those in competitive market or joint systems.

These observations are summarized in Table 4.2, which illustrates the differences among these four alternative managements with respect to the control of energy resources, the distribution of the products, the price of energy, and the underlying regulatory mechanism. Finally, it must be recognized that autarky represents still another option. But such a posture would, in effect, negate the possibility of developing a viable global exchange. A policy of

TABLE 4.2

The Management of System Requisites for Energy Exchanges

System Requisites	Alternative Exchange System			
	Competitive Market Mechanisms	Joint Exchanges	Multilateral Coordination	International Agreements
Control of energy resources	Profit maximization based on resource capital, and technology considerations	Based on resource availability and technological endowments	Based on agreed upon community principles	Institutionalized control of global management
Distribution of product	Competitive market principles	Market principles and accommodated national interests	Community interests and market principles	Social welfare function
Price	Supply and demand functions	Supply and demand functions	Community interests and supply and demand functions	International equity
Regulatory mechanism	Market price	Price and national interest	Community organization	International public organization

Source: Compiled by the author.

autarky amounts to a nonexchange and denies the necessity of developing viable means of interaction with other nations. Such a posture would be extremely costly and does not represent a viable option for the United States or any other nation. Energy needs can be accommodated only through a recognition of the linkages and interdependencies among nations, and through the development of some institutionalized means of regulating such transactions. The choice of such means is basically a question of alternative conceptions of world order.

NOTES

1. This section draws upon research notes for an ongoing Project on Access, Security, and Availability of Mineral Resources supported by the Rockefeller Foundation Fellowship Program in International Conflict.

2. This section draws upon Chapters 1 and 9 of Nazli Choucri with Vincent Ferraro, International Politics of Energy Interdependence: The Case of Petroleum (Lexington, Mass.: Lexington Books, 1975).

3. The following data are from United Nations, World Energy Supplies, ST/ESA/STAT/SER.J (New York: United Nations, 1960-73).

4. Ibid.

5. Amory D. Lovins, "World Energy Strategies," Bulletin of the Atomic Scientist 30, no. 5 (May 1974): 23.

6. Joel Darmstadter, "Energy," in Population, Resource, and the Environment, ed. Ronald G. Ridker (Washington, D.C.: U.S. Government Printing Office, 1972), p. 140.

7. James Ridgeway, The Last Play (New York: Mentor, 1973), p. 171.

8. United Nations, World Energy Supplies, ST/ESA/STAT/ SER.J/No. 18 (New York: United Nations, 1975).

9. Wall Street Journal, June 12, 1975.

10. United Nations, World Energy Supplies, 1970-73, op. cit.

11. U.S. Department of the Interior, Bureau of Mines, World Natural Gas, 1973 (Washington, D.C.: U.S. Government Printing Office, 1974).

12. New York Times, April 11, 1975.

13. New York Times, August 20, 1974.

14. Commissariat a l'Energie Atomique, Rapport Annual 1972 (Paris: Synelog, 1973).

15. United Nations, World Energy Supplies, 1970-73, op. cit.

16. U.S. Department of the Interior, Bureau of Mines, Mineral Facts and Problems, 1970 (Washington, D.C.: U.S. Government Printing Office, 1971), p. 239.

17. Irvin C. Bupp and Jean-Claude Derian, "The Breeder Reactor in the U.S.: A New Economic Analysis," Technology Review, July/August 1974, p. 27.

18. Allen Hammond, "Breeder Reactors: Power for the Future," Science 174 (November 19, 1974): 808.

19. Robert Gillette, "Nuclear Power in the U.S.S.R.: American Visitors Find Surprises," Science 173 (September 10, 1970): 1003.

20. Ibid., p. 1006.

21. Joseph A. Yager and Eleanor Steinberg, Energy and U.S. Foreign Policy (Cambridge, Mass.: Ballinger, 1974), p. 350.

22. Wall Street Journal, June 24, 1975.

23. New York Times, November 23, 1975.

24. Robert Gillette, "Uranium Enrichment: Rumors of Israeli Progress with Lasers," Science 183, no. 4130 (March 22, 1974): 1172.

25. Boston Globe, June 8, 1975.

26. New York Times, June 13, 1975.

27. New York Times, June 18, 26, 29 and July 20, 1975.

28. Dietrich E. Thomson, "Farming the Sun's Energy," Science News 101 (April 8, 1972): 238.

29. Allen Hammond, "Geothermal Energy: An Emergency Major Resource," Science 177 (September 15, 1972): 978.

30. National Petroleum Council, U.S. Energy Outlook (Washington, D.C.: the Council, 1972), p. 230.

31. Ibid., p. 225.

32. Nathaniel B. Guyol, Energy in the Perspective of Geography (Englewood Cliffs, N.J.: Prentice-Hall, 1971), p. 49.

33. Ibid.

34. National Petroleum Council, op. cit., p. 4.

35. Ibid., p. 219.

36. Ibid., p. 206.

37. Yager and Steinberg, op. cit., p. 335.

38. See, for example, Esteban Hnyilicza and Robert S. Pindyck, "Pricing Policies for a Two-Part Exhaustible Resource Cartel: The Case of OPEC," MIT Energy Laboratory, World Oil Project Working Paper, MITEL76-008WP, April 1976.

39. This section expands on themes presented in Chapter 9 in Choucri with Ferraro, op. cit.

40. New York Times, May 21 and 23, 1974.

41. New York Times, May 21, 1974.

42. Lincoln P. Bloomfield, "Nuclear Spread and World Order," Foreign Affairs 53, no. 4 (July 1975): 747.

43. "It Worked for the Arabs . . .," Forbes 115, no. 2 (January 15, 1975): 19-20.

44. Ryukichi Imai, "Nuclear Safeguards," Adelphi Papers, no. 86 (London: The International Institute for Strategic Studies, March 1972), p. 1.

45. William O. Doub and Joseph M. Duckert, "Making Nuclear Energy Safe and Secure," Foreign Affairs 53, no. 4 (July 1975): 756.

46. An earlier version of the following arguments has been presented in Analyzing Global Interdependence, Vol. II, Energy Interdependence, Nazli Choucri with Vincent Ferraro (Cambridge, Mass.: MIT Center for International Studies, 1974).

SUSTAINABLE GROWTH:
ACCIDENT OR
DESIGN

INTRODUCTION

People have speculated about the limits to sustainable economic growth for many decades. There are two main schools of thought on growth limitation issues and strategies. The first is at least loosely associated with the name of Thomas Malthus. "Neo-Malthusians" argue that lack of food, natural resources, and the fragile nature of ecosystems put real natural constraints that will inevitably be painful on the potential for economic growth. More refined versions of these limits-to-growth arguments stress limits due to structural factors and the law of diminishing returns. A second school of thought emphasizes a "steady-state" economy as both a physical necessity and a moral ideal. John Stuart Mill was one of the first philosophers of industrial society to argue the virtues of a steady-state economy. More recently, Kenneth Boulding, Herman Daly, and a small number of other social scientists have begun serious work on designing a transition strategy for shaping such an economy.

The two chapters that follow are rooted in these two different but related, schools of thought. Edward Renshaw argues that a transition to limited growth is already under way in the United States, although this is not yet generally realized. If this is indeed the case, it raises a long agenda of social, political, and economic issues that have been previously ignored when growth was assumed to be inevitable. Herman Daly, on the other hand, would probably agree with Renshaw, but he feels that the time has come to design a transition to a sustainable steady-state economy for both practical and moral reasons.

Whether one really agrees with Daly or Renshaw, a tremendous amount of evidence does exist indicating that advanced industrial economies will experience a period of social transition and slowing growth rates in the near future. The question is not whether industrial economies will change rather dramatically, but rather how the change will come about. One approach is to sit back and let natural processes reorganize industrial economies. An activist approach suggests confronting the issue agenda squarely and begs for the rational design of a transition to slowed growth. By actively intervening, some of the harshest social effects of such a transition might be mitigated.

Herman Daly is one of the best-known contemporary advocates of a designed transition to a steady-state economy. A steady-state economy would be characterized by a constant stock of people

105

and artifacts. The ultimate limitations on the size of the stock to be maintained are both environmental and social. The aim of such an economy is to minimize the "throughput" required to maintain a given stock. In an ideal steady state almost all raw materials would be recycled, necessitating minimal new inputs of natural resources.

Daly argues that a steady-state economy is both necessary and desirable. It is made necessary by the laws of thermodynamics, particularly by the entropy law. All work that is done requires energy and transforms low-entropy fuels into artifacts and waste heat. Growth is a process that depletes sources of low-entropy matter (fossil fuels) and fills waste systems with high entropy. Humankind has collectively reached a point where a return to a solar income economy is essential. Daly also argues that development of a steady-state economy is morally desirable. He feels that growth and throughput should be limited because of moral principles including religious ethics, stewardship, "enoughness," humility, and holism, and because of a need to overcome the emptiness of the growth society fostered by natural resource abundance.

Daly concludes by outlining three types of institutions that are essential to a steady-state economy. His aim is to maintain macro-stability while insuring microvariability. He would do this by stabilizing population, physical wealth, and by some sort of wealth redistribution. He suggests that marketable "baby licenses" would be one way to stabilize population and that resource depletion quotas would stabilize demand for natural resources. Auctions of deple-tion quotas would eventually drive up natural resource prices and thus encourage recycling and conservation. He also recognizes that some redistribution of wealth and income floors and ceilings would be essential to maintain social peace in a steady state.

Edward Renshaw demonstrates that a transition to a slow- or no-growth economy is already under way. Population growth and productivity are now much lower in the United States than in pre-vious decades and unemployment is on the rise. This results from the law of diminishing returns. There are limits to growth based on the substitution of inanimate for animate energy. No similar source of potential growth now exists.

Renshaw concludes, as do authors of earlier chapters, that spiraling prices for energy and nonfuel minerals will be a signifi-cant barrier to future growth. He suggests that we have few eco-nomic tools for combating the resulting "stagflation," simultaneous increases in prices, and unemployment. He concludes by arguing that resource conservation and new efficiency technologies are essential for further increases in the quality of life.

5

THE STEADY-STATE ECONOMY: WHAT, WHY, AND HOW
Herman E. Daly

WHAT IS A STEADY-STATE ECONOMY?

The steady-state economy is a physical concept. It is characterized by constant stocks of people and physical wealth maintained at some chosen, desirable level by a low rate of throughput. Throughput flow begins with depletion (followed by production and consumption) and ends with an equal amount of waste effluent or pollution. Benefits come from the services rendered by the stock of wealth (and people). This service or psychic income is unmeasurable, but it is clearly a function of the stock, not of the throughput flow. One cannot ride to town on the maintenance flow of the stock of automobiles, but only in an existing automobile that is a current member of the stock. Stocks yield services and require maintenance and replacement. The throughput flow is the maintenance cost of the stock. As such it should be minimized for any given stock size.

The psychic dimension of wealth, that is, its want-satisfying capacity, may forever increase as a result of increasing knowledge and technical improvement. But the physical dimensions are limited. It is obvious that in a finite world nothing physical can grow forever. Yet current policy seems to aim at increasing physical production indefinitely.

Stocks and their associated maintenance throughputs are limited by space, by the mass of the earth, by heat release, and far more stringently by the intricate web of ecological relationships which too large a throughput will destroy. Moral and social limits, though less definable, are likely to be even more stringent. For example, the social problem of safeguarding plutonium from immoral uses and consequences is more likely to limit breeder reactor

usage than is the physical constraint of thermal pollution. The
steady state will be socially desirable long before it becomes an
immediate physical necessity.

Economists usually disregard physical dimensions and concentrate their attention on value. There is no really satisfactory
measure of true value, since "utility" or "psychic income" simply
cannot be measured. Value is conventionally measured in terms of
money. Money serves as a kind of substitute for both "value" and
"commodities in general." Money, as a unit of account, has no
physical dimension. A sum on deposit in a bank can grow forever
at 5 percent. Why cannot real GNP, like money, also grow forever
at 5 percent? The concrete reality being measured is too often reduced to identity with the abstract unit of measure. But in fact,
wealth always has a physical dimension. Even knowledge requires
physical organisms with brains, calories to run the brain, and light
for the transmission of information. Knowledge can increase the
ability of the stock to satisfy wants, perhaps without limit, but the
physical stock that satisfies wants and the throughput that maintains
the stock are both subject to limits.

This role of money fetishism in supporting a growth ideology
has been noted by Lewis Mumford:

> Now, the desire for money, Thomas Aquinas
> pointed out, knows no limits, whereas all natural
> wealth, represented in the concrete form of food,
> clothing, furniture, houses, gardens, fields, has
> definite limits of production and consumption, fixed
> by the nature of the commodity and the organic
> needs and capacities of the user. The idea that
> there should be no limits on any human function is
> absurd: all life exists within very narrow limits
> of temperature, air, water, food; that services of
> other men, should be free of such definite limits
> is an aberration of the mind.[1]

Once a steady state is attained at some level of population and
wealth, it would not be forever frozen at that level. As values and
technology evolve, different levels might become both possible and
desirable. But the growth (or decline) required to get to the new
level would be seen as a temporary adjustment process, not a norm.
The momentum of growth in population and capital currently creates
our technological and moral development. In the steady state,
technological and moral evolution would be autonomous rather than
growth-induced. They would precede and pull growth in the most
desirable direction, rather than being pushed down the path of least

resistance by the pressure of autonomous growth. Growth (positive or negative) would always be seen as a temporary passage from one steady state to another.

WHY? ASSUMPTIONS AND VALUES UNDERLYING THE STEADY-STATE VIEW

The steady-state view is based on physical, biological, and moral first principles and is immediately deducible from them without the aid of computer simulations.

The physical first principles are the laws of thermodynamics, of which Albert Einstein said:

> A theory is more impressive the greater the
> simplicity of its premises is, the more differ-
> ent kinds of things it relates and the more ex-
> tended is its area of applicability. Therefore,
> the deep impression which classical thermo-
> dynamics made upon me. It is the only physical
> theory of universal content concerning which I
> am convinced that, within the framework of the
> applicability of its basic concepts, it will never
> be overthrown. [2]

From the first law (conservation of matter-energy) it is obvious that we do not produce or consume anything, we merely rearrange it. From the second law (increasing entropy) it is clear that our rearrangement implies a continual reduction in potential for further use within the system as a whole. In mining concentrated ores we convert usable energy to unusable energy. We concentrate and refine the material ores in "production," but then by way of "consumption" or depreciation we eventually, through friction, rust, accident, loss, decay, and so on, disperse the once-concentrated minerals all over the face of the earth so that they become forever useless. Entropy applies to materials as well as energy. For materials it means that order turns to disorder, the concentrated tends to be dispersed, the structured becomes unstructured. It is true that materials can be recycled and energy cannot, but materials recycling can never be 100 percent complege. Some fraction of useful materials will be irrevocably lost during each cycle of use. For energy, entropy means that usable energy is always diminishing, and useless (equilibrium temperature) energy is always increasing. The distinction between useful and useless energy is an anthropomorphic one--in fact an economic distinction. Thus the relevance

of entropy to economics is built into the very concept of entropy and
requires no further demonstration. The concept itself originated
with an economic problem: the maximum efficiency of heat engines.
Entropic constraints are not abstractions far off in the future. We
are not talking about the ultimate heat death of the universe. The
effect of the entropy law is as immediate and concrete as the facts
that you can't burn the same tank of gasoline twice, that organisms
cannot live in a medium of their own waste products, and that efficiencies cannot reach, much less exceed, 100 percent. The low
entropy of highly organized stocks of wealth and human bodies must
be maintained by the continual importation of low-entropy inputs
from the environment and the continual exportation of high-entropy
outputs back to the environment, where through the agency of solar-
powered biogeochemical cycles they are transformed into low-entropy
forms on varying time scales. The entropic flow, beginning with
depletion and ending with pollution (the throughput), is the necessary
cost of maintaining the stocks of commodities and people. Too
large a throughput can disrupt the biosphere and impair its capacity
to assimilate wastes. The world's sources of useful (low-entropy)
matter and energy become depleted, while the sinks for waste
(high-entropy) matter and energy become polluted. We live off of
the depletion-pollution throughput and cannot exist or enjoy life
without it. It is a necessary cost of existence and plentitude. But
this entropic degradation is a cost and must be reckoned as a cost
and minimized for any chosen level of population and per capita
wealth. Unfortunately, it seems that our present economic institutions and theories are more attuned to maximizing throughput than
to minimizing it. This results from the close association of throughput with GNP, which is taken as an index of welfare, and from our
failure to recognize any concept of a mature or sufficient level of
stocks.

It is true that we have a continual input of new low entropy in
the form of sunlight (our earth system is open with respect to solar
energy), so that it is possible to maintain and increase the order
and complexity of the earth, via photosynthesis and life processes,
at the expense of increasing the entropy of the sun. Solar energy
only arrives at a fixed rate independent of man's will, and the entire
biosphere has, over millions of years of evolution, adapted itself to
living off this fixed income of solar energy. But in the last two
centuries (a mere instant in the history of the biosphere) man has
ceased to live within the annual solar budget and has become ad-
dicted to living off his capital of terrestrial stocks of low entropy
(fossil fuels, minerals). Terrestrial stocks of fossil fuels represent
a minute fraction of the energy available from the sun, but unlike
the sun these stocks can be used at a rate of man's own choosing--

that is, we cannot mine the sun, but we can mine, and rapidly deplete, terrestrial stocks. As population grew, man needed more
food and undertook the work necessary to produce it, employing
draft animals to help. As population continued to grow man became
more reluctant to share his food-producing land to grow fodder for
draft animals. Instead he began to feed tractors with fossil fuels
and increased the ability of the land to support a larger population.
Also, new products were produced and standards of individual consumption increased along with population, further increasing man's
addiction to living off his terrestrial capital.

    Some big problems emerge from this addiction. Our terres-
trial capital will clearly become more and more scarce, and then
for all practical purposes available nonrenewable resources will be
used up. Our national income accounts treat consumption of geological capital as current income, thus sanctifying the addiction.
Substitution will extend the life of all resources, but will not "create
new resources" as metaphorically stated by many people. Whenever the net energy yield becomes zero (that is, it costs as much
energy to mine a ton of coal as can be got from a ton of coal) then it
becomes nonsensical to continue mining that energy source. This
consideration is unaffected by prices and clearly shows that we will
never be able to use all the resources in the earth's crust. Second,
since man is the only species living beyond the solar budget, it is
clear that such behavior will throw the human species out of balance
with the rest of the biosphere which, because of evolution over eons,
has become ever more elaborately adapted to the fixed solar flow.
Man is the only member of the biosphere who has broken this evolutionary budget constraint. It is only natural that this unique expansionary behavior should cause repercussions and feedbacks from
the rest of the system in the unhappy form of pollution and breakdown of local life-support systems. These systems are unable to
accommodate man-made energy and material flows that constitute
significant additions either to the local solar flux, or to that part of
the solar flux trapped by photosynthesis, or to the natural volumes
of solar-powered material cycles. The surprising thing is not that
these breakdowns occur, but that they have not occurred to a greater
degree. The ecosystem evidently has considerable slack, redun-
dancy, and resilience. But the slack is being used up in one dimension after another--no one doubts that man has the capacity to destroy the biosphere, whether directly by war or indirectly through
the growing commercialization of chemical and radioactive poisons
(DDT and plutonium), with which the biosphere had had no evolutionary experience and to which it is consequently unadapted. It is
not entirely correct to say that the biosphere is unadapted to DDT,
since a number of insects have become resistant to it. But this

adaptation is perverse from a human standpoint, because as the
target population of pests becomes less vulnerable, larger doses of
the poison must be used. While this may be good for pesticide
sales, it is not good for the nontarget populations who are increasingly affected by the larger applications and who often have longer
generations and are less quickly adaptable. No organisms have yet
evolved a resistance to plutonium toxicity, and although radioactivity
is naturally present in the environment, no one believes that more
of it is better. Man himself evolved in a hunting and gathering
economy, not an industrial economy. A growing proportion of industrial man's illnesses seem to be related to the adaptations which
his industrial growth-oriented economy has demanded, but which
were not supplied by his evolutionary formation under a hunting and
gathering mode of life. One cannot be sure of the degree of this
maladjustment, but to assume that an organism can change its customary environs and activities abruptly without paying significant
costs flies in the face of all we know about evolution.

     The upshot of these considerations is that we must move toward
an economy more dependent on solar energy. Our terrestrial capital should be used, but more and more in investments in ways to
capture solar energy. To burn up our fossil capital in trivial and
unnecessary consumption (such as transporting nonnutritional foods
in plastic throw-away containers in trucks traveling 70 mph across
paved-over farmland) is folly on wheels, not to mention the great
technological circuses of moon shooting and arms racing. Lewis
Mumford has likened rocket ships to the pyramids of ancient Egypt:
both are enormously expensive devices built by the sacrifices of the
many for the purpose of carrying an elite few into heaven.

     No one advocates an immediate or even a long-run return to a
berrypicking economy. Our current population size and life styles
make that quite impossible. But at least we can stop making things
worse at an exponential rate. We can stabilize population and eventually lower it to a more sustainable level. We can try to stabilize
our rates of throughput of energy and basic materials, and we can
force technology to look to solar energy and renewable resources to
a greater degree. The substitution of bicycles for cars for much
local transportation is only the most obvious example. Heat pumps,
solar space heating, and mass transit are other energy-saving possibilities for which the technology already exists. The "How" part
of this chapter suggests some institutions and policies for effecting
such a change.

     The physical and biological first principles just discussed
(that is, the first and second laws of thermodynamics, and the evolutionary adaption of the biosphere to solar energy) point toward the
eventual necessity of a stabilized economy (that is, ignoring the

first and second laws results in excessive depletion and pollution, which in turn provoke ecological disruption).

Independently, there are also some ethical first principles indicating the desirability of a steady state. Nearly all traditional religions teach man to conform his soul to reality by knowledge, self-discipline, and restraint on the multiplication of desires, as well as on the lengths to which one will go to satisfy a desire. The modern religions of technological scientism, magic, and economic growth seek to subjugate reality and bend it to the uninstructed will and whim of some men, usually to the uncounted detriment of other men. C. S. Lewis has reminded us that what we call the increasing dominance of "man" over nature is really the increasing dominance of some men over other men with knowledge of nature serving as the instrument of domination. This may not be intentional or always a bad thing, but it should be recognized for what it is. There is a limit beyond which the extra costs of surrendering control over one's environs and activities to the experts becomes greater than the extra benefits. This is not antiscience--it is merely a warning against the idolatry of science by some of its zealous fanatics who are consecrated to redoubling their efforts while forgetting their purposes. For scientism and growth-mania there is no such thing as "enough," even on the material plane. Indeed the whole idea seems to be to try to fill a spiritual void with material commodities. The usual objection to limiting growth, made in the name of the poor, only illustrates the extent of the void because it defends growth as an alternative to sharing, which is considered "unrealistic," if not inconceivable. For the traditional attitude there is such a thing as material sufficiency, and beyond that admittedly vague and historically changing amount the goal of life becomes wisdom, enjoyment, cultivation of the mind and soul, and of community. It may be that community requires a certain degree of scarcity, without which cooperation, sharing, and friendship would have no organic reason to be, and hence community would atrophy. Witness the self-sufficiency and lack of community of middle-class suburbs.

Another ethical first principle is a sense of stewardship for all of creation, and an extension of some degree of brotherhood to future generations and to subhuman life. Clearly the first demands on brotherhood are those of presently existing human beings who do not enjoy material sufficiency. The answer to this failure of brotherhood is not simply more growth, but is mainly to be found in more sharing and more population control, both of which are necessary. Without population control, sharing will simply make everyone equally poor. Without sharing, population control will at best reduce the number of the poor, but will not eliminate poverty. If, as often happens, the rich limit their numbers and the poor do not, then birth control worsens the distribution of income. Both sharing and population control are basically moral problems whose solutions require sound values far more than clever techniques.

The virtue of humility is also high on the list of moral first principles. Much of the drive to convert the ecosphere into one big technosphere comes from the technological hubris of ordinary men who think that the scientific method has somehow transfigured them into little godlings who can collectively accomplish anything--if only society will give them more and more research funds. At a more basic level the drive comes from the need for doing and controlling as a verification of knowledge. There is no reason why we must do everything we know how to do, but there is a sense in which we cannot be sure we know how to do something unless we have done it. If we are going to avoid doing certain things we will have to sacrifice the forbidden knowledge that would have been gained.

Another important virtue is "holism," the attitude that recognizes that the whole is greater than the sum of its parts, that reductionist analysis never tells the whole story, and that the abstractions necessary to make mechanistic models always do violence to reality. Those who habitually think in terms of abstract, reductionist models are especially prone to the "fallacy of misplaced concreteness"--that is, applying to one level of abstraction conclusions arrived at from thinking on a different (higher) level of abstraction.

In sum the moral first principles are some concept of "enoughness," stewardship, humility, and holism. In social science today one hears little of moral values or ethics (even though historically economics began as a branch of moral philosophy). Appeals to moral solutions, to a change in values, are considered as an admission of intellectual defeat, as a retreat from the rules of the game-- as cheating. The quest is for clever mechanistic technical solutions, not straightforward moral solutions. Power-yielding techniques have been assiduously sought for, while the cultivation of right purposes has been neglected--some even consider the latter "a meaningless question." We now have growing power in search of shrinking purpose.

If one accepts these biophysical and moral first principles, then it will be hard for him to reject the ideal of a steady-state economy. If one rejects the moral first principles, he may still be convinced by arguments of necessity arising from the biophysical first principles. If one rejects the biophysical premises, he may still be led to accept the steady state for reasons of desirability arising from the moral premises. If one accepts both sets of first principles then he should be doubly convinced.

HOW? THREE INSTITUTIONS FOR ATTAINING
A STEADY-STATE ECONOMY

The guiding design principle for the three institutions is to provide the necessary social control with a minimum sacrifice of personal freedom, to provide macrostability while allowing for microvariability, to combine the macrostatic with the microdynamic. To do otherwise, to aim for microstability and control, is likely to be self-defeating and result in macroinstability as the capacities for spontaneous coordination, adjustment, and mutation (which always occur on the micro level) are stifled by central planning with its inevitable rigidities and information losses. The micro is the domain of indeterminacy, novelty, and freedom. The macro or aggregate is the domain of determinacy, predictability, and control. We should strive for macrocontrol and avoid micromeddling. A second design principle, closely related to the first, is to maintain considerable slack between the actual environmental load and the maximum carrying capacity. The closer the actual approaches the maximum the less is the margin for error, and the more rigorous, finely tuned, and microoriented our controls will have to be. We lack the knowledge and ability to assume detailed control of the spaceship, so therefore we must leave it on "automatic pilot," as it has been for eons. But the automatic pilot only works when the actual load is small relative to the conceivable maximum. A third design principle, important for making the transition, is to build in the ability to tighten constraints gradually.

The kinds of institutions required follow directly from the definition of a steady-state economy: constant stocks of people and physical wealth maintained at some desirable chosen level by a low rate of throughput. We need: an institution for stabilizing population (the Boulding marketable license plan); an institution for stabilizing physical wealth and keeping throughput below ecological limits (marketable depletion quotas auctioned by the government); and a distributist institution limiting the degree of inequality in the distribution of the constant stocks among the constant population (maximum and minimum limits to personal income, and a maximum limit to personal wealth). Here is a brief outline of how each institution might function and how the three interrelate.

Distributist Institution

The critical institution is likely to be a minimum and maximum limit on income and a maximum limit on wealth. Without some

such limit private property and the whole market economy lose their
moral basis, and there would be no strong case for extending the
market to cover birth quotas and depletion quotas as a means of
institutionalizing environmental limits. Exchange relations are mutually beneficial among relative equals. Exchange between the powerful and the powerless is often only nominally voluntary and can easily
be a mask for exploitation, especially in the labor market, as Marx
has shown.

     There is considerable political support for a minimum income
financed by a negative income tax, as an alternative to bureaucratic
welfare programs. There now seems to be no such support for
maximum income or maximum wealth limits. In the growth paradigm there need be no uppoer limit. But in the steady-state paradigm
there must be an upper limit to the total, and the higher the minimum
per capita share, the lower must be the maximum per capita share.
A minimum wealth limit is not really feasible, since one can always
spend his wealth and can hardly expect to have it restored year after
year. The minimum income would be sufficient. But maximum
limits on wealth and income are both necessary, since wealth and
income are largely interchangeable, and since beyond some point
the concentration of wealth becomes inconsistent with both a market
economy and political democracy. John Stuart Mill stated the issue
very well:

> Private property, in every defense made of it, is
> supposed to mean the guarantee to individuals of
> the fruits of their own labor and abstinence. The
> guarantee to them of the fruits of the labor and
> abstinence of others, transmitted to them without
> any merit or exertion of their own, is not of the
> essence of the institution, but a mere incidental
> consequence which, when it reaches a certain
> height, does not promote, but conflicts with the
> ends which render private property legitimate.[3]

     According to Mill private property is legitimated as a bastion
against exploitation. But this is true only if everyone owns some
minimum amount. Otherwise private property, when some own a
great deal of it and others have very little, becomes the very instrument of exploitation, rather than a guarantee against it. It is
implicit in this view that private property is legitimate only if there
is some distributist institution (like, for example, the Jubilee year
of the Old Testament) which keeps inequality of wealth within some
justifiable limits. Such an institution is now lacking. The proposed
institution of maximum wealth and income, plus minimum income

limits, would remedy this severe defect and make private property legitimate again. Also it would go a long way toward legitimating the free market, since most of our blundering interference with the price system (for example, farm programs, minimum wages, rent controls) has its goal an equalizing alteration in the distribution of income and wealth. Thus such a distributist policy is based on impeccable respectable premises: private property, the free market, opposition to welfare bureaucracies, and centralized control. It also heeds the radicals' call of "power to the people" since it puts the source of power, namely property, in the hands of many people, rather than in the hands of a few capitalist plutocrats and socialist bureaucrats.

Maximum income and wealth would remove many of the incentives to monopolistic practices. Why conspire to corner markets, fix prices, and so on, if you cannot keep the loot? As for labor, the minimum income would enable the outlawing of strikes, which are rapidly becoming intolerable. Unions would not be needed as a means of confronting the power of concentrated wealth, since wealth would no longer be concentrated. Indeed, the workers would have a share of it and thus would not be at the mercy of an employer. In addition, some limit on corporate size would be needed, or else a requirement that all corporate profits be distributed as dividends to stockholders.

With no large concentrations in wealth and income, savings would be smaller and would truly represent abstinence from consumption rather than surplus remaining after satiation. There would be less expansionary pressure from large amounts of capital seeking ever new ways to grow exponentially.

The minimum income could be financed out of general revenues, which, in addition to a progressive income tax within the income limits, would also include revenues from the depletion quota auction and 100 percent marginal tax rates on wealth and income above the limits. Upon reaching the maximum most people would devote their further energies to noneconomic pursuits, so the latter revenues would be small. But the opportunities thus forgone by the wealthy would still be available to the not-so-wealthy, who would still be paying taxes on their increased earnings. The effect on incentive will be negative at the top, but positive at lower levels leading to a broader participation in running the economy. If the maximum and minimum were to move so close together that real differences in effort could not be rewarded and incentives were insufficient to call forth the talent and effort needed to sustain the system, then we should have to widen the limits again, or simply be content with the lower level of wealth that could be maintained within the narrower distributive limits. There may also be an increase in

public service by those who have hit the maximum. As Jonathan
Swift argued:

> In all well-instituted commonwealths, care has been
> taken to limit men's possessions; which is done for
> many reasons, and, among the rest, for one which,
> perhaps, is not often considered; that when bounds
> are set to men's desires, after they have acquired
> as much as the laws will permit them, their pri-
> vate interest is at an end, and they have nothing to
> do but to take care of the public. [4]

Marketable Licenses to Have Children

For maintaining a constant population an ingenious institution
has been proposed by Kenneth Boulding. Unfortunately, but under-
standably, it has been treated more as a joke than as a serious
proposal, and Boulding himself sometimes treats it seriously,
sometimes jokingly.

I think it is a good plan, but since so few people have supported
it I should say that the other two institutions (distribution limits and
depletion quotas) do not depend on it. The other two can be accepted
and the reader can substitute his own favorite population control
plan if he doesn't like this one. Also it should be noted that many of
the objections to the Boulding plan are neutralized by the other two
institutions.

The idea is to issue directly to individuals licenses to have
children. Each person receives certificates in an amount permitting
1.1 children, or each couple at marriage receives certificates permitting 2.2 children, or whatever number corresponds to replacement
fertility. The licenses can be bought and sold on a free market.
Thus macrostability is attained, microvariability is permitted.
Furthermore, those having more than two children must pay for an
extra license, those who have fewer than two children receive pay-
ment for their unused license certificates. The right to have children is distributed equally. Market supply and demand then redis-
tribute these rights according to differing preferences and abilities
to pay. People who do not or can not have children are rewarded
financially. People who wish to have more than two are penalized
financially. And the subsidies and penalties are handled by the
market with no government bureaucracy.

A slight amendment to the plan might be to grant 1.0 certificates to each individual and have these refer not to births but to
"survivals." If someone dies before he has a child then his

certificate becomes a part of his estate and is willed to someone
else, for example, his parents, who either use it to have another
child or sell it to someone else. The advantage of this modification
is that it offsets existing class differentials in infant and child mortality. Without the modification, a poor family desiring two children could end up with two infant deaths and no certificates. The
best plan of course is to eliminate class differences in mortality,
but in the meantime this modification may make the plan initially
easier to accept. Indeed, even in the absence of class differentials
the modification has the advantage of building in a "guarantee."
     Let me dispose of two common objections to the plan. First,
it is argued that it is unjust because the rich have an advantage. Of
course the rich always have an advantage, but is their advantage
increased or decreased by this plan? Clearly it is decreased. The
effect of the plan on income distribution is equalizing because the
new marketable asset is distributed equally, and as the rich have
more children their family per capita incomes are lowered, as the
poor have fewer their family per capita incomes increase. Also
from the point of view of the children there is something to be said
for increasing the probability that they will be born richer rather
than poorer. Whatever injustice there is in the plan stems from the
existence of rich and poor, not from Boulding's plan which actually
reduces the degree of injustice. Furthermore, income and wealth
distribution are to be controlled by a separate institution, discussed
above, so that in the overall system this objection is more fully and
directly met.
     A more reasonable objection raises the problem of enforce-
ment. What do we do with law-breaking parents and their illegal
children? What do we do with illegal children today? One possibility is to put the children up for adoption and encourage adoption by
paying the adopting parents the market value, plus subsidy if need
be, for their license, thus retiring a license from circulation to
compensate for the child born without a license. Like any other
lawbreakers the offending parents are subject to punishment. The
punishment need not be drastic, for example, a year's paid labor in
a public child care center. Of course if everyone breaks a law no
law can be enforced. The plan presupposes the acceptance by a
large majority of the public of the morality and necessity of the law.
It also presupposes widespread knowledge of contraceptive practices, and perhaps legalized abortion as well. But these presuppo-
sitions would apply to any institution of population control, except
the most coercive.
     Choice may be influenced in two ways: by acting on or "rig-
ging" the objective conditions of choice (prices and incomes in a
broad sense), or by manipulating the subjective conditions of choice

(preferences). Boulding's plan imposes straightforward objective constraints and does not presumptuously attempt to manipulate peoples' preferences. Preference changes due to individual example and moral conversion are in no way ruled out. If preferences should change so that, on the average, the population desired replacement fertility, the price of a certificate would approach zero and the objective constraint would automatically vanish. The current decline in the birth rate has perhaps already led to such a state. Perhaps this would be a good time to institute the plan, so that it would already be in place and functioning should preferences change toward more children in the future. The moral basis of the plan is that everyone is treated equally, yet there is no insistence upon conformity of preferences, the latter being the great drawback of "voluntary" plans which rely on official moral suasion and Madison Avenue techniques. Some people will never be persuaded, and their individual nonconformity wrecks the moral basis (equal treatment) of "voluntary" programs.

Kingsley Davis points out that population control is not a technological problem.

> . . . The solution is easy as long as one pays no
> attention to what must be given up. For instance
> a nation seeking ZPG could shut off immigration
> and permit each couple a maximum of two children,
> with possible state license for a third. Accidental
> pregnancies beyond the limit would be interrupted
> by abortion. If a third child were born without a
> license, or a fourth, the mother would be sterilized
> and the child given to a sterile couple. But anyone
> enticed into making such a suggestion risks being
> ostracised as a political or moral leper, a danger
> to society. He is accused of wanting to take people's
> freedom away from then and institute a Draconian
> dictatorship over private lives. Obviously then
> reproductive freedom still takes priority over
> population control. This makes a solution of the
> population problem impossible because, by defini-
> tion, population control and reproductive freedom
> are incompatible.[5]

The key to population control is simply to be willing to pay the cost. The cost of the plan here advocated seems to be less than the cost of Davis' hypothetical suggestion because it allows greater diversity--families need not be so homogeneous in size, and individual preferences are respected to a greater degree. Also should it become necessary to have negative population growth, the marketable license plan has a great advantage over those plans that put the limit on a flat child per family basis. This latter limit could be changed only by an integral number, and to go from two children to one child per family in order to reduce population is quite a drastic change. In the Boulding scheme of marketable licenses issued in "deci-child" units or one-tenth of a certificate, it would be possible to reduce population growth gradually by lowering the issue to 1.9 certificates per woman, to 1.8, and so on, the remaining 0.1 or 0.2 certificates being acquired by trade. Anyone advocating this will no doubt be accused of wanting to chop all babies into ten pieces.

There is an understandable reluctance to couple money and reproduction--somehow it seems to profane life. Yet life is physically coupled to increasingly scarce resources, and resources are coupled to money. If population growth and economic growth continue, then even free resources such as breathable air will either become coupled to money and subject to price or allocated by a harsher and less efficient means. Once we accept the fact that the price system is the most efficient mechanism for rationing the right to scarce life-sustaining and life-enhancing resources, then perhaps rather than "money profaning life" we will find that "life sanctifies money." We will then take the distribution of money and its wise use as serious matters. It is not the exchange relationship that debases life, it is the underlying inequality in wealth and income beyond any functional or ethical justification that loads the terms of free exchange against the poor. The same inequality also debases the "gift relationship" since it reduces the poor to the status of a perpetual dependent and the rich to the status of a weary and grumbling patron. Thus gift as well as exchange relationships require limits to the degree of inequality if they are not to subvert their legitimate ends. The sharing of resources in general is the job of the distributist institution. Allocation of particular resources and scarce rights is done by the market within the distribution limits imposed.

Depletion Quotas

The strategic point at which to impose control on the throughput flow seems to me to be the rate of depletion of resources, particularly nonrenewable resources. If we limit aggregate depletion, then by the law of conservation of matter and energy we will also indirectly limit aggregate pollution. Entropy is at its minimum at the input (depletion) end of the throughput pipeline, and at its maximum at the output (pollution) end. Therefore it is physically easier to monitor and control depletion than pollution--there are fewer mines, wells, and ports than there are smokestacks, garbage dumps, and drainpipes, not to mention such diffuse emission sources as runoff of insecticides and fertilizers from fields into rivers and lakes, and auto exhausts. Given that there is more leverage in intervening at the input end, should we intervene by way of taxes or quotas? Quotas, if they are auctioned by the government rather than allocated on nonmarket criteria, have an important net advantage over taxes in that they definitely limit aggregate throughput, which is the quantity to be controlled. Taxes exert only an indirect and very uncertain limit. It is quite true that given a demand curve, a price plus a tax determines a quantity. But demand curves shift and are subject to great errors in estimation, even if stable. Demand curves for resources could shift up as a result of population increase, change in tastes, increase in income, and so on. Every time we increase a price (internalize an externality) we also increase an income, so that in the aggregate the economy can still purchase exactly as much as before. Say the government seeks to limit throughput by taxing it. It then spends the tax. On what? On throughput. If government expenditures on each category of throughput were equal to the revenues received from taxing that same category, then the limit on throughput would be largely canceled out. If the government taxes resource-intensive items and spends on time-intensive items there will be a one-shot reduction in aggregate physical throughput, but not a limit to its future growth. A credit expansion by the banking sector, an increase in velocity of circulation of money, or deficit spending by the government for other purposes could easily offset even the short-run reduction induced by taxes. Taxes can influence the amount of depletion and pollution (throughput) per unit of GNP, but taxes provide no limit to the increase in the number of units of GNP (unless the government runs a growing surplus), and no limit to aggregate throughput. The fact that a tax levied on a single resource could by inducing substitution usually reduce the throughput of that resource very substantially should not mislead us into thinking that a general tax on all or most resources will reduce aggregate throughput (fallacy of composition). Finally, it is quantity that affects the ecosystem, not price, and therefore it is ecologically safer to let errors and unexpected shifts in demand result in price fluctuations rather than in quantity fluctuations. Hence quotas.

Pollution taxes also provide a much weaker inducement to resource-saving technological progress than do depletion quotas, since in the former scheme resource prices do not necessarily have to rise, and may even fall. The inducement of pollution taxes is to "pollution avoidance," and thus to recycling. But increased competition from recycling industries, instead of reducing depletion, might spur the extractive industries to even greater competitive efforts. Intensified search and the development of technologies with still larger jaws (for example, strip mining) could speed up the rate of depletion and thereby lower resource prices. Thus new extraction might once again become competitive with recycling, leading to less recycling and more depletion and pollution--exactly what we wish to avoid. This perverse effect could not happen under a depletion quota system.

The usual recommendation of "pollution taxes" would seem, if the above is correct, to intervene at the wrong end with the wrong policy tool. Intervention by pollution taxes also tends to be micro-control, rather than macro. There are, however, limits to the ability of depletion quotas to influence the qualitative nature and spatial location of pollution, and at this fine-tuning level pollution taxes would be a useful supplement, as would a bureau of technology assessment. Depletion quotas would induce resource-saving technological change, and the set of resource-saving technologies probably overlaps to a great degree with the set of socially benign technologies. But the coincidence is not complete and there is still a need, though a diminished one, for technology assessment.

How might a depletion quota system function? Let there be quotas set on new depletion on each of the basic resources, both renewable and nonrenewable, during a given time period. Let legal rights to deplete up to the amount of the quota for each resource be auctioned off by the government, at the beginning of each time period, in conveniently divisible units, to private firms, individuals, and public enterprises. After purchase from the government the quota rights are freely transferrable by sale or gift, and can be retained for use in subsequent time periods. As population growth and economic growth press against resources the prices of the depletion quotas will be driven higher and higher. Reduction of quotas to lower levels in the interest of conservation of nonrenewables and sustainable exploitation of renewables would drive the price of the quotas still higher. The increasing windfall rents resulting from increasing pressure of demand on fixed supply would be captured by the government through the auctioning of the depletion rights. The government spends the revenues, let us say, by paying a social dividend. Even though the monetary flow is therefore undiminished, the real flow (throughput) has been physically limited by the resource quotas. All prices of resources and of goods increase, with the prices of resource-intensive goods increasing relatively more. Total resource consumption (depletion) is reduced. Moreover, by the law of conservation of matter-energy, if ultimate inputs are reduced so must ultimate output (pollution) be reduced. The aggregate throughput is reduced and with it the gross stress it puts on the ecosystem.

With depletion now more expensive and with higher prices on final goods, recycling becomes more profitable. As recycling increases, effluents are reduced even more. Also higher prices make consumers more interested in durability and careful maintenance of wealth. The extra burden on the poor of increased prices can be more than offset via the distributist institution. Most importantly there is now a strong price incentive to develop new resource-saving technologies and patterns of consumption. If there is any static efficiency loss in setting the rate of depletion outside the market (a very doubtful point), it seems to be more than offset by the dynamic benefits of greater inducements to resource-saving technological progress.

The adjustment of depletion and pollution flows (throughput) to long-run ecologically sustainable levels can be effected gradually. In the first year depletion quotas could be set at last year's levels, and if necessary gradually reduced by, say, 2 percent per year until we reach an equilibrium level of stocks of wealth requiring that "optimal" throughput for its maintenance. Thereafter the goal is to maintain the constant stock with the minimal throughput. As we gradually exhaust nonrenewable resources their quotas will approach zero and recycling will become the only source of material inputs. By this time, presumably, the ever-rising price of the resource would have induced a recycling technology. Without quotas this resource exhaustion need not be gradual. Also, without quotas, the incentive to develop the new technology is less, since one must face the uncertainty that some newly discovered reserves will lower resource prices and make the resource-saving technology temporarily uneconomic. When the rate of depletion becomes a social parameter it can be taken as known, and uncertainty will be less. Discoveries of new reserves will increase the length of time until exhaustion, rather than lowering the price.

With depletion quotas the aggregate rate of depletion becomes a social decision. This can be regarded as the correction of a market failure. For renewable resources quotas can be set at a calculated optimum sustainable yield or maximum rent, thus correcting the market failure of overexploitation. The quota on renewables must be such as to avoid "eating into our capital." For privately owned and well-managed renewable resources the quotas would be redundant, and could be dispensed with. Since with nonrenewables mankind is always eating his capital the rate of depletion should be a collective decision based largely on value judgments --once we are below ecological disaster thresholds. Two considerations argue for lower rates of depletion and higher prices than now prevail: the conservationist's moral concern about future generations who cannot bid in present markets, and the idea that resource-saving technology can be induced by high resource prices. The rate of depletion of the stock of terrestrial low entropy is fundamentally a moral decision and should be decided on grounds of ethical desirability (stewardship), not technological possibility or present value calculations of profitability. By fixing the rate of depletion we force technology to focus more on the flow sources of solar energy and renewable resources. The solar flux cannot be increased in the present at the expense of the future. Thus let technology devote itself to learning how to live off our solar income, rather than our terrestrial capital. Such advances will benefit all generations, not just the present.

The issue is clarified by the following simple, yet insightful, observation by Nicholas Georgescu-Roegen:

> Man's natural dowry, as we all know, consists of
> two essentially distinct elements: (1) The stock of
> low entropy on or within the globe, and (2) the flow
> of solar energy, which slowly but steadily dimin-
> ished in intensity with the entropic degradation of
> the sun. But the crucial point for the population
> problem as well as for any reasonable speculations
> about the future exasomatic evolution of mankind is
> the relative importance of these two elements. For
> as surprising as it may seem, the entire stock of
> natural resources is not worth more than a few
> days of sunlight.[6]

The exosomatic or technological evolution of mankind over the last two centuries has almost entirely depended on the less-abundant stock source of man's "natural dowry," thus shifting our dependence away from the more abundant solar flow. How ironic, then, to be told by growth boosters that technical progress has reduced man's dependence on natural resources. But this does not mean that technical evolution cannot be redirected. Indeed, the main goal of the depletion quota plan is to turn technical change away from increasing dependence on the terrestrial stock and toward the more abundant flow of solar energy and renewable resources. As the stock becomes relatively more expensive it will be used less in direct consumption and more for investment in "work gates" which increase our ability to tap the solar flow. Instead of taking long-run technical evolution as a parameter to which the short-run variables of price and quantity continually adjust, the idea is to take short-run quantities (and hence prices) as a social parameter to be set so as to

induce a direction of technical evolution more in harmony with mankind's long-run interests.

This new direction of technical change is likely also to be in
mankind's short-run interests, if one accepts the view that man's
evolution in a solar-based and stable economy has programmed him
for that kind of life rather than for the stresses of a growing industrial economy. The future steady state could be a good deal more
comfortable than past ones, and much more human than the over-
grown, overcentralized, overextended, and overbearing economy
into which growth has pushed us.

The depletion quota plan should appeal both to technological
optimists and pessimists. The pessimist should be pleased by the
conservation effect of the quotas, while the optimist should be
pleased by the price inducement to resource-saving technology. The
optimist tells us not to worry about running out of resources because
technology embodied in reproducible capital is a nearly perfect substitute for resources. As we run out of anything prices will rise
and substitute methods will be found. If one believes this, then how
could one object to quotas, which simply increase the scarcity and
prices of resources a bit ahead of schedule and more gradually.
This plan simply requires the optimist to live up to his faith in
technology.

Like the maximum limits on income and wealth, the depletion
quotas could also have a trust-busting effect if accompanied by a
limit--for example, no single entity can own more than X percent of
the quota rights for a given resource, or more than Y percent of the
resource owned by the industry of which it is a member. X and Y
could be set so as to allow legitimate economies of scale, while cur-
tailing monopoly power.

A further effect of the quota scheme is that relative factor
prices would change, with labor becoming cheaper relative to natural
resources and capital. This effect by itself would tend to increase
employment, which in itself is not a benefit, but is necessary as long
as we maintain an income-through-jobs system of distribution.
However, reduced aggregate consumption would tend to reduce employment. If the latter effect predominated a job-sharing reduction
in the work week might be needed, or increased reliance on unearned
income, such as a social dividend financed out of receipts from the
auction of resource quotas, or capital income to the worker resulting
from wider distribution of capital ownership. But we have a distributist institution designed to accomplish these ends, which are
desirable on their own account.

The actual mechanics of quota auction markets for basic resources would present no great problems. The whole process could
be computerized since the function of an auctioneer is purely

mechanical. It could be vastly simpler, faster, more decentralized, and less subject to fraud and manipulation than today's stock market. Also, qualitative and locational variation among resources within each category, though ignored at the auction level, will be taken into account in price differentials paid to resource owners.

The depletion quota and birth quota systems bear an obvious analogy. The difference is that the birth quotas are equally distributed and privately held initially, and then redistributed among individuals through the market, while the depletion quotas are collectively held initially and then distributed to individuals by way of an auction market. The revenue derived from birth quotas is private income, the revenue from depletion quotas is public income.

The scheme could and probably must be designed to include imported resources. The same depletion quota right could be required for importation of resources, and thus the market would determine the proportions in which our standard of living is sustained by depletion of national and foreign resources. Imported final goods would now be cheaper relative to national goods, assuming foreigners do not limit their depletion. Our export goods would now be more expensive relative to the domestic goods of foreign countries. We would tend to a balance-of-payments deficit. But with a freely fluctuating exchange rate a rise in the price of foreign currencies relative to the dollar would restore equilibrium. It might be objected that limiting our imports of resources will work a hardship on the many underdeveloped countries who export raw materials. This is not clear, because such a policy will also force them to transform their own resources domestically rather than through international trade. Finished goods would not be subject to quotas. Also foreign suppliers of raw materials are treated no differently from domestic suppliers. In any case it is clear that in the long run we are not doing the underdeveloped countries any favor by using up their resource endowment. Sooner or later (sooner with the example of OPEC) they will begin to drive a hard bargain for their nonrenewable resources, and we had best not be too dependent on them. Eventually population control and environmental protection policies might become preconditions for membership in a new free-trade bloc or common market.

POLITICAL FEASIBILITY

Two questions about the above model must be kept separate. First, would it work if it were accepted, and second, would it be accepted if it were proposed? So far we have dealt only with the first question and have tried to show that the answer is yes. As of

1977 the answer to the second question is obviously no. But over
the medium run of, say, five to ten years, such institutions may
appear less extreme than the ecological costs of the trends generated by our current institutions. Consider, for example, that although the President's Commission on Population Growth and the
American Future did not advocate a marketable license plan for
population control, it did recommend that the nation "welcome and
plan for a stabilized population." Furthermore it listed some criteria for a good stabilization plan. The commission prefers "a
course toward population stabilization which minimizes fluctuation
in number of births; minimizes further growth; minimizes change
required in reproductive habits and provides adequate time for
such changes to be adopted; and maximizes variety and choice in
life styles, while minimizing pressures for conformity." On these
criteria the marketable license plan scores better than any alternative that I have seen or am able to imagine. If one accepts these
criteria then he should either accept the marketable birth license
plan or be prepared to suggest something better.

The National Commission on Materials Policy still put major
emphasis on increasing supplies, but recognized that a balance
must be struck "between the need to produce goods and the need to
protect the environment by modifying the materials system so that
all resources, including environmental, are paid for by users."
Depletion quotas were not taken seriously, but pollution taxes were.
Economists have made the case that pollution taxes are superior to
the alternatives of direct regulations and subsidizing pollution
abatement. But the alternative of depletion quotas has not yet been
widely debated. The 1952 President's Materials Policy Commission
(the Paley Commission), though acknowledging that "we share the
belief of the American people in the principle of Growth" [their
capital G], also went on to make the following enlightened observation:
"Whether there may be any unbreakable upper limit to the continuing
growth of our economy we do not pretend to know, but it must be a
part of our task to examine such limits as present themselves." This
would have been a good point of departure for the 1972 commission.

On the question of energy policy, the Ford Foundation's Energy
Policy Project took seriously the alternative of zero energy growth
and included it as one of their three possible scenarios for the future, thus giving a certain respectability to what the Materials Policy Commission and others evidently still consider a "far out" idea.

The minimum income part of the distributist institution already has political support. How much support one gets for the
maximum income and wealth depends partly on where the limits are
set. There are very, very few voters with more than $100,000 in-
come and $500,000 net worth, and not many citizens who really

believe that anything beyond those limits should not be classed as greed rather than need. The same could be said of limits set at one-half the above. Exactly where we draw the line is less important than the principle that such lines must be drawn. A widespread recognition of the general closure of growth should increase the appeal of maximum limits and perhaps revive our Populist heritage. If we really want decentralized decision making and participatory democracy rather than a "plutonium-powered corporate kleptocracy," some such limit is essential. Yet there is still ample room for the principle of differential reward for differential effort and contribution. A jealous homogeneity is not the goal.

All three institutions are capable of gradual application during the transition to a steady state. The birth quota does not have to be immediately set at replacement, but could begin at existing levels and gradually approach replacement or even lower fertility. Initially the price would be zero, and would rise gradually as the number of certificates issued to each person was cut from say 1.1, to 1.0, to 0.9, or to whatever level is desired. The depletion quotas could likewise be set at present levels, or even at levels corresponding to a slower rate of increase than in the recent past. They could be applied first to those materials in shortest supply, and to those whose wastes are hardest to absorb, and then gradually extended to include nearly all minerals and fossil fuels. Initial prices on quota rights would be low, but then would rise gradually as growth pressed against the fixed quotas, or as quotas were reduced in the interest of conservation. In either case the increased scarcity rent becomes revenue to the government. The distribution limits might begin near the present extremes and slowly close to a more desirable range. The three institutions are amenable to any degree of gradualism one may wish. However, the distribution limits must be tightened faster than the other two if the burden on the poor is to be lightened. All three control points are price system parameters and altering them does not interfere with the static allocative efficiency of the market.

But is it also the case that these institutions could be totally ineffective. Depletion quotas could be endlessly raised on the grounds of national defense, balance of payments, and so on. Real estate and construction interests, not to mention the baby food and toy lobby and the military, might convince Congress to keep the supply of birth licenses well above replacement level. People at the maximum income and wealth limit may succeed in continually raising that limit by spending a great deal of their money on television commercials extolling the "unlimited acquisition of everything" as the very foundation of the American Way of Life. And everyting would be the same, and all justified in the sacred name of growth. Nothing will work unless we break our idolatrous commitment to material growth.

A definite U.S. policy of population control at home would give us a much stronger base for preaching to the underdeveloped countries about their population problem, as would even more the reduction in U.S. consumption resulting from depletion quotas. Without such a base to preach from we will continue to waste our breath, as we did at the 1974 Population Conference in Bucharest.

Thus we are brought back to the all-important moral premises discussed earlier. A physical steady state, if it is to be worth living in, absolutely requires moral growth. Future progress simply must be made in terms of the things that really count, rather than the things that are merely countable.

NOTES

1. Lewis Mumford, The Myth of the Machine (New York: Harcourt, Brace, and World, 1967), p. 276.

2. P. A. Schlipp, ed., Albert Einstein: Philosopher-Scientist, Vol. 7 (New York: Harper, 1959), p. 33.

3. John Stuart Mill, "Of Property," in Principles of Political Economy (Toronto: University of Toronto Press, 1965), Book II, Chapter I, p. 208.

4. G. B. Woods et al., "Thoughts on Various Subjects," in The Literature of England (Chicago: Scott, Foreman, 1958), p. 1003.

5. Kingsley Davis, "Zero Population Growth, Daedalus 102, no. 4 (Fall 1973): 28.

6. Nicholas Georgescu-Roegen, The Entropy Law and the Economic Process (Cambridge, Mass.: Harvard University Press, 1971), p. 21.

6

SOME PROBLEMS
OF ECONOMIC
ADJUSTMENT
Edward F. Renshaw

In the late 1950s Robert Heilbroner noted:

> Amid the general celebration of the prospects for
> continued growth, something very much akin to the
> faith of the early Classical economists in the "in-
> evitability" of progress has come to pervade the
> atmosphere. There has been a change from the
> skeptical--no doubt too skeptical--attitude of the
> late thirties and mid-forties to an attitude which
> now seems reluctant to probe for anything which
> might throw a damper on the prevailing en-
> thusiasm. [1]

An example of this attitude is provided in a statement by
Sumner Slichter. He notes that "a large portion of technological
discoveries aid in the making of additional technological progress,"
and has asserted that "the process by which the making of technological discoveries enlarges the capacity of the economy to make
additional discoveries will go on indefinitely and will steadily raise
the ability of the economy to create investment opportunities."[2]
    The unlimited progress notion which has caused some writers
to suggest that per capita income in the United States might triple
in the next 35 years and that output in Japan might soon overtake our
own economy[3] is rapidly beginning to change. In his presidential
address before the American Association for the Advancement of
Science in December 1970,[4] Bentley Glass contrasted the Endless
Horizons[5] of Vannevar Bush in 1946 with the more recent Coming of
the Golden Age[6] by Gunther Stent. The question to be faced according to Glass is: "Are there finite limits to scientific understanding,
or are there endless horizons?"[7]

Stent, like Henry Adams and Roderick Seidenberg,[8] believes that there are limits to knowledge and that cessation of scientific advances will ultimately lead to an end to technological and social progress. Thoughtful questioning of the endless frontier concept in science[9] comes at a time when the growth in our population has slowed down, when evidence in support of retardation in the growth of labor productivity is widespread, and when the public, in general, has become more acutely conscious of pollution, congestion, and natural resource scarcity, problems which have not only led to a revival of interest in the steady-state economy[10] but to suggestions that laws should be passed to limit certain kinds of consumption[11] and help prevent industrialization from becoming an economic nightmare.

While most scientists are beginning to appreciate that there are constraints to technological progress and that economic growth may eventually cease, there have been very few with the courage of Jay Forrester[12] and some of his students and colleagues at MIT to suggest that this will happen in the near future, with or without human intervention.

The initial reaction of most economists to the report by the Club of Rome on the limits to growth[13] was not only skeptical but highly defensive of economic growth as being both desirable and necessary to achieve such worthwhile goals as a reduction of poverty and a cleaner environment.[14]

That it can be foolish simply to project past trends into the future without regard to inhibiting influences is suggested by population statistics. In 1950 our total population increased by more than 2.0 percent. The number of live births, which are only estimated to have equalled a little over 3.6 million in 1950, continued to increase to more than 4.3 million in 1957. Births remained on a high plateau until 1961 and then trended downward to less than 3.25 million in 1973. The even more dramatic decline in the birth rate per woman in the child-bearing age range has caused the growth of our population to decline by more than 50 percent to an average increase of less than 1 percent in the years since 1967. If the fertility of American women remains at the level experienced in 1973 there could be a peaking of our total population in a little over 50 years.

POPULATION GROWTH AND ECONOMIC ACTIVITY

The slowing down in the growth of population has not yet had a negative effect upon the growth of economic activity in the United States. The population aged 16 and over, from which our labor force is recruited, has been increasing at an average annual rate of about

1.7 percent in recent years. This growth rate peaked out in 1973, however, and can be expected to slump back to an increase of less than 1 percent per year by 1984 as the full effect of the birth-control pill and liberalized abortion become apparent.

This decline with other factors such as the labor force participation rate, the unemployment rate, and growth in labor productivity remaining the same would be sufficient to lower the economic growth rate for real GNP from about 3.5 percent from 1953-73 to less than 3.0 percent within the space of about one decade.

The labor force participation rate for our population aged 16 and over was about 60 percent in 1953 and has since increased about one percentage point to a little over 62 percent in 1972. If enough jobs can be found for older women and young people, the participation rate may continue to increase somewhat in the next decade but probably not enough to have a very significant impact on the overall growth of economic activity.

Unemployment averaged 4.9 percent in 1973 or almost a full percentage point more than the 4.0 percent rate that is commonly considered indicative of full employment. In the last 25 years, however, we have never been able to achieve a condition of 4.0 percent unemployment except during periods of active military involvement in Asia. With structural changes in the labor force making it more difficult to achieve a low unemployment rate and with inflation a very serious problem, it is questionable whether policy makers will even try to reduce the unemployment rate below 5 percent in the remainder of this decade. My own guess would be that increases in the unemployment rate will tend to offset most of the gain in the labor force participation rate in the next few years and that the more important determinant of economic progress will continue to be improvements in labor productivity.

In 1963 this author examined various factors which have contributed to a dramatic "Substitution of Inanimate Energy for Animal Power," noted that none of these factors seemed to be open ended or exempt from the law of diminishing returns, and suggested that real wages, which had doubled, redoubled, and then doubled for a third time in the space of about 100 years might "never double again."[15]

This conclusion was so out of tune with contemporary economic thinking as to be virtually ignored at the time. It has become increasingly clear, however, that labor productivity is no longer increasing as rapidly as was once the case. Output per man-hour in the private domestic economy, which had been increasing at a 3.5 percent annual rate from 1947-65, slumped to an average rate of only 2.0 percent from 1965-70. Of some 34 industries which were surveyed by the Bureau of Labor Statistics, only six had a higher rate of growth of labor productivity in the period 1965-70 than in the earlier period from 1953-65.[16]

The sharp decline in the growth of labor productivity raises some perplexing questions. Was retardation a transitory phenomenon which can be attributed to special circumstances, or was it the result of more fundamental constraints that are likely to persist in the future and eventually bring our economy to a state of economic maturity?

In the 1970 Economic Report of the President it was suggested that the decline in the growth of labor productivity in the late 1960s may have been the result of bottlenecks, labor shortages, inexperienced workers, absenteeism, a propensity to hoard skill workers, high labor turnover, and other factors which are mainly cyclical in character or adjustments which might be expected in connection with an inflationary transition from war to peace.[17]

Rapid productivity gains in 1971 and 1972 helped to alleviate concern about a fundamental change in the long-term growth of productivity and led the editors of Fortune to conclude that the "1969-70 lag was largely due to non recurring factors."[18] A number of studies have shown, however, that changes in labor productivity are highly correlated with fluctuations in the aggregate economy.[19] In an effort to adjust for changes which are mainly cyclical we have computed the annual percentage change in output per man-hour in the private economy for the years 1948-63 and related this variable to the associated percentage change in total output.[20] Where O equals output and M equals man-hours we observe on an establishment basis:

$$\% \triangle O/M = 2.1069 + .3488\% \triangle O \qquad \text{Correlation} = .6948$$
$$(.4848) \quad (.0965) \qquad \text{Durbin-Watson} = 1.8786$$
$$\text{Standard Error} = 1.2925$$

Almost half of the year-to-year variation in output per man-hour can be explained by fluctuations in the growth of total output. The actual percentage change in output per man-hour, the "normal" change estimated from the equation and the residuals for this equation during the original fitting period from 1948-63 can be found in the top half of Table 6.1. In the lower half of this table we present the same set of statistics when the equation is used to predict changes in output per man-hour in the more recent period from 1964-73.

It will be noted that there has only been one year since 1963 when the actual increase in output per man-hour exceeded the predicted increase. Output per man-hour in 1971 was abnormally large in relation to the growth of total output partly as a result of

TABLE 6.1

Percentage Changes in Output per Man-Hour and Related Data,
Private Domestic Economy, 1948–73

| | Percent Change from Preceding Year | | | Actual Minus Predicted Productivity or Column 2 - Column 3 |
| Year | Gross National Product in 1958 Dollars (1) | Output per Man-Hour | | |
		Actual (2)	Predicted[a] (3)	(4)
1948	4.8	4.5	3.8	.7
1949	-.3	3.2	2.0	1.2
1950	10.2	8.1	5.7	2.4
1951	6.3	3.0	4.3	-1.3
1952	2.5	1.9	3.0	-1.1
1953	5.1	4.2	3.9	.3
1954	-1.3	2.4	1.6	.8
1955	8.5	4.4	5.0	-.6
1956	1.9	.2	2.8	-2.6
1957	1.4	2.9	2.6	.3
1958	-1.3	3.1	1.6	1.5
1959	7.0	3.6	4.5	-.9
1960	2.4	1.6	2.9	-1.3
1961	1.9	3.5	2.8	.7
1962	6.8	4.7	4.5	.2
1963	4.2	3.6	3.6	.0
1964	5.7	3.9	4.1	-.2
1965	6.6	3.4	4.4	-1.0
1966	6.4	4.0	4.3	-.3
1967	2.3	2.1	2.9	-.8
1968	4.8	2.9	3.8	-.9
1969	2.8	.4	3.1	-2.7
1970	-.5	1.0	1.9	-.9
1971	3.5	4.1	3.3	.8
1972	6.5	3.8	4.4	-.6
1973[b]	6.2	2.9	4.3	-1.4

[a]Predicted output per man-hour equals 2.1 percent plus .35 times the percentage changed in real output, col. (1). The equation used to predict output per man-hour was fitted to the data for the years 1948–63.

[b]Preliminary.

Source: Economic Report of the President, February 1974, p. 287.

135

the General Motors strike which caused output per man-hour in the private nonfarm sector to decline 3.1 percent on an annual basis in the fourth quarter of 1970 and then leap upward at an annual rate of 7.4 percent in the first quarter of 1971.

It should also be noted that the difference between actual and predicted output per man-hour was very large in each of the four preceding years, implying that there may have existed some "catching up" potential in 1971 as businessmen began to take full advantage of the more than 70 percent increase in average annual real investment in producers' durable equipment which was achieved between 1960 and 1966 and then sustained throughout the recession of 1970. If the productivity increase which occurred in 1971 is averaged together with the increase which occurred in any of the four preceding years, the conclusion is that output per man-hour in the private domestic economy has been in a state of retarded growth for at least a decade and perhaps even longer.

One of the most dramatic ways to illustrate the large decline in the growth of labor productivity in the post-World War II period is to divide the last 25 years of change into three subperiods which bridge years of peak prosperity. For the subperiods 1947-53, 1953-66, and 1966-73 we obtain revised average annual growth rates of 4.1, 3.0, and 2.1 percent, respectively, for output per man-hour in the private domestic economy.

PRODUCTIVITY AND ENERGY SUPPLIES

There is reason to believe that the downward trend in the growth of labor productivity will continue and perhaps be even more dramatic in the remainder of this decade. One of the more important reasons is mounting evidence which suggests that the United States is now living off of productivity gains which, in a sense, were borrowed from the past. The evidence is particularly marked in the case of natural gas and oil production, where output per man-hour has been kept at high levels by drawing down reserves which were accumulated in previous decades.

Natural gas production, in terms of BTUs produced, surpassed petroleum production in 1963 to become our number-one source of domestically produced energy. In 1973 it provided almost a third of our energy consumption. Our reserves of natural gas were very large in relation to total consumption in the early post-World War II period and continued to increase each year until 1967. In the years since 1967, however, the net additions to our reserves have been less than half as large, on the average, as our consumption. By drawing gas reserves down we have been able to keep output per

person engaged in natural gas exploration at over twice the level
that would probably have prevailed if consumption were cut back to
equal new reserves or if drilling activity were expanded enough to
equal consumption.

Our petroleum industry is in a similar situation. In 8 of the
13 years prior to 1974 annual reserve finds for crude oil in the
United States were less than annual production. Total oil production
reached an all-time peak in 1970 and has since been trending downward. It was not until April 1972, however, that the Texas Railroad
Commission increased the allowable oil production from wells in our
largest producing state to 100 percent of their so-called maximum
efficient rate. Now that excess capacity is no longer available to
help offset the natural decline in production from existing wells, the
oil industry will have to increase its drilling activity substantially
merely to keep domestic production from declining.

The natural rate of decline, in the absence of advanced recovery technology and regulatory arrangements which limit production below the efficient rate, appears to be on the order of 10 percent
or more per year for existing onshore wells outside of Alaska. The
drilling of new oil wells in 1973 was apparently able to offset only
about 70 percent of this decline. This would imply a required increase in drilling activity of more than 40 percent simply to halt the
downward trend in domestic oil production in the United States, in
the interim before the Alaska pipeline is completed, if drilling efficiency were to remain the same as in 1973. Since total output would
not be increased by expanding drilling activity to offset production
losses from old wells, it is reasonable to conclude that efforts to
become more self-sufficient in basic energy production will tend to
substantially reduce output per man-hour in both the oil and natural
gas industries.

Shrinking supplies of domestically produced oil and gas have
made us more dependent upon energy that is imported from other
countries. The rapid increase in oil imports has not only allowed
the Arab world to embark upon a policy of oil diplomacy but has
also created an economic environment in which the Organization of
Petroleum Exporting Countries could raise the price of imported
oil dramatically.

In the 18-month period from the beginning of 1973 to the middle
of 1974 the wholesale price index for all fuels, related products,
and power (including the prices of domestically produced natural gas
and old domestic oil which were still regulated) more than doubled.
The substantially higher prices for almost all forms of energy make
it not unreasonable to suppose that energy consumption will increase
at a much slower rate in the future than in the last few decades.
This in turn can be expected to slow the growth in output per man-
hour in energy-distributing industries.

Total output for the gas and electric utility industries increased at an average annual rate of 7.8 percent from 1947-72.
The 6.8 percent increase in output per man-hour in these two industries was almost equal to the growth in total output. Once wires
and pipelines are in place, output per man-hour can be increased
by almost the same percentage as the growth of total energy consumption. If consumption grows at a slower rate in the future, it
follows that output per man-hour in the gas and utility industries
will also increase at a much slower rate.

The same sort of reasoning can be applied to other industries.
Since there are a large number of fixed costs or motions involved
in assembling and servicing automobiles, we can conclude that an
energy-price-induced shift to smaller cars, which use less gasoline
per mile, will tend to reduce labor productivity in both the automobile manufacturing and servicing industries. One could go on and
enumerate many other ways in which higher energy prices might be
expected to retard improvements in output per man-hour. The important point, it seems to me, is that the United States and other
nations, which are dependent upon oil imports for a significant share
of their energy needs, are not likely to grow as rapidly in the future
as was the case before the oil embargo. The process of adjusting
to a no-growth economy, in other words, is already upon us and is
not something that can be postponed until we have solved all our
economic problems, exhausted standing room, depleted most of our
high-grade mineral resources, drowned in our own industrial wastes,
or approached a worldwide heat limit which will not permit life to
be sustained on earth.

THE LIMITS TO TECHNOLOGICAL PROGRESS

To argue that economic optimists and even the authors of The
Limits to Growth are essentially wrong in assuming that economic
activity can continue to increase at a very rapid rate for several
more decades one must come directly to grips with a basic assumption that has often gone unchallenged in recent discussions of economic growth and environmental decay. That assumption is the
notion that progress in technology is essentially unlimited and
basically exponential in character or, if there are limits, that these
limits are fairly far off and not something that can be expected to
significantly retard economic progress in this century.

This assumption, it seems to me, can easily be refuted if one
examines some of the more important dimensions of economic
progress such as the speed, scale, and efficiency of converting inanimate energy into useful working effects. Of the factors that help

to restore one's faith in the law of diminishing returns, none has
been more neglected by economists than the substitution of inanimate
energy for animal power. This substitution provides an understandable basis for expecting improvements in output per man-hour, a
basis for suggesting that technological improvements can be reduced
or classified in terms of a few salient dimensions, and a basis for
guessing that we are probably closer to the end of strictly economic
progress than most persons engaged in research and development
would care to admit.

In 1928 C. R. Daugherty and others noted that

> it is manifestly impossible or at least impracti-
> cable to make a census of machines. They change
> and become obsolete too rapidly, and they cannot
> be reduced to any satisfactory common unit. But
> there is one way whereby an index of the installa-
> tion of machinery may be obtained--by ascertaining
> the total horsepower of the engines that drive the
> different kinds of machinery. The engines may be
> of many different types, but their ability to operate
> machines may be expressed in terms of a single
> unit, the horsepower. . . . It is recognized that
> improvement in the technique of production or in
> transmission mechanism may increase the amount
> of machinery which can be operated by the same
> amount of horsepower. Nevertheless, it is be-
> lieved that this difference is not large enough to
> impair the use of total horsepower as an index of
> the relative amounts of machinery in use over a
> period of years. [21]

This sentiment was again echoed in 1956 by Seymour Melman:

> The horsepower rating of electric motors used for
> direct machine drives or as prime movers, is a
> good average indicator of the degree of mechaniza-
> tion in manufacturing as a whole. . . . It is not
> implied that this criterion of change in production
> methods is effective apart from new organization
> methods, application of new raw materials, or
> qualitative improvement in given equipment.
> Rather it is the case that, on the average, in-
> creased horsepower per worker has accompanied
> such changes. They are two aspects of the same
> development. [22]

The horsepower of electric motors and other installed prime movers and the work performed by prime movers are among the few inputs of economic consequence that have increased more rapidly over time than total output. [23]

If one accepts the substitution hypothesis, growth in labor productivity can be considered a process which is partly self-generating, that is, induced by a spillover of wage benefits to a comparatively scarce supply of labor, raising the price of human energy relative to inanimate energy, and thus providing an economic incentive for innovations and adjustments leading to further substitution, [24] and partly the result of discoveries and inventions which cheapen inanimate energy by improving the efficiency of converting heat into work. Changes in conversion efficiency are important since they would appear to provide the "autonomous" force that is necessary to offset natural resource scarcity and diminishing marginal rates of substitution of inanimate energy for animal power. (A man or a horse can convert carbohydrate food energy into useful work with efficiencies ranging up to 35 percent. Without the development of internal combustion engines with efficiencies ranging between 20 and 30 percent we might still be using horses for work as well as pleasure and would not have entered the air age. A 1956 study of horse and tractor costs indicates that the horse was still more economical than a tractor in some agricultural situations, even in a country as technically advanced as Great Britain.)[25] Without improvements in the efficiency of converting energy into useful working effects, improvements in labor productivity would become analogous to a free-wheeling vehicle that is propelled on by its own momentum--a vehicle which will gradually lose momentum and inevitably coast to a stop as a result of friction and a natural scarcity of a good roadbed.

The limits of technological efficiency are well understood in the case of large-scale power plants and are rapidly being approached. [26] Higher fuel prices will no doubt stimulate a great deal of research in an effort to improve the combustion and work efficiencies of small-scale energy converters. It does not seem likely, however, that these efforts will be successful enough to fully offset natural resource scarcity without a relative sacrifice of some energy-intensive activities.

The importance of natural-resource scarcity in a longer-run context can best be illustrated by comparing the relative price of crude oil to vegetable oil. Crude oil, until recently, was only about one-tenth as expensive as cottonseed oil and soybean oil. As existing and yet-to-be-discovered supplies of liquid hydrocarbons are used up, however, caloric prices will eventually rise to equal and perhaps exceed the price of vegetable oil, which is more perishable and not as good a source of material for plastics and some essential chemicals. If our consumption of fossil fuels were valued not in terms of current extraction costs, but in terms of the long-run replacement costs suggested by conventional agriculture, the conclusion would be that the United States and most oil-exporting nations are becoming poorer instead of growing richer.[27] All of the investments we have made in factories, housing, roads, consumer durables, machinery, automobiles, refineries, transportation equipment, and public improvements--many of which appear to be dependent upon a cheap supply of liquid hydrocarbons--pale to a rather modest value in comparison to the relative cost of replacing the mineral wealth we have already used up, often--one suspects--for rather frivolous and unimportant purposes.

In 1857 John Stuart Mill noted: "It must have been seen, more or less distinctly by political economists, that the increase in wealth is not boundless; that at the end of what they term the progressive state lies the stationary state, that all progress in wealth is but a postponement of this, and that each step in advance is an approach to it."

Speaking before the Institute on Man and Science in 1970, Rene Dubos gave voice to a growing number of scientists and humanists who feel that the times have caught up with John Stuart Mill: "The ecological constraints upon population and technological growth will inevitably lead to social and economic systems different from the ones in which we live today. . . . Whether we want it or not, the phase of quantitative growth which has prevailed throughout technical civilization during the 19th and 20th centuries will soon come to an end."

INFLATION, UNEMPLOYMENT, AND ENERGY CONSERVATION

The end of quantitative growth, I believe, is not only in sight but has already created some rather painful problems of economic adjustment.[28] In the remainder of this chapter I would like to discuss briefly three interrelated problems: inflation, unemployment, and energy conservation.

Table 6.2 contains some least-squares regression equations which do a remarkably good job of explaining average annual percentage changes in the consumer price index (CPI) from 1948 to 1973. These equations suggest that the process of adjusting to a steady-state economy can aggravate the problem of inflation in several ways.

As fossil fuels and other high-grade mineral resources are used up and as world population presses against available food

supplies, the prices of farm products and other raw materials can
be expected to rise more rapidly than prices in general. The equations which are presented in Table 6.2 show that changes in the consumer price index are highly correlated with changes in the prices
of farm products and other crude materials which enter the wholesale price index. The coefficients, indeed, are much larger in
most instances than would be expected by the fraction of our gross
national product that is devoted to the production and consumption of
raw materials.[29]

TABLE 6.2

Equations Which Can Be Used to Explain the Average Annual
Percentage Change in the Consumer Price Index, 1948–73

Independent Variable or Statistic	Regression Coefficients and "t" Statistics for the Fitting Period		
	1948–73 (1)	1957–73 (2)	1948–73 (3)
Average annual percent Δ in crude material prices			
1948–73	.1606 (6.3081)		
1957–73		.0933 (5.3241)	
1948–52			.1924 (7.0391)
1953–63			.1457 (1.9847)
1964–73			.0904 (2.9783)
Average annual percent Δ in adjusted hourly earnings, private nonfarm economy	.7689 (5.0794)	.7780 (9.8831)	.7999 (6.6556)
Average annual percent Δ in total government expenditure	.0553 (1.8196)	.0613 (1.9898)	.0634 (2.5428)
Average annual percent Δ in output per man-hour, private nonfarm economy	-.2355		

Source: Data compiled by the author.

The value of raw materials in total domestic consumption in 1973, for example, was only about .07 or 7 percent of GNP. The relatively higher coefficients for raw materials suggest that a rapid increase in crude material prices will have a positive spillover effect upon other prices (in the absence of effective price controls) that will tend to accelerate the inflationary process.

In 1973 farm prices, which were not subject to price controls, rose at their fastest rate since 1917 and accounted for about 51 percent of the rise in the CPI. Another 11 percent of the rise in the CPI was accounted for by higher energy prices. For the year as a whole the wholesale price index for crude materials increased on the average by 36.2 percent compared to an average increase of only 6.2 percent for the consumer price index.

In January 1974 the members of the Organization of Petroleum Exporting Countries raised the price of imported oil more than threefold. The steep rise in food and energy prices in 1973-74 set the stage for a more general explosion of prices which is now causing organized labor to demand large, catch-up increases in wages which will further exacerbate price inflation.

The coefficients which are presented in Table 6.2 suggest that a 1 percent increase in wages, with other factors remaining the same, will in turn force businessmen to raise their prices an additional 0.8 percent. The end result of commodity inflation, in other words, has been the initiation of a price wage spiral that has been very difficult to control.

The negative coefficient which is associated with the percentage change in output per man-hour in the private nonfarm economy indicates that inflation could be moderated to a considerable extent by a large increase in productivity. We have already presented some evidence in Table 6.1, however, which shows that improvements in labor productivity have been in a state of retarded growth for more than a decade and have indicated that future improvements will probably be even smaller, on the average, than during the past decade.

The very small increases in output per man-hour which occurred in 1969 and 1970, more than any other factor, were probably responsible for the accelerated inflation which eventually caused President Nixon to implement a national system of wage and price controls in 1971. The dummy variable which we have included in our regressions for the control years of 1972 and 1973 suggests that wage and price controls may have been more effective than is commonly supposed. Their very success at suppressing inflation in the nonfarm sector at a time when some farm and other raw material prices were rising at unprecedented rates appears to have generated a decontrol explosion in wages and prices of such

proportions as to have helped tip the U.S. economy into a major recession. Is there any way of solving the problem of inflation without
a prolonged recession?

In response to this question, one must confess that our tools
for dealing with what some have termed a condition of stagflation
are rather weak. It is commonly supposed, for example, that a
cutback in the growth of government spending would help to reduce
inflation. The coefficients we obtained in Table 6.2 for changes in
total government spending at all levels of government are really
very small. A 1 percent decrease in government spending, with the
other variables in these equations remaining the same, would only
decrease the predicted value of the consumer price index by about
.06 percent. Depending on what happened to the other variables,
the cumulative sum of both the direct and indirect effects of a decrease in government spending could be either negative or positive.

If a decrease in federal expenditure for goods and services in
the private sector reduced output per man-hour in the nonfarm
economy sufficiently, the net effect of a decrease in government
spending might be inflationary. A decrease in government spending
which helped to reduce the demand for scarce raw materials, on the
other hand, might help to reduce the price of crude materials and
moderate consumer price inflation both directly and indirectly.

The U.S. Treasury has considered a proposal to raise gasoline taxes by as much as 10 cents a gallon to help fight inflation.
The main objection to such a tax is that it would tend to be regressive. This problem could be overcome, however, by using the proceeds to raise Social Security benefits and reduce payroll taxes,
which are even more regressive than the gasoline tax and in need of
basic reform.[30] Wage earners and retired persons who do not belong to the Social Security system could be given a tax credit of
about equal value to the reduction in payroll taxes which could then
be applied against their federal income tax or refunded by the Treasury in cash if no income tax is owed the U.S. government. The
overall progressivity of this shift in the structure of our tax system
could be increased by raising Social Security benefits by the amount
of the tax credit and by using the bulk of the proceeds to exempt,
say, the first $2,000 of wage and salary payments from Social
Security taxes.

Such a system could be implemented quickly, with very little
loss of consumer buying power, and would tend to benefit poor families and middle-income groups that endeavor to conserve gasoline
proportionately more than rich families. A 1969-70 survey by the
Bureau of the Census found that families in the $4,000-a-year income
bracket drive only 148 miles a week, on the average, compared to
a national average of 223 miles per week for all income groups.

Families with an annual income of $15,000 or more drove 288 miles per week on the average.

The United States is about the only "oil poor" industrial nation that does not levy a large tax on gasoline of 50 cents or more per gallon to limit the demand for imported oil. Drivers in other countries, as a consequence, have a greater incentive to buy smaller cars, organize car pools, drive at lower operating speeds, utilize mass transit, and in other ways help to conserve energy.

Excise taxes on gasoline are a particularly interesting weapon to employ against inflation since there is reason to believe that they might be socially beneficial in their own right. In a thought-provoking paper on the theory and measurement of the private and social costs of highway congestion, Alan Walters has argued that a minimum fuel tax of at least 33 cents a gallon ought to be charged in most urban areas of the United States to bring private costs, at the margin, into approximate equality with the marginal social cost of traffic congestion.[31] There is reason to believe that higher gasoline taxes would also help to reduce air pollution, reverse the deterioration of some of our central cities, and lessen the need for federal support for urban renewal and mass transit subsidies.[32]

There is an even more paradoxical reason for charging higher gasoline taxes and adopting other measures which will tend to conserve energy and raw materials. That is the possibility that by accepting the goal of a steady-state economy and developing the habits of thrift in the use of energy and materials which will be needed in the long run, we may be able to grow faster in the short run and experience less unemployment as well as less inflation.

Such factors as an almost chronic deficit in our balance of payments because of oil imports, the time and expense that will be involved in simply halting the downward trend in oil and gas production in the United States, and the huge capital costs that will be involved in obtaining synthetic oil and gas from coal and shale suggest that the United States cannot continue to grow as it has in the past. Whether we want to or not, we will simply have to be more conserving in the use of energy and materials.

There are many ways to reduce energy consumption and encourage conservation. I have chosen to emphasize the possibility of excise taxes since they would not only discourage wasteful consumption in the short run but could also be expected to provide consumers with an economic incentive to quickly replace large, gas-guzzling automobiles and inefficient appliances with smaller and more efficient vehicles and appliances. This in turn could help set the stage for a vigorous economic recovery, unimpeded by balance-of-payments difficulties or a severe shortage of capital, energy, and materials. Such a recovery is needed, I believe, to reduce unemployment and insure a condition of reasonable prosperity for all our citizens. If excise taxes on gasoline and, say, "excessive" amounts of electricity[33] were used to reduce Social Security taxes or in other ways provide disproportionate tax relief and/or benefits to families with low and moderate incomes, they could also help to improve the distribution of effective purchasing power and ameliorate other social injustices.

CONCLUDING REMARKS

Economists who have thought about a steady-state economy have differed widely in their personal regard for it. According to Adam Smith,

> it is in the progressive state, while society is advancing to the further acquisition, rather than when it has acquired its full complement of riches, that the condition of the laboring poor, of the great body of people, seems to be happiest and the most comfortable. It is hard in the stationary, and miserable in the declining state. The progressive state is really the cheerful and hearty state of all the different orders of society. The stationary is dull; the declining melancholy.

John Stuart Mill, on the other hand, was inclined to argue that a "stationary state" (by which he meant a constant population and a constant stock of physical wealth) was both necessary and desirable:

> It is scarcely necessary to remark that a stationary condition of capital and population implies no stationary state of human improvement. There would be as much scope as ever for all kinds of mental culture, and moral and social progress; as much and much more likelihood of it being improved, when minds cease to be engrossed by the art of getting on. Even the industrial arts might be as earnestly and as successfully cultivated, with this sole difference, that in serving no purpose but the increase of wealth, industrial improvements would produce their legitimate effect, that of abridging labor.

In a recent review of Jay Forrester's <u>World Dynamics</u>, William Bowen, president of Princeton University, has expressed similar thoughts:

> An end to growth in material output, moreover, would not necessarily be incompatible with economic growth of kinds not well measured by our present stock of indicators, notably growth in the quality of goods and services. With a renaissance of craftsmanship, of pride in work, of willingness to serve, a society poorer than ours by some statistical measures could enjoy goods of greater durability and higher aesthetic quality, and services performed with more courtesy, cheerfulness, and competence. And stability in material growth, finally, would not necessarily be incompatible with individual excellence, with devotion to one's craft, with love for one's children, with high achievement in the arts, with eloquence, with precise thought or careful expression, with enhanced sense of community, with deepened religious faith, or with care for the scarred yet still nurturing earth itself.

Human beings are extremely adaptable and also fairly nostalgic. While I rather doubt that a steady-state economy will be universally regarded as superior to the age of rapid economic growth, it does have the potential for being a better place to live in at least some respects. Whether it is indeed a heaven or a hell will no doubt depend in no small way on what we choose to make it.

NOTES

1. Robert L. Heilbroner, The Future as History (New York: Harper and Brothers, 1959), p. 133.

2. Sumner Slichter, Economic Growth in the United States (Baton Rouge: Louisiana State University Press, 1961), pp. 101-06.

3. In their book, The Year 2000, Jerome Wiener and Herman Kahn have published a "best estimate" for GNP which implies that per capita income will nearly triple by the year 2000. In his more recent book, The Emerging Japanese Superstate, Kahn suggests that per capita output in Japan will soon overtake the most advanced

Western countries. One wonders what they might do with all those
cars and other consumer goods--stack them on top of each other?

    4. Bentley Glass, "Science: Endless Horizons or Golden
Age?" Science, January 8, 1971, pp. 28-29.
    5. Vannevar Bush, Endless Horizons (Washington, D.C.:
Public Affairs Press, 1946).
    6. Gunther Stent, Coming of the Golden Age (Garden City,
N.Y.: Natural History Press, 1969).
    7. Glass, op. cit., p. 23.
    8. R. Seidenberg, Posthistoric Man (Chapel Hill: University
of North Carolina Press, 1950).
    9. Walter Sullivan, "Pioneer in Physics Sees Few Hidden
Discoveries," New York Times, December 13, 1971, p. 30. This
view of the future has led Harvey Brooks to seriously ask, "Can
Science Survive in the Modern Age?" Science, October 1, 1971,
pp. 21-29.
    10. Henry Jarrett, ed., "Economics of the Coming Spaceship
Earth," in Environmental Quality, ed. Kenneth E. Boulding (Balti-
more: Johns Hopkins University Press, 1966); Herman E. Daly,
"The Stationary-State Economy: Toward a Political Economy of
Biophysical Equilibrium and Moral Growth," Distinguished Lecture
Series No. 2, Department of Economics, University of Alabama,
1971; Edward F. Renshaw, The End of Progress (North Scituate,
Mass.: Duxbury Press, 1976).
    11. E. J. Mishan, The Costs of Economic Growth (New York:
Praeger, 1967).
    12. J. W. Forrester, World Dynamics (Cambridge, Mass.:
Wright Allen Press, 1971).
    13. Donella H. Meadows et al., The Limits to Growth (New
York: Universe Books, 1972).
    14. See, for example, Walter W. Heller, "Economic Growth
and Environmental Quality: Collision or Co-Existence?" (Boston:
General Learning Press, 1973); Peter Passell and Leonard Ross,
The Retreat from Riches (New York: Viking, 1973).
    15. Edward F. Renshaw, "The Substitution of Inanimate
Energy for Animal Power," Journal of Political Economy, June
1963, pp. 284-92.
    16. U.S. Department of Labor, Bureau of Labor Statistics,
Indexes of Output per Manhour: Selected Industries 1939 and
1947-70, Bulletin 1692 (Washington, D.C.: U.S. Government
Printing Office, 1971).
    17. Economic Report of the President (Washington, D.C.:
U.S. Government Printing Office, 1970), pp. 48-49.
    18. Fortune, June 1973, p. 30.

SOME PROBLEMS OF ECONOMIC ADJUSTMENT

19. Frank Brechling, "The Relationship Between Output and Employment in British Manufacturing Industries," Review of Economic Studies 32 (1965): 187-216; T. A. Wilson and O. Eckstein, "Short-Run Productivity Behavior in U.S. Manufacturing," Review of Economics and Statistics, February 1964; E. Kuh, "Cyclical and Secular Labor Productivity in U.S. Manufacturing," Review of Economics and Statistics, February 1965; and Edward Renshaw, "Why Economic Uptrend May Be Short Lived," Commercial and Financial Chronicle, December 3, 1970, pp. 1 and 10.

20. An association between labor productivity and output has been observed on a cross sectional basis by W. E. G. Salter, Productivity and Technical Change, Part II (Cambridge, Mass.: Harvard University Press, 1966), and by John W. Kendrick, Productivity Trends in the United States (Princeton, N.J.: National Bureau of Economic Research, 1961), Chapter 7. The degree of association appears to have been greater during the shorter periods studied by Salter than over the longer interval considered by Kendrick.

21. C. R. Daugherty et al., Power Capacity and Production in the United States, U.S. Geological Survey Water Supply Paper No. 579, 1928, p. 13.

22. Seymour Melman, Dynamic Factors in Industrial Productivity (London: Basil Blackwell, 1956), p. 109.

23. In addition to my own article on this subject, see Murray F. Foss, "The Utilization of Capital Equipment," Survey of Current Business, June 1963, pp. 8-16, and G. S. Maddala, "Productivity and Technological Change in the Bituminous Coal Industry, 1919-54," Journal of Political Economy, August 1965, pp. 352-65.

Maddala's index of output per employee in bituminous coal mining increased from 100 in 1919 to 228.5 in 1954; horsepower per employee rose from 100 to 772.0 during the same period. Index changes in gross farm output per person employed in agriculture and a combined index of animate and inanimate horsepower per person imply a marginal rate of substitution in agriculture from 1910 to 1955 that is about the same as that observed for the bituminous coal industry. Output per man-hour in manufacturing increased 381 percent between 1899 and 1962. The horsepower of installed prime mover per man-hour increased 556 percent during the same period of time.

Foss' finding that electric motors and other installed prime movers were utilized from one-third to one-half more hours per day in the mid-1950s than in 1929 suggests that the trade-off between human energy and inanimate energy--adjusted for changes in conversion efficiency--may have been quite a bit worse than that implied by the increase in inanimate prime mover.

24. Melman, op. cit., p. 26, has compiled statistics which show a very significant rise in the price of human energy relative to electrical energy and has emphasized the importance of this rise in inducing further substitution.

25. See Keith Dexter, "A Study of Economic Costs of Production: An Analysis of Horse and Tractor Costs," Journal of Agricultural Economics, June 1956, pp. 73-81.

26. Leonard G. Austin, "Fuel Cells," Scientific American, October 1959, p. 72; and Claude Summers, "The Conversion of Energy," Scientific American, September 1971, p. 151.

27. Some data in support of this conclusion are provided in "An Energy Tax and Other Essays on the Financing of Education," The Municipal Finance Study Group, State University of New York at Albany, August 1972, pp. 24-26.

28. Additional evidence and arguments in support of an early end to economic progress in the United States as well as a more extensive discussion of various adjustment problems are presented in Renshaw, The End of Progress, op. cit.

29. These results are discussed in greater detail in a paper by Daniel Egy and Edward F. Renshaw on "Alternative Strategies for Reducing Inflation," Albany Discussion Paper No. 16, Department of Economics, State University of New York at Albany, September 1974.

30. John A. Brittain, The Payroll Tax for Social Security (Washington, D.C.: Brookings Institution, 1973).

31. Alan A. Walters, "The Theory and Measurement of Private and Social Cost of Highway Congestion," Econometrica, October 1961, pp. 676-99.

32. Since mass transit consumes less than half as much fuel per passenger mile as most automobiles, an increase in operating subsidies would probably be deflationary on balance, provided Congress was willing to raise taxes enough to pay for the subsidies. See Edward F. Renshaw, "A Note on Mass Transit Subsidies," National Tax Journal, December 1973, pp. 639-44; "A Justification for Operating Subsidies," Traffic Quarterly, April 1974, pp. 197-207; and "A Note on Alternative Sources of Financing for Mass Transit Subsidies," Land Economics, May 1974, pp. 171-76.

33. In the last several years there has been a revival of interest in the concept of marginal cost pricing which suggests that consumers of electricity should pay a higher price for power during periods of peak demand than during off-peak hours. For an interesting discussion of these and other issues I would recommend a paper by Ernst Habicht, director of EDF's Energy Program, "The Social Origins and Economic Basis of the Demand for Electricity," which was presented at the New Zealand Energy Conference, University of Auckland, May 25, 1974.

III

THE POLITICS OF
SUSTAINABLE GROWTH

INTRODUCTION

Any attempt to create a sustainable society requires political action. Political leaders allocate scarce resources and decide who gets "what, when, and how." During the rapid economic growth of the Industrial Revolution, political leaders in industrial countries allocated pieces of an ever-larger economic pie. But slower growth, whether unanticipated or by design, means that leaders will not only decide who gets what, when, and how, but increasingly they will have to explain why.

Contemporary political institutions have been shaped in environments of growth. Mass democracy, for example, didn't exist prior to the onset of industrial abundance. In fact, the development of mass pluralist democracy is closely related to the compromises that have been made possible by economic growth. Demands from less-fortunate classes can be more easily met when they do not require dramatic redistribution of wealth and power.

A sustainable society presents many challenges to established political orders. It raises a new agenda of issues that have previously been buried by material affluence. It is this affluence that has legitimized self-interest in politics, laissez-faire economics, wealth as an indicator of worth, and rugged individualism. Population growth, resource depletion, and environmental pollution call all of these institutions into question. "Nonissues" of the twentieth century will become the critical issues of the twenty-first century.

There are several common themes implicit in the chapters that follow. All of the authors see future growth policy, whatever its nature, as having severe political consequences. The "frugal option" in growth policy requires a redefinition of political purpose and substantial changes in industrial politics. But even a continuation of "business as usual" may pose a threat to the future of democratic institutions. Democracy thrives on rapid growth, periods in which elected leaders can respond to citizen demands for increased material wealth. There is little experience to indicate that democracy prospers during protracted periods of slow growth or economic decline.

There also seems to be general agreement that continued population growth, environmental deterioration, resource depletion, and so on, call for a change in the scope of government activity. Minimal government or "nongovernment" can no longer be tolerated in an era when a number of pressing problems require political action. While each of the authors would like to see government play a more

153

active role in dealing with these problems, there is little indication that they feel rapid political change and initiative is imminent.

In Chapter 7 William Ophuls looks at some of the political implications of limits-to-growth arguments. He sees two options for industrial societies in meeting future demands. The first option is technological utopia characterized by high throughput of natural resources. This represents an extension of present trends and perspectives. But high-throughput utopia is predicated upon the rapid development of alternative sources of energy; most likely nuclear power. Ophuls argues that this means striking a "Faustian bargain" that will eventually lead toward some variant of "Brave New World."

The alternative is to develop a sustainable society based upon frugality. This society requires ordering priorities and represents a challenge to political systems long accustomed to burying rather than confronting critical issues. In a frugal society economics would be devoted to meeting human needs rather than encompassing all of social life.

Ophuls argues that the option that is chosen is not necessarily more important than the fact that a choice is made. Industrial politics has become "nonpolitics," an emphasis on process with little concern for outcomes. An attempt by politicians to ignore problems of resource depletion and environmental deterioration has become the most pressing problem.

Writing in a less-philosophical vein, Michael Kraft discusses political changes necessary in making a transition to sustainable growth as well as some political consequences of slowed economic growth. He argues that the limits-to-growth discussions have ignored many very fundamental political issues. Consciousness-raising efforts may have created an awareness of environmental problems, but political action is necessary to do something about them.

Kraft outlines an agenda of research questions relevant to slowed growth. In politics, as in ecology, everything is related to everything else and we must understand how political elements of the problem are interrelated. He concludes that it is important to stop abstract argumentation about limits to growth and to raise the proper questions about sustainable growth and political change. Advocates of change must work within an existing system for the foreseeable future and this means they must understand how the political system works, what it responds to, and what potential exists for changing it.

Davis Bobrow provides a vision of a "politics of coordinated redistribution" that he feels is essential to the political stability of a future society. He also suggests two different visions of a sustainable future: restraint-moderation and technology-abundance. Either of these visions requires a strikingly different type of politics.

Pursuing the restraint and moderation vision calls for an intrusive type of politics. Therefore certain policies are to be preferred if the onerous aspects of such a politics are to be avoided. A dependable flow of information must be maintained between citizen and government. There must be guarantees that redistribution will not foster the development of a new dominant class. And there must be continued emphasis on the welfare of future generations.

Bobrow claims that pursuing a technology and abundance vision also requires massive change. Saving and investment for the future must be encouraged. A world characterized by breeder reactors and nuclear parks is not likely to tolerate great diversity and freedom among individuals. Technology would remain paramount and citizens would be required to pull together to keep up with technology's needs.

In his lucid contribution on property, Peter Stillman concentrates on new justifications and definitions of property rights. He begins by noting a close link between property and Western politics. He argues that many of the justifications for private property found in political theory are no longer valid in today's overpopulated world. A new and more ecologically sound definition of property rights is clearly needed.

Three different approaches to redefinition of property rights are outlined: extension of some rights, limitations on others, and differentiations of categories of property. Thus, extending property rights could include new amenity rights, modification of rights to alienate, changes in standing to sue, expansion of the public trust, and even guaranteed subsistence. Stillman suggests that new limitations on property rights might include taxes on windfall gains caused by changes in growth policy and limitations on inheritance to create more equality of opportunity. Finally, differentiation of property could include tax breaks for property that increases use of renewable resources and a distinction in the treatment of property as capital and property for use.

Stillman concludes by suggesting a new set of justifications for property rights within a sustainable society. In the future property must liberate rather than enslave. It must also be seen as an instrument for human development and attitude change.

In the closing chapter of this section David Vogel raises some sobering questions about the link between politics and business. Corporate growth and investment is an essential component of growth policy. In fact, growth and diversification legitimize contemporary corporate management. Corporations also play a critical role in politics. Advocates of slowed economic growth are striking directly at corporate interests and can expect substantial opposition from the business community.

The political strength of the business community is increased by an alliance with the working class. The growth of business means increasing employment opportunities. More than 7 percent of the working force is presently unemployed and it is politically difficult to make a case for slowed growth. According to Vogel, it is up to the advocates of a sustainable society to specify more clearly what they mean and to come up with meaningful growth and employment alternatives.

7

THE POLITICS OF THE
SUSTAINABLE SOCIETY
William Ophuls

POLITICS AND NONPOLITICS

It is an existential given that human beings have to live in community. Even those who later choose to be hermits can do so only after having been born and raised in a community of other human beings. Community life is what makes us special. In addition, we are, as Aristotle said, inevitably political animals, for otherwise we would necessarily be either gods or beasts, not men. That is, human communities cannot exist without some agreed set of rules and procedures for ordering their community life. Without such a political "constitution," to use the word in its ancient Greek sense, there can be no successful community. Thus, there is, in addition to all the various individual interests of the members of the community, a community or common interest that is coexistent with, if not paramount to, individual interests. The fundamental task of politics then is, as it has been from time immemorial, the achievement of this common interest.

Men have gone about this task in a great variety of ways throughout their long years of living together in communities. At first their constitutions were implicit, buried within the cake of custom by which so-called primitive peoples have regulated their lives, right down to the present day in some cases. As a mode of politics, custom has been quite extraordinarily successful. Evolved over many generations by trial and error and furthered by a degree of intuitive understanding of man, nature, and the necessary and proper relationship between the two that we can only admire, custom created what were by and large highly successful adaptations--until circumstances beyond such peoples' control associated with the growth of civilization propelled their way of life along the path of extinction. The essential feature of this mode of politics is that the constitution is for all intents and purposes internalized by each member of the customary group. Politics is therefore carried out by the generality of cultural institutions, rather than by specific groups of people or sets of institutions. In fact, many of the first observers of primitive tribes were baffled by their inability to find anything they could call politics, and for many years it was usual to say of custom-ruled peoples that they did not in fact have any politics.

This parochial misunderstanding was probably to be expected, for the mode of politics practiced by so-called civilized man is quite different. Once development has proceeded beyond a certain point, the customary mode of politics becomes unworkable. There are too many people doing too many specialized things resulting in too many inequalities of condition and therefore too much potential for social turmoil for a customary regime to handle. Once past this critical point of transition, often subsumed under the rubric of "the Neolithic revolution," politics must become a self-conscious process of rationally directing the affairs of the human community. Thus, as Aristotle said, men are in effect condemned to be self-consciously political animals once they leave or are obliged to leave what the anthropologist Marshall Sahlins has called "the original affluent society" of hunting and gathering.[1]

Recorded history provides examples of the many ways in which this task of rationally directing community affairs can be performed. All were successful for at least a certain time, or they would not have become recorded examples. Ultimately, however, they all failed. Again, the causes are varied. Often the proximate reason was conquest, but in many cases conquest only ratified externally the process of internal decay. It seems to be a historical fact of the self-conscious political mode of community life that it is subject to decline into a form of nonpolitics. That is, the originally successful adaptation becomes gradually irrational and unable to cope with changed conditions, so the political community loses its direction. Sometimes the changed conditions are external, but just as often they are new internal circumstances created by the very success of past adaptation. The process is similar to that observed during ecological succession: pioneer species colonize a relatively abiotic environment and create soil and microclimate conditions that become increasingly favorable for species characteristic of more mature stages of succession and increasingly unfavorable for the pioneer species themselves, so that the latter are gradually excluded from the habitat. The pioneer species have in effect worked themselves out of a job, and political constitutions have a tendency to do much the same thing.

THE COLLISION OF NONPOLITICS AND
ECOLOGICAL SCARCITY

We have clearly reached such a point in our own political life. Thanks to the extraordinary success of a truly remarkable set of ideas and institutions, we have carried the process of development, with all that this word implies, to a transition point that makes our current political "constitution" (which includes more than the Constitution) into a form of nonpolitics. * That is, the political values, institutions, and practices we have inherited are no longer capable of achieving what any reasonable person would regard as the common interest.

The basic reasons why this is so are familiar (and I have argued the case in detail elsewhere),[2] so I will simply summarize the bare bones of the argument--about which there is little dispute, however much opinions may differ on the likely time and intensity of our final collision with environmental limits or on the social meaning of this impending collision. We see everywhere around us the inexorable logic of human ecologist Garrett Hardin's "tragedy of the commons"[3] in operation--in still uncontrolled population growth, in the desire for ever more material goods, in the scramble for resources in a limited environment, in the way that the "invisible hand" has become economist Herman Daly's "invisible foot" of pollution and ecological degradation,[4] and so on. We find that we have begun to reencounter scarcity in a new form--ecological scarcity, which comprises not only the physical limits of the planet, like finite material or ecological resources, but also such things as time pressures, lack of knowledge or artifice, managerial incapacity, as well as general human frailty, and many other social limits to growth. Because these limits cannot be indefinitely evaded, it is clear that somehow all those exponential growth curves that are the pride and joy of industrial civilization must start bending over toward some form of dynamic man-milieu equilibrium or steady state. Perhaps, also, we can now begin to understand how almost all our characteristic institutions--individualism and inalienable individual rights, the legitimacy of self-interest and the purely self-defined pursuit of happiness, laissez faire, majority-rule democracy designed to give individuals exactly what they want, wealth as the standard of worth, and the like--were largely predicated on an abnormal historic era of virgin resources, unspoiled environments, and rapid growth in

---

*I am speaking throughout particularly of the U.S. political experience, but almost all that I say could be easily transposed or extended comparatively and internationally.

applied knowledge that is now drawing to a close. To continue the
ecological metaphor begun in the previous section, our pioneer industrial civilization has undergone weed-like growth that has created
environmental conditions which make it no longer adaptive, and it
must soon give way to some kind of ecologically more mature form
of civilization that resembles the climax or true steady-state stage
of ecological succession. Thus, business as usual has become a
potentially deadly form of nonpolitics.

In fact, we can now see that in many ways U.S. politics has
been as close to being a form of nonpolitics as it is possible to get
and still have a viable community life. The very words we use
colloquially to describe our style of politics--"muddling through,"
"adhocracy," and the like--reveal the extent to which we have never
had a real concept of the common interest toward which our political
arrangements were designed to move us. Rather, we have had a
shared concept of what constituted a fair political process, and we
have assumed that whatever was generated by that process was the
just, or at least the only feasible, outcome. To use the language of
Rousseau, we have made the "will of all," the summation of all our
particular interests, into the "general will" or common interest,
and continuing along this path is a prescription for ecological ruin
via the "tragedy of the commons."

Of course, I am not such a fool as to imagine that human beings will ever conduct their politics as Plato wished--by careful,
rational planning in perfect social harmony. As Plato himself recognized, the beautiful city described in Republic is unattainable; humans
lack the knowledge and character to sustain such a utopia. Thus,
muddling through is inevitable. Moreover, muddling through has
undeniable virtues; in the absence of philosopher-kings, the alternative to politics as a series of minor blunders in a relatively decentralized system may be politics as a series of colossal blunders in
a centralized system. What is at issue, therefore, is not an either/
or choice between two extremes, but rather a movement of the political pendulum away from the pole of extreme individualism and laissez
faire typical of the modern era toward a politics informed by some
kind of ecological consciousness and some recognition of the imperatives of ecological scarcity.

Just what these new political arrangements will or ought to be
is, as discussed below, far from predetermined. However, some
of the general political consequences of the impending confrontation
with ecological scarcity seem virtually foreordained. In essence,
we shall be obliged to restore or reinvent a genuine politics--that
is, something resembling the premodern or classical polity. This
will involve abandoning process orientation in favor of political institutions that create and maintain some explicit conception of the

common interest that tells us who should get what out of the stock of scarce resources, how and when they should get it, and most important of all for the legitimacy of the constitution, why they should get it.

Implicit in this return to the classical political mode are a number of general requirements. For one thing, classical politics was characterized by hierarchy instead of equality. The few ruled the many; although considerable local autonomy was the rule, government was ultimately neither by the people nor of the people, even in Greek democracies. Second, the community had precedence over the individual; the emphasis was on individual duties to the community, rather than on an individual's rights from the community. Stated another way, the concept of freedom was positive ("freedom to") as opposed to negative ("freedom from").[5] Third, classical politics were bonded together by a strongly held, shared system of beliefs--that is, an ideology or, more commonly, a religion.* Thus to sum up, whatever its specific form, the politics of the sustainable society seem likely to move us along the spectrum from libertarianism toward authoritarianism, from individualism toward communalism, and from pragmatism toward ideology.

Given our prejudices, this is hardly a pleasant prospect. Rightly or wrongly, it is bound to call up the specter of a "closed" totalitarian society straight out of George Orwell's 1984. In fact, the very idea of classical political theory has been viciously attacked by the most eminent contemporary writers on politics, who profess to see Hitler and Stalin lurking behind every assertion of the common interest. And the evils of classical politics are undeniable. For example, government that was neither of nor by the people was frequently not for them either. Of course, taking the long-term philosophical view, one must probably concede that every age, tradition, and culture has its own joys and sorrows, beauties and uglinesses, virtues and vices. Those who came before us and those who will come after us would probably agree in condemning our own era for its sorrows, uglinesses, and vices while comparing its joys, beauties, and virtues unfavorably with their own. However, this philosophical stance may be small consolation to those of us who will not live in the long term--ourselves, our children, and our grandchildren. For we are going to have to live through the transition

---

*America's famous "pragmatism" is, of course, an ideology, all our protestations to the contrary notwithstanding. But because it is an antiideological ideology, it has practical consequences far different from the explicitly shared value systems of classical politics.

from one way of life to another: "caught between two ages," our
lives will be "reduced to real suffering, to hell."[6] The price for
living in a golden age of abnormal affluence is about to be exacted.

This is not, however, a counsel of despair. We could, of
course, do nothing, following the path of nonpolitics and letting nature take its course. If I thought this was inevitable, then I would
indeed despair, for the likely results are rather awful to contem-
plate--nuclear war, famine, pestilence, and social and ecological
collapse in various combinations and permutations, resulting in a
decisive and probably permanent reduction of the global carrying
capacity to a level that will support only agrarian civilizations. But
this is not inevitable. We are still at an early stage in the transition,
and if we act decisively and in good time, we still have a wide latitude
of choice available to us. Our collision with ecological limits is foreordained (although it has not yet fully occurred) but not its exact
character. We can still create a wide array of possible futures and
can still choose how we wish to meet the challenge of ecological
scarcity and what kind of sustainable society we wish to live in.
Let us explore some of these dimensions of choice.

THE MAXIMUM-FEASIBLE SUSTAINABLE STATE

To oversimplify, two basic types of sustainable society seem
possible. The first is the maximum-feasible sustainable state.
This concept denotes a society that aims to exist in equilibrium with
its environment, but that is still based on such fundamental "modern"
values as the dominance of man over nature, the primacy of material
and other hedonistic wants, and so on. In pursuit of these values,
such a society would try to squeeze the maximum out of nature with
a relatively high-throughput economy--that is, one in which per
capita use of consumable resources was high. Putting ourselves on
the path toward this type of society requires only that we do pretty
much what we are doing today--in fact, we shall have to do it more
intensively and on a larger scale than before--but that we simply do
it more intelligently from an ecological point of view. That is, we
must carry the rational exploitation of nature for human gain to its
ultimate limit by accepting the "Faustian bargain" of modern technology, turning the direction of society over to a "priesthood of responsible technologists," and rationalizing our social lives to accord
with the imperatives of ecology and technology.[7] Assuming that
these priests were decent and humane men, they would probably find
themselves impelled both by circumstances and inclination to begin
to actualize the utopian technological visions of such men as Buckminster Fuller and Glenn Seaborg--a totally planned and artificial
world designed to satiate the material wants of the multitude.

The end result of such a process seems likely to be a society resembling in all important respects Aldous Huxley's Brave New World. We would, of course, only realize (and probably rather dimly) that we were living in Brave New World after it had been created. Huxley was amazed in 1958 to discover how far the world had traveled toward his dystopia, which was written in 1932 and set six or seven centuries in the future.[8] He would be depressed to return today to find that the technology of test-tube babies, psychological conditioning, and the like is "progressing" at an astonishing rate; in a few years, all that will be necessary is our acquiescence.

To mention Brave New World is, however, to raise some doubts about whether we ought to acquiesce, because it is quite clear that its inhabitants are more or less subtly but completely enslaved by total psychological (and even physiological) conditioning in combination with the carefully planned satisfaction of so-called basic hedonistic wants. Men and women are "happy" in this near perfect world, but they totally lack autonomy or independent judgment; they are things, cogs in a megamachine who have sacrificed liberty and other goods to get peace and economic welfare. In most important respects, Brave New World is a model Hobbesian polity, a logical extrapolation ad absurdum of the basic premises of the modern world view that Hobbes did so much to create, but with the important difference that it is ultra-Hobbesian in its excessive concentration of absolute power far exceeding anything that Hobbes himself, no friend of totalitarian politics despite his fearsome reputation, would countenance. And if there is one lesson that the history of politics teaches, it is the great dangers of unlimited government. *

Yet, for many people, these things may not seem like crucial objections to Brave New World, for by many standards and by most historical yardsticks it is a highly desirable social order. Most of the ills that agitate reformers and revolutionaries are absent. At

----

*Indeed, is it even permissible to assume for the sake of argument, as I have done, that the technological priests will be decent and humane men with the interests of the multitude foremost in heart and mind? Does not history suggest that they will rapidly become a "new class" and use their power primarily to further secure their position and satiate their own social and material wants? In fact, despite some of its dystopian aspects, the extremely benign Leviathan of Brave New World may well represent something close to the best possible outcome of an attempt to travel the path toward the maximum-feasible steady state. Naturally far worse outcomes can be imagined--as George Orwell's 1984 makes inescapably plain.

least all are fed and clothed and housed decently, have work that exactly fits their capacities and that they "enjoy," have their sensual
desires fulfilled, and so on. Furthermore, at least in the novel,
the rulers are reasonable, humane men whose worst punishment for
misfits is exile to an interesting research laboratory. Thus, to
those who have accepted the basic mechanistic and hedonistic premises of the modern world, such a social order might seem to be a
desirable goal, giving us peace, economic welfare, and a variety of
social justice; that certain other human needs must be sacrificed
would appear to be a regrettable necessity (or are such things as
dignity and freedom really pseudo-needs, perpetuated by the backward state of our social technology?).

However, value considerations may be somewhat beside the
point, for Brave New World is almost certainly not a society in ecological balance over the long term (unless populations are drastically
reduced), so its existence is likely to be ephemeral. In fact, it
seems unlikely that we could even construct some of the important
elements needed to support Brave New World. We simply do not
know enough, nor do we have the technology or capital to compete
with nature in operating our life-support systems. Indeed, the very
concept "maximum feasible" violates the laws of ecology. Other requirements are also unrealistic. For example, a maximum-feasible
world must be a unitary global regime, for otherwise the measures
needed to rationalize planetary management and provide the quantity
of resources per capita required to run it would be impossible. In
reality, Brave New World is only a more thoroughgoing, utopian,
and therefore unrealistic version of our own, and trying to create
such a "utopia" seems likely to intensify the ultimate crisis, allowing us to climb further out on a limb we are sawing off behind ourselves.

Thus, even if desirable, Brave New World may not be feasible
after all. Nevertheless, it is seemingly the most probable or easier
path to the sustainable society precisely because it is an extrapolation
of the modern world view rather than a decisive break with it, and all
too many today appear ready to acquiesce at least tacitly in the
"Faustian bargain" provided this appears to permit them to keep
their dreams of "affluence" and most of their other received values.

THE FRUGAL SUSTAINABLE STATE

By contrast, the alternative to the maximum-feasible society
would involve a sharp break with the principles of the modern era,
for the simpler frugal sustainable society would be characterized by
a relatively low-throughput, income-energy economy designed to

elicit an optimal amount of material goods from nature--in other
words, a modicum or a sufficiency of material well-being rather
than a maximum. Although many different varieties of frugal sustainable society are conceivable, it seems likely that they would all
share more or less completely certain basic features (relative to
the maximum-feasible society)--decentralization and local autonomy;
a simpler, smaller-scale, face-to-face life closer to nature; labor-
intensive modes of production; a deemphasis on material things; individual self-sufficiency (versus dependence on complex systems
for the fulfillment of basic needs); and cultural diversity.

The political constitutions of "frugal" societies would be a
matter of social choice. Such societies could be either sacred or
secular, cosmopolitan or provincial, open or closed, according to
the wishes of the local population, so it is difficult to be precise
about what form their politics could or should take. However, for
Americans, the political ideas of Rousseau and Jefferson would
seem particularly appropriate for such circumstances, unlike the
Lockean and Hamiltonian ideas that have dominated U.S. history so
far. Also, any set of political institutions that aims to be ecologically viable over the long term would be very likely to have many features that Edmund Burke would approve of, for ecology is a pro-
foundly conservative doctrine in its social implications. One possible literary and utopian (yet quite realistic) model, with many attractive features, for what the frugal society could be made to look
like is contained in Island, another of Aldous Huxley's works. An
actual historical model, also with many attractive features, is
Switzerland. Naturally, less appealing models abound and should
be used to tell us what not to do. For example, although the widely
admired culture of Tokugawa Japan shows what miracles can be performed in a frugal society, we would probably judge that the price
in terms of political repression, especially of the peasantry, was
far too high.

To obviate any possible misunderstanding, it is necessary to
insist that most, if not all, of the dangers inherent in classical politics are avoidable in a well-ordered frugal society. As noted previously, most Americans are likely to see potential tyranny lurking
behind any suggestion that the rights we now enjoy be curtailed in
the slightest amount or that citizens should embrace moderation and
self-restraint in the name of the common good; any concession of
liberty seems to place us on a "slippery slope" toward fascist dic-
tatorship. This is an understandable but quite irrational reaction.
In fact, classical polities have run the entire political gamut, and
we have equal latitude of choice. Moreover, as the previous discussion of the maximum-feasible state ought to have made clear, it is
precisely the rejection of frugality that will create inexorable pressures toward totalitarianism.

Indeed, the great political virtue of the frugal society is that, even though we must accept certain restrictions, we can in principle retain most of our cherished liberties. For instance, there is absolutely no reason why a frugal society cannot be a constitutional polity in which all the key civil rights are upheld. What is not possible in a frugal society is a free-for-all system of wealth-getting and unrestricted property rights. Thus, although citizens can be made secure in their political liberty and in the ownership of their personal possessions or means of livelihood in a well-ordered frugal state, they probably cannot be allowed to use private property as capital, except in the most restricted fashion, or to treat land and other basic resources as commodities divorced from their critical ecological and environmental role. So, certain kinds of rights that we now enjoy will indeed have to be given up. But once we self-consciously adopt limits for the good of the whole and posterity, we would readily discover many humane yet effective means for operating a society of moderation and self-restraint. * Provided only that we accept the concept of self-imposed limits and plan to optimize our political values within those limits, nothing politically necessary for a full and dignified life need be yielded up.

Moreover, the wise use of technology would allow even "frugal" societies to enjoy a high level of material well-being relative to premodern societies. Thus, choosing this path need not constitute a regression in any important respect--unless any diminution of private affluence is regarded as intolerable. Indeed, with the technology that we now have or that we could readily develop without any fundamental breakthroughs, we could have societies that were quite utopian by historical standards. That is, ecological scarcity is not

---

*The trick seems to be to select key design criteria that make the system relatively automatic and self-enforcing--like natural ecosystems--so that detailed or day-to-day regulation by legislators and bureaucrats is unnecessary. Kenneth Boulding's famous "baby license" plan, which relies on the market to keep births at the desired level, is a prime example of such a design criterion (which does not mean that it is the best one for this purpose that we can find). Another example might be the personal energy quotas proposed by some; these would leave individuals free to allocate their quota as they wished but still insure that an acceptable overall social level of energy use was achieved. A more radical example is Ivan Illich's proposal for a universal 15-25 mile per hour speed limit; if implemented, this blanket proscription would become a design criterion virtually enforcing a type of rough frugality (and therefore, to use Illich's term, a more "convivial" society as well).

equivalent to classical scarcity, even though many of the political
implications are the same. The greater penury of classical scarcity
seems inevitably to have produced inequality along with the oppression necessary to maintain it (and to have made slavery overwhelmingly attractive as a source of energy). Ecological scarcity need not
be so stringent. Solar energy and other technological possibilities
denied to our ancestors will make the frugal society a radically new
form of civilization, not just a reversion to past patterns.

Utopian or not, however, life clearly will seem frugal in many
important respects. To take just one example, it seems evident that
in the long run agriculture will become more labor-intensive, both
because labor will be cheaper than energy in a frugal society and because horticultural agriculture as practiced in many parts of Asia is
less ecologically damaging than our current extensive, industrial
agriculture. This is likely to mean that a larger proportion of the
population will have to be "peasants" in a low-energy steady-state
society (or, alternatively, that most of the population will have to be
at least part-time peasants along Maoist lines), and this is a situation that will seem unpalatable and regressive to most moderns, for
whom toil has always been an enemy, even though Marx's "idiocy of
rural life" would not be inevitable with wise use of advanced technology.

Also, frugality will mean that we shall be obliged to choose
more carefully and stringently among competing goods, for we shall
no longer be able to afford the luxuries of choice made possible by
affluence. We could, for example, choose to retain an extremely
high degree of personal mobility (but certainly not the full-blown
private automobile system we now have). We could thus continue
casually to travel great distances to see friends or give academic
papers or bask on the beach or hear the symphony, but the substantial energy and resources devoted to such a transit system would
necessarily prevent high levels of support for other worthy but competing goals, such as the transmission and creation of knowledge or
the provision of certain social services. In addition, even in sectors on which we seem likely to place considerable social priority,
we shall be forced to scale down our expectations. For example, in
an economy of frugality, relatively cheap and resource-conserving
trains will certainly relegate expensive and energy-spendthrift jet
planes to oblivion as routine means of transport, so that personal
mobility will be more time-limited than it is now even if we continue
to give it very high priority. Similarly, although an impeccable state
of public health, extremely high standards of preventive medicine,
and even a high level of curative medicine are all compatible with the
frugal state, the future of high-technology, capital-intensive medicine, much less heart transplants for everyman, is cloudy--unless

we choose to place the same priority on the denial of death that the
ancient Egyptian pharoahs did. In sum, in the frugal state we shall
not be able to retain access to all the appurtenances of our current
"energy-slave" economy; we shall have to choose carefully and wise-
ly where to spend our limited resources in order to create and maintain those things we really value in life; some luxuries may be possible, but not mass luxury or all the luxuries we want.

The picture of the frugal society that thus emerges resembles
something like a return to the city-state form of civilization, but on
a much higher and more sophisticated technological base, especially
in the area of communications, which makes possible a simple yet
ample and humane life for all (but, of course, real life can only approximate such an ideal).

As with classical scarcity in the past, however, ecological
scarcity would create the potential for conflict between locally autonomous city states, "utopian" or not, so that microautonomy must inevitably be accompanied by some form of macroauthority capable of
preventing warfare or antiecological acts likely to produce the "tragedy of the commons." Thus, local polities would have to exist within
a regional or global empire of some kind.

Arguments for the frugal society are basically the inverse of
arguments against the maximum-feasible society. Naturally, it is
ecologically viable, for the frugal state is by definition one that re-
strains its material demands on nature to an optimal level that nature
can tolerate and that does not depend on the near-perfect operation of
artificial systems. In the area of values, it is clear that almost any
form of the frugal society would permit individuals greater freedom,
because there would be no necessity to plan and control all areas of
life in order to make the system work and because the kind of psycho-
social conditioning that Huxley describes would therefore not be necessary to make individuals fit into the system. Furthermore, although
some kind of macroauthority will be needed to keep ecological and
civil peace among local communities, there is no intrinsic reason
why its authority could not be limited solely to these essential tasks,
leaving local communities to proceed toward heaven or hell as their
own customs, predilections, and standards of religious or social
morality dictated.

Choosing the frugal option would also demote the economic side
of life to its proper place. Wise men have long suggested that the
purpose of the economic sphere is to give all members of the society
access to a fair supply of goods sufficient to support a dignified life
and to provide a basis for a stimulating community life that promotes
individual self-development (one part of which is genuine work, as
opposed to mere employment).[9] This ideal seems more likely to be
realized in the frugal state. Indeed, a much less "alienating" life

should be possible once human beings are no longer obliged by the system to be "economic men." Overall, it is difficult to think of any important aspect of the human potential that could not be fully realized in a properly ordered frugal sustainable society. Above all, unlike the maximum-feasible option, which will always be teetering on the ecological brink and must therefore adapt rigorously to ecological and technological imperatives, the frugal society would allow much greater latitude of social choice; the shape of institutions could reflect humane values instead of rational and technological exigencies.

Naturally, there are some drawbacks. For example, precisely to the extent that government was limited and local communities were free to govern themselves, the latter would be likely to contain many of the ills that agitate reformers and revolutionaries. Of course, certain standards of justice could be imposed by the macro-authority, but this dilution of limited government has its dangers, and exactly where to make the trade-offs between ecological values, social justice, and liberty will obviously be a major problem for the political theorists of the frugal state. Nevertheless, it is clear that total equality and social justice are at least conceivable in a total, centralized regime; just as clearly, they are not attainable in the basically decentralized frugal society. As compensation for this, however, the planet would be characterized by a certain spicy variety absent from the maximum-feasible variety.

Another possible drawback for many will be the very modesty of the frugal society. Naturally, men whose ambition it is to conquer the stars for the human race and undertake other equally great deeds will find frugality a little humdrum, but even the ordinary man of today might be reluctant to give up his power over the "energy slaves" that now do his bidding. On the other hand, the corrupting potential of power is well known, and so renunciation may be the better part of wisdom. In any event, frugality would inhibit only external conquest; there is no intrinsic reason why those living in frugal societies should ever lack for new fields to conquer in the arts and sciences and in the realm of spirit. Indeed, once we cease to be preoccupied with what John Stuart Mill, surely one of liberty's greatest friends, pejoratively called "getting on," then we should experience a considerable expansion of our possibilities in these areas.

RESTORING A GENUINE POLITICS

It thus appears that we do have a significant choice. Although in one sense the politics of the maximum-feasible and the frugal state converge--either way we will get a more authoritarian,

communalistic, and ideological set of political institutions--there
are clearly vast differences between the two basic paths to the sustainable state. For the reasons given, my own sympathies lie almost entirely with the frugal alternative, and I am convinced that it
is what we must necessarily arrive at eventually, even if we start
out in the opposite direction. Unfortunately, the frugal alternative
is alien to our current way of thinking and threatens many of the
material and psychological vested interests we all have in the current order, so it is quite "unrealistic" to believe that we shall
choose simplicity and frugality except under ecological duress.

This is a potential tragedy, for only if we use the bulk of what
is left from our stores of nonrenewable resources to construct the
material and scientific-technological infrastructure of the frugal
state is it likely to be a society existing at a high level in material
terms--and therefore a relatively utopian one in political terms as
well. Waiting for ecological duress could therefore be a very costly
mistake if we wish to consider the interests of posterity.

But what is the alternative to waiting for ecological duress?
There are many important and constructive things we can do. I have
tried to do one of them in this chapter: to project a vision of our
social possibilities. We know that we can only muddle through, but
if some kind of awareness of where we do and do not wish to go guides
our steps, then we can spring muddling through from the trap of nonpolitics, in which a political system inexorably grinds out an outcome
nobody really wanted. A social vision can warn us against some actions, even though they seem to be intuitively reasonable, and push
us toward others, even though they are counterintuitive and require
current sacrifice for the sake of future benefit. We can thus, in
part at least, help to create the future we want. Moreover, a social
vision will provide some justification for policy, the why of social
action, and in the coming time of troubled transition (when unlike
periods of "normal" politics there will be no shared, tacit agreement
on the "political paradigm"),[10] such explicit justification will be
essential to make the sacrifices of the transition meaningful and reduce the inevitable social turmoil.

However, projecting such an "unrealistic" social vision as the
frugal society is certain to be regarded as utopian and therefore quite
useless by many who are convinced that the only solution is to get involved in the rough and tumble of the muddling-through process itself.
True, the task of politics in the larger sense--that is, the achievement of the common interest--must inevitably be carried forward by
politics in the smaller sense--that is, by conflict in the political
arena over the interpretation and implementation of the common interest. However, it must be clear that it would be a fatal mistake to
accept the received definition of "reality," for this very "reality" is

in large part the essence of the problem we confront. In brief, as numerous poets and other observers wise in the inner workings of man have pointed out, the ecological devastation and degradation without simply mirror the wasteland within. In fact, reduced to its essence, the political struggle is about the definition of reality (which is remarkably plastic--as we know from post-Heisenbergian science). A changed consciousness that breaks the intellectual and psychic death grip of the self-destructive epistemological and psycho-logical assumptions that constitute our current "reality" is there-fore indispensable for the success of the political struggle to create a set of ecologically viable and yet humane institutions, and once this new paradigm comes to be widely shared, then institutional answers are likely to emerge as a matter of course. * Social vision-making of the type attempted here is therefore a vital complement, if not a prior necessity, to any effective political strategy for achiev-ing a sustainable society.

The reader, of course, may disagree on either analytical or normative grounds with much or even most of what has been said above about the alternative paths, their merits or demerits, and the rest. However, this is of lesser concern. What is important is that we begin to consider what kind of sustainable society is attainable and preferable, so we can determine how we are going to arrive at it, instead of remaining mired in nonpolitics, treating ecological scar-city in all its guises as just another problem to be merely muddled through on a totally ad hoc basis when what we confront is a civiliza-tional discontinuity. Until we somehow engineer the restoration of a genuine politics and begin self-consciously to redirect as best we can the march of history along lines that accord with our goals, there is little hope of meeting the challenge of ecological scarcity in any reasonable and humane fashion. Better that we should deliber-ately choose Brave New World and try to make it as benign as pos-sible than to continue along the path of nonpolitics, for this would surely earn us--quite justly--the enmity of posterity. If the neces-sity for the restoration of a genuine politics is fully understood and

---

*Naturally, until the new view of reality becomes predominant, a large part of the political struggle must be devoted to holding ac-tions and constructive time-biding--preventing as much overgrowth and irreversible damage as possible; stopping attempts to evade the negative feedback pressures on growth (for example, the current effort to buy continued growth with inflation); planting institutional seeds that will not flower until the shift of consciousness has oc-curred; and so on.

acted upon, then I will be well content, for I am fundamentally optimistic about the basic instincts of the human race and about what
can be done once humanity realizes its predicament.

NOTES

1. Marshall Sahlins, "The Original Affluent Society," The
Ecologist 4 (1974): 181-89.
2. William Ophuls, "Leviathan or Oblivion?" in Toward a
Steady-State Economy, ed. Herman E. Daly (San Francisco: W. H.
Freeman, 1973); "Locke's Paradigm Lost: The Environmental
Crisis and the Collapse of Laissez-Faire Politics," paper delivered
at the 1973 Annual Meeting of the American Political Science Association, New Orleans (to be published in revised form in a forthcoming collection edited by William R. Burch, Jr., and F. Herbert
Bormann entitled Growth, Limits and the Quality of Life); "The
Scarcity Society," Harper's Magazine, April 1974, pp. 47-52; and
Ecology and the Politics of Scarcity: Prologue to a Political Theory
of the Steady State (San Francisco: W. H. Freeman, 1977).
3. Garrett Hardin, "The Tragedy of the Commons," in Daly,
op. cit., pp. 133-48.
4. Herman E. Daly, "Introduction," in Daly, op. cit., pp.
1-29.
5. Isaiah Berlin, Four Essays on Liberty (New York: Oxford,
1969).
6. Herman Hesse, Steppenwolf, trans. Basil Creighten and
Joseph Mileck (New York: Bantam, 1969), pp. 24-25.
7. Alvin M. Weinberg, "Social Institutions and Nuclear Energy," Science 177 (1972): 27-34, and "Technology and Ecology--
Is There a Need for Confrontation?" BioScience 23 (1973): 40-44.
8. Aldous Huxley, Brave New World Revisited (New York:
Harper, 1958).
9. E. F. Schumacher, "Buddhist Economics," in Daly, op.
cit., pp. 231-39.
10. Sheldon S. Wolin, "Paradigms and Political Theories" in
Politics and Experience, ed. Preston King and B. C. Parekh (Cambridge: Cambridge University Press, 1968), pp. 125-52.

8

POLITICAL CHANGE
AND THE
SUSTAINABLE SOCIETY
Michael E. Kraft

It is difficult to imagine a serious discussion of such weighty
subjects as sustainable growth and steady-state societies without
substantial consideration of politics. Yet one does, on occasion,
find proposals for radical changes in economic and social institutions
which are almost totally uninformed by political realities. And one
commonly finds political exposition in this literature which is narrow, superficial, and naive. The purpose of this chapter is to complement the substantive chapters in the volume by exposing readers
to some important and challenging political ideas which might alter
these conditions in the future. Beyond that minimal goal, it would
also appear that if "subversive" concepts such as a steady-state
economy or sustainable growth are ever to gain much respect and
currency outside of university and elite intellectual circles, political questions must begin to occupy a much more central position
on the agendas for such discussions.[1]
    There are two major questions which are especially deserving
of increased attention. One is the focus of much of this chapter:
the political changes necessary to facilitate transition to a future
sustainable society. The other is discussed much less, but is equally
important: the largely unanticipated political consequences of moving toward a society with zero population growth and slowed, limited,
or organic economic growth. In both cases, our present knowledge
is very limited. We do not understand much about the political implications of these shifts from present levels of population growth
and economic growth, and, although much more has been written on
the subject, we are still quite ignorant about the kinds of political
changes necessary to further these developments, to hasten the
arrival of an ecologically sound future society. This is true not
only for the specifics of public policy (for example, what type of

federal policies will best reduce air pollution by automobiles) but also, and more significantly, for the larger and longer-range questions of the kind of governmental institutions and political values most suitable for such a transition and such a future polity.

Consider, for example, arguments over the extensiveness of change. Conventional political values and practices have been criticized for being highly inappropriate when measured by the task of meeting ecological imperatives. Environmentalists have argued that we need "fundamental" changes in our political institutions, attitudes, and behavior.[2] Others, perhaps less convinced of the severity of resource shortages, population growth, energy problems, and environmental threats, assert that "normal" politics is quite sufficient on the whole. They tend to argue that traditional American values (personal freedoms, private property, limited government) need not, and should not, be sacrificed so readily.[3] Might it be that we know less than we ought to if we are to resolve such disputes? Value differences will remain, of course, but some of the issues can be clarified, and better information can be brought to bear on the empirical questions of some contention.

Our present knowledge about such political questions is limited largely because of two conditions: political issues have not received the degree of attention in ecological or "limits to growth" discussions that they so clearly merit, and politics by its very nature raises some of the most complex and intractable of human problems. My primary concern here is to examine some of those neglected questions about the politics of ecology, chiefly by exploring the complexities of political change in adjusting to newly recognized limits to population and economic growth. The focus will be primarily on the United States, although the argument can be applied to other industrialized nations as well.

Since the main argument below will get a bit involved, it may be useful to provide a brief outline as a preface. I will begin by trying to clarify the role of politics in the sustainable-growth debate, will turn then to an agenda of concerns which might frame inquiry into these matters as well as guide political efforts, depart briefly from the direct line of argument for an overview and evaluation of recent environmental politics in the United States, and then return to the central issue of political change. Reviewing the work of a number of scholars on the obstacles to ecological change, I will offer a few critical observations as well as suggestions for how to analyze political constraints and promising paths to a new politics in a more meaningful and effective fashion. Toward that end, I will conclude with some references to fruitful points of departure for both research and political action. The concluding section will be a little more optimistic than the rest of the chapter, reflecting a conviction (actually, more of a hope) that there is still some value in rational inquiry if only the right questions are posed.

POLITICS AND THE LIMITS TO GROWTH

Since my purpose is to raise some questions about politics and political change, I leave the technical case for limited, slowed, sustainable, or organic growth to others (including some of the authors in this volume). It should be sufficient to say that I think the necessity of limiting conventional economic growth and of reaching a state of zero population growth in the not-too-distant future has been persuasively argued and is adequately supported by reliable data. Current evidence bearing on the pressures of population growth, the use of modern industrial technology, the limits to natural resources (including the availability of energy resources), the capacity for food production, the consequences of environmental degradation, and the constraints of the Second Law of Thermodynamics points to a number of severe problems to which we seem ill-equipped or unwilling to respond effectively.[4] If these positions are thought reasonable, it would seem that there is now a critical need to delve much more directly into the problems of transition to an alternative state of affairs--a sustainable society eventually-- rather than to spend quite so much time debating the question of growth versus nongrowth itself.

The most interesting and significant questions at this juncture, of course, are not simply whether population and economic growth must be limited, but what kinds of limits are necessary or desirable and when and how they should be imposed. These are in large part political questions. That is, they involve subjective preferences or choices among human values. These choices will inevitably be shaped by political processes. In the broadest sense politics is the process of resolving conflicts over the allocation of values, of determining priorities for society. To use Harold Lasswell's classic formulation, politics is the process of deciding who gets what, when, and how. It should be fairly obvious that there are at present, and will continue to be, major disagreements over ecological, economic, and social values. The sharp conflicts in recent years over issues of air and water pollution control, land use, strip mining, nuclear energy development, population control, and so on, should alert us to the fact that political battles of this nature are inescapably tied to ecological change. One might also add that if the outcome is to be more consistently favorable to limited-growth advocates, such decisions must receive more serious and sustained attention.

The role of politics is crucial not only in contemporary or short-term change, but in long-term developments as well. This is important enough to elaborate briefly. In terms of short-term policy making on, for example, energy or environmental policy, the political nature of ecological change is highly visible and easily understandable. Specific problems must be identified; they must be perceived, defined, and represented in policy-making institutions; specific action proposals must move through a legislative process usually characterized (in the United States) by bargaining, negotiation, and compromise; resulting public policies must be applied or administered; programs must be continually funded, putting them in direct competiton with all other policies which require public funds; choices must be made on how much to spend on what; standards and regulations must be promulgated and enforced, judicial institutions must settle conflicting interpretations and claims. At each step of this policy process the complex of human relations we call politics will inevitably be present, and political power or influence will greatly determine the final outcome.[5]

Once attention shifts to long-term ecological problems, however, politics often fades away as though it were no longer quite appropriate to discuss explicit political issues in such a speculative setting. To offer a recent example, Robert Heilbroner initially recognizes in An Inquiry into the Human Prospect that "the exercise of political power lies squarely in the center of the determination of [the human] prospect. The resolution of the crises thrust upon us by the social and natural environment can only be found through political action."[6] Yet, as is so often characteristic of such analysis, he does not go on to discuss the uses of this political power. While very effective as a personal, humanistic presentation of the ecological challenge, Heilbroner's book has remarkably little to offer on steady-state politics. He focuses chiefly on the importance of ethical and social change (part of politics to be sure) if man is to "summon up the will to survive." I wonder if we cannot go further than this.

Politics surely is as central to the kinds of long-range change Heilbroner and others suggest is so necessary as it is to contemporary policy disputes. We should not be too satisfied, then, with the issuing of calls for drastic policy change or the proposing of utopian social schemes in a veritable political vacuum. It should be said that such treatments do serve a very useful function in increasing public attention to and understanding of ecological and growth problems. Those as skillful, imaginative, and eloquent as Heilbroner and Rene Dubos carry off the job especially well. Nevertheless, consciousness raising and speculations over long-range scenarios carry us only so far. We need a fuller picture of what the future

holds and a better way to get a hold on the problems. For these
reasons, there is a clear need at this point to initiate more serious
political thinking, especially given the considerable uncertainty over
the two fundamental issues noted above: the consequences for government and politics of a transition to the sustainable society and the
kinds of political change or political actions seemingly prerequisite
for this transition.

AN AGENDA OF POLITICAL CONCERNS

If politics does indeed lie at the heart of ecological change or
achieving a sustainable society, what exactly should we be asking
about transitional politics, the form it will or should take? What are
the basic issues? What is or should be our agenda of concerns?
We must begin with these questions, I think. The answers will help
frame both further inquiry and future politics. As one approach I
would propose a fairly comprehensive and diverse list of questions
which may help clarify these core issues in political change. The
list also suggests what we need to know to be able to comment rationally about future consequences or effective courses of action.
The questions reflect four intellectual components of political
analysis: (1) normative considerations (value clarification, evaluation of political conditions, and prescription for reform); (2) scientific analysis (description and explanation of ecological problems
and political actions); (3) futuristic projections or predictions
(specification of likely consequences and possible alternative futures); and (4) strategic analysis (how change might be brought
about). While these analytical approaches are usually thoroughly
interwoven in practice, there are distinct orientations and skills
appropriate for each. All are significant for the issues raised here.
Our understanding of steady-state politics would be considerably
improved if we would begin applying these approaches in search of
answers to the following kinds of questions:

What is the nature of the ecological crisis? How do relevant
experts define ecological problems and in what ways, singly and
collectively, do these problems threaten us with what consequences
--social, economic, political, environmental? To what extent is
there agreement among various experts on the causes of these problems and on the severity of the threats? What are the long-range as
well as short-range consequences of major developments insofar as
we are able to determine them? In particular, what are the implications for government and politics of anticipated population trends
and of current economic growth patterns?

Toward what general and specific goals should we be aiming
and how much agreement is there on those goals? How does the
abstract concept of a sustainable society translate into a concrete
set of goals? What are the major conflicts between ecological
values implied in these goals and other values, for example, human
freedom and self-fulfillment, democratic political processes,
equality, justice, community, social and political stability, and
economic well being? What solutions are proposed for reaching
the goals? What are the political options (including, but going beyond, policy options), both for the short range and for the long
range? Their ethical or cultural acceptability? Political feasibility?
Economic feasibility? Administrative capabilities for implementation? What are the likely effects on ecological problems of adopting
those proposals? What consequences can we predict for government
processes and politics if the goal of a sustainable society is actively
sought?

What significant government (and private) actions have been
taken to date? How can we best explain those actions? Most importantly, how adequate do they appear to be? What actions can we
reasonably predict in the near future based on our understanding of
the political process? In particular, what public policies have now
been adopted, and what have been their effects, measuring policy
impact after a suitable lapse of time and as systematically as the
state of the art allows? How can we judge the adequacy of these actions? Against what standards or with what criteria shall such
evaluations be made?

If government and private efforts are deemed inadequate and
change is considered possible, what kinds of changes and of what
magnitude are necessary or desirable in public policies; in processes
of decision making; in the values, attitudes, and motivations of key
political actors; and in political institutions and political culture?
In short, if change is possible, what precisely do we need or want,
and how do we go about getting it? What is presently being suggested
or tried with what degree of success or failure? Under what conditions are necessary or desirable changes most likely to occur and
what strategies seem likely to make a difference?

I outline these concerns mainly to encourage the building of an
agenda for thinking comprehensively, holistically, and systematically
about the politics of ecology. The rationale is simple enough. Narrow, segmental approaches are extremely limited and prone to
enormous errors of both omission and commission, some of which
will be spelled out below. Of special interest in this respect is
Barry Commoner's observation that "everything [in an ecosystem]
is connected to everything else."[7] Extended to large-scale policy

issues, this perspective tells us that the many and varied environmental, energy, resource, population, and food problems on the
public agenda are intimately interrelated and ideally should be
approached systemically.

A similar argument can be applied to politics itself. The
political system, as conceptualized in contemporary political science, consists of more than a loose set of government institutions
and isolated individual actions subject to narrow criticism and re-
formist prescriptions. A systemic view of the political system
would suggest that political change might conceivably take place in
any or all of the interrelated "components" of the system: the basic
political culture and core values of the nation at large, the institutional arrangements of government, the specific beliefs and attitudes
of the people toward government and public problems, the values
and beliefs of political decision makers and other elites, the structure and distribution of power in society, and the decision-making
process from which public policies emerge. Each element in the
political system might be thought of as subject to some magnitude of
change (incremental, comprehensive, revolutionary) with some degree of speed (gradual, moderate, rapid).

A clear understanding of political change is made difficult,
however, because the component parts cannot be fully considered
in isolation from the rest of the system no more than can one part
of a complex ecosystem. Nor can one expect reform of one segment
of U.S. politics to work in isolation from other changes. For example, reform of lobbying by "special interests" will not be fully
effective without a corresponding change in the ability and willingness of the U.S. public to participate in politics, in the degree of
coverage of political decision making in the mass media, and perhaps most importantly, in the pressures on busy legislators to make
a wide variety of decisions under the burden of scarce time, information, and other vital resources (conditions favoring influence by
lobbyists).[8] The point is simply that political change is usually
much more complicated than it might appear at first glance. One
of the major tasks for students of politics, then, is to explore more
fully the kinds of "system" variables outlined and their key relationships, and to determine as far as is possible (and useful) what
sort of change is necessary or desirable, how it might best be
brought about, and how effective it is likely to be.

It is also important to note what may seem obvious. Politics
in the sustainable society must by definition be an ecological politics. Although no one is quite sure what an ecological politics would
look like, a reasonable definition would suggest a polity in which
individual behavior and government policy making are fundamentally
consistent with ecological principles. The various elements in such

a system would have to be based on a similar set of values and
would have to interlock more or less harmoniously. Within those
parameters, the extensive political possibilities are still to be explored. There are surely many options beyond the rather grim
authoritarian systems foreseen by some. We are more likely to
discover and promote them if greater thought is directed toward
these issues while time still affords us the choice.

I leave a more expansive treatment of this ideal future polity
to others.[9] For our present purposes, the very nature of this goal
should tell us that there is some wisdom in forcing ourselves to
think comprehensively and holistically about political change. Even
while concentrating on a narrow aspect of politics, we would profit
from bearing in mind the larger context and the longer-range future.

EVALUATING ENVIRONMENTAL POLITICS
IN THE UNITED STATES

The agenda of political concerns outlined above can be reduced
to two fundamental questions if our interest is focused on the long
range. Do present institutional structures and political processes
lend themselves to dealing effectively or adequately with the transition to a sustainable society? Is there now (or likely to be in the
not-too-distant future) sufficient political will among both the public
and political leaders to encourage or facilitate such an adaptation?
If the answer is in the negative (which is likely if one's demands are
set high enough--even for those who normally view politics optimis-
tically), the topic of political change flows logically from these conditions. This will be our major focus in the discussion below. One
prior question must be addressed first to provide some evidence that
the subject of political change is in fact a live issue of some consequence. This question is the response of the U.S. political system
over the past six or seven years to the environmental challenge and
what this may suggest regarding political obstacles or constraints
which prevent or inhibit realization of a sustainable society. Although space allows only a brief overview and a necessarily subjective evaluation, the exercise should be useful for what follows.

It seems neither inaccurate nor misleading to say that in spite
of some very impressive--and often unexpected--progress between
1969 and 1976, the predominant political response to the ecological
challenge has been characterized by (1) marginal and superficial
attention to, understanding of, and concern for ecological problems;
(2) weak and uncertain commitment to new environmental priorities
on the part of both the U.S. public and its political leaders; (3) reliance on palliative measures and technological fixes aimed at

relieving highly visible symptoms, rather than treating underlying
social and economic causes of environmental problems; (4) frequent
use by politicians of rhetorical and symbolic gestures as cheap and
safe substitutes for material changes in the quality of our environment; (5) timidity and moderation in public policy developments ad-
versely affecting economic growth, the interests of powerful groups,
and in conflict with traditional values of individual freedom and private control of property; and (6) adherence in the customary fashion
to disjointed incrementalism as the characteristic form of decision
making, that is, to "muddling through," and thus to preoccupation
primarily with short-range goals that are immediately "feasible" or
"realistic" given the constraints of present institutions, public
opinion, and the alignment of political forces in the country.[10] In
short, on balance the federal government has perpetuated business
as usual and old priorities rather than moving toward the vigorous
and innovative action and new priorities favored by environmentalists.[11]

If one must abstract prevailing national "goals" from a con-
fusingly large and diverse collection of public policies and from recent political actions of an enormously varied nature, the conclusion
would seem to be that we continue to favor increased economic
growth, physical comfort, and the maintenance of social and political
stability above all else. We are unwilling to sacrifice the material
conveniences to which we have grown accustomed; indeed, the most
affluent have yet to be satiated and the least-well-off are determined
to follow in hot pursuit. And we are also unwilling to violate traditional political sensibilities until literally forced to do so by the
exigencies of the moment.

Whether these patterns will continue is uncertain. Much depends upon changes in U.S. public opinion and in the proclivities of
elected political leaders. Public opinion on environmental issues
has changed markedly since 1970 and may be more supportive in the
future (more on this below). More significantly, for the entire period 1969-76, the presidential administrations of Richard Nixon and
Gerald Ford (neither with an impressive record of environmental
concern) have shaped much of the political response at the federal
level summarized above. A change of administrations could have
ramifications throughout the federal government which might well
lead to a quite different set of responses to the environmental challenge. One would not predict a continuation of the Nixon-Ford pattern with a Carter administration in the White House.

There have been some notable successes as well as major
defeats for environmentalists over the past seven years, of course.
The predominant pattern noted above reflects a selective and critical
review. The net conclusion one reaches in trying to identify such

patterns will be shaped by the particular events or cases considered, as well as by the criteria used to assess the "adequacy" or "sufficiency" of political actions. The more demanding the criteria, the more likely a critical or pessimistic conclusion. What are some of the significant cases in recent years which might support the picture drawn above or, conversely, which might suggest a greater social capacity for adjusting to new ecological demands? And what criteria are most appropriate for evaluating those actions?

The major failures, weaknesses, or omissions that come to mind are in the areas of land use, energy use, population growth, implementation of recently enacted air and water pollution control measures, construction of the Alaska Pipeline, and economic growth in general. Space prevents discussion of the particulars in each area, but a few comments should suffice. In what the National Wildlife Federation called--in something of an overstatement--the "most devastating defeat of the decade" for the environmental movement, the House of Representatives refused in June 1974 even to debate a very modest effort to develop a national land use policy. The bill's chief sponsor, Rep. Morris K. Udall (D., Arizona), defended the limited nature of what was in effect merely a proposal to encourage states to develop land use planning by claiming that the bill "does not include any authority for Federal planning of State or private land nor does it provide for any Federal review of substantive State or local decisions concerning land use."[12] Yet, extremely intense lobbying and eventually strong White House opposition sent the proposal down to defeat. Energy policy considerations in the last few years have continued to emphasize increased production rather than conservation and have focused on increased construction of nuclear power plants rather than on development of alternative and more sustainable (for example, solar) sources of energy. The population of the United States continues to increase and very likely will do so for at least the next 50 to 75 years. Assuming present low fertility rates continue (an unjustified assumption) and that immigration rates are lowered, there will be 280-300 million Americans before a zero rate of growth is reached. Yet we have no effective population policy, nor do we seem to pay much attention to the impact of population growth on environmental conditions and on our consumption of natural resources.[13] Perhaps most significant of all, movement away from the notion that conventional economic growth is desirable regardless of environmental consequences and toward some conception of the sustainable economy is barely perceptible in practical political arenas.

Environmental successes would have to include passage of the National Environmental Policy Act of 1969 (NEPA) and its creation of the Council on Environmental Quality in the Executive Office of

the president, the consolidation of previously dispersed environmental agencies into the Environmental Protection Agency in late
1970, the passage of fairly stringent air and water pollution control
legislation (the Clean Air Act Amendments of 1970 and the Water
Pollution Control Act of 1972), the defeat of the supersonic transport
in Congress in 1971 (although it reappeared in a European version in
1976), the strong opposition to the Trans-Alaska Pipeline proposal
between 1969 and 1973 and the eventual imposition of significant
environmental standards and safeguards on its construction, the
enormous impact of NEPA in the courts (far more than Congress
ever intended or has been happy with), and the adoption of the first
national strip-mining regulations by Congress late in 1974 and again
in 1975 (both bills, however, vetoed by President Ford).[14]

Any evaluation of the adequacy or success of these kinds of
actions must be based on several competing criteria or standards,
substantive as well as procedural. On the one hand, certainly the
necessity of meeting the ecological imperative, of satisfactorily resolving environmental problems is important. Given the purpose of
this chapter, we might also say that contemporary political actions
must be judged in part on how effectively they move the society toward an ecologically sound future. On the other hand, the usual
"process" criteria of democratic responsiveness, political legitimacy and consensus (usually indicated by widespread support of the
general public and various policy elites), and maintenance of traditional cultural or political values (for example, individual freedom
and property rights, social equality, economic well being) also condition our judgment--and rightly so. Environmental decision making
should not be assessed solely on the basis of efficiency or a narrow,
technical conception of problem solving. Conflicting interpretations
of our progress on the environmental front frequently arise out of
implicit reliance on these contrasting standards.

I have expressed my own fairly critical view at the beginning
of this section. Others would not entirely agree with these views,
mainly, I think, because they focus on different issues and assign a
different priority to these competing values. For example, advocates of a rapid transition to the sustainable society point, as I have
above, to incrementalism as a major obstacle to realizing the goals
they think necessary. In contrast, examining the more limited case
of air pollution politics, Charles O. Jones argues that this style of
decision making is well suited for settling moderate conflicts and is
to be valued as a means for helping to insure the building of political
support for new policy initiatives, for allowing sufficient time to
understand the nature of complex and technical environmental problems before rushing into action, and for encouraging the active consideration of important social and economic costs of new policies, all
of which are necessary, he says, if public policy is to be effective.[15]

Rather than argue here that some criteria are always more
appropriate than others--an unproductive exercise--I simply call
attention to the variety of standards by which we can and should
measure environmental progress. With these arguments in mind,
we can now return to the fourth set of questions set forth above: the
problems of political change in achieving a sustainable society.

POLITICAL CONSTRAINTS ON ACHIEVING
A SUSTAINABLE SOCIETY

Although not widely known, there is no real shortage of attempts to identify the major features of the U.S. political system
which prevent or constrain large-scale ecological change or the
achievement of a sustainable society. Many of these "obstacles" can
be viewed positively or negatively, of course, as we have just seen
with respect to incremental decision making. Such judgments reflect not only basic value differences, but our lack of knowledge
about the full consequences of present political patterns. Moreover,
even if there is substantial consensus that we need major change, do
we know how manipulable or elastic these political variables are?
Often there is a rather casual and simplistic assumption that fundamental change is not only necessary but is also perfectly feasible.
There appear to be few good reasons for these assumptions and very
little empirical data to support the expectations implied. The problem with analyzing political change at this level can be clarified by
briefly reviewing the main line of argument in much of the environmental politics literature.

In a fairly representative analysis of political difficulties environmental reformers in the United States face, Ronald Loveridge
identifies four major constraints: (1) decentralization and fragmentation of institutional structures and responsibility in the decision-
making process; (2) social and political pluralism; (3) bargaining and
coalition building as the dominant pattern of political interaction;
and (4) the pervasive presence of veto groups ("special interests").[16]
Others have added administrative or bureaucratic rigidity and inertia
to this list to round out a picture that suggests a political process
producing primarily incremental or conservative decisions; what
emerges as politically "feasible" in such a process is invariably only
marginally or incrementally different from existing practice. Thus,
it is argued, we see the adoption of short-range, uncoordinated,
conflicting, and often ineffective public policies.

Along with these explicitly political obstacles, a number of
scholars include the familiar and powerful constraints of American
culture which tend to inhibit ecological change. Pirages and Ehrlich,

for example, offer the following perspective on the values and beliefs of both elites and masses in their reference to the dominant
social paradigm (DSP, the collection of norms, beliefs, values, and
habits that form the "prevailing world view"):

> Despite many . . . differences, citizens in most
> industrial countries share with Americans a belief
> in progress, faith in the steady increase of mate-
> rial affluence (which unfortunately is often equated
> with progress), and belief in the necessity and
> goodness of growth. Other central features of the
> industrial DSP seemingly include high values placed
> on work, the nuclear family, and career-oriented
> formal education; a strong faith in the efficacy of
> science and technology (as opposed to religion) to
> solve problems; and a view of Nature as something
> to be subdued by mankind.[17]

Others add to this description of cultural constraints a firm public
belief in the value of individualism and achievement (including competition), a strong suspicion of and skepticism toward government
planning, and a cynical view of government capabilities and intentions in general.

The similarity of analyses of these kinds of constraints by
Loveridge, Rosenbaum, Brenner, Caldwell, Henning, Ophuls, and
Pirages and Ehrlich, among others, seems to suggest that there is
a consensus of sorts on these fundamental "deficiencies" of the U.S.
political process.[18] And if such agreement exists, one might further conclude that the analysis is basically correct, and thus we
know the main features of the route to ecological salvation. While
there is indeed substantial agreement on these constraints, the
second conclusion is premature. The last few years have seen the
renewal of conventional defensive arguments by those economists
and political scientists who tend either to support the status quo or
to be advocates of gradual, moderate change at best.[19] And even
ecological enthusiasts have had second thoughts about their initial
positions.[20] One should have expected both. The lesson would
appear to be that there is some virtue in a skeptical reading of
first-generation responses to newly recognized crises.

To give proper credit where it is very much due, these early
analyses did much to dispel unwarranted optimism over our institutional capabilities to cope with environmental problems. They also
served as initial and highly important guides to political change
strategies. Yet one also needs to appreciate the very real limits to
what we can expect from the compilation of such constraints. There

are two major reasons for raising some doubts about the utility of
these exercises in political analysis. First, while these factors or
conditions are undeniably prominent and significant features of U.S.
politics, there is neither universal agreement nor an especially convincing case at present for their wholly negative effects. Indeed, it
should be instructive that political scientists who are neither uninformed nor particularly hostile to environmental progress have
often celebrated precisely the same political characteristics (for
example, decentralization, "fragmentation," pluralism, incrementalism) for their contribution to the maintenance of a moderate degree of consensus in policy making, freedom, diversity, and political stability. Can we so easily ignore those long-standing and quite
respectable arguments? At what cost?

The second reason for inclining toward a skeptical position on
these questions is closely related to the first: the adequacy of
present knowledge of the causes of our ecological difficulties (especially the political causes), the reforms necessary to reverse past
behavior, and the consequences of adopting those reforms. It should
be examined at much greater length.

Most of the authors cited above conclude their discussions with
a set of recommendations which they predict (or simply hope) will
alter the unfavorable climate of present politics. For example, we
are advised that we need more central coordination of policy making
and possibly national planning agencies, or even extremely powerful
new forms of government--largely authoritarian in nature; that we
need to reform Congress and the "captive" regulatory and administrative agencies to "open up" or democratize U.S. government; that
we need to turn from excessive dedication to individualism and
laissez-faire economics to more cooperative social values and socialistic economies; that we need to arouse and educate the U.S.
public and create a new environmental consciousness and a new environmental ethic--borrowing heavily from Eastern philosophical
and religious traditions to challenge Western rationalized, mate-
rialistic cultures. [21] These suggestions--and many others--may
seem highly attractive and likely to be effective. The key question,
however, is whether we can know with any reasonable degree of
certainty that the right reforms are being promoted and will have the
expected consequences. And if we do know that, do we also know how
such ideas can be converted from broad goals to specific action
proposals. In short, how do we begin moving from here to there,
when "there" implies as fundamental a shift as achievement of a
sustainable society?

These omissions and inadequacies are not insignificant. One
need not go as far as cautious academic purists who insist that we
know everything possible before taking an initial first step in a new

and controversial direction. But some advancement over present
knowledge is certainly necessary if the conventional defense of U.S.
political processes is to be effectively addressed, if the general
public and its representatives are to be impressed with the importance and urgency of change, and if those currently opposed to
environmental initiatives are to be persuaded to reevaluate their
position. How might this advancement take place?

The change, I believe, requires a shift in the way we pose
these key political questions and in the level of analysis pursued.
Let me illustrate the point by reviewing once again the kinds of
factors thought to be inhibiting movement toward a sustainable society. Attention is usually called to incremental, satisficing, and
piecemeal decision making; symbolic or rhetorical politics; bureaucratic rigidity; social and political pluralism; fragmentation of
authority; the power of special-interest groups; the conservatism of
the mass public; the timidity of political leaders; the general inertia
in political institutions; and the negative effects of our Lockean
heritage of individualism and competition, including, of course, a
capitalist or free market economy. The message has been repeated
frequently and at great length. Yet, as important as the insights
have been, it is simply not sufficient to point to these conditions,
assert therein lies the problem, and issue a call for reform. Even
assuming that the diagnosis of institutional and public failings is a
completely accurate one—and I am by no means convinced that it is,
can we not do better than this? A different approach might move
beyond this first step to a more constructive and useful level of
inquiry and prescription.

The central problem is that these partial and limited descriptive analyses of current politics and probable "deficiencies" do not
provide the necessary information and guidance. To improve upon
this work we need more expansive and more fully developed ex-
plorations, including critical examination of the full ramifications
of these political characteristics. Put most broadly, what we need
is more and better explanatory, evaluative, prescriptive, and
strategic analysis to begin providing some meaningful and useful
answers to the questions of what changes are really necessary and
how they might be implemented. [22] The argument should be summed
up before venturing some specific (though necessarily limited) suggestions for how that new line of inquiry might proceed.

Our knowledge of U.S. environmental politics is fairly extensive, having increased dramatically in the last six years. In contrast, our understanding of the political implications of moving
toward a sustainable society (politics and government as the dependent variable) is very limited. Available insights into the political
constraints on achieving such a society and into fruitful levers for

political change (politics and government as the independent variable) fall in between those two extremes. We need especially to improve our capabilities in this last area. We can begin doing that by raising some doubts about the overly casual first-order political prescriptions noted above. A healthy dose of skepticism is called for. We need to reappraise some of the conventional wisdom regarding political change and to think more imaginatively about how to generate momentum during a period of increasing public cynicism, apathy, and distrust of new political demands.

There are two critical requirements to move toward these goals: better knowledge of the politics suitable for transition to a sustainable society and improvement in how well the essential arguments for this shift are communicated to the U.S. public and its political leaders. These two needs create an agenda of future tasks both for students of politics and for political activists. Properly approached, the former need not conceive of such analysis as merely another opportunity to expand personal and disciplinary rewards, and the latter need not restrict themselves to short-range and uncertain defensive battles.[23] Let me make a few suggestions to inspire some confidence in these remarks.

TOWARD A SUSTAINABLE-STATE POLITICS

There is much truth to the proposition that the ecologic crisis arises fundamentally from man's world view or dominant social paradigm and the political and social arrangements he has developed over time based upon that world view. One of the greatest challenges for students of politics is the contradiction between ecological imperatives and the philosophical foundations of modern industrial political systems. William Ophuls is one of the few individuals to begin exploring that issue. His comprehensive and original treatment hopefully will provoke others to seek answers to the question of what an ecologically sound future society will, or should, look like; what kinds of problems, conflicts, and choices are likely; and perhaps most significantly, how we can move through the uncertain period of transitional politics to whatever lies beyond with minimal cost and maximum gain in human values.[24]

Whether through excursions in utopian thought and the construction of scenarios of possible ecological futures, through practical discussion of shorter-range innovation in U.S. government institutions, or through any of the possibilities between those extremes, this kind of dialog can be enormously valuable. Clearly some distinction must be made between short- or intermediate-term change and long-term change. Ophuls and others may be correct in

suggesting that the most we can really hope for at present--given
the revolutionary character of the change they think necessary--is
that construction of alternative paradigms and circulation of the
ideas will eventually pay off, most likely at a time when the U.S.
public becomes sufficiently disenchanted with current political-
economic-social behavior and the consequences. The new alternative
would then clearly be preferable to present paradigms. We need
utopian thinking, of course, much as we need a full-scale reevalua-
tion of our traditional assumptions, values, and behavior. One
wonders, however, whether much faith should be placed in the
proposition that when the basic ideas of ecology and the necessity of
a steady state catch on, the required changes in values, goals, institutions, and behavior will somehow spring forth automatically.
Those of us who dwell in a world of political realism find the notion
difficult to accept. One must also question whether comfortable,
affluent Americans find it too easy already to ignore difficult political choices. Should they be encouraged to limit further their excessively modest interest in important decisions taking place in
Washington and in state capitols across the nation?

     In the short term, while waiting for the new consciousness to
take hold, traditional political action is called for, at least in the
hope of ameliorating present conditions and minimizing the human
cost of present political priorities. This is precisely what active
environmentalists have been concerned with for the past six or
seven years. Seemingly endless battles have been fought in Congress, in the bureaucracies of national, state, and local governments, and especially in the nation's courtrooms. At this level,
action must be highly specific with concrete and "feasible" goals.
Winning requires the same kind of knowledge, skills, and tactics
used so well by the "opposition." As the late Senator Philip Hart
remarked: "Congress can endure with composure that mass assault
by well-meaning citizens demanding generalities such as world
peace or a change in the system. But it almost always responds to
determined coalitions that are driven by self-interest into a sustained effort to hammer through a couple of specific bills.''[25]

     The narrow defeat in 1974 of the first national effort to en-
courage land use planning policies is a case in point. Lobbying by
opponents of the measure was so intensive that even the final watered-
down version of the bill was rejected. Environmentalist success on
the SST in 1971, the very narrow defeat on strip-mining legislation
in 1974 and again in 1975, and most of the cases cited above illustrate the stakes as well as the possibilities of victory. To be sure,
the issues in such political arenas are normally quite limited compared to the requirements of sustainable growth. They are hardly
trivial issues, however; and the very intensity of conflict over such

modest proposals as the land use bill indicates the degree of opposition to large-scale change and the necessity, therefore, of developing better strategies for political action.

The fact that short-term environmental change requires working "within the system" raises two related questions. How do we gain the political support of the mass public and how do we insure that political leaders act responsibly? Success requires an effective combination of government assertiveness and leadership on ecological issues and a public which demands, supports, and reinforces the right kind of behavior on the part of political elites.

There is good reason to suspect that no matter how extensive institutional change or what kind of political leaders come to power, without the strong support and willing cooperation of the U.S. public major efforts at ecological change will amount to little. Fundamental social and political change in a democracy does not occur without support of broad segments of the population, including the mass public. Ecological change cannot be forced down the throat of an unwilling or hostile public, nor will democratically elected leaders attempt to do so. The great reluctance of both former Presidents Nixon and Ford to move beyond voluntary efforts in our national energy "policy" (especially in 1973 and 1974) provides a lesson in the importance of public opinion. And most certainly, any proposals for restricting economic growth or possibly reducing standards of living will face the same barrier. Often accused of ignoring public opinion, politicians are very responsive to public preferences on questions of this sort. They prefer to follow public opinion rather than attempt to lead it.

These conditions suggest that we need to know much more about public attitudes toward the environment, and more about the processes of attitude formation and change. How does such change occur? What will promote the kind of alteration in human values and attitudes necessary for movement in the direction of a sustainable society? What is the role, for example, of early socialization, personal experience, formal education, exposure to religious and cultural institutions, the mass media, and government or political leadership (especially presidential leadership)? The innumerable public opinion polls on environmental matters over the past few years have told us amazingly little in this regard. We have few good measures of public values, beliefs, and commitment in these polls. We don't know much about the role public opinion actually plays in influencing political decisions or how much support or opposition can be expected from various segments of the public for new policy initiatives (always a matter of concern to politicians).

Frequent allusions to an unconcerned, reluctant, or hostile public are somewhat misleading and, in any event, not terribly

informative. The public is certainly capable of recognizing its interest and has supported environmental change in many communities
and states when the problems were quite visible and the consequences
clearly perceived as related to quality of life.[26] Rather than settle
for general comments on public opinion and assume the worst, we
would be better advised to ask more about the reality of public attitudes and the prospects for change. For example, how aware of
environmental problems is the public? How serious are growth,
resource, and environmental problems considered to be? How
salient are these issues? What is the public willing to pay for corrective actions? How intensely do people feel about such matters?
How resistant to change are these attitudes? Empirical studies of
these kinds of questions may provide some valuable information,
especially if social scientists can control their frequent inclination
to concentrate on the inconsequential.[27]

There may be some basis for cautious optimism about potential public support for ecological change. Nevertheless, in the short
run the greatest burden clearly is on citizen activists and political
leaders. It is up to them to persuade the American people to find
some identity between personal quality of life and a national need to
begin coming to terms with ecological scarcity. In the immediate
future these kinds of appeals must be put in terms the public can
understand and support; they cannot be general and abstract, nor in
direct conflict with the public's strong attachment to traditional
values, for example, individualism and private property. Furthermore, in building broader coalitions with those segments of the
public less concerned with environmental or growth issues than with
their still-unsatisfactory standard of living (including, of course,
the developing nations), effective political leadership is indispensable. George McKenna's conclusion to a fascinating case study in
local coalition-building is instructive in this regard:

> Somewhere there must be environmental mystics
> who will give up everything they have or want for
> the sake of our collective ecological future. But
> I doubt we can ever build viable ecological move-
> ments out of them. There aren't enough of them
> to go around, and the attempt to generate more by
> conversion will only produce hypocrites.[28]

For the most part, political elites are responsible for the
initiation and shaping of ecological or growth policies, even though
policy preferences and behavior are sometimes greatly conditioned,
or severely restricted, by the U.S. public, and even more by various politically active and influential citizens and groups. Students

of politics could profitably inquire into the values, attitudes, perceptions, motivations, and behavior of these elites. Why do elites
or decision makers hold the values and attitudes they do? What are
their perceptions and definitions of ecological or growth problems?
How well informed are they (for example, on technical aspects or
on underlying social and economic causes)? How do they respond
to policy advice from environmental and social scientists? Why are
they motivated or not to adopt particular policy preferences? What
personal or political rewards attend commitment to, and action on,
ecological issues? It would hardly be reasonable to expect normal
political behavior to be suspended merely because the issues loom
so large. Recognition of the limitations or constraints under which
political elites operate (institutional, political, and behavioral) can
at least make for more effective prescription and action.

Much of this chapter, including this final section, has consisted
of a series of questions. At this stage in our understanding of
sustainable-state politics, raising such questions may be more
valuable than engaging in narrowly focused empirical inquiry or
continuing to debate in the abstract the wisdom of limiting growth.
Even if the answers prove unproductive or elusive, the search
represents an important change from inattention to the issues or
complacency with the status quo. And if I have raised the wrong
questions, others might respond by proposing more interesting or
productive ones. That would at least signal the beginning of more
widespread and serious efforts to confront steady-state issues.
Hopefully, such efforts will help shape and speed the emergence of
a new politics suitable to the age of ecological scarcity.

NOTES

1. I will use the terms sustainable, or equilibrium society to
refer to a society having a steady-state-type economy approximately
that defined in Herman Daly's work: "An economy in which the total
population and the total stock of physical wealth are maintained constant at some desired levels by a 'minimal' rate of maintenance
throughout (i.e., by birth and death rates that are equal at the lowest feasible level, and by physical production and consumption rates
that are equal at the lowest feasible level)." See Herman E. Daly,
"The Steady-State Economy: Toward a Political Economy of Biophysical Equilibrium and Moral Growth," in Toward a Steady-State
Economy, ed. Herman E. Daly (San Francisco: W. H. Freeman,
1973), p. 152. A much fuller treatment of the physical necessity of
a state state as well as the political and social implications can be
found in William Ophuls, Ecology and the Politics of Scarcity:

Prologue to a Political Theory of the Steady State (San Francisco: W. H. Freeman, 1977).

2. See, for example, Ophuls, op. cit.; Daly, op. cit.; Dennis C. Pirages and Paul R. Ehrlich, Ark II: Social Responses to Environmental Imperatives (San Francisco: W. H. Freeman, 1974); Robert L. Heilbroner, An Inquiry into the Human Prospect (New York: W. W. Norton, 1974); and Edward Goldsmith et al., Blueprint for Survival (Boston: Houghton Mifflin, 1972).

3. A good example would be Charles O. Jones, Clean Air: The Policies and Politics of Pollution Control (Pittsburgh: University of Pittsburgh Press, 1975). The same perspective (by economists) can be found in Mancur Olson and Hans H. Landsberg, eds., The No-Growth Society (New York: W. W. Norton, 1975).

4. The evidence is reviewed in Ophuls, op. cit., and in Pirages and Ehrlich, op. cit.

5. A lucid discussion of the steps in the policy-making process can be found in Charles O. Jones, An Introduction to the Study of Public Policy (Belmont, Calif.: Wadsworth, 1970).

6. Heilbroner, op. cit., p. 100.

7. Barry Commoner, The Closing Circle (New York: Alfred A. Knopf, 1971), p. 33.

8. John W. Kingdon, Congressmen's Voting Decisions (New York: Harper and Row, 1973), Chapters 2 and 5.

9. Ophuls has made an excellent beginning in Ecology and the Politics of Scarcity, op. cit.

10. The major statement on, and defense of, incrementalism in American politics is Charles E. Lindblom, The Intelligence of Democracy (New York: The Free Press, 1965). For a critique of incrementalism based on ecological criteria, see Ophuls, "The Limits of American Economic and Political Institutions," in Ecology and the Politics of Scarcity, op. cit.

11. Obviously it is still early to assess the full "political response" to the ecological crisis in any systematic fashion, but the following works contain evidence supporting the summary judgment: Lynton K. Caldwell, Environment: A Challenge to Modern Society (Garden City, N.Y.: Doubleday, 1971); J. Clarence Davies III, The Politics of Pollution (Indianapolis: Bobbs-Merrill, 1970; 2d ed., 1975); Walter A. Rosenbaum, The Politics of Environmental Concern (New York: Praeger, 1973); Ronald O. Loveridge, "Political Science and Air Pollution: A Review and Assessment of the Literature," in Air Pollution and Social Sciences: Formulating and Implementing Control Programs, ed. Paul B. Downing (New York: Praeger, 1971); Richard A. Cooley and Geoffrey Wandesforde-Smith, eds., Congress and the Environment (Seattle: University of Washington Press, 1970); Roy L. Meek and John A. Straayer, eds.,

The Politics of Neglect: The Environmental Crisis (Boston: Houghton Mifflin, 1971); James Rathlesberger, ed., Nixon and the Environment: The Politics of Devastation (New York: Village Voice Books, 1972); John C. Exposito, Vanishing Air (New York: Grossman, 1970); and David Zwick and Marcy Benstock, Water Wasteland (New York: Grossman, 1971).

12. Conservation Report, March 8, 1974, p. 79.

13. John Holdren, "Population and the American Predicament: The Case Against Complacency," in Olson and Landsberg, op. cit., pp. 31-43, and "U.S. Population in 2000--Zero Growth or Not?" Population Bulletin 30, no. 5 (Population Reference Bureau, Washington, D.C., 1975).

14. It may be worth noting that the most useful sources for information on environmental developments of this sort are the New York Times, Congressional Quarterly Weekly Report, National Journal, the National Wildlife Federation's excellent weekly, Conservation Report, the annual reports of the Council on Environmental Quality, and various congressional documents (especially hearings before relevant committees or subcommittees).

15. For a thorough discussion of this perspective see Jones, Clean Air, op. cit.

16. Loveridge, op. cit.

17. Pirages and Ehrlich, op. cit., pp. 43-44. Whether these norms, beliefs, and habits are as widely held now as they used to be is an empirical question. Clearly social and cultural changes are underway which may make descriptions of this sort inaccurate in the future.

18. Loveridge, op. cit.; Rosenbaum, op. cit.; Michael J. Brenner, The Political Economy of America's Environmental Dilemma (Lexington, Mass.: D. C. Heath, 1973); Caldwell, Environment, op. cit., and In Defense of Earth: International Protection of the Biosphere (Bloomington: Indiana University Press, 1972); Daniel H. Henning, Environmental Policy and Administration (New York: American Elsevier, 1974); Pirages and Ehrlich, op. cit.; and Ophuls, Ecology and the Politics of Scarcity, op. cit.

19. Jones, Clear Air, op. cit.; Olson and Landsberg, op. cit.

20. Cf. Mihajlo Mesarovic and Edward Pestel, Mankind at the Turning Point: The Second Report to the Club of Rome (New York: E. P. Dutton, 1974), especially p. 55, and Donella H. Meadows et al., The Limits to Growth (New York: Universe Books, 1972).

21. Most of those proposals are very effectively reviewed in Pirages and Ehrlich, op. cit.

22. A wide-ranging discussion which helps to clarify the meaning of change in U.S. politics and offers a framework along this line is Kenneth M. Dolbeare, Political Change in the United States: A Framework for Analysis (New York: McGraw-Hill, 1974).

23. An overview of current efforts by political scientists in
the environmental politics area (though rather limited in terms of
steady-state questions), can be found in Stuart S. Nagel, ed.,
Environmental Politics (New York: Praeger, 1974), and a compre-
hensive list of research suggestions in Lester W. Milbrath and
Frederick R. Inscho, "The Environmental Problem as a Political
Problem: An Agenda of Environmental Concerns for Political Scien-
tists," American Behavioral Scientist 17 (May/June 1974): 623-50.
See also Michael E. Kraft and Peter G. Stillman, "Environmental
Politics and Political Science: Issues and Opportunities," Polity 8
(Spring 1976): 443-53, for other references to bibliographies and
research topics.

24. For a discussion of these questions see Michael E. Kraft
and Peter G. Stillman, "Toward a Political Theory of Ecological
Survival," paper delivered at the Annual Meeting of the American
Political Science Association, New Orleans, September 1973.

25. The Progressive, February 1973, p. 35. The popular
literature of the early 1970s not surprisingly offered more on political tactics than found in most scholarly analysis. Much of that
work can still stand as practical political advice, although it is
geared more to short-term change and conventional politics than to
long-term adaptation to the steady state. See Sam Love, ed., Earth
Tool Kit: A Field Manual for Citizen Activists (New York: Pocket
Books, 1971); John Mitchell and Constance Stallings, eds., Ecotac-
tics: The Sierra Club Handbook for Environmental Activists (New
York: Pocket Books, 1970); Garrett DeBell, ed., The Voter's Guide
to Environmental Politics (New York: Ballantine Books, 1970); and
Norman J. Landau and Paul Rheingold, The Environmental Law
Handbook (New York: Ballantine Books, 1971).

26. See Karl Lamb, As Orange Goes: Twelve California
Families and the Future of American Politics (New York: W. W.
Norton, 1974); George McKenna, "Ecology, Economy, and Ecumen-
ism: A Case Study," Politics and Society, Spring 1973, pp. 379-407;
Carol E. Steinhart and John S. Steinhart, Blowout: A Case Study of
the Santa Barbara Oil Spill (North Scituate, Mass.: Duxbury Press,
1972); and Lester W. Milbrath, "Environmental Beliefs: A Tale of
Two Counties: (Monograph, Buffalo, New York: Social Science Research Institute, SUNY, Buffalo, January 1975). Perhaps there is
some significance in the findings of a recent Gallup opinion poll
which showed a majority of Americans "think population and economic growth will have to be regulated, both globally and in the
areas where they live to avert resource shortages, pollution and a
lowered quality of life" (New York Times, December 1, 1974, p. 47).

27. An excellent bibliography containing illustrations of useful
public opinion analysis as well as of the tendency toward politically

insignificant research is Riley E. Dunlap, "Sociological and Social-Psychological Perspectives on Environmental Issues: A Bibliography" (Monticello, Ill.: Council of Planning Librarians, November 1975). See also Dunlap's "Directory of Environmental Sociologists" (Pullman: College of Agriculture Research Center Circular No. 586, Washington State University, August 1975).

    28. For one attempt to address these kinds of questions with a sample of congressmen serving on environmental subcommittees, see Michael E. Kraft, "Congressional Attitudes toward the Environment: Attention and Issue-Orientation in Ecological Politics," Ph.D. dissertation, Yale University, 1973. A shorter report of the findings appeared in "Congressional Attitudes toward the Environment," Alternatives 1 (Summer 1972): 27-37, reprinted in Arvin W. Murch, ed., Environmental Concern: Personal Attitudes and Behavior toward Environmental Problems (New York: MSS Information Corporation, 1974).

9

THE POLITICS OF
COORDINATED
REDISTRIBUTION
Davis B. Bobrow

With remarkable speed, intellectual discourse about policy needs has become full of talk about a steady-state earth, about moderated growth, about the need to balance population with planetary resources, about the progress of and direct and second-order consequences from radical technologies to replace natural, depletable materials.[1] Much about these discussions may be unclear, inconsistent, and lacking in factual or theoretical foundation. However, the concern of this chapter does not lie with the soundness of the arguments about resources, technology, population, and their interactive consequences. Rather, the following pages are about the politics called for, at least implicitly, by two of the major positions in the public debate. For convenience we shall call these the doctrine of restraint and moderation (Vision I) and of technology and abundance (Vision II).

EVALUATING ALTERNATIVE FUTURES

The two doctrinal positions we shall deal with, and indeed almost all major suggestions about the future, cannot be achieved or sustained through individual action alone. All then are assuming or hoping (praying?) for some sort of collective action and institutional performance. That is, they all require for success some public policies, some administrative organizations, and some sort of

---

The author is obliged for particularly helpful suggestions to Warren Phillips, Dennis Pirages, and John Ruggie. Dewey Covington assisted in background research for this chapter.

political process. Accordingly, politics should matter to us when
we try to evaluate the desirability and feasibility of alternative
futures.[2] Matters of politics are not mere mundane, subordinate,
nitty-gritty details of implementation which can "be taken care of"
at will by well-intentioned people.

With regard to desirability, much of the appeal of different
visions of the future lies in their indications of "who gets what,
when, and how." We are all free to decide to pay little attention to
questions of governance, freedom, and safeguards to insure equity
and adaptiveness to unfolding problems. Yet surely we should not
place our total evaluation of the desirability of alternative futures
on aggregate economic and environmental outcomes without facing
up to possible costs and dangers involving political power.

With regard to feasibility, it seems reasonable to see if certain policies are likely to work within existing political arrangements. If our estimate is negative, we had best begin promptly to
generate the needed arrangements. To do so we must recognize
what they are. If we cannot envision the needed policies, institutions, and processes then we are in a poor position to evaluate the
practicality of some suggested future. If we can envision those aspects of the future and if we know that current political realities are
inappropriate, we still have the task of formulating a transition
strategy to transform the politics we have into the politics any particularly appealing vision of the future requires.

Given agreement on the importance of politics broadly construed in the design, appraisal, and realization of alternative futures, there may still be disagreement about what to do about such
matters. One familiar line of argument contends that we simply
cannot say anything very meaningful. Accordingly, we should grace-
fully admit uncertainty and accept the inevitability of a "muddling
through" approach. We will set this position aside because it begs
the question of the public policies, administrative organizations,
and political processes needed to insure that one will indeed have a
politics of incrementalism and muddling through.

A second line of argument has found favor with both the advocates of restraint and moderation and of technology and abundance.
It supports what can be called the politics of centralized authoritative institutions to bring "selfish and unreasonable" people to behave in terms of the collective interest and thus avert the "tragedy
of the commons." Technology and abundance partisans, to continue
the illustration, call for centralized authority to override local objections to siting of new energy technology. Both groups tend to support a technocratic elite which will do the long-range detailed, comprehensive, and binding planning to make us all act in ways consistent with their preferred future. Neither group contends that such a

modernized model of Hobbes' Leviathan is normatively attractive.
They do imply that the problems which must be overcome are so
serious, and democratic governments so ineffective, that only
Leviathan can do the job.[3]

    This argument scants some serious questions about the desir-
ability and effectiveness of modernized Leviathan. The restraint
and moderation advocates do have a strong theoretical basis for arguing that without centralized authoritative planning, social systems
pursue the common interests of their members to less than an optimal extent.[4] And the advocates of technology and abundance can
point out numerous instances where decentralized market forces and
demands for immediate consumption operate to divert resources
from the pursuit of long-run abundance.[5] However, embracing
Leviathan too quickly can easily lead us to overlook some important
issues. First, there are relatively few examples of commodities or
situations which in practice are good or bad from everyone's point
of view at the same time and which impact on everyone to the same
extent. Accordingly, common interests are by no means easy to
identify. Opting for modern Leviathan does not suffice to provide
that Leviathan with the ability to identify genuine common interests
and ignore illusory possibilities. Second, if we say that the business of Leviathan is to see to the production and distribution of private rather than public goods or bads, we then need a large number
of distributional decisions. Also, we will have to move toward centralized authoritative planning in a context where many people are
dissatisfied with, and less than quiescent about, existing distributions. What characteristics of centralized authoritative planning institutions will lead them to engage in redistributive acts which are
fair by any particular standard and which are legitimate enough to
avoid pouring resources into coercive instruments to maintain power?
What are the incentives in the politics of modern Leviathan to shut
out those who demand redistribution by withdrawing into isolation--
that is, the lifeboat solution--or to acknowledge obligations other
than those imposed by force or the threat of force? Finally, what
properties of the centralized technocracy will induce large numbers
of people to engage in the endeavors and to internalize the particular
life style which each vision of the future demands rather than engaging in a continuing battle of wits with central authority?

    Clearly we should not be sanguine about Leviathan doing the
"right thing" or winning the "hearts and minds" of populations.
Some would still contend that Leviathan will be effective at what it
does. This argument as grounds for turning to the Leviathan alternative is of course not new--for example, Mussolini was admired
for making the trains run on time. Yet is it so easy to tell a Leviathan from a dinosaur? I think not. Mussolini was not on average

conspicuously successful at most things he tried. More importantly, the arguments for centralized authoritative planning assume tremendous capabilities for forecasting, handling information without distortion, and diversity and flexibility about policy alternatives. Centralization beyond some point in a large and complex social system does not produce prompt compliance and it surely does not produce creative initiatives from below. The more skeptical we are about the likelihood of providing the required capabilities, the more skeptical we will be about the argument for centralized, authoritative technocracy.

These reservations suggest that we should explore a third line of argument which can be called the politics of coordinated redistribution.[6] It seems to have little appeal to the zealots of restraint and moderation or to those of technology and abundance. The politics of coordinated redistribution are decentralized in relative terms. The center provides information for planning, with the notion that dispersed parties will arrive at appropriate courses of action, that is, indicative planning. Notions of some generalized common interest provided by centralized authority are reduced in importance. Instead, numerous bargains are being struck more or less explicitly for the exchange of private goods and bads. The emphasis on de facto, dispersed adaptation reduces the requirements our previous alternative levied for information and institutional capacity of a unified, fixed kind.

Of course, coordinated redistribution does not eliminate the problems of political prescription discussed with respect to centralized authoritative planning. It does, I believe, provide a conducive framework for thinking through the politics implied by Vision I (restraint and moderation) and Vision II (technology and abundance). Intense pursuit of either doctrine calls for continuing changes in the distribution of money, power, and information across persons, classes, and institutions. Mutually reinforcing redistributions seem necessary if we are to shift from our current mode of societal operation to one called for by either doctrine. And even after the transition to one or another future, continuing redistributions will probably be needed if the vision is to be sustained with dynamism and popular legitimacy. Otherwise, pursuit of either vision will be seriously hampered by the massive drain of resources into coercive institutions and into a new "administrative class."

Our discussion of the politics involved in successful pursuit of Vision I and Vision II will necessarily be very qualitative and descriptive. If the intuitive and impressionistic sketches presented in the rest of this chapter are compelling, others hopefully will go on to treat the politics of alternative futures in a more technically rigorous and abstract fashion, for example, through the use of

approaches from the literatures of public choice and of hierarchical
decision systems.

In our sketches of political requirements certain themes will
occur frequently. Some are of course the classic dimensions of any
discussion of politics. Who are the participants and how are they
organized? What commodities or matters of value are being allocated
through the political system? Who gives and who receives in what
amounts and at what times? What are the processes for changing the
answers to any of these questions for the political system involved?
Other themes merit more attention than they sometimes receive because of the extended, futuristic nature of our topic. First, we are
concerned with both the transition to particular futures called for by
each doctrine and maintenance of each future after it is initially attained. With respect to politics, several questions become salient.[7]
First, how are the politics conducive to transition different from or
similar to those appropriate for maintenance? How do politics present at any one temporal point in a purposeful attempt to change the
future affect the probabilities of one or another kind of politics at
subsequent points? How long will the politics called for take to come
into being for each of the steps involved in transition and maintenance?
Second, we need to deal with the geographic domain of the futures
under discussion. Do we require a politics for the globe or for only
one nation-state, for example, the United States? Even if we opt for
the latter, what sorts of interactions do we assume between the country on which we focus and the rest of the world?

The advocates of each vision often mention global interdependence and international benefits. Yet most examples they provide of
policies, administrative organizations, and political processes are
national or limited to the industrialized countries. This inconsis-
tency surely is understandable. If we really adopt the global perspective, the necessary politics become even more dominated by
conflicts of interest. The redistributions called for are even more
likely to involve sharp, absolute cuts in the shares of scarce goods
held by the white, rich parts of the world population. The difficulty
of the political design problem increases by orders of magnitude.
Yet the normative and pragmatic consequences of acting as if the
rest of the world can be left out of the political design problem are
also severe.[8] We tend to assume that the doctrines do not differ in
their moral implications for our relations with others. We tend to
assume that the doctrines do not differ in the extent to which they
depend on at least passive tolerance by others (for example, raw
material supply) and in the likelihood that they are likely to trigger
actively hostile responses by others. After all, both visions require
some substantial changes in contemporary emphases in the United
States and the Organization for Economic Cooperation and Development

(OECD) member states in general. There is no reason to assume
that such changes on our part will not lead to changes in the way
others relate to us. Also, the tendency to ignore the rest of the
world leads us to ignore the national security resource requirements
for effective pursuit of either doctrine. Even if these requirements
are the same for each vision of the future, meeting them may impose
a very different burden on Vision I than on Vision II. There is no
obvious reason to treat the political design problem in an artificial
context which assumes a complete absence of external threat.

VISION I: RESTRAINT AND MODERATION

The restraint and moderation vision of the future centers
around the notion of a steady state, "defined as an economy in which
the total population and the total stock of physical wealth are maintained constant at some desired levels by a 'minimal' rate of maintenance throughput (i.e., by birth and death rates that are equal at
the lowest feasible level, and by physical production and consumption
rates that are equal at the lowest feasible level). . . . Minimizing
throughput implies maximizing the average life expectancy of a member of the stock."[9]
This vision of material limits seems to call for public policies
which

produce and maintain low birth rates and adjust birth rates to changes
    in life expectancy;
conserve natural resources by exploitation rates consistent with re-
    newal and substitution rates, by recycling, and by labor rather
    than capital or raw material intensive production strategies;
weigh benefits and costs to future generations as or more heavily
    than benefits to those currently alive;
insure against further deterioration of the physical and biological
    environment;
restrict the differences between and the absolute wealth of individuals,
    including ceilings as well as floors on wealth.

To adopt and effectively implement such public policies, administrative organizations and the political process must be complex
and conducive to a multigeneration time perspective. The challenge
posed by complexity, while reflecting the large and diverse number
of issues and actors involved, compounds because the policies call
for attaining and maintaining ratio relationships where the rates of
change in the elements which produce each side of the ratio differ
widely.

There is little doubt that those who put forward Vision I are opposed to stagnation, conformity, dullness, and oppression. They tell us that we need instead, "a dynamic equilibrium affording ample scope for continued artistic, intellectual, scientific and spiritual growth."[10] What sort of politics will help combine the policies and management they call for with an open and dynamic society which they also call for? Clearly, it must be a politics which excludes extermination of major population segments by acts of commission or omission, which does not generate mass apathy and depression (a survival mentality), and which does not violate civil liberties as that term is customarily construed in Western democracies. And it must achieve and maintain low throughput.

The goals of Vision I call for a society most of whose members comply with the notions of material restraint and moderation and also are vital and in large measure satisfied with their lot. At the same time, the policies called for are highly intrusive on individuals. Participation of a rewarding kind seems necessary to avoid massive withdrawal and alienation. For participation to seem rewarding it must seem efficacious to the citizenry. That is, it must seem to produce results which are on balance positive and which would probably not have been achieved without citizens playing an active part. For participation to be relevant to policy questions, it must manifest itself in relation to them. The meaningfulness of participation to achieve a society of restraint and moderation depends in important ways on two information flows. The first must provide specialists and executives with accurate information about the preferences of participants including intensity of support and opposition to different germane policy alternatives. The second must provide the participant citizenry with evidence that policy has responded to their preferences.

Taken together, these requirements have some strong implications for modes of participation. First, individuals must have participation opportunities and ways of aggregating their opinions which reflect interests in what are for Vision I the major issues of public policy. For example, since population is a major issue area, and since interests in population policy vary with age-grades, participation must at least in part be organized along age-grade lines. There are important implications for the demarcation of voting populations, the selection system for representatives in relation to identified constituencies, the reliance on issue-specific rather than personality-specific institutions to ascertain popular mandates.[11] Second, participatory settings must be small enough for individuals to perceive that their actions matter. Accordingly, opinions should be aggregated by small units, and individual voters should not simply be immersed in a voting population in the millions. Issues need to

be broken down into local alternatives. Third, there must be channels for direct communication between citizens and specialists and
executives. These channels do not have to involve face-to-face, one-
on-one interchange. Modern technology provides numerous other ways
to short-circuit anonymous intervening bureaucracies and to report on
how citizen preferences entered into policy choice. And a host of organizational devices are available to provide such communications if
there is the will to employ them.

One major task of the transition to the goals of Vision I involves
providing the foundation for sustained acceptance by most citizens of
the reasonableness of continuing moderation and restraint. This
seems to me to be an impossible task in the absence of substantial
steps to equalize the standard of living in terms of which persons are
expected to be moderate and restrained in their material appetites.
Since we start far from a uniform standard of living, there seems a
substantial need for major redistributive actions which, given limits
on throughput, will require lowering the standard of living of some
in favor of others. Some forms of participation and its instrumentali-
ties can make such redistributions relatively feasible and conducive
to a generalized acceptance of restraint and moderation. These include: (1) communication flows which create awareness of distributional inequities; (2) hard-to-break guarantees that redistributions
will stop with equality and not simply change ranks in a class hierarchy by making top dogs into underdogs; and (3) clear, prompt, and
very public reporting systems which check on the extent to which re-
distributional programs do in fact contribute to their proclaimed goals.

All of these emphases run directly counter to the familiar patterns in which moderation and restraint are imposed and urged with
particular vigor on those already less favored. Compliance leads if
anything to more rather than to less equitable distributions. Those
who already have the most are treated as deserving special privilege.
The politics of noncoercive redistribution cannot help but suffer when,
for example, motorists are urged to use less gas while oil companies
make record profits, or when a new administrative class with special
privileges takes the cream off the top of the resources for redistribution, or when pivotal, rich countries in the world economy call for
efforts to limit growth but not to share the wealth from existing economic development.

The severity of the problems imposed by redistribution at any
given level of throughput increase to the extent that everyone wants
more of the same commodity at the same time. Accordingly, the
politics of noncoercive redistribution are more feasible when preferences for particular commodities differ widely as do the preferred
times for their receipt. Diversity across commodities and delivery
times increases the possibilities of adequate supply and of consensus

that restraint and moderation are working out well. Uniform preferences make general satisfaction unlikely in the absence of high
throughput. Diversity makes possible a number of nonidentical
benefit packages. In order for citizens to see these complex benefit packages as part of the politics of restraint and moderation, they
must see the allocation of the benefits in question as itself a political
act. Otherwise the allocation will not help to create generalized
support for the restraint and moderation objective and attendant distributional policies. Accordingly, noncoercive redistribution by
satisfying diverse preferences operates best when citizens perceive
that many sorts of benefits are in fact distributed by the political
system--if only through indirect subsidy. Of course, a particularly
conducive situation prevails when large groups in the population come
to value highly those benefits which involve little throughput (symbolic rather than material rewards) and which favor future generations (low discount rates), and see the allocation of symbolic rewards
and guardianship of the welfare of future generations as a major
raison d'être of the political system.

The emphasis on diverse benefit packages also has implications for participation as does the concern with symbolic and deferred rewards. The concern with symbolic rewards calls for open
access to them and expression of preferences about the criteria to
govern their allocation. For example, if authority over production
is one form of symbolic reward, access to authority cannot be restricted to a small fraction of employees of an enterprise but must
involve greater industrial democracy. Similarly, criteria for recognition of individual accomplishment should not eliminate the large
mass of the population automatically. Instead the citizenry should
have the opportunity to indicate what sorts of accomplishments and
social contributions merit reward. Acceptance of largely deferred
awards coupled with low throughput seem to call for general conviction that members of future generations will have similar opportunities to participate in the enjoyment of those rewards. This implies
effective elimination of the transfer of wealth from the better-off of
any current generation to their descendants. While participation in
relation to diverse benefit packages does not require a particular interest group for each and every package, it does imply that the organization of interests is not limited to seeking shares in the current
allocation of a few material commodities. Otherwise it is difficult
to see how the political system can avoid polarization and continual
conflict. A more durable state of affairs for citizen satisfaction
and loyalty to a restraint and moderation regime will result if members of any group with particular preferences for the immediate allocation of material benefits are also members of groups which differ
markedly in their other preferences. If they are not, participation

will divert the political system to a focus on the immediate material
gratification which Vision I advocates deplore.

If our emphases on participation, distribution, and diverse
values are to lead us to the Vision I goals of restraint and moderation, they must be complemented by appropriate administrative organizations, grounds for policy choice, and incentives for citizens
and for specialists and executives. Administratively, organizations
need to be structured and assigned missions in line with the major
policy objectives associated with low throughput. In the U.S. case,
for example, this would call for a different set than now exists of
executive departments and congressional oversight committees.
And it would call for sharp deemphasis or even dissolution of some
that now exist. Coordinating institutions, for example, the Office
of Management and Budget, the Congressional Budget Office, would
focus on division of resources within a throughput pie and not only a
budgetary pie. Reorganization at the federal level would be accompanied by substantial decentralization of control. This seems necessary given the demands posed by participation and the complexity of
the policy problems. Central government would limit itself to establishing broad resource constraints, adjusting the consequences
of the actions of local bodies, and producing and distributing the information these tasks and those of local units would require. The
nature and scope of local institutions would also have to be adjusted
to fit with the nature of newly central issues rather than with historically established boundaries, for example, with regional air
sheds rather than with existing state jurisdictions. One might well
have a set of local control institutions within a framework of central
tax collection, public statistics and forecasts, and administrative
law to limit externalities from and secure compensation for actions
of one local authority which impact unfavorably on others, for example, by exporting pollutants.

Grounds for policy choice will also have to be in keeping with
the five major policy objectives central to Vision I. Policy assessments will as a matter of standard operating procedure address net
effects on population, natural resource consumption, and environmental quality. They will explicitly identify immediate distributional
consequences for different groups in the population and estimate their
impacts on each of several future generations. Automatic review
procedures will be built into policies to insure that these estimates
are updated and used to modify earlier policy choices as warranted.
Whether or not these sorts of evaluative information are embodied
in an extended set of impact statements or rather become embodied
in routing policy appraisals is less important than their becoming
the bread and butter of policy formation and evaluation.

Of course, administrative organization and policy criteria fare no better than those charged with operations and implementation desire. Their incentives must also be adjusted appropriately. Personal conviction is of course one notable incentive. Historical experience gives us little reason to rely primarily on it as social change movements pass through their normal maturation from an emphasis on mobilization and agitation to an emphasis on administration.[12] We need to build in additional incentives to induce specialists and executives to behave in line with Vision I. Clearly, there have to be ways to link their rewards to low throughput criteria rather than to the familiar "bigger is better" criteria, for example, the larger the budget and the greater the number of subordinates, the higher are the rewards. Sanctions must be imposed for throughput overruns rather than treating them as justifications for larger resource shares. And the personnel system characteristics which decouple individual specialists and executives from policy consequences must be weakened. Useful instruments to provide appropriate incentives include zero-base budgeting, multiyear performance contracts, and personal visibility rather than anonymity.

Large numbers of citizens must also be provided with incentives in order to maintain participation and support for noncoercive redistribution. The proponents of Vision I cannot afford widespread desperation and pessimism about the future, convictions that individuals will fare badly whatever their current behavior because of their previous share of benefits, and perceptions that specialists and executives are hypocrites in distributional terms. A variety of constructive actions should be taken to achieve and maintain Vision I. First, the focus should be on the future of individuals and their offspring rather than on that of large institutions and social classes. For example, individual Americans may have positive expectations about their own life styles even though some large institutions will lose their accustomed autonomy and the United States as a whole will consume less in the way of depletable resources. Second, access and public information must be sufficient to deny credibility to charges of extremist conspiracies. Third, checks and balances which guarantee that distributional policies are reversible in response to citizen preferences must seem strong. Fourth, it will be important to stress the feasibility and efficacy of social action and political reconstruction rather than the inefficacy of noncoercive steps. Finally, it will be important to have as political leaders personalities whose past performance and personal affiliations fit with these emphases, that is, individuals who seem moderate and in touch with the life concerns of most of the population.

In managerial and political terms, it seems tempting to act as if Vision I can be achieved unilaterally and that the rest of the globe

can be ignored for practical purposes. It may indeed be easier to
achieve a coalition of the whole in this rich country if the problem
is defined as the United States in isolation from the rest of the world.
However, much of the balancing of population, resources, and environment called for by Vision I advocates cannot be achieved unilaterally. Also, it is difficult to see how the low-throughput objective can be achieved if there is massive external threat with a resulting need for massive allocations of resources to military programs.[13] Unless other powerful nations also move toward Vision I,
it may well be the case that U.S. restraint and moderation will not
culminate in the free and diverse society sought by Vision I advocates. We can accept this point without denying that some unilateral,
internal actions by the United States are needed to generate momentum toward restraint and moderation globally.

Global achievement and maintenance of Vision I have the general requirements noted earlier compounded by even greater existing distributional inequities and even more deep-seated fears and
antipathies. Also, problems of coordination multiply as the number
and diversity of participants increase. Some critical administrative
organizations, policies, and political processes are easily recognized.
First, it will be important to foster diversity rather than uniformity
in preferences for different commodities to be received at different
points in time. Universal desire for a "consumer society" will make
Vision I well nigh impossible. The instruments for fostering diversity fall in the realms of cultural and human rights policy. Diverse
content in cultural media calls for managing international and internal communications so that alternative models and values are presented to audiences. There is then a need to avoid domination, especially of the most powerful media in conveying images, by pro-
gramming which fosters any one set of commodity preferences. It
is equally important to provide access to the media as audience and
programmers to viewpoints held by those who do not control large
amounts of wealth and/or political power. Cultural policy can make
it possible for people to be exposed to diverse preferences. It does
not make it safe to espouse them actively. Short of centralized in-
trusion to protect dissent, a state of affairs unlikely to come about
and even less likely to be sustained, policies and institutions should
provide refuge for those who express preferences unpopular in a
particular local setting and lessen the costs they incur by having to
take refuge. By requiring diverse preferences globally, Vision I
implies international acceptance of the rights of persons to move
from one to another political unit with their property rights respected
through compensation.

Second, global restraint and moderation violates its throughput
objective unless it also provides effective measures to provide

security against those who reject restraint and moderation. Some
sort of quarantine capability is needed which does not in and of itself
require high throughput, which prevents the party in quarantine from
engaging in seriously damaging coercive actions, and which compensates parties who bear a disproportionate cost of implementing the
quarantine. This all amounts to collective security and seems unattainable without drastic amounts of disarmament (as distinct from
arms control) and a sufficient redistribution of military power so
that the efficacy of quarantine did not rely on the decisions of two or
three national regimes. In principle the leveling-down process of
disarmament could provide the high-throughput military items to
support quarantine actions. Beyond collective security, the effective deterrence of potential quarantine also requires collective subsidy for any party which bears heavy costs of cooperation in a quarantine action, for example, by financial transfers to defray the cost
of troops committed to a peace-keeping force or by raw material
transfers and market shares to those economically dependent on the
target of the quarantine.

Third, noncoercive strategies for global restraint and moderation will have to have strong and credible redistributive elements.
Otherwise injunctions to restraint and moderation will be interpreted
as a stratagem to preserve the status quo. Two directions seem important, if not in themselves sufficient, to deal with this obstacle to
Vision I. As an earnest of commitment to collective welfare, it will
be important to develop emergency stocks of scarce commodities for
the survival of populations in the poorer countries in shortage situations. Management institutions for the accumulation and distribution
of these stocks will have to be designed and staffed in ways which
constrain them from using the stocks for purposes other than pressing mass needs, for example, to eliminate indigenous producers.
As a more long-run step, it will be important to develop international terms of exchange institutions which insure that distributional
improvements as the result of shifts in relative prices do not recede
or simply serve as token changes. The hammering out of the values
to be embodied in international terms of exchange, beyond those the
more or less competitive market provides, will play a crucial role
in the transition to restraint and moderation. If the institutions involved are committed to preserving existing terms and their fluctuations, there seems little chance for noncoercive redistribution on a
global basis and thus for Vision I.

Obviously, the costs involved in generating arrangements of
any of the three kinds called for will be very substantial. They will
have to be borne primarily by those already rich in capital and
power very much including groups in the poorer countries who have
risen on platforms and personal desires far different from moderation

and restraint. And of course, the feasibility of redistribution across national lines without coercion can be no better than the extent to which it is accompanied by progress toward equity domestically.

VISION II: TECHNOLOGY AND ABUNDANCE

The advocates of our second vision, technology as the source of ever-greater abundance, are by no means advocates of business as usual. They do believe that massive development and application of relatively new technologies can effectively relax otherwise severe limits imposed by existing, economically accessible global resources. At least with regard to material wealth, they call for a high-throughput solution based on notions of technologically extending the set of inputs to production, expanding their stock, and essentially avoiding the constraints of depletion.[14] The breeder reactor is a familiar example. The vision of technology and abundance seems to call for public policies which

generate and maintain massive flows of resources into new technologies;

weigh material benefits in the future more heavily than material benefits in the present;

weigh material benefits more heavily than negative second-order effects on other values;

insure support for and acceptance of new technologies regardless of their negative second-order effects or unresolved questions about their control, costs, and effectiveness;

maintain and stimulate aspirations for material abundance for future generations;

set aside correction of inequitable distributions to pursue growth in the absolute supply of inputs to the production of finished goods and in the volume of production material items.

These public policies once again require a policy process with a very long time perspective compared to that normally found in U.S. politics. The type of complexity required, while also substantial, differs in some important respects from that implicit in Vision I. The scope and complexity recognized by Vision II proponents is that of systems management in the development of complex systems where analogues are the Manhattan Project and the role of NASA in the heyday of the U.S. space program.[15] That is, technical specialists are amply funded to engage in intricate management of the technology system and its human operators but only relate to most of society as highly valued magicians. Indeed, a major administrative and political

task is to maintain such splendid isolation until the horn of plenty
is fully ready to produce.

There is little doubt that those who put forward Vision II also
are strongly opposed to stagnation, conformity, dullness, and oppression. Indeed they present themselves as more opposed to these
bad, gray states of affairs than the advocates of Vision I. However,
once again much remains undiscussed about the needed politics.
Vision II proponents say little about how we can have a political system which will provide the resources and latitude called for in a
time of absolute shortages and still have an open and generally vital
society. They apparently are not loath to propose Faustian bargains,
in Weinberg's phrase, with technology.[16] But they say little about
the essential selfishness of the Faustian bargain, the morality of
making future generations its signatory, or our limited ability to
know the probability that the bargain will turn out to have been a
disastrous mistake.

The goals of Vision II call for a society most of whose members accept the programs of their leaders and participate primarily
as members of a disciplined work force. Alienation and active discontent run counter to Vision II since they will reduce the productive
energies required to develop and procure the abundance bearing new
technologies. They will drain resources from this goal by creating
pressures for current consumption, requirements for coercive institutions to maintain the civic order, diversions from rational systems management practices. Decisions should be left to specialists
and executives.

Participation beyond the contribution of labor and a variety of
pride-taking activities in national technological progress runs counter to Vision II. So too do diverse values intensely pursued. These
can only fracture the consensus required for the efficient pursuit of
abundance through technology. Vision II calls for a homogeneous
preference for material abundance available to succeeding generations. While orderly development and phasing in of successive generations of technology does call for some diversity about when in the
future the benefits should become available, preferences for current
material gratification are unacceptable. Secondary values may vary
widely so long as they do not impede the expeditious development of
new technologies. For example, a value on environmental quality
which impedes the development of new energy sources runs counter
to Vision II strategies. Individuals wishing to spend some leisure
walking a nature trail while others prefer attending rock concerts
does not. Indeed, some preferences for values which can be met by
low throughput in the present help damp current consumption demand
and thus aid the quest for Vision II so long as these preferences are
subordinate to the value of future material plenty.

Some implications for politics begin to emerge from the need for a disciplined, patient, and quiescent labor force. First, citizens must believe that their descendants will be able to benefit from the future abundance, whatever differences in the material position of their parents--that is, there must be social confidence in the principle of equal opportunity. Second, citizens must believe in the competence of the autonomous specialists and executives who are directing technological change and in their commitment to future general abundance--that is, they must respect and trust ruling elites and technocrats. Third, there must be sufficient economic abundance for most citizens to forego pressing for additional immediate material goods or coming to feel that their labor is not justly rewarded. In part, this requires secure provision of the necessities of life after years of productive labor--for example, social security. Fourth, while the previous implication does not call for complete economic equality, it does limit the differential economic incentives which can be available for specialists and executives. Minimally, it implies that differential wealth should be awarded only for contributing to the technology which will provide future abundance and not for other activities. Fifth, current acceptance by the labor force of their material situation must not damp aspirations for their descendants to have more or nourish beliefs that the existing material state of affairs will last without continuing labor discipline and hard work. If the prod of higher aspirations for future generations is unavailable or weak, Vision II advocates require widespread recognition of threats (from man or nature) to current levels of material consumption. If the incentives provided by such aspirations and threats become too weak, the resources for new technology and the autonomy its managerial midwives seek will vanish.

It is worth noting some corollaries of the previous discussion. After a generation of massive increases in abundance, the likelihood of unmet material aspirations on the part of its beneficiaries declines. So too does the willingness of population segments which have not benefited proportionately to accept their lot quietly. In this situation, threats provide badly needed stimuli to pursue Vision II. The threats which are perceived by Vision I advocates can suffice admirably for this purpose. They are particularly valuable because they do not seem manageable by the military expenditures which might otherwise drain resources from the development of civil technologies to provide abundance. The extent to which such threats will provide the momentum Vision II advocates require will of course depend on the treatment of the other implications discussed above. If citizens perceive changes for the worse in equal opportunity, social security, and the basis for differing material incentives, the threats will have to be especially credible to motivate the labor force. Of course, credibility will suffer if citizens widely believe that the very same specialists and executives who proclaim the threats have played falsely with the citizenry in the past about equal opportunity, social security, and the basis for special economic benefits.

Vision II like Vision I requires appropriate administrative organizations, grounds for policy choice, and incentives for citizens, specialists, and executives. Administratively, organizations need to be structured and assigned missions in line with the technology and abundance goals, that is, by major resource and technology families. A highly centralized authoritative organization should exist for each major technology family under intensive development and have the authority to secure from the resource departments what it needs in terms of capital, materials, and manpower. The tasks of coordinating institutions will be to monitor potential shortages in the resources needed by the technology directorates, enforce efficiency according to systems management standards in the development of new technologies, and vigorously assess the extent to which alternative possible technologies will contribute to abundance. Human resource tasks will be centralized increasingly to insure the availability of needed skills and the various welfare and compensation standards necessary for continued labor-force morale. The role of local administrative organizations, other than monitoring compliance with central plans and directives, will vary. To the extent that the population can be imbued with an ideology of effort in the service of future plenty--or the belief that it is crucial for national survival--the forms of local discretion will be observed within a guiding line from the center. In the absence of such an ideology or perception of necessity, all authority will have to reside in central, specialized institutions. Whatever the degree of centralization of control, the systems management approach implies that administrative organizations will be staffed by technocrats, including management scientists, more than by lawyers and will arrive at decisions more through a set of formal analytic procedures than by adversarial litigation.

Grounds for policy choice will have to be in keeping with the six major policy objectives of Vision II. Policy assessments will routinely address net effects on resources available for pursuit of new technologies including capital, skilled manpower, entrepreneurial energy, raw materials, and machinery. They will compare new technology possibilities with each other with respect to the future provision of material abundance given resource constraints but will not compare them on other grounds. They will consider the probable effectiveness of different presentation strategies to gain popular acceptance and keep attention away from nonmaterial consequences. These policy desiderata will be used in the context of a warning system about decay in labor force morale and in material aspirations for descendants.

Incentives for specialists and executives will also have to complement the requirements of Vision II. Rewards should be tied to the development and use of new technologies and not solely to budget and organizational size. Some mode of calculation of individual contributions to such developments which looks at the criticality of a person's contribution will need to be developed and used. Since the point of the new technologies is to achieve abundance, there will need to be incentives which support concern with the net contribution of the technology to abundance, that is, ones which subtract the consumption involved in creating and operating the technology from its output. Efficiency will be valued more than spectacular technical innovation. Given that the results will not be known for many years, specialists and executives must be placed in a regime which compensates them for their efforts in relation to their eventual consequences and not their current popularity. Devices for contingent benefits and penalties such as "stock" in the new technology held in escrow for the participant specialists and executives until ten years after it goes into operation illustrate this principle.

Incentives needed for citizens are those which follow from the points we discussed earlier to meet the need for a cooperative labor force. Some of these can be provided by familiar governmental programs or government-induced programs, for example, equal opportunity, social security. Others have to do directly with conceptions of the good citizen and obligations to society. The life style of hard work and delayed material gratification inherent in Vision II requires a supportive belief system and will crumble under socialization and ideology which stress the right to be supported by others and to secure as much in the way of material benefits as one can as fast as one can.

Once again, unilateral pursuit of a preferred future, in this case that of Vision II, seems more tractable than dealing with the globe as a whole. And once again treating the problem as if the United States existed in isolation seems impractical. The resources required for the development of appropriate new technologies may have to be procured abroad. Foreign cooperation may well be required to maintain flows of current consumables at prices which allow for massive investment in new technologies and to insure that the new technologies will prove useful to their owners. Issues involving energy well illustrate these kinds of dependency. And foreign regimes and movements will have to behave with sufficient restraint so that the resources needed for civil technology and maintaining labor force morale do not have to be diverted into military preparedness. There seems little reason to expect others to unilaterally sacrifice their sources of abundance--for example, deplete their mineral reserves--or to fail to defend their market position

vis-a-vis the new technologies--for example, by cutting oil prices--
or to refrain from developing military establishments which can be
used to bargain for an increasing share of global wealth. Even if
they somehow agree to leave the rich members of OECD alone to
develop and acquire the abundance-producing technologies while the
rest of the world pursues current consumption and military investment, it seems reasonable to expect that the long-run consequence
will be demands to benefit from that abundance from those who did
not contribute to its realization. An illustrative, if perhaps unduly
dramatic, instance might be the future behavior of a heavily armed
but food-deficient Soviet Union toward a militarily inferior but food-
surplus United States.

The international politics conducive to Vision II are analogous
to those for its pursuit by a particular nation. There must be the
international equivalent of an equal opportunity doctrine for future
generations as distinct from the perpetuation of current wealth
classes. There must be international confidence in the commitment
of the developers of new technologies to abundance in all continents
and for all races. There must be a tolerable current standard of
living and general belief in the efficacy of work and delayed gratification rather than an atmosphere of intense privation and desperation. These requirements clearly cannot be met if the development
of the new technologies remains monopolized by the rich countries
and their diffusion lies under the control of existing multinational
corporations. Significant authority over development and diffusion
or transfer must lie with bodies responsible to a global constituency.
The new technologies should not be treated as proprietary to their
national developers or private-sector manufacturers. That state of
affairs will not give most national leaders confidence in widespread
abundance. Institutions which promise widespread dispersion of
future benefits must be accompanied by short-term measures to
lessen current stringencies for a large share of the world's population. Concern with the future is a luxury available only to those who
have a tolerable present.

How can we combine immediate transfers of wealth from the
populations which must provide the new technologies and at the same
time secure commitments by donors and recipients to the sort of
labor discipline which Vision II must have? Simple notions of equal
standards of living for all or even automatic ceilings on current consumption to allow a surplus for the global poor will not suffice. No
labor force will work for others unless it believes that they are also
making a significant contribution to their own needs and are showing
commitment to the future of technology and abundance. Accordingly,
transfers will not happen in ways which facilitate Vision II unless
there is compliance with a number of conditions, compliance perceived

by the donor population. These conditions include: (1) sturdy safeguards to assume that the resources transferred are not used to
bolster regimes which themselves are channeling massive resources
into military expenditures or to the current gratification of the indigenous rich; (2) serious efforts by the recipients to build consensus
in their own society in support of the work discipline and orientation
toward the future which characterizes the donor population; and (3)
integrative actions which forge bonds to insure that the recipients
will not move into alignments hostile to the donors on grounds not
open to distributive reconciliation, for example, on grounds of race
or territorial aspiration.

The measures necessary for the effective global pursuit of
Vision II require all parties to share influence over current and
future policies. Just as they do not allow for the rich to maintain
exclusive property rights in the technologies for abundance, they do
not allow for the poorer nations to maintain claims on the labor of
others regardless of their own efforts.

Our sketch of the politics and policies inherent in the vision of
restraint and moderation and that of technology and abundance suggests three common elements. First, both suffer if massive resources go to coercive instruments. The garrison state is not the
appropriate strategy in either case.[17] Second, both call for actions
which span national boundaries and recognize global interactions.
Third, both are to be achieved in situations where there are genuine
problems of differing interests and notable grounds for doubting the
good faith of other parties. Taken together, these points argue
against a transition strategy emphasizing monolithic central authority. There seems little reason to expect such an authority to develop
or survive without massive suppression which neither vision can afford. We are left with the alternative of coordinated action on a
global basis resting on increased recognition of the set of realities
which impinge on the successful pursuit of Vision I and Vision II and
demonstrations of willingness to proceed accordingly on a recipro-
cal, matching basis.

NOTES

1. For examples, see Kenneth E. Boulding, "Is Scarcity
Dead?" The Public Interest, no. 5 (Fall 1966): 36–44; Herman
E. Daly, ed., Toward a Steady-State Economy (San Francisco:
W. H. Freeman, 1973); Jay W. Forrester, World Dynamics (Cam-
bridge: Wright-Allen, 1971); "The No-Growth Society," Daedalus
102 (Fall 1974); National Goals Research Staff, Toward Balanced
Growth (Washington, D.C.: U.S. Government Printing Office, 1970);

H. S. D. Cole et al., Models of Doom (New York: Universe Books, 1973); Donella H. Meadows et al., The Limits to Growth (New York: Universe Books, 1972); Mihajlo Mesarovic and Edward Pestel, Mankind at the Turning Point (New York: E. P. Dutton, 1974); The Planetary Product in 1972, U.S. Department of State News Release, RESS-46, December 15, 1973.

2. An exceptionally extensive discussion is provided by Dennis C. Pirages and Paul R. Ehrlich, ARK II: Social Responses to Environmental Imperatives (San Francisco: W. H. Freeman, 1974), 117-87.

3. For more or less supportive and critical evaluations of Leviathan in this context, see William Ophuls, "Prologue to a Political Theory of the Steady State," Ph.D. dissertation, Department of Political Science, Yale University, 1973 as well as his "Leviathan or Oblivion," in Daly, op. cit., pp. 215-30, and "Locke's Paradigm Lost," paper presented at the 1973 Annual Meeting of the American Political Science Association, New Orleans, September 4-8, 1973; Desmond P. Ellis, "The Hobbesian Problem of Order," American Sociological Review 36 (August 1971): 692-703; John M. Orbell and Brent M. Rutherford, "Can Leviathan Make the Life of Man Less Solitary, Poor, Nasty, Brutish and Short?" British Journal of Political Science 3 (October 1973): 383-407; David Robertson, "Well, Does Leviathan . . .?" British Journal of Political Science 4 (April 1974): 245-56; John M. Orbell and Brent M. Rutherford, "Social Peace as a Collective Good," British Journal of Political Science 4 (October 1974): 501-10.

4. For illustrative discussions, see Garrett Hardin, "The Tragedy of the Commons," in Daly, op. cit., pp. 33-48; Thomas C. Schelling, "On the Ecology of Micromotives," The Public Interest, no. 25 (Fall 1971): 61-98, and "Hockey Helmets, Concealed Weapons, and Daylight Saving," Journal of Conflict Resolution 17 (September 1973): 381-428.

5. For illustrative discussions, see Alfred E. Kahn, "The Tyranny of Small Decisions," Kyklos 19 (1966): 23-45; Albert O. Hirschman, "The Principle of the Hiding Hand," in his Development Projects Observed (Washington, D.C.: Brookings Institution, 1967), pp. 9-34.

6. For general treatments of the issues involved in coordination and redistribution, see Charles E. Lindblom, The Intelligence of Democracy (New York: The Free Press, 1965); Robert E. Goodin, Political Rationality (London: Wiley, 1976); Harold M. Hochman and George E. Peterson, eds., Redistribution through Public Choice (New York: Columbia University Press, 1974), as well as Hochman's paper with James D. Rogers, "The Simple Politics of Distributional Preference," presented at the Conference on Income and Wealth of

the National Bureau of Economic Research, Ann Arbor, May 15-16, 1974; and Benjamin Ward, "Majority Rule and Allocation," Journal of Conflict Resolution 5 (December 1961): 379-89.

7. For a discussion at greater length of the issues involved in political design, see Davis Bobrow, "Transitions to Preferred World Futures," in Planning Alternative World Futures, ed. Louis Rene Beres and Harry T. Targ (New York: Praeger, 1975), pp. 93-130.

8. For useful overview discussion on international interdependence, see Hayward R. Alker, Jr., Lincoln P. Bloomfield, and Nazli Choucri, Analyzing Global Interdependence, Vols. I-IV (Cambridge: Massachusetts Institute of Technology, Center for International Studies, November 1974); David S. Blake and Robert S. Walters, The Politics of Global Economic Relations (Englewood Cliffs, N.J.: Prentice-Hall, 1976); "Symposium: New Directions for International Institutions," International Organization 30 (Spring 1976): 309-72.

9. Herman E. Daly, "The Steady-State Economy," in Daly, op. cit., p. 152.

10. William Ophuls, "Leviathan or Oblivion," in Daly, op. cit., p. 223.

11. For some especially suggestive discussions of election and representation systems, see Arthur Levenglick, "Fair and Reasonable Election Systems," Behavioral Science 20 (January 1975): 34-46; Edwin T. Haefele, Representative Government and Environmental Management (Baltimore: Johns Hopkins University Press, 1973).

12. See Harold D. Lasswell, Daniel Lerner, and C. Easton Rothwell, The Comparative Study of Elites (Stanford, Calif.: Stanford University Press, 1952).

13. Any attention to the immediate and long-term costs of military preparedness and waging war provides "evidential overkill" on this point. For example, see the Stockholm International Peace Research Institute (SIPRI) Yearbooks entitled World Armaments and Disarmament published by the MIT Press, and the U.S. government estimates of the costs of wars the United States has participated in including an estimate for the Vietnam War of $352 billion in Congressional Record-Senate, February 8, 1974, pp. S1598-9.

14. For some illustrative views, see Robert L. Heilbroner, "Growth and Survival," Foreign Affairs 51 (October 1972): 139-53; Carl Kaysen, "The Computer That Printed Out W*O*L*F," Foreign Affairs 50 (July 1972): 660-68; Harold J. Barnett, "Economic Growth and Environmental Quality Are Compatible," Policy Sciences 5 (1974): 137-47 and his volume with C. Morse, Scarcity and Growth (Baltimore: Johns Hopkins University Press, 1965); Alvin M. Weinberg, "Social Institutions and Nuclear Energy," Science 177 (July 7,

1972): 27-34; Glenn T. Seaborg and William R. Corliss, Man and Atom (New York: E. P. Dutton, 1971).

15. On doubts about the feasibility of systems management in this context, see Daniel C. Drucker, "The Engineer in the Establishment," Bulletin of the Atomic Scientists 27 (December 1971): 31-34; and Richard Nelson, "Intellectualizing about the Moon-Ghetto Metaphor," Policy Sciences 5 (December 1974): 375-414.

16. Weinberg, op. cit., p. 33.

17. Harold D. Lasswell, "The Garrison State and Specialists on Violence," American Journal of Sociology 46 (January 1941): 455-68.

10

PROPERTY RIGHTS, ECOLOGICAL LIMITS, AND THE STEADY-STATE SOCIETY

Peter G. Stillman

Issues that relate to property are central to modern life. The questions of the rights to and distribution of property have always been crucial in social, economic, political, and legal debates and struggles. Similarly, property rights and ecological problems are closely tied; ecological problems, sometimes caused in part by a particular definition of property rights, may frequently be only or best resolved by a redefinition of those rights. For instance, by regarding air and water as free resources without exclusive ownership, that is, by regarding the air and water as a commons on which the "tragedy of the commons" could be played out, society established property rights such that pollution was facilitated, since the costs of polluting were not borne by the polluter. To mitigate such pollution will require a change in rights.

Despite the importance of property, however, property rights are studied only infrequently,[1] and current conceptions of property tend to be fairly crude. The standard dichotomy in most laymen's minds is that between private property--as in capitalism--and state-owned property--as in (especially Russian) socialism. But it is easily apparent that neither extreme of the dichotomy has ever existed. "Free and complete" capitalistic private property has in fact always been limited by the state--by taxes, eminent domain, the common law about nuisances, and the police power, which forbids

This chapter owes much to many individuals and institutions. It was supported by grants from the American Philosophical Society and Vassar College and by suggestions and comments from Natalie Marshall and Michael Kraft, as well as the general assistance of my colleagues in the Political Science Department and of many of the participants at the Conference.

the ownership of certain items, like LSD or counterfeit money. Conversely, socialistic or state-owned property has never extended to include personal property like clothes, toothbrushes, and sometimes luxury villas on the Black Sea.

Further, in ecological matters this dichotomy may be positively misleading. Robert Heilbroner is only one of the many who see current human problems as stemming not from one particular economic system but from the general system of industrialization, whose values include the "vandal ideology" of homocentric economic growth, abetted by highly rationalized and efficient means of production, and whose ideology shapes the goals of the unindustrialized.[2] That communist Russia, economically mixed Japan, and capitalist United States all share serious ecological problems is evidence to support Heilbroner's view. In short, the usual dichotomy between private and state-owned property is inaccurate and misleading.

A clearer understanding of property may be gained from a study of some explicitly articulated definitions of property. In general, "private property" has been the usual form of property in the Western world since the end of feudalism. Private property has usually been defined in fairly absolute terms in principle, though these terms have always been limited by other details of the law and by other legal principles. The Austrian Civil Code of 1811, for instance, defined ownership as the "right to use, abuse or ignore, destroy, transfer or abandon" any thing;[3] this code remained in effect for much of central Europe for a long time--until after World War II in Czechoslovakia. Blackstone, the English jurist, saw the right of property as "that sole and despotic dominion which one man claims and exercises over the external things of the world, in total exclusion of the right of any other individual in the universe."[4] In these legal definitions, the right to property is the right to use a thing in any way; contained in the right to use is the right to exclude others from use; and the right also includes the right to alienate, relinquish, or transfer the thing. In short, private property involves the rights to use, to exclude, and to alienate.

These traditional definitions of private property had a variety of traditional justifications. Locke, for instance, justified private property because it was a reward for human labor.[5] Andrew Carnegie, among others, saw private property as a public trust, of which the owner was the temporary trustee; by his work and skill, he increased the wealth of the earth, and what he owned he had for his use for a limited time. Thus, of Carnegie's vast stock of wealth, little went as inheritance to his children; most went as charitable gifts, to fulfill the public trust.[6] Hegel saw in private property one major means for the individual's exercise and development of his human faculties of, for instance, unfettered creativity and rational choice, in that private property guaranteed the individual an exclusive locus in which to act.[7]

But the traditional definitions cannot accommodate one of the major changes of the twentieth century: the development and prolif- eration of the large corporation. In the modern corporation, prop- erty is bifurcated: The link is dissolved that bound the formal own- ership of property with the power, responsibility, and substance of ownership.[8] While the stockholders are the formal owners, the managers of the corporation are the effective controllers of the assets and power of the corporation. The shareholders have legal ownership without personal control: Managers, lacking legal owner- ship, nonetheless have the control--of use, exclusion, and aliena- tion--over the assets of the corporation, within very broad limits.

The bifurcation between ownership and control in the modern corporation is an important change in the definition of property, with many implications, two of which are important in this context. The first is that the traditional justifications of private property no longer apply. For Locke, an individual's property was an expression of his own labor and efforts. Now, however, the wealth of an owner, that is, a shareholder, is primarily an expression of the efforts of others-- his managers. For Carnegie, the individual's property was a public trust. Now, however, the individual is in no position to act as trustee, because the managers control the assets of the immortal corporation. (Any manager acting as trustee--which is done to some extent--is limited, much more than was Carnegie, by the requirements of his corporate role and the immortality of his corporation.) For Hegel, property was valuable because its exercise extended and developed the human personality; but Adolf Berle is explicit that modern prop- erty has none of that potential: "When an individual invests capital in the large corporation, he grants to the corporate management all power to use that capital to create, produce, and develop. . . . He is an almost completely inactive recipient . . . he must look else- where for opportunity to produce or create."[9] The traditional justi- fications of private property no longer justify private property.

The second important implication of the separation of owner- ship and control is the breaking of whatever responsibility to self and others may derive from the direct link whereby the controller of a thing is also its owner. The owner of a small business lives in the same community as his business. He thus has feelings toward his community and his fellows; he must see and live in the output, of goods (and bads), of his business; and he is subject to social pres- sure when the bads become too great. The managers of a large corporation, on the other hand, are usually independent of the com- munity in which their plants are located; and their representatives in those communities, the local managers, are subject to pressure

from the top managers to fulfill quotas, pressure that frequently op-
poses and overpowers the community's pressure. In other words,
in a large corporation the ultimate managers are absentee managers,
insulated from community feelings and pressure; and the local managers are subject to pressure from the top managers. Before the
large corporation or outside its sphere, there remains some link between ownership and responsibility; but where large industrial units
exist, that link is broken; and the large units are irresponsible.

The split between ownership and control has led to a loss in
the responsibility that can inhere in private property and to the in-
validation of traditional justifications of private property. The new
justification of the large corporation--that it can deliver the goods
for the consumers--has also been laid open to serious doubt. Berle,
overoptimistically, dreamed that "in broadest outline we are plotting
the course by which the twentieth century in America is expected to
produce an evolving economic Utopia, and, apparently, the potential
actually exists, bringing that dangerous and thrilling adventure within
human reach for the first time in recorded history."[10] Yet the ecological unsoundness of this impending "utopia," this imagined cornu-
copia of consumer goods, has been shown, in the other chapters of
this book, to be almost transparently clear. Similarly, the modern
corporation seems empirically to lack the guiding "conscience,"
asserted for it by Berle, that would limit ecological transgressions.[11]

It is important to note that the same analysis holds for communist countries. There, "the people" or "the workers" have formal
ownership, the managers the actual control. This bifurcation between ownership and control undermines the Marxian justifications
for communist property. While Marx justified communism because
it would produce equality and eliminate alienation, the rise of a
managerial stratum in communist countries means inequalities in
wealth, authority, and social influence; it also results in the worker's
being alienated (in Marx's terms), since he produces not for himself
but at the command of an other. Replacing Marx's justification is
the promise that communism can produce more consumer goods than
capitalism--that is, that communism can bring about Berle's "economic Utopia" more rapidly than capitalism. But this communist
ideal is as ecologically unsound as its noncommunist counterpart.

The "twentieth-century capitalist revolution" of Anglo-American,
Western European advanced industrial society (and its communist and
Third World idolaters) has a new definition of property which lacks the
traditional justifications, lacks the responsibility of property, and
bears a large measure of responsibility for the ecological problems
of the present. That conception of property, then, must be rejected
as invalid for the contemporary world and certainly inadequate for an
ecologically sound world in which limited growth might be conjoined

with some modicum of political freedom, social community, legal
justice, and individual development.

TOWARD AN ECOLOGICALLY SOUND
CONCEPTION OF PROPERTY

A simple but superficial way to solve the theoretical problem
of property rights within a limited-growth economy is to posit that
all ownership and control be vested in a strong central government
that is to use its power in an ecologically sound manner. But there
are a number of problems with the idea of the ecological efficacy of
a strong, interventionist government controlling all property. Such
a government would have to be expert in all matters of ecological
fact; it would have to be well-intentioned (and not, for instance, out
to destroy individuals on an "enemies list," nor corrupted by power);
it would have to be effective in implementing its policies; and it
would have to maintain popular support, or at least not produce a
lack of popular consent. Merely to state these requirements is to
indicate how tenuous it is to postulate an expert, well-intentioned,
effective, popular government that actively intervenes and controls
all property. [12]

A different approach to ecological soundness and limited growth
is to analyze property rights in some detail. Rather than conceptualize private property as the free and complete right to use (and abuse,
ignore, and destroy), to exclude, and to alienate, it may be helpful
to conceptualize property as containing various degrees and kinds of
rights to use, exclusion, and alienation, or, to employ a different
terminology, to conceptualize private property (and all property) in
terms of "property rights," where the owner has some rights, and
is prohibited some others. In any concrete situation of private property, such as my owning my car, I have certain rights of use--I can
use it almost at will on my own land, I can use it on public highways
so long as I obey traffic laws--but certain rights of use are prohibited
me by the state--for instance, I cannot use by car on highways if it is
unlicensed or if I am under 16, I cannot use it to run over another
person, or to create a nuisance designed to annoy my neighbor; the
criminal and civil laws prohibit these uses, and thus they are not
part of my rights of use of my car. Similarly, while I can exclude
most others from using my car, I cannot exclude a policeman from
commandeering and using it. I can sell my car to whomever I
please; but if the object in this example were a gun and not a car, I
would have the right to sell it only to certain classes of persons (for
instance, those who are not convicted felons). In contemporary
society and in any sustainable society, individuals have and will have

certain rights to use, exclude, and alienate certain things, and will
be prohibited certain other "rights" by society and government.

When property-related issues are conceptualized in terms of
legally defined property rights, then it can be seen that many reforms are matters of property rights, that is, the expanding or con-
tracting of the number or conditions of the rights to use, exclude,
and alienate. Thus, some means whereby to reform a society from
being a resource-squandering "cowboy" economy to an ecologically
sound limited- or no-growth economy, and some ways for maintaining that economy, are to extend, reformulate, and--where necessary--
limit property rights.   (Since property rights are so closely bound
not only to strictly ecological issues but also to so many aspects of
the social order, the effect of the proposed property rights changes
on the distribution of wealth, political freedom, and the like are
frequently noted. In general, the proposed changes would enhance
freedom, reduce wealth inequalities, and develop human capacities.)

SOME EXTENSIONS OF PROPERTY RIGHTS

Some ecologically sound changes involve extending property
rights. In general, these extensions are reforms more likely in the
short run than most proposed reforms, since they build in a dominant U.S. ideology and since they frequently involve extensions of
current trends. Likewise, they are reforms which, once legislated,
in effect carry their own enforcement with them, since the injured
individual has a direct interest in suing to have his rights upheld--
unlike, for instance, a regulatory agency, which might be interested
primarily in helping the "regulated." Since most of the extensions
of property rights discussed below have been treated elsewhere at
length, the presentation here will be brief.

1. Amenity rights.[13] From the point of view of both ecological problems and the quality of life in a limited- or no-growth society, amenity rights--the rights to a clean and quiet environment--
are important. Basically, amenity rights are an extension of the
right to exclude; the individual has the right to exclude power-
lawnmower noise, or electric-power-plant pollution, from his ears
and air, and the right to sue if his property right of exclusion is infringed. Particularly in light of J. K. Galbraith's analysis of how
the affluent society cannot produce for public wants the way it can
for private wants,[14] amenity rights give the individual a chance to
sue to enforce what ultimately turn out to be public wants (or at least
public benefits), since not only the individual but also most of his
neighbors benefit from the individual's enforcing his amenity rights.

2. Modifying the right to alienate. Traditional property rights theory sees the origin of the right to alienate (or sell) in the right to relinquish, that is, to let a thing fall ownerless by abandoning it. Most traditional property rights theories also see the right to relinquish as being rare, now that contracts are common and things can be sold. Unfortunately, it is frequently forgotten that much pollution is, basically, property that has been relinquished (and not sold, because it has no positive economic value). To eliminate the right to relinquish would be to insist that a producer--of pollution of any sort--continues to own the pollutants and thus is responsible for any damage done by the pollutants. (Since a specific polluter's exact liability might be difficult to prove, a different version of a class-action suit might be instituted: The suit is filed as at present, but it can be filed against a single polluter or, where specific liability cannot be proven, against a class of polluters. Also, of course, the government could act against the polluters.)

3. Standing to sue.[15] One central part of property rights--part of the right to use--involves the right to sue, if the individual thinks his right to use has been infringed. Despite the unpopularity of the Mineral King decision (where the Sierra Club was denied standing in its attempt to enjoin the grant of federal permits allowing Walt Disney, Inc., to develop a resort on National Forest land), and despite the difficulties, ambiguities, and inconsistencies in the decision itself,[16] it is clear that the Supreme Court would have granted standing to an individual user of Mineral King or to the Sierra Club as representative of its members who are users. In any case where the public trust may be threatened with misuse, an individual user of the trust in question may be found, and he can serve as the (formal) plaintiff in the suit.

Another crucial aspect of standing to sue--crucial especially because of recent adverse court rulings--is the continuation and expansion of the class-action suit. When illegal ecological damage has occurred, legal recourse should be possible no matter how little the damage or how numerous the class of plaintiffs. When all members of the class cannot be located and thus informed or paid, or when the costs of doing so are prohibitive, the award should go into a general environmental trust fund, to further ecologically sound practices.

4. The public trust.[17] Especially air and frequently water have been regarded as goods in infinite supply, and therefore free. It is, of course, now obvious that neither clear air nor clean water are in infinite supply. Furthermore, a sort of Gresham's law applies when there are competing uses for air and water: The bad use drives out the good, as, for example, the polluting factory or municipal sewerage plant kills the fish, makes swimming unpleasant, and

fouls tap water. Rather than air and water being unrestricted common property which each and all have the property right to use, it
is necessary to establish some limits on the right of use, in order
both to limit pollution and to assure that all users have the effective
right to use.

For instance, the Germans, in the Ruhr Valley, have effectively established limits on the right of use of rivers. Some rivers
can be polluted almost at will (that is, can be used for pollution only);
others, kept unpolluted, are available for neutral or positive uses.
The German approach, far from a desirable solution in the long run,
is an advance.

Some of the U.S. environmental legislation of the past five
years seems to be moving, if haltingly, in a slightly different direction in limiting the rights of use of common property. This legislation returns in part to the ancient Roman tradition that public waters
and lands (and air) are held in trust by the government for the people,
that it is the responsibility of the government to guarantee their reasonable use in the light not of particular interests but of the general
good, and that individual citizens can insist that the government live
up to its trusteeship, in procedure if not in substance (for example,
an environmental impact statement is necessary in government
projects). In order to guarantee continuing rights of use to its citizens, the government limits the right of use to polluters, by holding
the common property in trust.

5. The new property.[18] Charles Reich's long and able article
about the new property--rights or privileges that an individual can
claim from the government or its agencies because he holds a certain status--strongly suggests that the rights of property ought and
must be expanded to these granted privileges. The mazes of privileges allocated by regulatory boards and licensing bureaus in the
modern administrative state are very complex, unbounded by the
rule of law, and fraught at present with inequities and injustices
that are irremediable; the individual can obtain justice and equity,
predictability and assurance, only if these privileges come to be
treated like most property rights and include, for example, recourse
to the courts in the case where they are revoked by a board acting
as prosecutor, judge, and jury. Among these "new property" rights,
one crucial right--for a limited- or no-growth society necessarily
concerned with the distribution of income--is the right to a guaranteed annual income. Almost equally important, "new property"
rights that involve governmental relaxing of ecological laws or allowing pollution must explicitly be rights of limited, not eternal,
duration.

6. Guaranteed subsistence. In a world in which essential
items--fuels and foods--are coming to be in scarce and erratic

supply, subsistence rights are important, as an aspect of or addition to a guaranteed annual income. Each family unit would be given the right to obtain, at reasonable cost, enough of given commodities in order to subsist--for example, enough fuel to heat a small-to-average-size house with adequate insulation to 65°, enough gasoline to drive the average distance to the supermarket once a week. The rights would be stringently set, to encourage people to insulate their homes adequately and to live near food markets; but they would be generous enough to assure subsistence in time of scarcity and need. (Implicit in this proposal is a Pareto optimal definition of justice: everyone is equal in having his essential needs met; beyond essential needs, however, inequality prevails.)

7. The elimination of existing commons. Much of the world is still a commons, open to exploitation by all. Merely to extend some property rights in that commons to some party would help limit environmental degradation. For instance, the oceans will almost surely be ecologically more sound and economically more productive when states' offshore limits are expanded and states' rights over fish established.

EXCURSUS: LIABILITY, EXTERNALITIES, AND RONALD COASE

The suggestions in the previous section (especially items 1-4) generally place the legal liability for pollution on the producer of pollution. While this locating of liability may seem prima facie to make sense, it does not take into account the influential argument by Ronald Coase, who deals at length with the "problem of social costs."[19] Basically, Coase argues that liability for externalities will be handled most efficiently by the market, that is, that the total social cost-benefit will be maximized when individuals are left to negotiate among themselves on how to deal with externalities, including pollution. While this chapter is not the place to criticize Coase's argument at length, at least two crucial problems are directly relevant.

The first is an ecological one. Basically, Coase asserts that the free market with free negotiation will lead to the optimal allocation of resources to competing uses, where some of the uses are polluting and some are not. Even if Coase's theoretical argument about optimality be correct, it is crucial to note that Coase assumes that the costs of pollution are measurable, that they are measurable by the parties who are negotiating, and that--so long as the negotiating parties can agree--the pollution can continue. But there is doubt that economists can accurately measure pollution costs--and this doubt is based not only on technical or practical problems (which are great) but on essential theoretical reasons. Economic cost-benefit analysis takes into account the idea that a pleasure deferred into the future is worth less than one enjoyed today; future costs and benefits are "discounted," the way loans are. When the usual economic discounting is applied to ecological costs (or any other costs and benefits), the effect is to reduce (or "discount") to zero all costs (and benefits) that are more than about 20 years in the future. For every-day economic planning and for the usual benefits and costs, this discounting is effective, indeed necessary and valuable. But for measuring ecological costs, this discounting can be totally misleading. If it is true that Freon is slowly separating the ozone in the upper atmosphere so that eventually the lethal X-rays from the sun will make their way in great numbers to earth, then economic cost analysis is misleading, because the disaster coming from Freon, being more than 20 years in the future, is, in economics, discounted to zero. In short, although it is sensible to discount in most cases (and necessary for economic efficiency and rationality), the use of discounting is misleading in the case of gradually accumulating and eventually irreversible costs, like some ecological costs.

There are additional important problems in terms of measurement. Even if economic cost analysis could take care of the problem of a too-hasty discounting of disaster, would the negotiating parties know the measurement? Indeed, in the case of many potential problems, does anyone know the costs? For instance (though to say it is to say the obvious), no one knew that Freon might be ecologically dangerous, indeed disastrous, until someone discovered its potential danger. Especially in terms of ecological damage, which can be so insidious and thus so difficult to discover and predict, the problem of man's knowledge (or lack thereof) of the ramifications of his actions turns out to be crucial.

The second problem with Coase's analysis is not directly ecological, though it is central to a limited- or no-growth society. Coase basically accepts the initial distribution of wealth as a given, in his analysis and prescription; similarly, he does not care what change in the distribution of wealth is brought about by his prescription. The theorist of limited growth, however, must be concerned with the resulting distribution of wealth. Among other things, therefore, the limited growth theorist might well want to adopt a non-Coasean rule, which aims not at economic optimality but at economic redistribution. For instance, the rule might be: Once ecological matters are settled, then adopt the liability solution that most favors the redistribution of wealth.

In short, even if Coase's analysis be accurate, his conclusion-- that the free market and negotiation should settle all externality

issues, including pollution--is acceptable only if there are no debilitating ecological problems and if there is no concern with the ultimate distribution of wealth. But the serious ecological problems of
the present mean that Coase's analysis, regardless of its logical ac-
curacy, must be rejected; and his conclusions ought to be replaced
by a rule for externalities and liability that takes into account the
possibility of serious, long-term ecological problems and the desirability of a consistent, predictable redistribution of wealth.

SOME LIMITATIONS ON PROPERTY RIGHTS

In addition to the extensions of property rights proposed above,
some limitations are ecologically sound. These limitations, in general, would have beneficial side effects; in addition, some of them
build on existing trends.

1. Taxes on windfall gains from government action. Gains in
property value resulting from much government activity--for example, highway construction--ought be taxed at a rate approximating
100 percent. Such gains come about through no merit or wisdom of
the property owner; further, the prospect of such gains leads to much
political corruption--the proverbial "honest graft." One easily administered equivalent of such a tax in highway construction would be
to exercise eminent domain not only for the width of the current
right-of-way but also for an extra two lots (or so) of width on either
side. The chief ecological benefits would be to allow the government
to establish green belts and maintain farms where possible, to permit services where necessary, and to use the profits (of reselling
the land for services) for transportation generally.
2. Zoning. Where noncoercive techniques of land use control
are inapplicable or inefficacious, zoning is possible. Zoning has had
some notable ecological successes--for example, in California's
coastal land plan--and holds some promise--especially in Vermont,
Oregon, and Colorado. Unfortunately, zoning boards are subject to
the sort of special-interest pressures so common to regulatory agencies, where only the special interest--and not the other interests--
are effectively represented.[20]
3. Inheritance. To the extent that it helps maintain a static
inequality of wealth, the right of inheritance should be limited. Thus,
large inheritances ought be severely taxed, and the proceeds directly
distributed to the population, at income-tax time, for example, in
inverse proportion to the effective tax rate, in order to aid the redistribution desirable in a limited- or no-growth society. But moderate inheritances ought to be treated as leniently as at present,

since inheritance does assist family unity, feelings of community, and especially individual concern for other generations; it thus helps provide an effective anchor in times of dislocation that resource scarcity and economic transition may bring, and it produces a pros-pective vision toward humans yet unborn, that is, the sort of future orientation necessary for wise ecological action.

SOME NEW OR REFORMULATED DIFFERENTIATIONS

Like some expansions and most limitations on property rights already suggested in this chapter, the first two differentiations pro-posed in this section--about land and renewable resources generally--are already being put into effect in some places. Thus, if success-ful, the changes may be accelerated and may spread relatively quick-ly--for example, within a couple of decades in the United States. On the other hand, the last two differentiations proposed--about the corporation and capital--have broad implications for the economic and social order, have not yet been begun, and must thus be seen purely as long-term speculations and goals for, perhaps, the next century.

1. Land. For food production, environmental stability, and esthetic reasons, land--especially farmland--deserves special treat-ment in terms of property rights, as has been historically the case, except for the last two centuries.[21] At present in the United States, two methods of modifying property rights in farmland are underway. Both give some promise of success. One, being tried in Suffolk County, New York, and elsewhere, is to separate the property right to subdivide and develop the land from the other rights of use, and then to have the government buy the development rights. After the development rights are alienated to the government, the land can be farmed, left fallow, or turned to forest; it can be sold to someone who will not develop it; but it cannot be turned into a subdivision. (It also can be taxed only as undeveloped and undevelopable land.) Another (and indeed complementary) method, in use in upstate New York, is to establish "agricultural districts," wherein farmers alienate to the state their property right to subdivide and develop their land in exchange for expanded property rights of use--such as unrestricted (from zoning) farming practices--and in exchange for certain exemptions from property taxes.[22]
2. Renewable resources generally. These changes in prop-erty rights in connection with farms might be extended, in one form or another, to all economic activities that involve renewable (and renewed) resources. In general, then, economic activities where

the object is used, without destroying or being destroyed, would receive property rights benefits (and/or tax benefits). Conversely,
those activities where the use involves destruction (and thus non-
renewability) would receive no benefits or even disabilities in terms
of property rights (and/or taxes).

Especially in the energy field, these changes would be important for a limited- or no-growth society. Regardless of the amount
of coal under Midwestern wheat fields or of shale oil in Western
hills, those resources are not renewable. But trees, wind, and sun
are (and the wind and sun are quite clean, as well). Thus, any tax
and property-rights benefits should go to the renewable resource development and use. Tax and property-rights limitations should go to
the others--limitations such as, for instance, allowing the extraction
of coal only on the condition that the (renewable farm and pasture)
land be let alone or restored, with the burden of proof and the liability on the coal-mining concerns.

Essentially, the underlying aim of the reform of property
rights in connection with land and renewable resources is to try to
maintain both, so that they will be useful and available to people not
only this year and next, but in a decade and a century as well. Food
and energy are scarce; consumption patterns of each must change;
but both continue to be needed, in great measure. Property rights
modifications can help assure the existence of both farmland for
food and renewable resources for energy.

3. The corporation. The great burst in growth of the Industrial Revolution was propelled at first by entrepreneurs; very quickly, however, the limited-liability, joint-stock company--the corpora-
tion--became the vehicle for industrial development. It had many
advantages. One simple negative advantage was limited liability:
While the partners in a partnership are each individually liable for
the full extent of the partnership's debts, investors in a corporation
have no liability beyond their original investment. The corporation's
positive advantages are legion. By law, the corporation--an artificial person--has most of the same privileges as a natural person;
but it also has or can have immense resources to back up those
privileges (if an individual sues General Motors [GM], both the individual and GM are equal in the eyes of the law--although their
available resources differ drastically); it can provide individual investors with anonymity (and thus no responsibility); it can hire
managers to provide continuing managerial expertise; and it can
generally grow much larger than a partnership. Further, the corporation can be immortal; since it never need die, it never need be
subject to the inconveniences, upsets, and taxes that befall a partnership or individually owned business on the demise of any important individual.

In part because corporations have shown themselves to be such
an excellent means by which to attain industrial growth and to satisfy
(and create) consumer wants and whims, the corporation--with its
rights as now constituted--is not suited for ecological responsibility
nor for a society with limited growth. Nor is the corporation's pen-
chant for growth its only disqualification from such a society. For
the rationales for large corporations have been thrown into doubt by
many recent corporate developments.

For instance, the rise of conglomerates--groups of companies
in fields unrelated to each other--seems not to have produced any
discernible "synergy" or any other purely economic benefit; indeed,
in some ways conglomerates are economically inefficient. Similarly, even well-integrated large corporations--like GM--no longer
have the traditional justification of economies of scale, as the corporations themselves have realized and shown by subdividing themselves into many fairly autonomous divisions. Further, large size
seems to lessen innovation; most major advances in cars and com-
puters have come, not from GM and IBM, but from smaller companies; the excellence of GM and IBM is primarily in marketing. In
addition, large corporations present the serious monopolistic problems of economic inefficiency and inordinate political power. Economic inefficiency also pervades regulated corporations.

There are many different means of trying to make the large
corporation less ecologically unsound and less economically inefficient. One approach to the problem of the large corporation is to
alter property rights. Since the corporation is "an artificial being,
invisible, intangible, and existing only in the contemplation of the
law, "[23] the property rights that attend the corporation are legally
modifiable.

Such modification could be done in any of a number of ways.
One type of change would be to alter the property rights of the shareholder in the corporation. At present, shareholders vote for management on a one-share, one-vote principle, and then management makes
all the decisions. An alternative model, suggested by F. A. Hayek,
would vest property rights of control, not voting rights, in the shareholders.[24] Each shareholder would be "annually called upon individually to decide what part of his share in the net profits he was
willing to reinvest in the corporation." Among the many advantages
of the reform, Hayek thinks, would be to "limit the growth (and probably the existence) of individual corporations to what is economically
desirable." No longer would management be able to act in its own
self-aggrandizing self-interest (and perhaps against the interests of
the shareholders, that is, against the most efficient use of their
capital) by reinvesting all corporate profits in order to increase the
size of the corporation that the management directs.

A second type of change would be to limit the property rights of corporations, so they do not have the same rights as natural persons. (Indeed, since artificial persons have so many benefits over natural persons, equity would suggest that corporations not have as many rights as natural persons.) One means of limiting corporate growth by limiting their property rights is Hayek's idea that corporations should not be allowed to have voting stock (and thus frequently effective control) in other corporations.[25] Another change would be to prohibit corporations from establishing subsidiaries that are also limited-liability and for which the parent corporation assumes no liability. Ultimately, perhaps, the immortality of the corporation must be modified; one possible--though clearly radical--proposal would be to stop granting the privilege of immortality to corporations: after a life-span (perhaps the Bible's "three-score years and ten"), the corporation would be dissolved or liquidated, and its assets divided up among the shareholders.

Since the line that divides property rights from taxes is so faint, a third type of change in corporation rights would be to change taxation practices. For instance, one incentive to corporate growth is that the present tax system allows a variety of "business deductions." If the number of legitimate business deductions were carefully reduced, some of the tendency to growth would lessen. For instance, retained earnings and new capital investment (at least beyond depreciation) ought to be taxed. So should be the money now spent (and deducted) on marketing.

Taxation reform would be even more important in the case of the multinational corporation, which has even more privileges over the natural person than does the purely one-nation corporation. Tax law changes could lessen some of those advantages. For instance, there is no real reason why overseas taxes (and royalties as well, for oil companies) should be a tax credit on U.S. tax returns. At most, they should be a deductible expense; better, they ought not be deductible at all, but be viewed as a cost for the privilege of multi-nationality. In short, the property rights of the multinationals involve so many privileges that equity can require some reduction in privilege.

The above suggestions start to get at some of the ways in which a property rights approach can be used to limit the size and the propensity to growth of corporations. Other property rights ideas, while of less importance in terms of corporate growth, might be important in terms of the amenities of life in a no-growth society. For instance, a corporation, not being a natural person, cannot "use" much of its property in any way other than to (hope to) make a profit on it; a natural person can enjoy the beauty of the forest he owns, in a way that, for example, the Diamond Match Company simply cannot.

Forests owned by corporations, thus, provide less human utility
than forests owned by natural persons, because corporations lack
the esthetic sensibilities or athletic abilities of natural persons.
Thus, to increase human utility, the property right of corporations
to exclude individuals from forests should be modified.

4. Property as capital and property for use. Related in part
to the distinction between natural and artificial persons is the distinction between capital (property invested to make more money) and
property for use (for a livelihood and for consumption). Here, as
with the corporation (which is capital embodied in an institutional
and legal form), the question is how to modify property rights so
that the tendency for capital to behave in ecologically unsound ways
is limited, that is, so that the tendency for capital incessantly to
seek to grow is limited. In general, property rights in capital should
be modified at least by subjecting capital gains to a higher tax than
other forms of income, that is, by limiting the individual's right
freely to use his capital gain by taking some of it by taxation. A
blanket change in the capital-gains tax rate would probably lead to
some decrease in large-scale capital formation immediately, as
some funds shifted from capital to consumption. If the tax continued
and the proceeds were used as part of a redistribution scheme, long-
term capital formation would decline, at the same time as the redistribution lessened inequalities. The capital-gains tax rate could be
modified, at a set pace and within broad limits, in order to keep investment at the necessary level. Further, capital investments that
result in the same good or service being produced with less pollution
or natural resource use could gain an exclusion from or a reduction
in the tax (that is, a sort of reverse depletion allowance).

Ultimately, the requisite and goal of a limited- or no-growth
society would be the drastic modification of some property rights
associated with capital. This change is necessary because of the
relationship between capital and industrial growth; it is also necessary because, unlike property rights in items used for consumption,
property rights in capital involve potential control, by the capitalist
(or his managers), of the means of production and of other human
beings (the workers), who sell their services for wages. But capital need not involve such control as a permanent feature. For there
is no reason why capital--and the control it brings--should always
remain in the hands of the original investor.

For instance, it might be desirable to establish a property
rights system whereby the capitalist can maintain and retain his
capital (and its control) only until it has returned to him its value
and some additional multiple of that value. After that return, the
capital would pass into other hands: to the workers in the factory,
perhaps, who could establish a system of "industrial democracy,"[26]

or to the citizens of the country equally. The capitalist would thus
gain one of his major objects--an increase in his money--and yet,
since capital no longer included the right to permanent control, the
capitalist would have to relinquish control eventually. With that re-
linquishment, the inequality of power and of the distribution of
wealth in society would be lessened.

Essentially, the underlying aim of the reform of property
rights connected with capital and with the corporation is to establish
a system wherein property for use will predominate, corporations
will generally be small, and capital will be unable to grow immortal-
ly and will lack the element of control it now has--in short, a system
where there is much private property, but little capital. Historically, such systems existed prior to the advent of capitalism; they can
exist again.[27] To establish such a system in the contemporary
world would be a difficult and lengthy process. But the proposals
herein suggested do provide a beginning. Moreover, such a system
would contain within itself a justification of property rights that is at
present lacking.

CONCLUSION I: THE JUSTIFICATION
OF PROPERTY RIGHTS

Earlier, this chapter argued that, with the rise of the modern
corporation, private property lost its traditional justifications.
Some of the suggestions about property rights in this chapter provide the basis for a new justification of a new system of property
rights wherein there is much private ownership, with extended
rights, and little capital.

The suggested system of private ownership aims at cutting
down the size and control of corporations and capital, and thereby
returning property rights and economic issues to a human, personal,
and humane scale. With the decline of large concentrations of capi-
tal--for example, electric utilities with nuclear power plants--will
come the proliferation of small units of property--for example,
solar power units, in each dwelling, with present electrical lines
preserved for emergencies; just as individuals have individual furnaces in houses, so they will have individual solar power units.
With the decline of large concentrations of capital will also come the
decline of a complex division of labor and a complex technology,
both of which--especially when combined with the current "service
economy"--serve to narrow and stultify individuals by narrowing the
range and diversity of their activities both on and off the job. By
placing property and economic issues generally on a smaller and
more human scale, ownership can become a locus in which the

individual owner can have--as some earlier justifications of private property tried to argue--scope for self-development. Some property is necessary for the individual to have some liberty of action, some context in which he can arrange his life in advance, some freedom of choice, and some certainty of experiencing the results of his choice. In more philosophic language, ownership is in some ways essential, on a personal level, because it is "the indispensable counterpart to being actual," to living and acting with some freedom and direction.[28] When small scale and personal, "the forms of ownership are liberating, sustaining the individual's freedom of identity and participation," because they express a "lived relationship of belonging."

With the decline of the large corporation and its concern for growth, and with the lessening of capital and the desire for having money make more money should come a concurrent change in the human psyche, a change perhaps best described by John Stuart Mill a century ago in his newly famous discussion of the stationary state:

> I cannot, therefore, regard the stationary state of capital and wealth with the unaffected aversion so generally manifested towards it by political economists of the old school. I am inclined to believe that it would be, on the whole, a very considerable improvement on our present condition. I confess that I am not charmed with the ideal of life held out by those who think that the normal state of human beings is that of struggling to get on; that the trampling, crushing, elbowing, and treading on each other's heels, which form the existing type of social life, are the most desirable lots of human kind, or anything but the disagreeable symptoms of one of the phases of industrial progress. . . .
>
> [In the stationary state,] there would be as much scope as ever for all kinds of mental culture, and moral and social progress; as much room for improving the Art of Living, and much more likelihood of its being improved, when minds ceased to be engrossed by the art of getting on.[29]

In addition to serving as a means for human development and of the change in human attitudes, the system of ownership herein suggested would retain, in large measure, the major political and economic benefits attributed to the traditional private property system--benefits probably lacking, indeed, in the twentieth-century capitalist revolution. The major political benefit is that ownership provides individuals with some of the psychological, social, economic, and political means of effectively resisting or ignoring some of the decisions made by those in authority over them. The major economic benefits are that a system of ownership, on a small scale with basically free markets, provides individual freedom of choice and social (or systematic) adaptability to changing needs.

CONCLUSION II: THE POSSIBILITIES FOR CHANGE

Some of the changes suggested in this chapter, like the changes suggested or required in other chapters, may seem impractically far-fetched and so incongruent with the ideas and interests of those who hold power as to be incapable of realization. It is certainly true that to effect some of these changes would require far-reaching political and government action, which itself would probably require much popular pressure and popular education.

Most of the proposals of this chapter, however, have been made with the problem and possibilities of practical political change in mind. First, some of the changes involve extensions of property rights, or are the proposals of strong supporters of a laissez-faire, free-enterprise system (like F. A. Hayek); these changes are thus squarely within one part of the U.S. political tradition. Second, some of the changes are intended to try to increase citizen participation, in part because it seems likely that, ultimately, the government will be unable to act consistently, effectively, and fairly without the development of citizen activity. Third, some of the changes are aimed directly at individual self-interest, such as buying farm development rights. Fourth, these changes are various and not interdependent, so that they can separately appeal to wide constituencies. Further, some suggestions build on changes already underway. None of these suggested changes will come about quickly. But definitions of property rights do change and are changing; and these suggestions can serve as goals, some short-term and some long-term, for incremental--or faster--policy changes.

NOTES

1. Eirik G. Furubotn and Svetozar Pejovich, "Property Rights and Economic Theory: A Survey of Recent Literature," Journal of Economic Literature 10, no. 4 (December 1972): 1142.
2. Robert L. Heilbroner, An Inquiry into the Human Prospect (New York: W. W. Norton, 1974).

3. Erazim Kohák, "Possessing, Owning, Belonging,"
Dissent, Spring 1974, p. 344.

4. Blackstone, Commentaries, Book II, opening section.
For other ramifications of this type of definition, see Peter Stillman, "Hegel's Idea of Property," forthcoming.

5. John Locke, Two Treatises of Government, Second
Treatise, Chap. V, sec. 27.

6. Carnegie's is also the attitude of the Bible, that all be-
longs to God and is simply held, in trust, by humans; see I Chron.
xxix.14.

7. G. W. F. Hegel, The Philosophy of Right, secs. 41-53.

8. The locus classicus for this now common interpretation
is Adolf A. Berle and G. C. Means, The Modern Corporation and
Private Property (New York: Macmillan, 1933).

9. Adolf A. Berle, The 20th Century Capitalist Revolution
(New York: Harcourt, Brace & World, 1954), pp. 30-31.

10. Ibid., pp. 174-75.

11. Ibid., Chapter 3.

12. For this argument detailed, see Peter G. Stillman, "Ecological Problems, Political Theory, and Public Policy," in Environmental Politics, ed. Stuart S. Nagel (New York: Praeger, 1974),
pp. 49-60.

13. Here see the work of E. J. Mishan, especially Technology
and Growth: The Price We Pay (New York: Praeger, 1970).

14. J. K. Galbraith, The Affluent Society (New York: Mentor
Books, 1958), especially Chapter 22.

15. Here see the work of Joseph L. Sax, especially "Standing
to Sue: A Critical Review of the Mineral King Decision," Natural
Resources Journal 13, no. 1 (January 1973): 76-88.

16. Ibid., where Sax argues brilliantly that the Court's "user
test" is crude and muddled.

17. Here also see the work of Joseph L. Sax, especially De-
fending the Environment (New York: Knopf, 1971), pp. 158-74.

18. Charles A. Reich, "The New Property," Yale Law Journal
73, no. 5 (April 1964): 734-87.

19. Ronald Coase, "The Problem of Social Cost," Journal of
Law and Economics 3 (October 1960). This brilliantly reasoned
article really deserves a full rejoinder, for which there is unfortunately not space here.

20. This thesis is argued persuasively by Theodore Lowi,
The End of Liberalism (New York: W. W. Norton, 1969), and
seriously undercuts the descriptive power and justifications of both
The Federalist No. 10 and pluralism, each of which requires all
parties to be in the arena for the result to be democratic and fair.

21. See Karl Polanyi, The Great Transformation (Boston:
Beacon, 1957 [1944]).

22. On the New York State experiments, see especially <u>NYS Environment</u>, published monthly by the state's Department of Environmental Conservation—for example, Vol. 4, no. 6 (December 1, 1974): 12.

23. F. A. Hayek, <u>Studies in Philosophy, Politics and Economics</u> (New York: Clarion Books, Simon and Schuster, 1966), p. 311.

24. Ibid., pp. 306-08.

25. Ibid., pp. 308-11.

26. See, for example, G. David Garson, <u>On Democratic Administration and Socialist Self-Management</u> (Beverly Hills, Calif.: Sage Professional Paper, 1974), especially pp. 45-53.

27. See Polanyi, op. cit.; M. I. Finley, <u>The Ancient Economy</u> (Berkeley: University of California Press, 1973); and Aristotle, <u>Politics</u>.

28. Kohák, op. cit., pp. 349-50.

29. John Stuart Mill, <u>Principles of Political Economy</u>, Book IV, Chapter 6, sec. 2.

BUSINESS AND THE
POLITICS OF
SLOWED GROWTH
David Vogel

This chapter discusses some of the political implications of limiting economic growth. More specifically, it attempts to explore the present and future response of the business community in the United States to the political and economic challenges posed by the advocates of slowed growth. The reaction of corporate managers and owners to critics of economic growth is important for two reasons. First, the investments of corporations are themselves a critical component of the nation's rate and direction of economic development. Second, the ideologies and institutional objectives of large-scale profit-making enterprises play an important if not decisive part in the formation of public policy. The interests of business corporations present a major "limit to nongrowth" and ecologists require a more careful analysis of the political dimensions of their vision.

The chapter is divided into four parts. The first section places the current environmental movement in the context of the growing public antagonism to the business corporation in the United States. The next two sections distinguish between the issues raised by the movement that are, in principle, compatible with the long-run interests of the business system and those that are not; zero economic growth falls into the latter category. The final section outlines some of the political obstacles that confront advocates of slowed growth.

THE EVOLUTION OF PUBLIC OPINION

With amazing rapidity, man's relationship to his physical environment has been placed upon the nation's political agenda. As recently as 1965 only 28 percent of the public considered air pollution a "very or somewhat serious problem." By 1970 the number had increased to 69 percent. Comparable statistics for water pollution reveal a similar pattern: an increase in public concern from 35 percent in 1965 to 74 percent five years later.[1] The most dramatic shift in public consciousness took place between 1969 and 1971. During these two years, which include the Union Company oil spill off the coast of Santa Barbara--"the ecological shot heard around the world"--and the first Earth Day, April 22, 1970, the public's awareness of mercury residues increased 54 percentage points; oil spills, 26 points; fish kills, 22; and lead poisoning, 20. By 1971 over three-fifths of the population indicated that they had "heard or read a lot about" the following environmental problems: air pollution, smog, unsafe drugs, water pollution, auto accidents, earthquakes, littering, and garbage.[2]

An analysis of public opinion surveys over the last decade suggests a close relationship between popular awareness of environmental issues and growing public antagonism to business. According to a content analysis of major national periodicals, conducted by the Battelle Seattle Research Center, only 25 percent of the articles critical of business they recorded in 1965 focused on environmental issues. While the total "volume" of criticism increased significantly between 1965 and 1969, the proportion stemming from environmental concerns remained between one-fourth and one-fifth. In 1970, however, the environmental percentage more than doubled to 42 percent. By 1971, 58 percent of the articles that appeared in the national mass media critical of business focused on the impact of corporations on the environment.[3]

There has also been a significant shift in public perception of the causes of pollution. According to Opinion Research Corporation, "blame on traditional sources--dirt from roads, septic tanks--declined or remained stable, while criticism of industrial sources rose sharply." Their studies reveal that public awareness of the role of factories and plants in causing air pollution increased from 34 percent in 1965 to 64 percent in 1970. The shift in responsibility for water pollution was even more decisive: from 42 percent in 1965 to 69 percent five years later. The most dramatic shifts in public perception of the causes of environmental problems focused on two areas in which the responsibility of industry has been particularly visible: exhaust from automobiles and insecticide sprays. In 1976, 27 percent of the public saw the former as a source of air pollution; five years later the figure became 62 percent. The comparable statistics for the latter are 19 percent and 48 percent.[4]

In 1972, 66 percent of the population stated that a company's efforts in "working to control air and water pollution" formed the

most important component of their opinion of a particular firm.[5]
According to Lou Harris and Associates, controlling air and water
pollution ranked first among 16 public problems whose solution
"businessmen and companies should give some leadership to"; in
1972 over 92 percent of the public listed it as an appropriate problem for business initiative.[6]

To the extent that the public is concerned not only with air and
water pollution, but also with the impact of technology per se, its
confidence in business is weakened even further. California voters
were recently asked to evaluate eight "decision-actors"--technical
experts, government leaders, consumer groups, the courts, congressmen, the public, no one, and business--in terms of the influence they should exercise in four critical areas of technological innovation. The authors of the study conclude:

> A substantial portion of the public seems to be
> asking business and government leaders to with-
> draw from the field of decision-making about
> technologies. This attitude is particularly
> directed toward business leaders, who are in a
> sense the biggest "losers" in the legitimacy
> dimension: in every case, the public wanted
> them to stay out of decisions if they were out
> and to get out if they were perceived as having
> any influence in them.[7]

THE ENVIRONMENTAL MOVEMENT

The initial reaction of the business community to the criti-
cisms of the environmental movement was largely a defensive one.
This reaction is understandable. American businessmen are remarkably insecure; proposals that are perceived as compromising
their autonomy or challenging their stewardship of the nation's productive machinery are automatically greeted as harbingers of the
imminent collapse of the free enterprise system.[8] While obviously
exaggerated, this response also has a basis in reality. For the
entrepreneur or manager, pollution control legislation, like the
regulation of wages and hours a generation ago, introduces an unmeasurable and unpredictable factor into the decision-making calculus. By making the firm vulnerable to a whole new set of pressures and constraints, it threatens to upset corporate planning. In
addition, there is also an ideological challenge: the very existence
of an environmental movement suggests the shortcomings of the
proverbial invisible hand. Business Week wrote in 1970: ". . . the

price system is seen to be defective when it deals with environmental factors. . . . For those trained in the tradition of Adam Smith, the divergence of private and social costs is of major environmental significance."[9]

Although an immediate priority of business was to deflect the critical thrust of public concern with the deterioration of the environment by identifying the corporation and the business system with the movement's goals--a process that has been uncharitably described as "ecopornography"[10]--the consensus of opinion among executives was that ecologists had indeed raised a legitimate issue and that it was appropriate that "the political and social ground rules within which business is conducted . . . be drastically amended."[11] Thus a poll of Fortune 500 executives in 1970 reported that 57 percent believed that the federal government should "step up regulatory activities"; in addition, very few executives reported they were impressed with the efforts of their peers to improve their industry's performance.[12]

The conflict between the goals of business and the efforts of environmentalists to ameliorate some of the more obvious by-products of industrial production and consumption, particularly air and water pollution and the accumulation of solid wastes, essentially reflects a tension between the interests of particular firms and industries and that of the business system as a whole. While this conflict is endemic to a market system, it is particularly exacerbated by the pressures of the environmental movement. The policies and programs required to improve the quality of the environment involve costs that fall disproportionately upon specific industries, most notably, utilities, oil and steel, chemicals, utilities, and paper. Executives representing the interests of firms in these industries can therefore be expected to seek to delay the enforcement of regulations that limit pollution emissions: These types of conflicts presently define most of the politics of environmental protection.[13]

Yet there is no inherent tension between the concern of the public with these issues and the interests of corporate capitalism as a whole: A clearer environment is in the interests of all citizens, including businessmen. The current projections of investment for environmental improvement by business--most recently estimated at $113 billion over this decade--do not threaten to interfere with the economy's overall rate of economic accumulation.[14] On the contrary, there is growing evidence that, for the economy as a whole, corporate expansion and the reduction of the levels of air and water pollution are entirely compatible. They may even be reenforcing: The larger the rate of economic growth, the more funds that are available to reduce pollution levels; pollution control expenditures, by stimulating employment and encouraging technological innovation,

in turn contribute to improved earnings for many corporations.[15]
Thus, a study in Fortune suggests:

> Over the longer term, pollution abatement seems
> likely to increase real G.N.P. A significant de-
> crease in air pollution, for example, can be ex-
> pected to reduce absenteeism and turnover and
> improve production . . . many industries might
> have to pay out less in sickness and death bene-
> fits. . . . If these longer-range savings were put
> through benefit-cost analysis, many corporations
> might discover that pollution control yields a
> profit.[16]

As Forbes magazine put it somewhat more crudely: "There's cash
in all that trash."[17] Ironically, the growing market for pollution
control equipment has created a "pollution-industrial complex" consisting of firms with considerable financial stake in strict environmental standards. Carl Gerstacker, chairman of Dow Chemical
Corporation, recently defended federal regulations against criticism
from other industrialists. He told the New York Times: "We have
been making a profit from pollution-control investments."[18]

THE CHALLENGE OF SLOWED GROWTH

Air and water pollution and solid waste disposal are "first-
generation" environmental issues: Their solution is essentially
technical and threatens only the short-term financial interests of
particular firms. To criticize business performance on these issues
is to challenge some of the effects of corporate production, not the
principles that underlie that production itself. Advocates of limited
growth, however, pose a qualitatively different challenge to business:
They threaten the essential purpose and justification of the business
system and hence the values that underlie the survival of every
profit-making institution.

Both mercantile and laissez-faire capitalism rested on a vision
of infinite economic accumulation; given a supportive political environment, there was no limit to the increase in material living
standards. Keynesian economics challenged the neoclassical faith
only to suggest a more expeditious means for achieving its objective;
the legitimacy of the goal itself was reinforced. Not surprisingly,
most commentators who have addressed themselves to the theoretical
relationship between capitalism and zero economic growth usually argue that they are incompatible. The rate of profit is closely linked to

that of economic growth. A reduction in the rate of profit, not
simply for some sectors, but for the economy as a whole, would
invariably result in a decline in the rate of capital accumulation,
thus threatening both "the engine and the fuel of the capitalist system." A study of this issue by R. O. Heiser, an Australian economist, concludes:

> The dilemma posed for capitalism by the promise
> of zero population growth, with zero accumulation
> and zero profits, does not stem necessarily from
> the greed misguidance of capitalists. It resides
> in the very nature of the system itself. There-
> fore, it is not a question of conservationists per-
> suading "reasonable" men to behave in a most
> uncapitalist manner. It calls for a radical re-
> structuring of the whole economic system. . . .
> It is well that conservationists and ecologists
> (and economists) should recognize the full mea-
> sure of their aspirations.[19]

Although economic growth is built into the dynamics of capitalism, its importance to business is reinforced by the organizational
and financial context of accumulation in an advanced industrial society. The debate between J. K. Galbraith and his critics on the left
about whether growth or profits are more important to the managers
of the contemporary business corporation has become a sterile one:
The most recent consensus is that the two are interdependent.[20]
Yet by placing such emphasis on management's perceived stake in
growth, Galbraith has identified a novel characteristic of the business environment in the post-World War II industrial state. Due to
the increased influence and visibility of the investment community--
which includes individual and institutional shareholders as well as
security analysis and money managers--corporate management operates in essentially an economic fishbowl.[21] The professionaliza-
tion of management, whatever its implications for the legitimacy of
the corporation, has not reduced the economic pressures on management; on the contrary, it has enhanced them. The manager of a
publicly held firm, unlike his (or her) entrepreneurial counterpart,
has relatively little discretion about the goals he should strive for:
One's "performance" is judged exclusively by the firm's current
and potential rate of growth.
      The growing internationalization of capital markets in the post-
war period has exacerbated these pressures: Managers whose performance is found to be lagging now experience pressure--including
the possibility of take-overs, not only from their compatriots but

also from foreign investors. Any unilateral attempt on the part of businessmen in one nation to reduce their economic expectations would immediately result in an influx of foreign capital, thus bringing the performance of these firms up to that of international capitalism as a whole. The growth of multinational enterprises means that not only is the individual firm a "hostage" to the rate of growth of its competition, but that the entire business community of any capitalist nation is similarly vulnerable.

The relative perfection of capital markets has a further implication. In an advanced capitalist society, economic accumulation takes place largely within the context of large bureaucracies. While the operations of a firm's various divisions frequently have some relationship to each other, the modern corporation, unlike the typical enterprise of a generation ago, is not committed to any particular product or service. Rather, its primary commitment is to its own institutional viability. If the demand for the products or services which comprise a major share of its future growth declines (as is currently the case for the manufacturers of baby foods faced with a declining birth rate), it can use the capital markets to diversify into those sectors that will enable it to continue its growth unabated. (Thus, Gerber, the principal manufacturer of baby foods, is currently seeking to expand its sales of nonfood baby products as well as to develop a new line of products for the growing "singles" market.)[22]

This strategy is completely rational: In a relatively large firm, management compensation tends to be higher. Moreover, a profitable growing firm is likely to be more innovative, more tolerant of incompetency and failure, and to provide greater opportunities for promotion--in short, a much more pleasant place for everyone, from chairman to secretary, to work. The problems of staff morale associated with universities currently experiencing "steady state" are indicative of the kinds of problems that would confront profit-making institutions whose growth was restricted. If anything, these problems would be multiplied in a corporation since, unlike the university, it lacks any other institutional definition of achievement goals.

As a political issue, the possibility of a nongrowth economy remains highly abstract. To the extent that the publication of books such as The Closing Circle and Technology and Growth have injected the issue into public discourse, the public reaction of the business community to the prospect has been uniformly negative.[23] Meadows, Commoner, and Mishan have been attacked both for being unduly pessimistic and for overlooking the unpredictable benefits of future technological innovation. In addition, editorials in the business press have stressed the importance of continued economic growth for the reduction of social conflict: the larger the pie, the less dispute over

how it is to be divided.[24] Nonetheless, the very fact of business
sponsorship of the Club of Rome's report suggests that the idea that
the world's resources are finite is being taken increasingly seriously
by many business leaders. More importantly, the energy crisis, although precipitated by political factors rather than natural shortage,
has dramatized the prospect of future resource scarcities. As
Louis Lundborg, former chairman of the board of Bank of America,
remarked:

> We have been on a binge--a spree that has been as
> reckless as a three-day drunk. We have been in-
> toxicated by the game of production. . . .
>   The present energy crisis is only an index, a
> gauge of our excessive use of all kinds of irre-
> placeable resources. It is our D.E.W. Line--our
> Distant Early Warning of what lies ahead. . . .
>   The current scurrying around to find alterna-
> tive sources of energy focuses attention only on the
> visible tip of the problem, not on the underlying
> causes. Copper, manganese and other nonferrous
> metals are already in short supply . . . there is a
> worldwide shortage of pulp. . . .[25]

Yet for the individual firm, the higher prices created by the
relative scarcity of many raw materials simply become another obstacle to be confronted in its pursuit of growth. The objectives of
corporations do not change, only their strategy for achieving them.
Thus, the response of the oil industry to a threatened reduction in
the nation's rate of consumption of oil and natural gas caused by
higher prices is to diversify into other areas, both energy- and
nonenergy-related, to enable its growth to continue uninterrupted.
"Oil" companies have been rapidly increasing their holdings in coal
and uranium reserves in order to become "total energy" institutions.
In addition, to compensate for future declines in the rate of energy
use, Mobil recently purchased Montgomery Ward, and Standard Oil
of California has partially merged with American Metal Climax.
(Characteristically, during the winter of 1974-75 when the scarcity
of oil was to some extent alleviated, the industry began to promote
gasoline consumption. One station owner, succinctly articulating
the tension between resource conservation and corporate growth,
told the New York Times, "It's very confusing; the government says
'conserve' and the oil companies say, 'sell.'")[26] The utility industry confronts a similar dilemma. Its slower rate of growth, attributed
to both government-encouraged conservation measures and the increased costs of electricity, is placing it in considerable financial

jeopardy. Unlike the oil companies, however, its regulated status forbids it from diversifying and thus severely compromises its ability to attract additional capital.

For business as a whole, the growing scarcity of many natural resources, particularly oil, has stimulated research into ways in which economic growth can be maintained with a reduction in the rate of resource consumption. While their findings are necessarily speculative, two independent studies contend that the nation's growth of energy consumption could be reduced significantly, by perhaps one-half--with no major adverse impact on corporate growth and profits.[27] Whether economic growth rates could be maintained in the face of significantly reduced consumption of other natural resources is somewhat more problematic. To be sure, there is considerable waste in the economy. Vance Packard's The Waste Makers, written nearly 15 years ago, presents a bill of particulars against American habits of production and consumption that have by now become a part of our conventional wisdom.[28] Planned obsolescence, conspicuous consumption, frequent style and model changes, the promotion of private as opposed to social consumption, the identification of personal well-being with material possessions--all are critical features of an economy whose success depends upon the deliberate squandering of resources. Yet these marketing practices--most of which were first identified by Thorstein Veblen in the 1920s--exist only because they have proven critical to the expansion of the consumer goods sector. The waste of irreplaceable resources is not a by-product of consumer demand; it is essential to its creation. The problem is not whether Americans could be induced to consume in less-environmentally destructive ways--to the extent that the current consumption habits satisfy artificially induced needs and result from manipulated expectations, they could clearly be altered without any real decline in living standards--but what would replace the industries that would disappear in the process? Walking through the woods on a snowy evening may be just as pleasant as riding in a snowmobile, but is it as marketable?

An economic and political system committed to reducing or eliminating economic growth would thus radically challenge, in the literal sense of the word, the prerogatives and privileges of U.S. business. Not only would the scope of state intervention be dramatically expanded as investment decisions became socialized, but more importantly, the direction of that intervention would change: It would cease making the goal of a healthy, prosperous economy--as measured by corporate profits--the essential objective of economic policy. Instead, investments in both the private and public sectors would be made using criteria that discouraged, or at least did not purposely abet, the essential objective of production in a capitalist

society, namely accumulation. The authority of corporate managers
and owners, justified largely in terms of their contribution to economic efficiency and productivity, would accordingly suffer a serious
erosion.

To fully understand the corporate position on slowed growth,
it is important to distinguish between slower growth rates that occur
as a result of economic and political forces beyond the control of the
business community and a reduction in economic growth due to the
effectiveness of environmental or slowed-growth political pressures.
In the opinion of many economists--and businessmen--the former is
a distinct possibility over the next decade. From the perspective of
the mid-1970s, it appears unlikely that the U.S. standard of living
will increase over the next two decades at a rate comparable to that
of the 1950s and 1960s. Accordingly, the U.S. public may well have
to lower its economic expectations. Convincing the public of the
necessity of consuming less so corporations can have the funds they
want for capital investments will prove a difficult challenge to business leaders, since through corporate advertising the public has become all too convinced of both the desirability and the feasibility of
a steady rise in levels of personal consumption.

Ironically, the antigrowth movement can be seen as a potential
ally in this effort. At a series of private meetings of corporate executives held in 1975 and 1976, a number of business leaders commented
favorably on "the antimaterialism of the young." One noted: "We
should take the message of the young more seriously. Maybe the
quality of life is not identical with the quality of goods." It seems
apparent that at least a few businessmen and conservationists have
found a common ground: Both want the American people to cease to
regard their personal and social well-being as a function of the size
of the Gross National Product. Their motivations, of course, remain
quite distinct: Some businessmen find the values of ecologists and
the counterculture acceptable because they provide a way of legitimating a redistribution of wealth and income away from consumption--
which benefits the mass of citizens--toward investment--which directly benefits a small and already relatively affluent minority.
Their "enlightenment" is largely one of expedience. They still want
the full potential growth of the economy realized: They are willing
to consider the virtues of the principles of the environmental movement while remaining unalterably opposed to its practices and policies. If the rate of increase in levels of personal consumption is
going to be retarded in any event, why not help rationalize it to an
unenthusiastic public by employing the very arguments of some of
the economic system's most articulate and principled critics? Needless to say, this "alliance" remains an awkward one for both slowed-
growth advocates and businessmen. It is not, however, completely

fanciful. For example, some environmental organizations have supported utility rate increases because they reduce consumption and
thus energy use--a position that allies them with industry and
against consumer interests.[29]

THE POLITICS OF SLOWED GROWTH

Ironically, objective conditions are uniquely favorable to the
advocates of slowed growth. The declining international economic
position of the United States--and the advanced capitalist nations in
general--will likely result in a lower long-run rate of growth, in
spite of the best efforts of business leaders to avoid this prospect.
Indeed, one could argue that this development is probably more
functional to the cause of planetary survival than most attempts at
pollution control: By reducing the demand for goods, it lowers production and thus scarce resources are exploited at a slower rate.
(Thus the recession of 1975 almost completely eliminated the critical
shortages of raw material that confronted business six months earlier.) Yet, politically, its immediate effect is the opposite: The
consequence of a slow-down in the rate of economic growth--either
temporary or permanent--is to reinforce the economic importance
of business. The organized working class, like business, has always been ambivalent about the environmental movement. It will
not actively oppose the demands of ecologists only as long as the
economy remains relatively prosperous: Reduced economic growth
means increased unemployment for the vast number of workers
directly dependent on corporate expansion for economic survival.
If corporate growth declines, workers and their employees will come
to perceive a common interest in "hunting ecologists with hounds" in
order to stimulate economic recovery. (Ironically, the no-growth
movement itself is indirectly dependent on economic growth: The
more rapid the growth of corporations, the more money that is available for studies, conferences, research projects, and so on, on how
to limit that growth.)

To the extent that the significant expansion of employment in
the public sector in the postwar decades frees a significant segment
of the middle class from direct dependence on corporate growth for
employment, a political constituency exists to advocate the reduction of economic growth rates. It is these individuals--the so-called
conscience constituency: relatively affluent, well-educated, and
usually employed outside the corporate sector--who constitute the
basis of political support for the environmental movement. Yet although their sources of income--usually from nonprofit institutions--
have enabled them to develop values that are independent of those of

the business community, their very distance from the profit sector also brings those values into conflict with the priorities of people who work for corporations. Moreover, even though they may be relatively critical of capital accumulation as a national objective, they remain ultimately dependent on the welfare of the profit sector. A decline in the fortunes of the nation's large corporations--with a consequent reduction in security values--means that less money is available for educational expansion, foundation grants, contributions to public-interest law firms, and so on.[30]

One of the principal factors that underlies the political and intellectual impact of Marxism is that Marx, unlike the utopian socialists, sought to define the economic and political preconditions that made socialism an actual historical possibility rather than simply a utopian ideal. A similar challenge can be made to the advocates of slowed growth. If they are serious about a society that satisfies reasonable material requirements without straining the finite resources of the planet, they have two responsibilities. The first is to describe the social, economic, and political characteristics of such a society, that is, its means of allocating resources, of regulating technological innovation, of interaction with other economic systems organized around different principles, and so on. Proponents of more restrictive growth policies will only succeed in mobilizing sufficient political support if they propose economic programs that somehow manage to attack the basic source of corporate power, namely the link between the rate of expansion of the corporate sector and the economic welfare of virtually the entire population. To prevail, their vision of society must unite the interests of organized labor and middle-class ecologists by convincing them that an economy that is both socially and environmentally responsible is indeed feasible. Second, they must attempt to specify the political conflicts through which such a system will be created. The politics of slower growth involve several sets of political actors, including businessmen, ecologists, workers, and the consuming public. Our brief analysis suggests that a variety of alliances and tensions are likely among these interested parties on both ideological and practical levels. We may all be inhabitants on a dying space ship, but this observation is unlikely to persuade those who benefit disproportionately from its rate of death. (Even on the Titanic some people traveled first class.) An environmental movement without a sophisticated sense of its potential allies and antagonists--and the circumstances that create each--will be unlikely to produce much beyond apocalyptic rhetoric. That is a commodity whose rate of growth appears to be unlimited.

NOTES

1. "Pollution: A Five Year Perspective," Opinion Research Findings--A Report on Timely Topics, Opinion Research Corporation (ORC, 1971), p. 3.

2. Thomas W. Benham, "Trends in Public Attitudes Toward Business and the Free Enterprise System," White House Conference on the Industrial World Ahead, Washington, D.C., 1971, pp. 13-14.

3. R. Coppock, M. Dierkes, H. Snowball, H. Thomas, Battelle Seattle Research Center, "Social Pressures and Business Actions: An Empirical Study of Corporate Social Responsibility in the U.S. 1965-71," revised version of a paper presented to the Seminar on Corporate Social Accounts, November 10-11, 1972 (unpublished), p. 14.

4. "Pollution: A Five Year Perspective," op. cit.

5. ORC, Public Opinion Index, April 1972, p. 7.

6. Lou Harris, "More Active Role Expected of Business in Solving Nation's Problems," The Harris Survey, February 10, 1973.

7. Daniel Metlay, "A Study of the Attitudes and Behavior of Technological Dissent," paper presented at the Annual Meeting of the Western Political Science Association, April 7, 1973, p. 16.

8. See Robert Lane, The Regulation of Businessmen (New Haven, Conn.: Yale University Press, 1964), for a study of the relationship between perceived challenges to management autonomy and the compliance of businessmen with government regulations. American businessmen have historically been granted far more autonomy than their counterparts in other capitalist societies. Andrew Schonfield, Modern Capitalism (New York: Oxford University Press, 1965), especially Chapter 13, pp. 298-329.

9. "Who Will Foot the Clean-Up Bill?" Business Week, January 3, 1970, p. 63.

10. See "Corporate Advertising and the Environment," Economic Priorities Report, September-October 1971.

11. Max Ways, "How to Think About the Environment," Fortune, February 1970, p. 99.

12. Robert Diamond, "What Business Thinks," Fortune, February 1970, p. 139.

13. See, for example, David Bird, "Ford Official Urges a Major Loosening of Emission Regulations to Avert 'Shutdown' of U.S. Auto Industry," New York Times, February 16, 1973, p. 9; Gene Smith, "Steel Chief Sees Threat in Antipollution Program," New York Times, December 6, 1972, p. 63.

14. For the 1974-83 decade, the Council on Environmental Quality estimated expenditures attributable to federal laws will be

about $217 billion--an average of $21 billion per year. Gladwin Hill, "Cleaning Up the Environment Is a Money-Making Proposition," Nation, April 17, 1976, p. 457. "Since 1971 there have been only 75 plant closings--involving 13,900 workers--in which cleanup requirements were even purported to be a factor," ibid. This total is considerably less than expected and suggests that even for the individual firm the tension between growth and pollution control may be less than originally anticipated. At a conference in Washington held in December 1975, Russell Peterson, Chairman of the White House Council on Environmental Quality, stated that the American people and government do not have to make "a choice" between environmental protection and the economy. E. W. Kenworthy, "$15 Billion Seen Going to Pollution Fight," New York Times, December 11, 1975, p. 37.

15. For documentation of this relationship, see Stanford Rose, "The Economics of Environmental Quality," Fortune, February 1970, pp. 120-23, 184-86. Many of the benefits of environmental improvement, such as the increase in property values, the opening up of waterways for recreation, tend to be unreflected in GNP but, nonetheless, can be considered economic benefits. Indeed, the ability of the market system to reflect the costs of environmental improvement but to obscure the benefits underlies the existence of environmental problems in the first place.

See also James Quinn, "Next Big Industry: Environmental Improvement," Harvard Business Review, September-October 1971, pp. 120-29. The article is subtitled, "Far From Being a Costly Drain on the Economy, the Ecology Movement Could Produce Profitable New Markets for Business Expansion."

The Environmental Protection Administration estimates that sewerage treatment construction projects alone are currently creating 55,000 jobs, Gladwin Hill, "Environmental Outlays and Inflation: Is There a Link?" New York Times, November 9, 1974.

According to a report prepared by two Wall Street analysts, entitled "The Environmental Control Industry," environmental-control-related employment has been one of the relatively few areas of job strength during the recent recession. Kenworthy, op. cit. Based on Bureau of Labor Statistics data, it has been estimated that pollution-control activity of all sorts currently account for more than one million jobs. Hill, "Cleaning Up the Environment," op. cit., p. 456.

16. Rose, op. cit., p. 186. According to EPA estimates, air and water pollution costs the nation upward of $30 billion a year. This compares quite favorably with current expenditures of $20 billion per year.

17. Quoted in Martin Gellen, "The Making of a Pollution-Control Complex," Ramparts, May 1970, p. 22. See, for example, Pamela Hollie, "Paper Companies Boost Their Profits by Recovering Expensive By-Products," Wall Street Journal, February 7, 1975, p. 28.

18. Quoted in Hill, "Environmental Outlays," op. cit. The compatibility of pollution abatement and capitalism is suggested by the fact that the business community is bitterly divided about the economic effect of increasing expenditures for environmental improvement. Some firms, by virtue of their recycling efforts or their production of pollution-control equipment, favor strict environmental standards.

19. R. O. Hieser, "The Economic Consequences of Zero Population Growth," The Economic Record, June 1973, p. 260. This appraisal is echoed in Barry Commoner, The Closing Circle (New York: Alfred A. Knopf, 1971), Chapter 12, and in Robert Heilbroner, Between Capitalism and Socialism (New York: Vintage, 1970), pp. 269-86.

20. See Paul Sweezy's review of Economics and Public Purpose, in New York Review of Books, November 15, 1973, p. 5.

21. This argument was suggested to me by Louis Lundborg, chairman of the board of Bank of America, retired. It is presented in a different form in Paul Baran and Paul Sweezy, Monopoly Capital (New York: Monthly Review Press, 1966), Chapter 2, especially pp. 20-28.

22. See "The Lower Birthrate Crimps the Baby-Food Market," Business Week, July 13, 1974, pp. 45-50.

23. Commoner, op. cit. E. J. Mishan, Technology and Growth--The Price We Pay (New York: Praeger, 1969). Donella Meadows et al., The Limits to Growth (New York: Universe Books, 1972).

24. "The MIT Report--Is Doomsday Really That Close?" Business Week, March 11, 1972, pp. 97-98. Lewis Beman, "Can Society Survive Technology?" Business Week, April 25, 1970, p. 8. "Growth? Or No Growth?" Forbes, May 15, 1974, pp. 116-17. "Zero-Growth--and Nothing," Dun's, June 1972, p. 136. "Not Surprisingly the Refutation of the No-Growth Position," in The Retreat from Riches, Peter Passell and Leonard Ross (New York: Viking, 1971), was greeted with visible relief in the business press. See Michael Gartner, "The Advocates of Growth," Wall Street Journal, April 10, 1973, p. 20.

25. "How Do We Get From Here to There," address to American Association for the Advancement of Science, San Francisco, February 25, 1974. Lundborg is among the relatively few business

leaders who has publicly confronted the possibility that the scarcity
of resources may require a major reversal of the principles with
which business currently operates.

26. Robert Lindsey, "Oil Companies Promoting Consumption
of Gasoline," New York Times, November 11, 1974, p. 1.

27. See Stephen Shepard, "How Much Energy Does the U.S.
Need?" Business Week, June 1, 1974, pp. 69-70.

28. Vance Packard, The Waste Makers (New York: David
McKay, 1960). Packard's book, which in many ways anticipates
our current concerns about scarcity, was a best seller in the early
1960s. Its criticism of marketing was primarily a moral one and
the book had little economic impact.

29. This paragraph is based on the author's research on the
political and social thinking of businessmen. For a complete exposition, see Leonard Silk and David Vogel, Ethics and Profits:
The Crisis of Confidence in American Business (New York: Simon
and Schuster, 1976), especially Chapter 2.

30. There has always been some tension between the environmental movement and organized labor. See Byron Galame, "Fear-
ing Loss of Jobs, Unions Battle Efforts to Clean Environment,"
Wall Street Journal, November 19, 1971, p. 1.

A slowdown in the rate of economic growth makes these tensions much more visible. The United Auto Workers, for example,
a traditional supporter of strong pollution regulations, reversed its
position when the economy began to decline in 1974: It favored a
relaxation of government requirements in order to reduce costs
and thus increase sales.

The steady growth of industrial economies has been accompanied by a period of social stability. The vision of Karl Marx, who saw an increasingly stratified society eventually overthrown by a restive and unemployed working class, has been repudiated by steady economic growth. Class conflict has been obviated by economic expansion. Instead of a finite world in which the gains of the poor could only come about through direct redistribution of the fortunes of the rich, growth has created a world in which relatively painless reallocation of a growing economic pie has de-fused potentially serious issues of equity and redistribution.

Prosperity has covered over many potentially divisive social issues that persist beneath the surface in industrial societies. Any deliberate change in the rate or direction of economic growth will raise serious problems of equity. Growth has been a great equalizer and largely responsible for closing the gap between rich and poor in U.S. society by putting floors under incomes of the poorest. But the record indicates that, while there was growth in equality of income in the nineteenth century in the United States, there has been no similar growth in income equality in the United States over the last 30 years, a period of relative economic prosperity. Although economic growth makes greater income equality possible, the issue of equality is clearly separable from growth. But, if there is to be less growth in a future society, this will raise some very fundamental problems of income distribution, incentives, social stratification, and equality of opportunity.

Aside from income there are many other social issues that must be faced. Intergenerational equality of opportunity must be preserved. If history is any guide, slowed economic growth would witness greater rigidity in class structures. Resolute attempts must be made to preserve social mobility in any future society. The structure of economic and social rewards must be a rational one. Where great differences in wealth and income persist, there must be a morally acceptable reason for them. A revolution of rising expectations is a worldwide phenomenon. Since expectations are anchored in what other people are perceived to have, a transition to a sustainable society must be accompanied by a new definition of social reality.

Lee Rainwater addresses these questions in Chapter 12. He claims that people in industrial societies are fairly sophisticated about what their money buys. A large paycheck has little objective meaning since most people feel that the cost of maintaining a decent standard of living has been increasing just as rapidly as have wages and salaries. Furthermore, human expectations are anchored in what others are perceived to have. Thus, feelings of prosperity or happiness are related to how well others are perceived to be prospering.

Rainwater has both good and bad news for advocates of sustainable growth. The good news is that Americans are much more egalitarian than they are usually given credit for being. The mythology holds that Americans want a highly inegalitarian structure of rewards, but empirical data indicate the opposite. On the other hand, Americans also question some of the ways in which rewards are apportioned. They feel that they have worked hard for what they have and must be shown why they should accept less than they get.

Rainwater concludes that greater equality is necessary before a sustainable or slow-growth society can be established. A more egalitarian society, on the other hand, is possible prior to a transition to slow growth and would facilitate development of a sustainable society. But to grow slowly first and worry about equality later is to put the cart before the horse. Thus, designing a sustainable society requires attention to the distribution of wealth (a lifetime income spread of no more than four to one from the highest to the lowest classes is suggested), a separation of income inequality from social inequality, and real equality of opportunity within a morally legitimated structure of rewards.

In his visionary chapter on social innovations, John Platt outlines a research and development agenda for a sustainable global society. He claims that humankind is faced with a complicated design process since components of a new society must all fit together. Innovations will be required in both the physical and social sciences. Platt discusses a myriad of changes that could take place in moving toward a sustainable society including innovations in energy conservation, life styles, political and economic structures, and belief systems. Life in a sustainable society characterized by planned growth need not be boring. In fact, Platt's suggested innovations would make life in a future society vital, lively, innovative, and in many ways a much preferred alternative.

The final chapter in this section examines the very important, largely neglected, issue of growth policy and intergenerational equity. Victor Lippit and Koichi Hamada argue that economic analysis as represented by the Coase theorem and Pareto optimality cannot handle controversies among generations. Conventional economics concentrates on exchanges among living persons. But bargains struck among persons in this generation do have an impact on the welfare of future generations. Future generations, however, have no one to represent their interests effectively. Furthermore, even if they did have representatives they have nothing to offer to this generation in return for maintenance of a healthy environment.

The authors also fault conventional economics for its concentration on efficiency at the expense of equity. In their search for rules that would establish an "intergenerational" code of conduct they embrace some of the ideas found in John Rawls' theory of justice. Rawls would maximize the well-being of the most handicapped, in this case the most-handicapped generation. This raises the controversial question of which generation is most handicapped. It seems that in the most industrially developed countries an argument could be made that the present generation is the least handicapped and that future generations will suffer because of contemporary pollution activities. But in the less developed countries it might well be that the present generation is the most handicapped.

CHAPTER

12

EQUITY, INCOME, INEQUALITY, AND THE STEADY STATE
Lee Rainwater

In the past decade, as an outcome of the Civil Rights struggle, the War on Poverty, and the various liberation movements which these set off, there has been a rebirth of hope about the possibility of achieving a more equalitarian society and a rebirth of interest in reforms that are broader than the various War on Poverty measures, which aimed at alleviating the worst damage of inequalitarian patterns of income distribution. To some extent, also, this renewed commitment to the goal of equality came about from a sharper understanding of the fact that inequality in modern industrial societies was not being automatically abated. Instead, evidence began to pile up during the 1960s that existing patterns of inequality were in fact highly stable and that there had been relatively little change over the past half century.

Patterns of inequality exercise a profound and pervasive influence on the quality of life in modern society. When sociologists discuss inequality they have in mind a complex patterning of resources for living, even though this complex is often indexed by a single dimension like occupation or income.

Thus, John Goldthorpe observes that

> social inequality in all its manifestations can be
> thought of as involving differences in social power
> and advantage: power being defined as the capacity
> to mobilize resources (human and nonhuman) in
> order to bring about a desired state of affairs; and
> advantage as the possession or control over whatever in society is valued and scarce. . . . Power
> can be used to secure advantage, while certain advantages constitute the resources that are used in

> the exercise of power. Moreover, different forms
> of power and advantage tend in their very nature to
> be convertible: economic resources can be used to
> gain status or to establish authority; status can
> help to reinforce authority or to create economic
> opportunities; positions of authority usually confer
> status and command high economic rewards, and
> so on. . . . Differences in social power and ad-
> vantage, simply because they imply differences
> across the whole range of life chances, always tend,
> other things being equal, to become generalized
> differences.[1]

Income and wealth are the most easily measured of the resources involved in patterns of social inequality, and given our relatively good measures of these resources the discussion of income
inequality and its trend over time has the greatest precision.

CHANGES IN ECONOMIC INEQUALITY

It seems well established that income and wealth inequality
have not declined significantly over the past half century, and probably have not declined at all in the past quarter century. This recently discovered stability has been an embarrassment to many.
Economic growth in the minds of many social commentators had been
a force for steadily diminishing social inequality. As the pie got
larger and larger, those who were less well off were also supposed
to be getting slightly larger proportions. Such apparently is not the
case.
Some would argue that the stability of inequality does not really
matter, that even if you are in the same relative place on the totem
pole, the fact that you have a great deal more now than you did 20 or
50 or 100 years ago means that the quality of your life has improved
in a roughly proportional way. However, there is an increasing
amount of evidence from research into the sociology and social psychology of inequality to suggest that this is not the case. Two kinds
of illusions, a "money illusion" and a "growth illusion, " enable
people to argue that the lot of the poor man, or the man who is just
getting along, or the average man improves in some fundamental
way as the economic pie gets larger. Economists have talked about
the money illusion as an important factor in creating acceptance of
one's relative position in the structure of income and wealth--in
periods of moderate inflation, the man who gets a wage that enables
him just to keep up with the rising cost of living may nevertheless

feel that he somehow is better off than before, because his attention is fixed on the dollars and cents on his paycheck rather than on what it will buy. Similarly, the growth illusion seems to have functioned to distract people's attention from the fact that although their incomes command more in the way of goods and services, their relative shares have not changed.

The money and growth illusions were probably much more powerful as people came out of the Great Depression, through the period of World War II, and into the relatively sustained period of postwar economic growth than they are now. Sophistication about inflation and the cost of living seems to have grown quite a bit. More basic is the folk wisdom which enables people to perceive that if everyone has more--so that having more becomes a requirement-- improvement in your physical standard of living does not necessarily represent an improvement in your social standard of living.

There are several different kinds of suggestive, though not conclusive, evidence on this point. In a recent interview study dealing with people's perceptions of how life had changed from the late 1940s to the present and how it was likely to change from 1971 to the 1980s, a very striking dominant theme in the responses was that while everyone had higher incomes, somehow the cost of living had risen as fast as incomes had.[2] People also believed that this was likely to be true into the future. It was clear that the people we interviewed did not mean the cost of living in the sense of economists' dollars of constant purchasing power, but rather the cost of living in a more social sense of the kind of access to housing and automobiles and food and education for one's children and the like that an individual has to have in order to consider himself a full-fledged participant in the American dream.

More along the line of hard data, I assembled for that study the answers since 1946 to a Gallup Poll question that has been asked almost every year: "How much does a family of four need to get along in this community?" In analyzing the average amounts given by Gallup's national samples, I discovered that the average as a proportion of per capita disposable personal income had varied hardly at all in that 25-year period. The amount considered necessary for the family of four to get along averaged almost exactly 50 percent of disposable income for four persons in that year.

This result, I think, suggests how powerfully our sense of whether we have an acceptable, adequate standard of living is a function of what everybody else has. The money illusion and the growth illusion serve to distract consciousness from this fact, but in the end people's conceptions of how well they are doing point not so much

to improvements over the past as to their current situations vis-a-
vis their fellow citizens.

One final example of this point comes from a study conducted
by Richard Easterlin in which he posed for himself the question,
"Does money buy happiness?"[3] He observed that various public
opinion polls had asked people in a number of countries varying
widely in their level of economic development a question about
whether they were happy. On assembling data from these studies he
discovered that in general, as any classical economist would predict, within each country those who had high incomes were somewhat happier than those with average incomes; those with average
incomes considerably more often said they were happier than those
with low incomes. Thus, it seems that the more you have in the
way of income and all that money buys, the greater your sense of
subjective well-being. This economists' logic would also predict
that people in countries with high per capita incomes will, on the
average, be happier than people in countries with low per capita income. Here, however, the relationship between income and happiness disappears. Examining the proportion of the population who
consider themselves happy in relation to per capita GNP, one dis-
covers that the correlation is essentially zero. So though within any
one country the level of well-being is correlated with economic resources, across countries it is not, suggesting very powerfully,
Easterlin argues, that what is important in people's sense of subjective well-being is their relative position vis-a-vis those in their
own group rather than the absolute resources which they command.

IMPLICATIONS FOR SUSTAINABLE GROWTH

One can take from findings such as these both good news and
bad news. The good news is that there is no necessary connection
between economic growth and personal well-being. There is no
reason why in a low-growth society people cannot be as happy as in
one that experiences 5 percent growth per year. People do not have
to have more and more in order to find satisfaction in life. Indeed,
folk awareness operates even now to discount much of the gain that
people experience from growth.

The bad news is that there is no connection between economic
growth and decreasing inequality. The whole notion of "progress,"
to the extent that it is assumed that modern industrialization and
economic growth would produce ever more equalitarian societies,
is clearly wrong.

PUBLIC VIEWS CONCERNING EQUALITY
AND INEQUALITY

If one turns from the question of patterns of inequality and relative position to that of public conceptions of the structure of inequality, one finds that the public has very mixed feelings about the massive inequalities which exist in U.S. society. The dominant view among Americans is one that holds that there are in fact many important unjustified inequalities in the way our system operates, that far too many people have less than any human being should have, that too many of the fat cats are selfish and rapacious. Many people disapprove of the level of inequality, wish it were different, but accept things as they are as nearly the best one can hope for in an imperfect world.

They believe there is much room for improvement and particularly that the world ought to be put together in such a way that no one is confined to a life as a low wage-earner or as a wife and child in a low wage-earner's family. Americans are remarkably generous in the kinds of social and economic policies they are willing to consider to bring about a change in that kind of situation, so long as policies seem to reinforce the value of working for a living rather than subverting it.

As John Goldthorpe observes of Britain, in the United States there is no clearly established legitimation of the particular pattern of inequalities that exist.[4] There is a general sense that some people work harder than others, that some people have greater talents than others, that some people have greater enterprise than others, and that therefore it is right that some people have more income, wealth, and power than others. The minute one begins to examine the structure of rewards closely, the lack of a moral basis for the distribution as it exists is readily apparent. The distribution of rewards is understood to be partly the result of moral forces (hard work, enterprise, creativity), and partly the result of immoral ones (cheating, undeserved luck, selfishness, and viciousness). In such a situation, no one need feel embarrassed about asserting his own claims on the system.

Exactly because the work ethic is alive and well in the United States, because most people feel that they work hard for what they have, that they have tried hard in the past, and that they have built up some skill, they feel justified in pressing their own demands for more income, more benefits, and the like. Goldthorpe, in his analysis of labor relations in Britain, makes the profound observation that the juxtaposition of one's own sense of doing one's best on the job coupled with the lack of any overall sense of moral regulation of the structure of rewards is conducive to endemic economic conflict, an economic conflict which can be expected to continue so long as there is merely acquiescence to but not acceptance of the structure of rewards as morally based. Further, there is good reason to believe that the only possible moral basis for a structure of rewards would involve a much more egalitarian distribution than now exists, as well as a greater degree of equality of opportunity to achieve whatever unequal rewards might still exist.

I've reviewed here the question of public views concerning the patterns of inequality in order to suggest that the often-repeated conservative notion that inequality is demanded by the public has little basis in fact. Most Americans would like to see a more egalitarian distribution of income than in fact exists, and they have fairly clear and quite realistic reasons: They believe that the more egalitarian society would not only be more just, but would also be more comfortable both for those who are advantaged and those who are disadvantaged. It would be a more humane society, one in which individuals could be more fully themselves because they wouldn't be caught up in the rat race of keeping up with the Joneses.

The problem of achieving a more egalitarian society, therefore, is more the problem of transition to it than of its maintenance once achieved. And it is here, in connection with the question of the transition from a system of glaring inequalities to a more equitable system, that the question of growth is most salient.

GREATER EQUALITY WITH SLOWED GROWTH

Though those interested in achieving a more egalitarian society have learned that economic growth is no automatic ally of equality, optimists still believe that economic growth could be a powerful facilitator of the transition to a more egalitarian society. There is nothing automatic about the move toward equality, but economic growth could be harnessed to achieve a markedly more equal society without the advantaged classes losing in other than a relative sense.

A little simple arithmetic will show you that if personal income grows at 5 percent a year in real terms--slightly biasing that rate upward for income classes below the median and slightly biasing it downward for those with incomes above the median--it could produce a situation within a decade in which no one in the society earned significantly less than the median income, while everyone above the median was nevertheless slightly better off in absolute terms. Phrased another way, if half of the increment in personal income that would come from ten years of economic growth at 5 percent a year were distributed to those below the median, those above the median could divide the other half and still be somewhat better off than before. (By biasing the growth in income in the direction of the group below the median I am not referring only or even primarily to policies such as the guaranteed income or family allowances, though those would play an important part, but principally to changing the demand for labor in such a way that there would be virtually no unemployment for people in low-income positions and their wages would rise relative to the median income.)

In this sense, economic growth if properly managed could realize the reformer's dream of helping the unfortunate but not making anyone else absolutely worse off. Such a program is, I believe, imminently feasible in a world of what has been considered reasonable economic growth, although the fact that it is feasible does not, of course, mean that the political will exists to do it.

This kind of movement toward greater equality would be oriented to inequalities in advantage, rather than social power (although of course there would be effects on social power). Another aspect of moving toward a more egalitarian society involves reducing the social power of those who are far above the median in terms of income and other economic resources. Even during a period of rapid economic growth there can be no question of producing greater equality without an absolute decline in the power exercised by the very affluent, since power is preeminently a relative matter, a zero-sum game. Nevertheless, to some extent the bite that would come from higher marginal tax rates on the incomes of the rich, and from wealth taxes on the wealth of those with great fortunes, would he reduced in a situation of continuing economic growth.

In any case, in terms of the equality of the daily lives of those who are disadvantaged by our current patterns of socioeconomic inequality, it is clear that the most important goal is that of raising incomes of the disadvantaged relative to those in the middle, rather than lowering the incomes of the overprivileged. The average citizen now believes that families with incomes over about $30,000 a year are rich. It is not at all difficult to devise tax programs which heavily redistribute income toward families with incomes below the median and are paid for exclusively by higher taxes on families with incomes over that amount.

What happens if we enter a low-growth world with roughly the same level of inequality that we have today; what then are the prospects for transition to a significantly more egalitarian society? My guess is that the probability of such a transition is considerably less than in a world of moderate economic growth (ignoring the case in which the probability of such a transition, even in a world of growth, is zero and egalitarian hopes are simply pipe dreams).

In a sustainable society we no longer have the possibility of moving toward whatever equality is desired without individuals in the advantaged half of the population ever having to suffer an absolute decline in income. In order to produce a distribution in which no one has a living level very far below the median, the income of those above the median would have to be cut by some 30 percent. What is to be our strategy in such a world, then? To persuade the better-off proportion of the population to give up 3 percent of their relative position a year through various redistributive strategies and achieve the redistribution over a decade? Or to give up 1 percent a year and achieve the redistribution over a quarter of a century?

Offhand, it does not seem likely that any kind of consensual democratic politics could produce such an altruistic result. (Maybe this would be possible in a society such as Sweden where there is a broad-based ideological commitment to the idea of equality of result and nothing like the romantic individualism which has characterized the United States.)

The problem is that the economy of slowed growth does away with the two illusions which make it somewhat easier to swallow the pill of redistribution. The growth illusion is by definition gone. In the case of inflation, the slow-growth society achieves zero or very low rates of inflation, or exactly because there is no growth people become hyperaware of what inflation means in terms of their consumption and push toward a kind of de facto indexing.

Without these illusions, it seems likely that the lack of moral regulation of the rewards people receive from the system will become more and more a focus of attention. Therefore the competitive demands of different groups are likely to precipitate more and more conflict, and that conflict is likely to become increasingly politicized as opposed to being fought out exclusively within economic institutions.

One of the first casualties of the sustainable society may be the rather high level of equality of opportunity enjoyed in the modern industrial societies. Much of the social mobility which exists in our world is "forced" by economic growth and the lower relative level of the higher classes' birth rates. In a society with uniformly low birth rates and little or no economic growth, the proportion of any generation that felt itself to have realized parental ambitions and sacrifices so that the kids could do better in life would be smaller than today. Further, it is very likely that parents with advantages would work much harder than they do today (and in ways that would be regarded as illegitimate as well as legitimate) to insure that their children at least maintained the family's status. Slowed growth, therefore, would exert great strain on our already imperfect system of social classes. One would not have difficulty

finding today individuals ready to perfect an ideology for such a sys-
tem--it would be all too clear that society's stability, our cultural
heritage, and having things run by the best minds required it.

EQUALITY THROUGH SOCIOPOLITICAL COLLAPSE

There are some egalitarians who believe that the increasing
conflict and the decreasing legitimacy of the corporations and government would be a useful development, that the more conflict there
is the more the basic injustice of the system is revealed and the
more also is revealed the pernicious role of those with great power
in the large corporations and in the government institutions which
serve that power. According to this scenario, from the outrage at
the discovery that "the system" is no longer capable of producing
ever higher material levels of living would come significant moves
to limit the power of those at the top, and in the case of large corporations to deprive them of the power to ignore the public interest.
The elite have been the principal salesmen of growth, so the argument goes, and once growth disappears they will lose their legitimacy as movers and shakers.

Then, so the argument goes, after the current power elite has
been stripped of its power, perhaps after significant nationalization
of large corporations and after the infusion into position of political
leadership of persons whose goal is to serve the people rather than
to serve the powers, significant egalitarian policies can be adopted.
There will be no more large fortunes, no more six-figure salaries
and stock option deals, the lower upper class will pay a more reasonable proportion of their income in taxes, and redistribution will bring
into the mainstream of American life those who now live below it.

I wish I could believe that scenario, but it seems to me a less-
attractive one is more probable. During the crises which must attend any transition to a much different type of economy, the disappearance of the growth and money illusions will establish an even
more intensive awareness on the part of each class in society of
where its own selfish interests lie. In particular those with even a
modicum of social power will bend their every effort toward using
that power in alliance with other groups to preserve and solidify
their privilege. Large groups of workers in the middle will be
sorely pressed to make use of their bargaining power to maintain
or improve their incomes a bit. It will be easier for some of them
to strike bargains with small groups with great power than it will be
to confront the powerful head-on. One possible outcome is that public and private policies will be pursued which render more and more
of the population superfluous (unemployed or employed in only a

marginal labor market) in order to preserve the security and privilege of the middle majority.   It might well be, depending on the particular political cast of the times in which this takes place, that the
very rich suffer a bit from this turmoil--one can even imagine a
fairly hefty wealth tax being adopted--but such a slight reduction in
inequality at the top would not at all contraindicate an increase in
inequality between the middle and the bottom of the scale.

For all these reasons, the egalitarian is not likely to welcome
the coming of slower economic growth or to view the slowed-growth
society with any optimism.   This is not, however, because slowed
growth and egalitarianism could not coexist once established.

SLOWED GROWTH IN A MORE EQUAL SOCIETY

Suppose, therefore, by some miracle, U.S. society were to
become much more egalitarian in the distribution of socioeconomic
resources. Suppose in the course of a lifetime almost everyone in
society experienced at least the median level of income, and no one
had great wealth. Suppose also that a society had very little economic growth.

We should probably find that in this kind of society the well-
being of the population, in fact, had increased considerably over the
well-being of the population in our present inegalitarian society with
economic growth. The fact that there is diminishing marginal utility
to increasing economic resources means that for any given level of
aggregate economic resources, the more equally distributed the
income, the higher the overall level of well-being of the group. An
elegant mathematical statement of this general point by Atkinson
allows us to make some estimates of how much better off a population would be with given levels of inequality. It's possible, that is,
to compare income distributions in terms of how much aggregate
well-being could be increased by redistribution or, on the other
hand (and this is particularly important when one is concerned with
issues of slowing economic growth), how much less aggregate income would be necessary to achieve the same level of aggregate
well-being in a more egalitarian society. For example, given some
recent work on the marginal utility of aggregate income, it looks
like aggregate well-being with egalitarian distributions would require only about 70 percent of the present level of personal income
to produce an equal aggregate level of well-being.[5]

At a more sociological level, in the more egalitarian society
the instigation to status-striving through the use of material goods
and services (so-called conspicuous consumption) would be greatly
limited.   Much of what we think of now as conspicuous consumption

is more defensive in character than it is intrinsically rewarding. It involves keeping up with the Joneses, and is in fact experienced as a burden by a surprisingly large proportion of families.

Therefore, societies with much more equality than our own are the only kinds of societies that are likely to be able to live with slow growth without a totalitarian government. In fact, it is unlikely that even totalitarian societies would be interested in maintaining slowed growth since such governments are seldom far-sighted and would be under constant pressure to make use of economic growth to buy off incipient opposition.

This more egalitarian society that could live with less growth would be strikingly different from our own. It would probably require a lifetime income spread of no more than four to one from the highest to the lowest level of income classes. (Of course, some people might choose to take their "income" in the form of voluntary leisure--but the leisure would have to be truly voluntary and not involve the assignment of some people to a forced leisure class.) It would have to be a society in which there was no private wealth other than the private goods and provisions for retirement and disablement that individuals make. No large fortunes. Finally, it would need to be a society in which the exacerbation of inequality in income by linking it with inequalities of social capital like education was much reduced. And it would need to be a system in which equality of opportunity to achieve whatever conditions of leadership and higher reward existed was truly open in terms of recruitment, careers, and decision making. Given this kind of society, the maintenance of a low-growth society would be much easier than it would be, if indeed it is possible, in a society with high levels of economic inequality.

There is nothing to be learned from spinning out these scenarios much further. The essential point is that achieving the goals of equality is made more difficult by the disappearance of economic growth. This is no argument against the sustainable society, since if we are to believe the information that has been developed in recent times, the alternative is first the declining society then possibly no society. My argument does suggest that those who participate in bringing about the transition to the no-growth situation should have the utmost sensitivity to equality issues, to the needs and possibilities of that third of Americans who never have had the chance to enjoy the pleasures of overabundance, and whose experience in the labor force is one of insecurity, marginality, and superfluity except in times of rapid economic growth. There will be a great danger in the low-growth society that better-off people will seek to monopolize work as a way of monopolizing the economy's product.

It would help if those who make the transition understood that while there is no necessary connection between a given amount of material resources and personal well-being, the dynamics of human society (modern or primitive, growing or steady) are such that people who have relatively less than whatever is the going mainstream standard of their society are being deprived of crucial resources to live a reasonable life, are indeed being robbed of a decent life by their more affluent fellow men. It would be shameful if the exigencies of saving the planet for the future of mankind became an excuse to perpetuate the injustices some men now inflict on their fellows.

NOTES

1. John H. Goldthorpe, "Social Inequality and Social Integration in Britain," Advancement of Science 26 (December 1969): 128; reprinted in Social Problems and Public Policy: Inequality and Justice, ed. Lee Rainwater (Chicago: Aldine, 1974).

2. Lee Rainwater, What Money Buys (New York: Basic Books, 1974).

3. Richard A. Easterlin, "Does Economic Growth Improve the Human Lot," in Nations and Households in Economic Growth: Essays in Honor of Moses Abramovitz, ed. Paul A. David and Melvin W. Reder (Stanford, Calif.: Stanford University Press, 1974).

4. Goldthorpe, op. cit. Rainwater, What Money Buys, op. cit.

5. A. B. Atkinson, "On the Measurement of Inequality," Journal of Economic Theory 2 (1970): 244-63; Joseph E. Schwartz, "Taking a Look at Income," unpublished paper, Department of Sociology, Harvard University, September 1974.

CHAPTER

13

SOCIAL INNOVATIONS
REQUIRED FOR A
SUSTAINABLE GLOBAL SOCIETY
John Platt

The list is endless. Society is at least as complicated as an automobile. And an automobile has something like 10,000 parts that must be designed by R&D teams, tried out, corrected or thrown away and redesigned, fitted together, and continually changed as cars change. Today we are in the midst of a great world transformation carrying us into a new kind of future, because of our new technological changes in the powers and speeds and intensities of human interaction. All the old institutions are changing before our eyes and they must be revised or new institutions must be created by the best designs we can make, if we are not to leave them to be created by force and accident. Every level of organization, from the individual and the family to the global system, and every functional relationship, from belief systems to international money, must be reexamined in the light of our new needs and new knowledge. The task is urgent because these relationships are changing so fast. Within 20 years, new structures, good or bad, and new stresses of the deepest and most dangerous sort may become frozen or locked-in together so they would be almost impossible for our children to change for many generations. And even in these very responsive times, there is still a long lead time, of ten years or more, to get any new design or institutional response studied, planned, pilottested, and adopted, no matter how promising it may seem. The result is that there is no time to be lost, and leadership groups such as the Institute for World Order, Pugwash Conferences, or the Club of Rome, or more specialized local, regional, or functional groups, need to get hundreds or thousands of such studies started and funded.

It is important--as with an automobile--that the new designs of different components should fit together. Individual images and

behaviors must fit the pattern of a sustainable global society, and
vice versa. Groups working on such problems must interact so that
they can get as much agreement as possible on a common philosophy
and common goals; or where agreement is not possible, a metaagreement or framework within which to disagree (like parliamentary rules), so that the contending groups will not destroy each other
or all the rest of us. A tolerance of diversity, as in the Treaty of
Ghent that ended a century of Protestant-Catholic wars, is obviously
an essential component for any sustainable global society.

A few examples of needed studies will be given here in several
areas to illustrate the range of things that must be done and to suggest
some approaches. But obviously no single individual can imagine all
the structures and relationships that need to be studied and perhaps
redesigned in all parts of the world, any more than a single individual
could design an automobile today. Every group that gets to work on
any of these areas or on the general problematique will soon come up
with its own lists, and they will evolve as the studies proceed.

ENERGY-CONSERVING METHODS AND INSTITUTIONS

Energy costs in this century have been so low that conservation
has not been very important for the industrial West, either in design
or in methods of use. In many cases, fairly trivial redesign or
changed patterns of use could effect large energy savings, and it
seems almost certain that such changed patterns will characterize
a sustainable future that has greatly increased energy and environmental costs.

In architecture, buildings are likely to use less materials,
more locally produced and less highly processed, but with less external surface, better insulation, less wasteful furances, and more
use of solar heat or of waste heat from other processes. It will move
toward the "maximin" architecture that Buckminster Fuller has emphasized, to get maximum usefulness with minimum materials. This
does not necessarily mean stone buildings that would last for 200
years; it might mean modular constructions, easy to move or rearrange or recycle. The cost of some minimum recycling might be
a cost that each generation would gladly pay to fit its own new technological changes or new images and life styles, or to be rid of the
mistakes of its predecessors.

We have also been wasteful in our use of buildings. Offices and
schools are in use only about one-third of every day, although there
are round-the-clock factories and hospitals and airports and, more
recently, supermarkets and laundromats. Some people are nightin-
gales, some are skylarks. Why not allow for their diversity by

having work and play and transportation facilities around the clock
and around the week and around the year? It would take leadership
and government design and incentives, but it might almost cut in
half our need for new buildings and roads and public transport, with
their energy requirements. It would cut overcrowding in schools
and traffic jams, and it would fit well into round-the-world networks
of business and transportation, which are necessarily around-the-
clock.

    In our use of energy, we have been wasteful in designing in-
dustrial processes. There is great waste in wash water and cooling
water (as in agricultural irrigation). Much energy is lost in the
inefficient burning of trash or in cleaning up dispersed wastes, often
thrown onto the public sector, when these wastes could be reduced
or recycled much more efficiently. The failure to design automobiles and other consumer goods for automatic return and easy
separation and recycling of components is wasteful of both materials and energy.

    We need to distinguish clearly between unnecessarily large
uses of energy and the small uses which give their full measure of
human and home satisfactions. Automobiles, for example, cost $4
to $5 per car per day in the United States--which is at least a crude
measure of their cost in energy consumption of materials and gasoline and highways. This cost might be cut almost in half by using
smaller cars with less gasoline consumption and more mass transport. But even a 10 percent reduction would be more than enough to
pay for all the human and home satisfactions and leisure enhance-
ments of lights, automatic dishwashers, clothes washers and dryers,
refrigerators, and radio and television, all of which cost only a few
cents per day. When energy grows more scarce and expensive, we
should, and probably we will, concentrate on the uses that give us
more abundant personal satisfactions.

    In transportation, it is clear that we need more and better
mass transportation to reduce our need for private cars, and of
course enormous efforts are now going into such developments. In
the public sector it is not usually realized how much each additional
private car costs the community in highways, police, parking space,
congestion, and air pollution. Often this money could better be
spent in subsidies for free buses and trains, as many communities
have now realized. Cheap and abundant taxicabs, possibly subsidized, are much more convenient and efficient than private cars in
high-density cities, as New Yorkers have always told us. But we
also need faster and more universal Dial-a-Bus systems (computerized mass-taxi service) and Rent-a-Car systems, to keep cars
in service around the clock, for door-to-door family needs and privacy and bad-weather service that mass transit cannot provide.

LIFE STYLES

No species and no society can be sustainable for long against our numerous and unexpected developments and threats in creating a more interconnected global society, unless it practices systematic diversification. This principle is well-known in evolution, and it has recently been reemphasized for society and culture by B. F. Skinner in Beyond Freedom and Dignity.[1] A rigid society is a dead-end society, unable to discuss or cope with changes necessary for survival. We have seen this repeatedly in the dictatorships of the last 50 years, which have failed again and again to deal with complex problems and changes, by comparison with the more open and flexible democracies with their continual cries of alarm and adaptations.

So in the years ahead an excessively unified world might easily drift into locked-in technological madness or ecological madness or into psychologically suicidal retreat-from-the-world or unnoticed genetic deterioration or into more sophisticated dangers which we cannot even imagine today. The only hope for long-run human survival is in the active encouragement of tolerance and diverse experimentation of different individual and group attitudes, beliefs, and life styles, often in isolation or in what seem to be very undesirable directions. Only thus can we create the social mutations necessary for important improvements or response to changed circumstances.

A sustainable society is also likely to require a return to many Puritan virtues such as simplicity of living styles and conservation practices, as Edward Goldsmith and his colleagues emphasized in Blueprint for Survival.[2] We may not only turn off lights and pick up aluminum foil and carry European net shopping bags, but we may become string savers again, like our grandmothers. The Puritan pattern included a lot of education and apprenticeship in the home, because of the distance and cost of schooling, and mutual services between neighbors: sharing pies, barn-raisings, and barn dances. Many of our families and neighborhoods today need such a rebuilding of relationships, to make a psychologically sustainable society.

And certainly we will have to enlarge the nuclear family in various ways, in some forms of group living such as communes, extended families, or family clusters. The Victorian houses had 14 rooms and 10 to 20 people of several generations, playing various roles. The nuclear family of the 1920s, with its two young adults and two to four children in a small apartment or suburban house, was an important escape from rigid Victorian grandparents and morality toward freedom and scientific ideas and modernity. But it destroyed the psychological supports of close relationships across the whole life cycle--with the children locked-in to their peer group and the little box, with the parents forced into too many roles, and

with old people having to leave their big empty nest for a trailer or
a Sunset Colony. No wonder the alcoholism and divorce rates are
so high.

What is perhaps worst about the stereotypical nuclear family
is that it is such a standard image of American life for advertisers
and the media, business, banks, and officials and yet is so far from
reality for most people. Tens of millions are in college dormitories
or the army, or are single, widowed, divorced, or are children in
broken families, or are old people, isolated or in retirement homes.
The nuclear family, with relatives hundreds or thousands of miles
away, doubles the burden in the life crises of separation or illness
or death, at precisely the times when an extended family or a tribe
is most needed. We suddenly realize that the human species, like
all the primates, has lived for most of its existence in larger troops
and tribes and is probably not genetically or psychologically designed
for this artificially separated modern world. What is urgently needed
for a sustainable society is study to find a way back, a synthesis that
will give us both the freedom and enlightenment of the nuclear family
at its best and the total psychological support of an extended living
group.

To make such a synthesis we need the knowledge and innovative
ideas of many different fields. We need architects to design for
both privacy and communal rooms; economists to examine new costs
and new savings and the balance of work and leisure and income between in-group and outside activities; lawyers on group contracts,
equity, transfers, insurance, divorce, and children; psychologists
and child psychologists and behaviorists on group reinforcements,
decision making, interpersonal and community friction, and leadership; and so on. It would be of great value to bring such experts
together for study, along with religious or social or neighborhood
groups that would like to take part in extended-family living experiments, to see how various types of ongoing and self-correcting
groups might be launched and successfully kept going.

In another direction, we need innovations to make optimum
use of the new "electronic surround" that is now enfolding all of us
with television and audio and video cassettes. More than 1.5 billion
people--nearly two-fifths of the world's population--saw the Olympic
games telecast from Munich in 1972 and Montreal in 1976. As the
number who are simultaneously linked together in this way to the
world's excitements and crises passes the 50 percent mark in the
next year or two, their collective on-going responses may make a
sustainable global society much easier--or much more difficult. In
a deep sense, "the medium is the message," as it crosses all
boundaries and brings the story of the electronic sciences and the
communications network and the world weather map and literacy and

skills and the knowledge of how other people live, regardless of how propagandistic the individual programs are. Study of the international effects of this tremendous change in simultaneous human consciousness is urgently needed.

But it is clear that many of these effects can be beneficial in terms of personal growth, value-sharing, study, and work. The electronic surround, with cassettes of choice, can transform schooling--as in the British Open University on television--and increase diversity and mutual consciousness of different interest groups, in the same way that long-playing records have increased the diversity and coherence of audio and music enthusiasts. Our current "movements of consciousness," such as the ecology and consumer movements, women's liberation, black power, and the ethnic movements, have grown rapidly under the impact of video controversy. If work can also be brought back into the home by electronic methods, the destabilizing effects of national and world business operations on family patterns may be greatly reduced.

But this simplification and increased neighborhood bonding of life in the new world should not go so far as to prevent all travel. Marx warned against "rural idiocy," and an electronic society can also have a dangerous loss of relationships, understanding, and breadth of vision if people everywhere are tied too closely to one local group or one television set. It is important for the young to break away from families, to travel or to go to college to become deprovincialized, and in a global society it will be important to go to other countries to learn other languages and ways by living in them for a year or two. A part of that commuter travel of 10,000 miles a year could well be transferred to occasional vacation travel or sabbaticals, for the working classes as well as for management, to other countries and climates. A sustainable world order will require world networks and massive popular sympathies that reach beyond the nation-state and are continually renewed.

POLITICAL AND ECONOMIC STRUCTURES

John Rawls' A Theory of Justice, the central principle of which is to maximize the lot of the least-well-off, may become a powerful political bargaining principle for both rich and poor, since it justifies inequality within limits while demanding improvement for the poorest.[3] With intense debate and improvement aiming at more widespread consensus, such a theory might play the role of Montesquieu and Locke in making a philosophical base for the laws, politics, economics, and participatory sharing of the next century.

The U.S. Constitution gave us the first designed, self-correcting society with feedback stabilization by "checks and balances." But it urgently needs to be brought up to date to fit our new problems, dangers, and knowledge. Political science departments everywhere should be examining what new checks and balances are available or could be devised to help stabilize good government and make it responsive in an age of nuclear terror, television, data banks, multinational corporations, and international interdependence with respect to food, energy, resources, inflation, and unemployment.

Some thought needs to be given specifically to the "rules of order" of parliamentary bodies, which mostly go back two centuries to a time when orderly debate was the first requirement. It seems possible that a conference on this problem, bringing in our new knowledge of small group processes, management and decision theory, game theory of conflict and cooperation, lock-ins and social traps, could speed up our parliamentary decision making, reduce legalistic confrontations, anger, and boredom, and increase the sense of effective mutual decision. Various new designs could be tried experimentally for a few years, and the most promising ones might then spread like wildfire to thousands of democratic bodies, faculty senates, city councils, and state and national legislatures to give us all a new sense of mutuality and confidence in the democratic process.

A systems analysis of our legal system, courts, and police is urgently needed to see if we could not deal more fairly and at the same time more expeditiously with deviant or dangerous behavior than we are doing now with our old-fashioned theories of crime, guilt, and punishment. The decriminalization of drunkenness, homosexuality, consenting sex acts, gambling, divorce, and auto accidents is an important start, but the whole system needs to be reexamined. Reinforcement theorists say that a nonpunitive society is possible. Is it? Can the energies of protesting subcultures that entrap the young, or entrepreneurial criminal services to the society, be prevented or redirected by increasing justice or reducing profits or positively reinforcing other activities by these subgroups? Can violence and terrorism be made less influential and less attractive? Can upper-class crime be better revealed and better prevented?

Many of our economic structures may change radically in the next 20 years, because they seem incompatible with a sustainable global society. In a world of scarce resources and great population pressure and public needs, the private control of land use or building design or use for private profit will become increasingly intolerable, and so will the control or manipulation of industries, stocks,

and money. New mechanisms will be needed to reconcile the public
need for design and planning and the public good with the useful flexibility of private bargaining and market mechanisms in promoting
efficiencies and adjusting to new desires and values.

In economics a number of new developments may make it
easier to convert to "real-time flow-system accounting," much
closer to the ideas of the early socialists. Credit cards and computerized check-offs of purchases, moving toward a "moneyless"
society, will fit together with daily interest accruals and daily
adjustments to inflation by the Brazilian method of "indexing," and
perhaps soon with daily wage credits or rent or installment-plan
credits, to make a "real-time" daily flow of all living expenses and
earnings credits. It might only be a short step then to put all social
transfers, from primary wage-earners to children, students, the
sick, the old--as represented today by time-delayed debts, insurance, welfare, savings, and investments--on a similar real-time
basis, to give considerably increased clarification, rationality, and
justice to our personal and national economics and social accounting.

Another change in production and trade in the last few years
has been the change from "stockpiling" of surplus goods to a "pipeline" system in which there is continuous feedback adjustment of
production to anticipated demand, as in the blood system of a biological organism. Unfortunately this makes the system much more
vulnerable to blockages in essential pipelines or "bottlenecks," with
what could be called "throttleneck" behavior by groups demanding
justice or blackmailers or terrorists. This is a principal reason
for the numerous crises that have disrupted society recently from
strikes by teachers, firemen, police, bridgetenders, longshoremen,
taxi drivers, coal miners, and oil producers.[4] Obviously a method
is needed for calling attention to needs and for achieving justice and
equity without such desperate measures and convulsions of civil life.
But in addition, society may need new methods of preventing blockages and protecting essential pipelines. And it probably should
create multiple parallel or alternative pipelines in many cases, like
the parallel arteries that supply the brain, to keep the blockage of
any one from being fatal. Coal-plus-oil-plus-nuclear-power and
railroads-plus-trucks-plus-airlines.

In addition, it is clear, as many have said, that we need "a
new Keynes" to analyze international economics and the strange new
global coupling of inflation and unemployment. Global computer
simulations may be needed to find policies that will not have "counterintuitive" consequences that make the disease worse, and new
forms of international cooperation on such policies may be necessary and inevitable.

NEW GLOBAL STRUCTURES TO MEET
GLOBAL CRISES

There are many pressures now, of need, self-interest, conscience, and concern for the prevention of foreseeable collective disasters, for the creation of new world management structures of several different kinds. World food stockpiles against massive famines are called for by many authorities, and some efforts are being made for agreement on the law of the sea and ocean resources. McGeorge Bundy has suggested some plausible scenarios in which a series of disasters--megafamines, or terrorist Hiroshima explosions--finally motivate the major powers to make realistic and enforceable "covenants" for food supply, population leveling, and nuclear peace-keeping. He sees these as leading to a great covenant for world planning and management by about 1989--the 200th anniversary of the democracies.

That these prospects are not hopeless is suggested by the results of the oil and energy crisis created by the oil producers' price rise in 1973, which has already led to a general realization of world economic interdependence, a massive redistribution of wealth, and calls for a better international monetary system and increased aid to developing countries, as well as for multiple long-range energy planning. And, just as hunters and fishermen have a common interest in setting up fish and game commissions to manage these resources for maximum sustainable yield, so the nations of the world may see a similar common interest in setting up superordinate authorities to manage the oceans and other resources for maximum long-run use.

The future role of the multinational corporations (MNCs) is especially interesting. On the one hand, they represent useful and necessary production and trade networks for exchange of resources and peaceful operations large enough to interpenetrate and stand against the military threats of the nation-states. But on the other hand, they are so large that they can buy and sell small countries and subvert governments, or maximize profits by sweat-shop methods indifferent to human or ecological considerations. It seems likely that checks and balances against these dangers must and will develop, including political checks from world opinion and the superpowers, countervailing multinational efforts against cartels, and multinational labor unions and consumer and ecology movements.

It seems likely that these new global structures will be fairly narrow, functionally organized networks in the beginning, and only later will begin to interact strongly as a kind of world government under some great covenant or world structures management council. At that stage there could come constitutional provisions for representation and reform.

BELIEF SYSTEMS FOR SURVIVAL

The last few years have seen the rapid growth of a strong
humanistic and secular ethics oriented toward responsibility and
mutual survival. This is exerting strong pressures for change on
the older religions. Along with their lofty beliefs in love or the
eightfold way or the unity of mankind, they are seen as holding many
primitive and dangerous or immoral doctrines from their patriar-
chal beginnings--hierarchical, pronatalist, antiwomen, antioutsiders
and "heathen," prowar, proproperty, and antiland-reform, antiex-
perimental, predeterminist, dogmatic, and full of irrational taboos.
By contrast, the new ethics emphasize ecology, the stewardship and protection of the "seamless web" of nature around the globe,
rather than the attempt to "have dominion" over it. It means a religious respect for life, not polluting the oceans or killing off the
whales or tigers or flies; and at the personal level, having two
children or less, recycling the bottles, and leaving the land better
off each generation. The human-potential movement, emphasizing
personal awareness and growth, love, and transactional relationships, is the interior side of the new consciousness. And it emphasizes an existential responsibility for one's own values and acts
creating the future, along with a goal-directed cybernetic attitude
of continual reassessment, growth and development, both for the
individual and for societies.
Survival also demands a metaagreement of mutual religious
tolerance and respect, a framework within which religious disagreements can be uplifting and fruitful. It is no accident that our local
wars today all have a religious component--Protestant versus
Catholic, Jew versus Moslem, Greek Orthodox versus Moslem,
Hindu versus Moslem, Buddhist versus Catholic. Often the political
and economic differences could be resolved to the mutual advantage
of all, if the religious differences did not make each side think of
the others as unclean and untrustworthy dogs. And many valuable
old cultures and old religions have been destroyed in large measure
by the patronizing intolerance of Protestant and Catholic mission-
aries. Humanity cannot survive or build a world together if we
allow these most immoral attitudes of mutual contempt to continue
to be propagated by old or new religious groups. The formal heal-
ing of old schisms by the Vatican is a step in the right direction,
but it must be extended in doctrine and in personal and national
practice to all the schisms of the human race.
Many other such reforms within the churches are necessary
in this new world and are coming rapidly, with changed attitudes
toward the equal participation of women, birth control, divorce,
centralized hierarchy, dogma and forbidden reading, property and
land reform in many countries, and ancient food and Sabbath taboos.

A new reformed Catholic church might easily spring up among the
millions of communicants who are divorced or practice contracep-
tion, aided by the thousands of nuns and priests who have left the
church. This would inevitably lead to an intense and valuable public
debate over ethical and structural reforms in all our older religions.

Finally it should be noted that there is a serious danger of
fanatic religious-revolutionary movements in times of crisis like
the present with turmoil and the breakdown of old rules and structures.
Harvey Wheeler suggested that such armed prophets, like Mohammed
and Cromwell, might be more common in history than political or
national revolutionary movements of the Nazi or Communist type.
A sustainable global society will have to find ways of preventing early
the unemployment and alienation and sense of injustice, either among
the poor or the middle class, that form a seedbed for such passionate
movements for purification and change. Yet at the same time, it
must find ways for purification and renewal of individuals and groups
and the whole society to take place without treading on the rights of
the ungodly and the unconvinced.

The theory and practice of a sustainable global society and of
the transition paths to it must blend together many innovations of
these kinds within a framework of increased justice, hope, renewal,
mutual design, and mutual effort to bring these components urgently
into being.

NOTES

1. B. F. Skinner, Beyond Freedom and Dignity (New York
Knopf, 1971).

2. Edward Goldsmith et al., Blueprint for Survival (Boston:
Houghton Mifflin, 1972).

3. John Rawls, A Theory of Justice (Cambridge, Mass.:
Harvard University Press, 1971).

4. The author is indebted to the late Jacob Bronowski for
most of this analysis.

14

**EFFICIENCY AND EQUITY
IN INTERGENERATIONAL
DISTRIBUTION**
Victor D. Lippit
Koichi Hamada

In economics, questions concerning the distribution of income and wealth are commonly resolved into their efficiency and equity aspects. Equity is commonly dismissed as beyond the purview of economics. Efficiency is understood in terms of Pareto optimality, according to which distribution is efficient only when all possibilities for exchange that will improve the lot of both parties to a transaction (or one if the other's welfare remains unaffected) have been exhausted. This concept of efficiency is widely used in economic theory and analysis. With regard to negative externalities, instances in which an unintended by-product of one's activity is damage to others, and with regard to problems of pollution in general, an extensive literature analyzing conflict in terms of efficiency has grown up. This literature might be expected to cast light on the problem of intergenerational distribution, especially insofar as the central issue here is the incidental damage each generation inflicts on future generations by destroying nature, using up nonrenewable resources, and polluting the environment. In fact, however, much of the existing economic literature and even such basic economic concepts as Pareto optimality are of limited usefulness in analyzing intergenerational conflicts. The purpose of this chapter is to indicate some of the inadequacies of orthodox economic analysis vis-a-vis questions of efficiency and equity in the intergenerational distribution of income and wealth (including natural wealth), and to indicate a basis upon which such questions can be pursued more fruitfully. In this context we will argue that economic growth has become increasingly suspect where the welfare of future generations is at issue.

In a celebrated article, Ronald Coase has proved that in the absence of transaction costs, negotiations between polluters and sufferers will lead to Pareto optimal resource allocation regardless

of which party is liable for the damage.[1] If, for example, the air is
regarded as belonging to the owner of a factory, the public is liable,
and if it wishes to restrict his polluting activities it must bribe him
to stop. If the air is regarded as belonging to the public, the factory
owner is liable for his polluting activities and must compensate the
public for the damage he causes. According to the Coase theorem,
regardless of the liability rule, negotiations between the two parties
will lead to efficient distribution if the costs of negotiation can be
neglected. This is so because it will be in the interest of both parties
to negotiate with each other until they reach some point on the contract curve, the locus of all points of Pareto optimality. Alternatively stated, exchange will take place as long as it is in the interest
of both parties to engage in it and will result--if transaction costs
are neglected--in efficient allocation, regardless of the initial
assignment of property rights. Warren Nutter has argued that the
same mechanism will bring about efficient allocation in the intertemporal allocation of resources, again regardless of the liability
rule.[2] The Coase theorem and its derivatives suggest the efficacy
of the market mechanism in resolving distributional conflicts, especially where negative externalities are present.

In considering problems of intergenerational efficiency and
equity, however, the practical meaningfulness of the theorem, if not
its logical validity, is open to question. If negotiations to restore
efficiency are to take place, there must be some entity to represent
the interest of future generations. However, since it is very difficult to find an agent to represent the interest of future generations,
as we shall argue, the laissez-faire solution to intergenerational
conflict could lead to an inefficient use of resources in a dynamic
sense.

In fact, as Coase himself recognizes, in the presence of transaction and negotiation costs, the liability rule does make a considerable difference as far as efficiency is concerned.[3] In the case of
intergenerational conflict, the negotiation cost for future generations
is effectively infinite, and the laissez-faire solution with some liability rule is not sufficient to achieve intergenerational efficiency.

INTERGENERATIONAL IMPLICATIONS OF
ENVIRONMENTAL DESTRUCTION

Many of the pollution damages that are a result of the producing activities of firms or of the consuming activities of households
will affect not only the interest of the contemporary generation but
also the interest of future generations. Polluting the air with jet
aircraft wastes or water with detergents may not be counted as

explicit social costs by the present generation. But after these
wastes accumulate for some time, they may suddenly turn out to be
critical to the living condition of the human race. As most problems
of environmental deterioration are associated with cumulative effects, and as the harm done tends to increase disproportionately
faster than the increase in pollutant levels, environmental problems
typically have strong connotations of intergenerational conflict.
That is to say, most problems of environmental destruction involve
significant elements of intergenerational efficiency and equity.

It is impossible, of course, to forecast precisely what the
long-range, worldwide effects of the current rate of increase of
pollution will be. Some significant consequences of existing conditions and trends, however, are already clear. It has been predicted
that, at current rates of pollution-increase, U.S. surface waters
will, in a typical case, lose the power to sustain life by the year
2000.[4] The survival of the oceans, which have served as convenient
cesspools for all nations, has also come into question and the issue
may also be determined by the turn of the century. CO_2 in the atmosphere is growing at a compound rate of 0.02 percent per year
and may affect the world's weather.[5] Waste-heat generation is
already having such an effect. Most of the fish caught in Japanese
waters contain chemical residues that are not ordinarily recommended as dietary supplements. The hazards of pollution are sufficiently clear to suggest that the magnitude of the hazard to future
generations is substantial.

In the Los Angeles area of the United States, high school foot-
ball teams practice and play at night. They do so for reasons of
health: physical activity in smog-laden air is injurious to the body
and smog levels fall at night. The shift of school sports to the
evening represents one form of social adaptation to an unclean environment. Logically, if society chooses to adapt to pollution rather
than eliminate it, there is no reason why other activities might not
be shifted to the nighttime; or, alternatively, man might secure his
existence more firmly by living underground. It is, moreover,
quite conceivable that irreversible polluting activities--as with the
release of atomic radiation--will force man to create an artificial
environment. There is, then, the distinct possibility that decisions
of the present generation will transform the life of future generations in ways that would be unacceptable to them if they were capable
of choosing. Even without such dramatic possibilities as underground
living being realized, current rates of commercial development suggest that people will live in a world without pure nature.

In analyzing the structure of intergenerational conflicts generally, an intrinsic asymmetry soon becomes evident. The present
generation establishes the environmental and living conditions for

future generations. Indeed, every act with significant future conse-
quences--including therefore most acts of production and consump-
tion--affects the welfare of future generations. On the other hand,
however, no act of future generations can affect the welfare of past
generations. Thus there is nothing that future generations can offer
the present generation to influence its decisions in a direction that
will promote future welfare. In the extreme case, future generations cannot compensate the present for foregoing the mildest satisfactions, even if the very survival of mankind is at stake. Thus
there is no possibility of a genuine intergenerational bargain or
transaction; the necessary parallelism is lacking.

Future generations cannot bargain with the present generation
because, first, they have nothing they can offer in exchange to the
present generation and, second, there is no way to represent their
interest adequately. The second point will be elaborated in a later
section. With regard to the first, the objection might be raised that
future generations can offer the survival of mankind, which at least
some people of the present generation may value highly. In reality,
however, people of the present generation cannot find out what happens after their lifetimes. While their actions will certainly affect
future possibilities, the issue of conflict is an internal dialog within
the present generation and the question is one of whether its actions
are consistent with its values rather than any intergenerational
transaction.

In fact, the relations between present and future generations
are not relations among men, but between gods and men. Like gods,
the present generation holds the destiny of future generations in its
hands. But if afflicted by the actions of the present generation,
future generations can do no more than curse their fate.

PARETO OPTIMALITY AND INTERGENERATIONAL
DISTRIBUTION

Now let us consider the concept of Pareto optimality applied to
intergenerational problems, particularly in the environmental context. As stated in most textbooks, a situation is Pareto optimal if a
member of society cannot increase his satisfaction without reducing
that of at least one other member. Stated in this positive form, the
concept of Pareto optimality sounds like a useful and at least innocent
concept. However, in the presence of external diseconomies, situations that are Pareto optimal can be truly brutal.

A situation is Pareto optimal if an individual's sufferings from
pollution can be reduced only when others suffer from a reduction of
real income. Thus if the people of a town are suffering from mercury

poisoning, the consequence of a chemical company polluting the local waters and fish with its wastes, the situation remains one of Pareto optimality despite their death and agony if measures to alleviate their plight would reduce the income of the company owners even nominally. In the intergenerational context, the elimination of human life is Pareto optimal (that is, economically efficient) if the survival of a future generation depends on reducing the income or satisfaction of the present generation. That is to say, the situation in which all life ceases to exist in 100 years is one of Pareto optimality if preventing catastrophe would require any reduction in the real income or satisfaction (for example, using ceramic plates instead of paper ones) of the present generation.

The fundamental propositions of welfare economics can be stated as follows: under certain conditions, in particular under the assumptions of the absence of externalities, perfect competition achieves a Pareto optimal situation; conversely, under certain conditions any specific Pareto optimal situation can be achieved by perfect competition provided that income redistribution by a lump-sum tax is possible.

Needless to say, the applicability or relevance of these propositions is rather limited in the intergenerational situation. The present generation does not know the technology of the future or the taste of the members of future generations. The propositions are relevant only under the presupposition that the taste or preferences of future generations are represented by the present generation through the bequest motive or through the above-mentioned internal dialog within the present generation. The permanent-income hypothesis theory of consumption originated by Milton Friedman, for example, illustrates the point. [6] Consumption behavior is explained in terms of rational calculation by households taking account of income flows up to the infinite future. The household is assumed to take account of the entire course of the future and to reflect the preference orderings of the children and grandchildren of the present members of the household. Thus the basic structure of price theory, on which most of the arguments of legal economists depend, assumes that the interest of future generations is sufficiently reflected in the preference ordering of the present generation.

This procedure may not be totally unrealistic in the absence of external diseconomies. The rationale for this presumption breaks down, however, as soon as we introduce external diseconomies into the intergenerational problem. People may, at least partly, take account of the benefit of their sons and grandsons who will inherit their wealth. But do they also take account of the damage to a third person in the future who will suffer from the activities of the present generation, and from the combined effect of its activities and those of his contemporaries? Even if the present generation should happen to take account of this, does it reflect it in its actual consumption or production behavior at present?

THE COASE THEOREM AND INTERGENERATIONAL DISTRIBUTION

The Coase theorem states that even in the presence of external diseconomies, the market mechanism combined with the negotiation process achieves a Pareto optimal situation if transaction or negotiation costs can be neglected, and that it does so irrespective of the rules of assigning the liability to either party involved. If the polluter is liable, he will compare the cost of foregoing the polluting activities with the cost of compensation and choose the cheaper one between continuing the activity and refraining from it. If the victim is liable, that is, if he cannot sue the polluter, he will choose between suffering from pollution and negotiating with the polluter over paying a "bribe" to stop the polluting activities. In either case, Coase has demonstrated that the Pareto optimal situation will be achieved in the absence of negotiating costs.

In the context of the intergenerational problem, however, this mechanism does not work at all. In the intergenerational environmental problem, who will represent the interest of future generations? As indicated in the last section, how can the interest of the future generation that will be suffering from polluted water be represented in the current allocation mechanism? Neither consumers of the product produced with a polluting process, nor stockholders of the producing firms, nor the business managers of the plants would consider the interest of the future generations.

Thus laissez-faire dealings to achieve the Pareto optimal situation are not possible in practice. Even in the case where members of future generations would have paid a "bribe" to stop polluting activities because it is cheaper to avoid the pollution now than to deal with it later, the future generation cannot express or find representation for its interest. From the standpoint of intertemporal efficiency, therefore, the market mechanism combined with the negotiation process will not restore the efficient allocation of resources.

In the static problem of intragenerational allocation, the Coase theorem holds true if potential victims are able to negotiate costlessly. By way of negotiation, the externality is "internalized" and accounted as a cost item in the budget by either polluters or victims. In the actual world, the negotiation cost is not negligible and the liability rule makes a great difference in resource allocation.

In the problem which we are considering, that of intergenerational allocation, the potential victims are scattered not only spatially but also temporally, so that the externality has an expanded dimension. Most important of all, potential victims do not have an agent to represent their interest. In terms of Calabresi's approach, the negotiation cost for the members of future generations is infinite, thus negating the possibility of any kind of bargaining.[7]

In this intergenerational situation, what are the consequences of alternative liability rules? First, suppose that the victims are liable. How can they bribe the current polluters for foregoing polluting production activities if these activities are foregone hundreds of years before their birth? There is no agent to represent their interest to negotiate with the current generation. Second, suppose polluters are liable. It does not improve the situation very much. As there is no way for a victim living hundreds of years from now to sue a polluter, the "polluters-pay principle" (PPP) is not enough. It is difficult to apply because there is no agent to sue the present generation right now, and because there is no possibility of suing the present generation after hundreds of years have passed. Thus an alternative approach to pollution control based on absolute limitations on polluting activities offers greater potential relief for future generations. That is, the "polluters-stop principle" (PSP) should be adopted to safeguard the interest of future generations.

It is not completely impossible, of course, to conceive of hypothetical bargaining schemes that will give partial representation to the interest of future generations. Environmental agencies of the government may be regarded as representatives of the interest of future generations that negotiate with the present generation accordingly. The bribing process in Coase's argument could be regarded as being realized by the flotation of bonds for antipollution expenditure. The increase in public debt this involves, however, can be interpreted more straightforwardly as a decision of the present generation to shift the burden of financing to future generations. As J. M. Buchanan argues, there is a tendency for governments choosing between monetary and fiscal instruments for economic stabilization to rely on easy budgets for stimulation and tight money for restraint.[8] This leaves a burden of public debt to be borne by future taxpayers. Moreover, this policy mix tends to increase consumption at the expense of investment over the course of the business cycle as a whole, thereby increasing present consumption at the expense of future consumption.

Whether such policy measures are really detrimental to future generations, however, remains ambiguous, for if a higher level of investment increases throughputs or economic activity over time it will also tend to increase environmental pollution accordingly. Be

that as it may, government behavior can be understood more readily
as representing some interest within the present generation than as
representing the interest of future generations. In this light, the
efforts of environmental agencies to preserve and protect the environment for posterity must be understood as representing a certain humanitarian value within the present generation. While this
value fortuitously coincides with the interest of future generations,
environmental agencies cannot properly be represented as their
bargaining agents. Such agencies, moreover, like all their government counterparts, are subject to intense political pressures that
reflect conflict within the present generation rather than between
generations.

THE ISSUE OF EQUITY IN INTERGENERATIONAL DISTRIBUTION

We have indicated that the Coase theorem cannot be applied
on intergenerational environmental problems because the future
generations have no agent to represent their interest. That is to
say, polluting activity may not be avoided at present even though it
is cheaper to do so now than in the future. This leads to an inefficient point from the standpoint of Pareto optimality.

At the same time, we have shown the inappropriate nature of
the concept of Pareto optimality itself when it is applied to the intergenerational problem. Therefore it remains for us to comment on
the issue of fairness or equity in matters of intergenerational conflict. It still remains an extremely difficult question whether economists can have anything useful to say about this matter. It will be
suggested here, however, that there are several lines of approach
that may prove useful. While all of them incorporate considerations
of equity or fairness, it is no longer possible for economists to
evade such issues in the name of positive science.

Abba Lerner has demonstrated that probable total satisfaction
in society can be maximized by equalizing incomes.[9] Since no time
rate of discount can be applied when comparing satisfactions experienced by different generations,[10] the equal distribution of real
income and nature among generations can be sought as a desirable
goal. Market forces cannot be relied upon in pursuing this goal,
for as they tend to bring about a positive rate of time preference
within any generation, the market mechanism discounts the needs
and satisfactions of future generations and becomes an unsatisfactory mechanism for determining distribution among generations.

Another possible approach to the question of intergenerational
relations lies in the establishment of rules based on shared values

and experiences, rules that would modify the predatory behavior of
the present generation. Perhaps the simplest analogy can be drawn
with regard to the use of campsites by hikers. The hikers arriving
at a campsite can expect to find it clean and with firewood cut and
neatly stacked. They are expected to leave it in the same condition.
If hikers in general do not observe these rules, then nature will be
destroyed, the purpose of such journeys defeated, and the experience
of hiking, of creating a special relation between man and nature,
will disappear from the earth. (Of course this is happening quite
frequently now as improved road communications bring many people
who are ignorant about the rules or do not care about them into contact with formerly remote places.) It should be possible to establish
fairly simple rules, akin to those for hiking, to govern the relations
among generations. For example, each generation must leave behind water, air, and soil that are at least as pure and unpolluted as
when it arrived on the scene. Further, each generation must leave
behind substantially as much undeveloped nature ("pure nature") and
the same species it found on earth. As we will show below, such
propositions do indeed have a philosophical underpinning in the theory
of justice.

Any such rules must have a theoretical basis to avoid the problem of arbitrary choice. It will be necessary then to have a theory
of equity upon which principles of distribution, particularly among
generations, can be based. Perhaps the most useful work along
these lines has been done by John Rawls in <u>A Theory of Justice</u>;[11]
Rawls' "justice" is the economist's "equity."

Rawls' theory of justice presumes that people enter into a social contract to establish the rules governing society under a "veil
of ignorance"; that is, people do not know what their social position
will be in actuality. It is easy to extend this concept to situations
involving intergenerational distribution; people do not know into
which generation they will be born. Rawls presents two principles
of justice which he argues will be acceptable to rational people under
the contract conditions. First, "each person is to have an equal
right to the most extensive total system of equal basic liberties
compatible with a similar system of liberty for all."[12] Second,
"social and economic inequalities are to be arranged so that they
are both: (a) to the greatest benefit of the least advantaged, consistent with the just savings principle, and (b) attached to offices
and positions open to all under conditions of fair equality of opportunity."[13] It is the first part of the second principle that is of particular relevance to the problem of equity in intergenerational distribution. (While Rawls himself explicitly excludes intergenerational
issues from the scope of this "maximin" principle, his grounds for
doing so are unsatisfactory. If indeed a principle of economic

justice is to be established such that inequalities are to be arranged
to the greatest benefit of the least advantaged, there seems to be no
reasonable basis for excluding intergenerational distribution, and
Rawls' efforts on this score are not convincing. He argues that it
must be excluded because there is no way for later generations to
aid the least fortunate first generation, which has the smallest capital stock.[14] But if the state of nature becomes a more important
determinant of welfare than the level of capital accumulation, it is
future generations that are the most disadvantaged--and they can
indeed be aided by the actions of the present generation.)

   According to Rawls' second principle, we should maximize the
well-being of the most handicapped generation. If we return to the
hikers' site example, the probability or the likelihood of visiting the
site at a particular turn is identical for a member of any generation
born on earth. The issue is who are in the most handicapped generation. As far as technology is concerned, future generations are
more or at least as well advantaged. The same is true with regard
to the capital stock. But as far as the natural environment is concerned, future generations are less or at most as well advantaged.
The quest for the just distribution principle depends on how we balance these advantages and disadvantages of future generations.

   The more limited capital stock, technological capabilities, and
output of the present generation compared to future ones is undoubtedly of great significance in the case of the developing countries.
In this instance, the least-advantaged generation is almost certainly
the present one. In the case of the advanced countries, however,
conditions appear to be quite the opposite. One may not agree with
J. K. Galbraith's argument that, over a wide range, the marginal
utility of consumption is zero compared with the point before new
demand is created,[15] but the contrary remains to be demonstrated,
and that is surely where the burden of proof must lie. Of course it
is difficult to show changes in utility, but rational men have not even
tried on a priori grounds to attach any great utility to the consumption of two cars, two television sets, and so forth. Some survey
efforts dealing with the relationship between happiness and income
have been undertaken in a number of countries. Although they reveal a correlation between utility or happiness and one's relative
income standing, they reveal no correlation between utility or happiness and per capita national income, whether the comparison is
made internationally or at different times (and income levels) within
a given country.[16] If added material consumption is not worth much
in the advanced countries, then the advantages of future generations
on this score are minor.

   By comparison, the disadvantages of future generations include living in an increasingly polluted environment and in a

homogenized, commercially developed world where wild and natural
beauty exists only in fiction. In what seems the most likely case,
if current trends are not reversed future generations will live by
making grotesque adaptations to a polluted environment or not live
at all. What the environmental crisis has done is to change the position of future generations from the most advantaged to the least
advantaged. A just principle of intergenerational distribution must
take this into account, according to Rawls' second principle.
        In his well-known essay, "The Economics of the Coming
Spaceship Earth," Kenneth Boulding contrasts the "cowboy economy"
of the past--"reckless, exploitative, romantic and violent"--with the
"spaceman economy" of the near future,

> in which the earth has become a single spaceship,
> without unlimited reservoirs of anything, either
> for extraction or for pollution, and in which,
> therefore, man must find his place in a cyclical
> ecological system which is capable of continuous
> reproduction of material form even though it
> cannot escape having inputs of energy.[17]

In the cowboy economy, production and consumption, roughly measured by GNP, are considered positive, while in the spaceman
economy, throughput is

> to be regarded as something to be minimized rather
> than maximized. The essential measure of the suc-
> cess of the economy is not production and consump-
> tion at all, but the nature, extent, quality and com-
> plexity of the capital stock, including in this the
> state of the human bodies and minds included in the
> system. In the spaceman economy, what we are
> primarily concerned with is stock maintenance, and
> any technological change which results in the main-
> tenance of a given total stock with a lessened
> throughput (that is, less production and consumption)
> is clearly a gain.[18]

        Boulding's argument has considerable intuitive appeal for
those prepared to accept the humanist assumptions that underlie it:
that human life is worth preserving, that the quality of human experience takes precedence over the quantity of consumption (presuming
basic needs are met), and that future generations have a claim to
scarce resources that is equal to that of the present generation.
The assumptions, it should be noted, overstep the bounds that

economists have traditionally set for themselves, transgressing
the realm of equity. Given the inability of the market mechanism to
resolve problems of intergenerational conflict, this is unavoidable.

CONCLUSION

Until quite recently, the issue of equity or justice in intergenerational conflict could be avoided because of the predominant harmony of interests that governed relations between generations. In
the earlier stage of modern capitalism, the instinct of capitalists to
accumulate profit, or the spirit of capitalism with the Protestant
ethic, may really have represented the interest of the future generations.[19] The massive capital stock of the developed countries
today reflects the positive value that past generations placed on saving and the accumulation of real capital. This is a case where intuitive or religious motives as well as the cool calculation of self-
interest achieved the representation of later generations, including
our own. But nowadays, accumulation itself is not beneficial but
harmful to the well-being of future generations. What they really
need seems not to be an abundance of physical products, but unpolluted air, water, soil, and so forth. (As indicated above, the argument here applies more forcefully to advanced countries than to
less developed countries.)

Under such circumstances, the dominant character of the relations between present and future generations has shifted from
harmony to conflict. As we have argued, there is no liability rule
or market mechanism that can secure a Pareto optimal resolution
of the intergenerational conflict--the Coase theorem cannot be applied. Moreover, even if it were possible to apply the theorem,
Pareto optimality does not offer a satisfactory criterion for distribution where intergenerational conflicts are involved. If there is
to be any protection for the interest of future generations, then it
must be carried out on the grounds of equity or justice. Rawls'
criteria seem to provide the most useful basis for establishing rules
to protect intergenerational distributive justice.

His first principle of assuring equal rights is based largely on
political considerations but can easily be applied to the problem of
environmental deterioration. Everyone, in future generations as
much as in the present generation, has an equal right to breathe
clean air, drink and use unpolluted water, and maintain his existence
in an unpolluted environment generally. Rawls' second principle
establishes a standard of justice that puts the burden of proof on the
present generation. From the standpoint of the environment, it is
future generations that are the most disadvantaged and thus a principal

criterion for judging present actions is the extent to which they serve
to promote the greatest benefit of the future generations.

From these general principles of intergenerational distributive
justice we can derive the simple rules outlined above: the polluters-
stop principle and the requirement for each generation to leave the
earth's environment no more polluted than it was at the time of that
generation's arrival on the scene. The limit to these rules would
become operative only if maintaining them resulted in a disadvantage
to the present generation so severe that it rather than future generations would become the most disadvantaged. Accordingly, some
environmental disruption might be justified to assure adequate food
supplies, but never to assure a second car for every family--or even
a first. Thus the adoption of these rules would affect the behavior of
the more developed countries to a significantly greater degree than
it would that of the developing countries, although it would by no
means free the latter of all constraints.

We have suggested that government agencies cannot, except in
a highly restricted sense, be considered agents of future generations.
That argument was not meant to belittle the central role such agencies must assume in environmental preservation. This role, however, should be understood rather as upholding the principles of
justice and the humanitarian values of preserving the culture and
environment of mankind in the face of activities by production and
consumption decision-making units that neglect such considerations.

A final point to consider in determining what constitutes equitable relations between generations derives from the gods-man
analogy between present and future generations discussed above:
The present generation can do anything to the future generations,
even to the point of destroying them, while the latter can do nothing
to the former. Where the power in a relationship is all on one side,
the responsibility and ethical burden it places on the powerful side
cannot be avoided.

As long as capital accumulation benefited future generations
substantially and the environment's pollution-absorpition capacities
remained largely untested, the accumulative instinct of existing
generations served the interest of future generations as well. Now
that the preservation of a finite environment has become more important than the added consumption of material goods, the dominant
character of the relations between generations has shifted from
harmony to conflict. The market mechanism, even admitting its
ability under certain circumstances to bring about efficient distribution where negative externalities exist, is capable of resolving intergenerational conflicts neither efficiently nor equitably. Moreover,
the very concept of economic efficiency as a normative criterion for
economic analysis must be called into question as far as intergenera-

tional distribution is concerned. Under these circumstances, alternative mechanisms and criteria for treating the problems of intergenerational distribution are necessary. In this chapter we have argued that a theory of justice can provide the philosophical basis for a fairly simple set of rules governing intergenerational distribution. These rules do not directly deny the possibility of further growth taking place, but the priority they assign to environmental preservation inevitably suggests the curtailment of growth and indicts those social arrangements that perpetuate it unnecessarily.

NOTES

1. Ronald H. Coase, "The Problem of Social Cost," Journal of Law and Economics 3 (October 1960): 1-44.

2. Warren G. Nutter, "The Coase Theorem on Social Cost: A Footnote," Journal of Law and Economics 11 (October 1968): 503-07.

3. For the elaboration of this point, see Guido Calabresi, "Transaction Costs, Resource Allocation and Liability Rules--A Comment," Journal of Law and Economics 11 (April 1968): 67-74.

4. Barry Commoner cites a U.S. National Academy of Sciences report that projects the yearly rate of increase of the amount of organic wastes intruded into U.S. surface waters and the amount of oxygen needed to degrade them. This is contrasted with the oxygen content of the waters. Based on this projection, the total oxygen supply would be exhausted by about the year 2000 if the oxygen supply and pollution rates were everywhere the same. The Closing Circle (New York: Knopf, 1971), p. 219.

5. Donella H. Meadows et al., The Limits to Growth (New York: Universe Books, 1972), p. 73.

6. Milton Friedman, A Theory of the Consumption Function (New York: National Bureau of Economic Research, 1957).

7. Calabresi, op. cit.

8. J. M. Buchanan, "Easy Budgets and Tight Money," Lloyd's Bank Review, April 1962.

9. Abba Lerner, The Economics of Control (New York: Macmillan, 1944), Chapter 3.

10. This proposition has been explicitly endorsed by a number of economists. See, for example, Robert Solow, "The Economics of Resources or the Resources of Economics," American Economic Review, May 1974, pp. 8-9.

11. John Rawls, A Theory of Justice (Cambridge, Mass.: Harvard University Press, 1971).

12. Ibid., p. 302.

13. Ibid.

14. Ibid., p. 291.

15. John K. Galbraith, The Affluent Society (Boston: Houghton Mifflin, 1958).

16. Richard A. Easterlin, "Does Money Buy Happiness?" Public Interest, Winter 1973.

17. Kenneth E. Boulding, "The Economics of the Coming Spaceship Earth," reprinted in Toward a Steady-State Economy, ed. Herman Daly (San Francisco: W. H. Freeman, 1973), p. 127.

18. Ibid.

19. See Max Weber, The Protestant Ethic and the Spirit of Capitalism, trans. T. Parsons (London: Allen and Unwin, 1930).

Growing interdependence among nations places moral constraints on growth options for the United States. Increasing trade
among industrial countries has created a situation in which recession or depression in one major economic power has serious ramifications for all other industrial countries. Major decisions regarding growth made in the United States will not be restrained by national boundaries. Thus, there is an obvious need for coordination
of any sustainable growth policies among OECD countries.

An even more serious issue must be faced in relations between the industrial and less developed countries. Decisions to slow
or redirect growth in industrial countries can have a serious impact
on the fragile economies of the less developed countries. The less
developed countries trade primarily with industrial countries; only
about one-fifth of their exports go to other less developed countries.
The bulk of their exports and their main hope for earning development capital are raw materials and agricultural products, the demand for which fluctuates dramatically with weather and economic
fortunes in the industrial countries. Unless adjustments in growth
policy are carefully conceived, slowed growth could erase hopes for
industrialization among the presently less developed countries and
resign most of them to the ranks of the never-to-be-developed world.

The major recession of 1974-75 following on the heels of a
sharp increase in the price of petroleum illustrates this point. As
industrial growth slowed and then reversed in OECD countries,
prices of raw materials began to plummet. Most less developed nations export only one or two basic commodities and their economies
were struck by a combination of lagging demand for exports and related declining prices. Copper-exporting countries such as Zaire,
Zambia, and Chile, for example, saw copper prices drop by more
than 60 percent in only a few months. In addition, slowed economic
growth in the industrial world led to reductions in official foreign
assistance and to some hard questioning of commercial loans to less
developed countries that are teetering on the edge of bankruptcy.

Any plan for limiting world consumption of natural resources
must take the plight of the less developed countries into account.
For them growth is just beginning and arguments about the pernicious
side effects of growth or resource depletion fall upon deaf ears.
Even meeting the most basic needs of people living in these countries will require a major jump in natural resource consumption.

Jack Barkenbus analyzes the implications of slowed growth from the perspective of the Third World. He points out that Third World scholars have universally rejected the <u>Limits To Growth</u> analyses as being irrelevant to their concerns. They argue that if growth is slowed at all it certainly should be slowed only in the highly industrialized countries. But even slowed growth in industrial countries creates a dilemma for Third World policy makers. Restricted consumption of fuels and minerals in industrial countries can be justified on equity grounds, but if consumption is reduced this will destroy markets for LDC exports and eliminate a source of development capital.

Barkenbus suggests that one of the little-noticed but potentially most important aspects of the New International Economic Order is a call for Third World self-reliance efforts involving selected and limited participation in the global economy. It is difficult for countries to decouple themselves immediately from the international economy, and development of self-reliance will be a long-term process. Some less developed countries such as Sri Lanka and Tanzania have already begun decoupling experiments. Others are certain to follow. It is likely that greater efforts will be made to set up regional common markets, to develop mineral processing facilities in these countries, and to diminish the role of multinational corporations in Third World affairs. Barkenbus concludes that increasing Third World self-reliance makes growth limitation in industrial societies without damaging Third World welfare a possibility.

In the final chapter James Kuhlman emphasizes that there are serious differences of opinion within the industrial world about the need for further industrial growth. He points out that in the Soviet Union and the socialist countries of Eastern Europe growth in consumption is still an accepted sign of progress. East European countries feel they must grow in order to reduce the domination of the Soviet Union. The Soviet Union, in turn, feels that its economy must grow in order to compete effectively in the international system. This raises the very important and sobering question of international economic competition. Is it possible for a peaceful world to long exist if one or two major capitalist powers seek to limit growth while their socialist competitors move into the resulting economic vacuum? It would be ironic if Western capitalist nations were the first to voluntarily limit their growth on grounds of equity while socialist countries would forsake their ideology in order to pursue rapid growth in a highly inegalitarian international economy.

15

**SLOWED GROWTH
AND THIRD
WORLD WELFARE**
Jack N. Barkenbus

The pronouncement that further economic growth is essential for the eradication of widespread global poverty would not ordinarily be expected to show up in newspaper headlines. But when Aurelio Peccei, founder of the Club of Rome, made this pronouncement in 1976, it was heralded on the front pages of major U.S. newspapers. The reason for this, of course, was the Club of Rome's sponsorship in the early 1970s of the Massachusetts Institute of Technology (MIT)-based study on the "predicament of mankind" which found its final form in the book The Limits to Growth.[1]

The Peccei announcement that further growth is necessary for peace and prosperity in the nonindustrial nations (hereafter referred to in conventional terms as the Third World) represented a significant recognition of a major weakness in The Limits to Growth and much of the associated "steady-state" literature, namely: an exclusive concern with global resources and global pollution without the insight that comes from analytical disaggregation.[2] In other words, in most slowed growth literature, Third World conditions and prospects are not separated from those existing in the industrial nations. Viewed from this "global" or aggregate perspective, one gets the mistaken impression that overconsumption of resources characterizes life on earth today when, in fact, most individuals still suffer from an underconsumption of resources. Peccei has served notice that the Club of Rome will not neglect the particular conditions and interests of the Third World in subsequent sponsored projects.

There are two major reasons for the neglect of Third World conditions in the limits-to-growth literature which has emanated from the campuses of industrial nations, particularly the United States. First, many analysts consider the Third World as simply irrelevant to the industrial-growth issue. In a first-order sense this is certainly true. The nearly 25 percent of the earth's population that inhabits industrial nations consumes nearly 75 percent of the world's annual material resource production (the United States with only 6 percent of the world's population consumes nearly 30 percent of all material resource production). It has been estimated that the "pollution and natural resource load" placed on the environment by each individual in the industrial nations is from 20 to 50 times greater than that generated by individuals in the Third World.[3] Obviously, if growth is to be limited as a matter of policy, slowed growth must first begin in the industrial nations to have a positive and appreciable ecological effect.

The second reason for the neglect of the Third World, I suggest, is that most analysts would prefer not to grapple with the dilemma of Third World Welfare in a slow-growth economy. It is far simpler and more straightforward to concentrate upon the evils of superfluous consumption in the rich nations than to raise complex issues of how a steady-state world economy would impact upon Third World development. It is understandable, therefore, why analysts have not faced the second-order issue of Third World welfare, but nevertheless regrettable. Without consideration of Third World conditions and interests in an economy of slowed growth, the analysis is incomplete and seriously flawed. This chapter offers a preliminary inquiry into the subject. It first examines carefully how limited-growth advocates have handled the Third World dilemma in the past, if at all, and then explores how recent Third World demands for a new international economic order can have important implications for the establishment of a sustainable economy.

THE BASIC DILEMMA

The basic dilemma facing growth-limitation advocates when considering the Third World can be stated simply: If resources are so limited and finite--or if current proposed levels of resource utilization place an unbearable strain upon the environment--so as to require a policy of limited resource consumption, what fate can be held out to those Third World inhabitants barely surviving at current resource levels? In other words, is the strain upon our resource base, and our environment, which is occasioned by economic growth, of sufficient magnitude and danger that it precludes further economic enrichment for those millions who have very real and immediate material needs? It is impossible at this time to assess with certainty the magnitude of global resource and environmental dangers, but several scholars have painted a bleak scenario, indeed, should economic growth rates continue. According to a distinguished geologist, if a world population were consuming mineral resources at the rate the United States is today, it would require from 200 to 400 times the present annual rates of mineral resource consumption.[4] Kenneth Boulding has stated:

> There is not enough of anything. There is not
> enough copper. There is not enough of an enor-
> mous number of elements which are essential to
> the developed economy. If the whole world de-
> veloped to American standards overnight, we
> would run out of everything in less than 100
> years. . . . Economic development is the pro-
> cess by which the evil day is brought closer,
> when everything will be gone.[5]

Given this stark scenario it may be of some comfort to limited-growth advocates that the performance of the Third World in reaching the economic levels of the industrial world has not been all that spectacular. Yet to gain comfort in the belief that our ultimate survival is dependent upon the inability of Third World nations to provide fundamental services to the majority of its citizens is cold comfort indeed. Moreover, the belief that there will be continued acquiescence in the striking (and increasing) disparities in national economic levels is shortsighted. Since the dilemma facing the Third World in a slowed-growth economy is so apparent, some advocates have proposed solutions to the dilemma. It is worth examining the efficacy of these solutions briefly.

One of the more novel approaches to the Third World dilemma was provided by MIT systems theorist Jay Forrester who viewed the lack of Third World economic growth as positive, not only in global terms but for Third World nations themselves. Forrester singles out industrialization as the most fundamental ecologically disturbing force today and exhorts the Third World to forego greater industrial advancement, saying:

> The present efforts of underdeveloped countries
> to industrialize may be unwise. They may now
> be closer to an ultimate equilibrium with the en-
> vironment than are the industrialized nations . . .
> [and] may be in a better condition for surviving
> forthcoming world-wide environmental and eco-
> nomic pressures than are the advanced countries.[6]

Forrester's approach to the Third World dilemma, then, is to claim that there is no dilemma. In effect, he is saying that Third World interests coincide with limited growth.

The authors of The Limits to Growth present a scarcely more enlightened solution for the Third World. While advocating a global equilibrium, the authors suggest a redistribution of wealth among nations in order that everyone can be "maintained" at least at a subsistence level.[7] Since growth would not be allowed beyond a certain level, the only way to ensure the earth's population of subsistence food and material resources would be to take from the richer nations and give to the poorer nations. While the idea of taking excess consumption from those in the rich nations and distributing it to the poor in Third World nations has obvious altruistic appeal, it does not sufficiently take political realities into account. Even in our currently expanding world economy the level of resource transfers among nations is minuscule. Current levels of development assistance from industrial nations average 0.3 percent of their Gross National Product (GNP), falling far short of the UN official development assistance target of 0.7 percent of GNP.[8] Industrial nations were enjoined to boost the level of development assistance up to the UN target at the Seventh Special Session of the United Nations, but several representatives from industrial nations went on record to stress their government's inability to reach such a target.[9]

One can, in fact, make a more compelling case that, as we approach a global equilibrium, less and not more development assistance will be forthcoming. Greater competitiveness and possessiveness over a limited pot of resources seems a much more likely development than a resurgence of altruism. It is not strange, but predictable, that global food scarcities in recent years have triggered discussion in the United States of "lifeboat ethics"[10] and "triage."[11] According to the lifeboat ethic, the United States and other rich industrial nations are metaphoric lifeboats in a sea of world poverty. Because of the sea's expanding population, it is said, the attempt to share finite resources with the growing population of the sea is folly and will exhaust the resources of all. "Triage," or the sacrifice of the weak and wounded for the preservation of the strong, is still another rationalization which can be marshalled for the hoarding of one's own resources. There is little reason to believe, therefore, that under a system of global equilibrium anything approaching economic parity among nations would ever be achieved.

Rejection of the MIT systems models from Third World scholars has been unambiguous and universal on account of the aforementioned inadequacies in the Forrester and The Limits to Growth analyses.[12] While a rise in Third World GNP levels may not be a sufficient condition for the creation of a better society, it appears to be a necessary condition, nonetheless. The momentum of population growth in the Third World requires continued economic growth policies. Even if Third World birth rates declined to the replacement

level characteristic of the industrial world, as early as 1985 population growth would continue for decades and come close to doubling
its 1970-level population.[13] The argument of certain limited-growth
advocates that the pursuit of affluence should be foregone has not
found a receptive audience in the Third World for good reason. A
group of Third World scientists made their position clear before the
UN Stockholm Conference on the Human Environment in 1972, stating:

> We strongly reject models of stagnation, proposed
> by certain alarmist Western ecologists, economists,
> industrialists and computer fans; and assert that
> holding economic growth, per se, responsible for
> environmental ills amounts to a diversion of atten-
> tion from the real causes of the problem.[14]

The true picture which comes through the elaborate systems
models is of a cemented world order, based and sustained upon existing differences in economic levels. To use the popular metaphor
of "spaceship earth," it means the construction of a permanent com-
partment within this spaceship which separates first- and second-
class passengers.[15] First-class travel would, of course, be re-
served for the minority of the earth's inhabitants found in the rich
industrial nations.

LIMITING GROWTH IN INDUSTRIAL COUNTRIES

Several limited-growth advocates have attempted to escape the
dilemma posed by Third World economic growth by suggesting that
limited or zero growth need only be a policy goal of the rich industrial nations. They recognize that economic growth is a necessary
condition for the elimination of vast poverty in the Third World. The
steady-state spokesman of the nineteenth century, John Stuart Mill,
was not indifferent to the economic needs of the poorer countries,
stating: "It is only in the backward countries of the world that increased production is still an important object: in those most advanced, what is economically needed is a better distribution."[16]
The case for continued Third World growth is stated even more
forcibly by the twentieth-century steady-state advocate, Herman Daly:

> Extra GNP in a poor country, assuming it does
> not go mainly to the richest class of that country,
> represents satisfaction of relatively basic wants,
> whereas extra GNP in a rich country, assuming
> it does not go mainly to the poorest class of that

> country, represents satisfaction of relatively
> trivial wants. For our purposes the upshot of
> these differences is that for the poor, growth in
> GNP is still a good thing, but for the rich it is
> probably a bad thing. [17]

One must admit that this argument has considerable appeal
even if it doesn't ultimately come to grips with the issue of finite
resources and global pollution. First, it addresses itself to the
most immediate problem source, the rich industrial nations. As
stated previously, the industrial world is by far the major consumer
of materials and polluter of the environment. Moreover, at current
rates of growth, advanced economic societies in the Third World
will not grow overnight. If a viable and equitable sustainable society
in the rich countries were achieved, it would no doubt have a powerful "demonstration effect" upon other countries, and hence be a significant force for the eventual establishment of a global equilibrium.
Finally, continued growth in the Third World, combined with zero
or limited growth in the industrial nations, would gradually narrow
the economic gap between nations, thereby reducing Third World
antagonism toward richer nations.

As desirable as this solution might appear in theory, it suf-
fers in practice from the interrelated nature of economic transactions among nations. Assuming that slowed growth was made economic policy in the industrial world tomorrow, it is difficult, at
present, to perceive how Third World growth rates would not be
negatively affected by its implementation. Historically, there is a
high correlation between growth rates in the industrial and Third
World nations. [18] Periods of recession and depression in the industrial nations inevitably produce severe unfavorable impacts upon the
Third World. It is worth briefly examining the interrelationship between national economies since it is crucial to an understanding of
why growth in the Third World cannot, at present, be easily separated from growth in the industrial nations.

The essential fact is that few Third World nations possess the
resources and capacity to allow them currently to be independent of
the world economy. Because of this, and historical processes, their
welfare or development efforts are very much dependent upon export
earnings which in turn can be used to buy needed imports. It is well
known that many Third World nations are highly reliant upon only a
single (or very few) export items for the bulk of their export receipts.
This reliance is heightened by the concentrated nature of the markets
for exported commodities. As can be seen in Table 15.1, nearly
three-fourths of all Third World exports go to industrial world markets. In short, Third World exports are normally distributed to a

TABLE 15.1

World Exports, by Origin and Destination, 1961-72
($ billions and percentages)

| | Exports to | | | | | | | |
| Exports from | Developed Market Economy Countries | | Developing Market Economy Countries | | Centrally Planned Economy Countries | | World Total | |
	Percent of Total	Growth Rate	Percent of Total	Growth Rate	Percent of Total	Growth Rate	Value	Growth Rate
Developed market economy countries								
1961-66 average	73.8	10.8	22.0	6.3	3.8	13.0	$112.6	9.8
1967-72 average	76.7	15.3	19.1	12.2	3.8	12.9	213.4	14.6
Developing market economy countries								
1961-66 average	71.9	7.5	21.3	5.7	5.7	11.1	33.0	7.2
1967-72 average	73.6	11.2	19.8	10.3	5.4	11.7	52.7	11.0
Western hemisphere								
1961-66 average	74.7	5.2	18.1	8.8	7.1	10.0	10.2	6.2
1967-72 average	73.8	11.9	19.9	11.4	5.7	7.6	15.8	11.7
Africa								
1961-66 average	80.7	9.4	11.9	8.8	6.4	14.6	6.7	9.7
1967-72 average	81.6	12.8	10.3	11.0	6.8	15.5	11.8	12.6
Middle East								
1961-66 average	73.4	10.9	21.1	7.4	2.2	12.4	5.7	10.1
1967-72 average	76.5	11.9	19.0	12.5	2.3	18.2	10.4	12.4
Other Asia								
1961-66 average	58.7	6.8	33.5	3.5	7.3	9.7	8.6	5.6
1967-72 average	63.9	13.5	29.4	10.4	6.1	11.1	13.5	12.4

Source: James W. Howe et al., The U.S. and the Developing World: Agenda for Action 1974 (New York: Praeger, 1974).

limited number of industrial-nation buyers, creating a high degree of partner concentration.[19] The precariousness of this dependency is exacerbated by the fact that over 75 percent of Third World exports are raw material commodities--agricultural or mineral--and subject to the severe price fluctuations characteristic of the primary commodity market.[20] These compounded dependencies in the trade sector produce an extreme vulnerability to conditions and policies outside the Third World which might alter existing trade volume and relationships.

The dependence of the Third World upon the influx of foreign capital, management, and technology--increasingly being provided by multinational corporations (MNCs)--is also well known. Though most private capital and technology transfers take place among the highly industrial nations, that portion which is transferred to the Third World often occupies a disproportionately large and visible place in the economy. A decrease in export earnings, therefore, means a consequent decrease in the purchase of technology so necessary to spur economic growth.

Given the web of Third World-industrial nation interests briefly described, it is clear that growth in the industrial nations cannot now be curbed without seriously affecting Third World economic development. The broad solution to environmental decay and pollution posed by Mill, Daly, and several other observers, while seemingly more enlightened than other steady-state advocate solutions, fails, in itself, to address the real needs and interests of the Third World. Attention, which has not yet been forthcoming from slowed-growth advocates, must be devoted to how the Third World would develop independent of the industrial nations. Despite admirable intentions, inadequate attention to the mechanics of economic growth can produce effects nearly as disturbing as total neglect.

A NEW INTERNATIONAL ECONOMIC ORDER

Recognition of the ties that bind Third World development to the economic performance of industrial nations has led several individuals (quite unconnected to the growth-limitation debate) to suggest that continued economic growth in the industrial world is the crucial factor influencing future Third World welfare.[21] U.S. representatives in international forums have repeatedly made this claim in response to those who advocate changing the international economic system. Besides being self-serving, the argument is both an incomplete and inadequate response to long-term global welfare. First, calls for continued growth in industrial nations ignore the resource and environmental dangers inherent in these policies, as highlighted

by advocates of limited growth. It is obvious that no nation stands
to gain in the long run from resource depletion and environmental
degradation. Third World welfare, therefore, should not be used
as a rationalization for the necessity of continued economic growth.
Second, economic growth in the industrial world, by itself, does not
ensure Third World nations of ever reaching acceptable living standards. The fact that these nations cannot develop simply in response
to industrial-nation growth should now be clear from the record of
the past 20 years. Continued economic growth under the current
economic system, therefore, cannot be viewed--as many in the
United States would prefer to view it--as a "solution" to world poverty. "Growth as usual" is neither a direct nor a sufficient means
of eliminating global poverty.

Fortunately, one can begin to perceive of means by which Third
World development can be furthered without requiring that industrial
nations pursue environmentally destructive growth policies ad in-
finitum. The rest of this chapter will explore what these means are
and the basis for their support. There need not be the contradiction
between Third World welfare and the evolution of a sustainable
economy in the industrial nations--a contradiction just described in
the previous section. What is required, however, is a commitment
by the international community to the central principles of a new international economic order, the base of which Third World nations
are now attempting to form in various international forums. Limited growth advocates would do well to examine these principles carefully and determine how they are congruent with global resource interests. In this way, global solutions to "the predicament of mankind" would not ignore the needs of that part of mankind facing the
largest predicaments.

The call for a new international economic order emanated
from the final resolution of the Sixth Special Session of the United
Nations in May 1974.[22] Further clarification of what would constitute an acceptable new economic order has been elaborated at subsequent UN and UN-related sessions, and at various meetings of
nonaligned nations.[23] The demands of Third World countries for a
new economic order contain both old and new reform elements.
These are old reform proposals in the sense that they have been advocated by the Third World for at least ten years, primarily before
UN Conference on Trade and Development (UNCTAD) meetings.
They include demands for an improved trading position with the industrial nations (for example, industrial-nation extension of trade
preferences and the elimination of nontariff barriers to trade); demands for increased levels of development assistance; demands for
an increase in international raw-material commodity arrangements
by which the risks of free-market commodity exchange for Third
World suppliers could be moderated.

The above proposals are also old in the sense that they represent the heart of the 1960 Third World development strategy, namely: aspirations to become fully and equitably integrated into the existing international economic framework. The hope was to coax industrial nations into giving them a "better deal" in trade relationships because of their special needs. The result of such a strategy would be greater economic growth rates in the Third World and the bolstering of economic ties which bind North and South nations. The strategy was not particularly successful in the 1960s, however, because industrial nations could not be compelled to provide the "better deal" desired by the Third World. It was felt that preferences given to Third World suppliers could only come at the expense of domestic interests. Events of the 1970s, however, have altered the perspectives of the industrial nations. The strength and actions of the OPEC cartel have abruptly brought industrial-nation resource dependencies to light. As a result of this lever, Third World nations have been increasingly successful in bringing industrial-nation representatives to international forums to discuss their mutual interests. In recognition of their own dependency and vulnerability, industrial nations are likely over the coming decades to grudgingly make significant-- though incremental--economic concessions to Third World nations.

It is ironic that just as the industrial nations inch toward accepting many of the elements of the 1960 Third World development strategy, the Third World should be preparing to venture upon a new development strategy. One might say that Third World nations are now beginning to perceive their long-term development interests not in a "better deal" but in a "new deal." Further integration into the international system and the subsequent increased dependence upon industrial-nation economic performances and policy inherent in such integration is now being seriously questioned. On account of this, there are some new proposals within the Third World demand for a new international economic order which foretell a genuinely new development strategy. Two such proposals have raised particular controversy: First is the demand for full permanent sovereignty of every nation over its natural resources and all economic activities. The demand is aimed, of course, at ensuring full state control over MNC investment and operation in Third World countries. The Charter of Economic Rights and Duties of States passed by the United Nations in December 1974 stated: "Each State has the right to nationalize, expropriate or transfer ownership of foreign property. . . . In any case where the question of compensation gives rise to a controversy, it shall be settled under the domestic law of the nationalizing State."[24] Many industrial nations have fervently opposed granting states the right to establish levels of compensation for expropriated property, insisting that compensation be determined through

international law. The second proposal which is hotly disputed is
the Third World desire for a greater role and participation in functional international organizations. The industrial nations, on account of their abundant expertise and technical capabilities, have
played dominant roles in these organizations since their founding.
As such, the operation of these organizations has very much reflected the interests of the industrial nations. Recognizing this fact
and the need for organizations which will address the needs of Third
World nations directly, calls for a new international economic order
proclaim "the sovereign equality of States" and "full and effective
participation on the basis of equality of all countries in the solving
of world economic problems."[25] Particularly relevant examples of
the attempt to put this principle into practice are current Third
World efforts to gain a larger share of decision-making power in
the World Bank, the International Monetary Fund, and the proposed
International Seabed Authority.

Industrial nations have not been nearly as forthcoming in response to these new proposals as they have to the old, cited previously. This is not surprising, since what Third World nations are raising in their "new deal" is a fundamental shift of power--both in state-
state and MNC-state relationships. Industrial nations have found it
in their interests to accede to purely economic demands, since they
actually work to perpetuate the existing economic system and the
powers behind it. The newer proposals are more far-reaching in
their effects, however, and if accepted would create a new arena
for international relationships.

Perhaps the most fundamental element of the new international
economic order, and one which illustrates the Third World vision of
a "new deal" or new development strategy better than any other, has
thus far drawn scant notice. This is the call for national and collective Third World self-reliance efforts to bring about indigenous or
self-sustaining development. Unlike the 1960s development strategy
which emphasized Third World integration into the global economy,
the new strategy's hallmark is a giant step back from full participation in the international economy. Selective and limited participation
in the global economy is emphasized until such time that economic
relationships between nations become more symmetrical.

There are two main reasons why the theme of self-reliance
has not been emphasized more in discussions of the new international
economic order. First, it does not make any immediate demands
upon the industrial nations as do some of the other elements. Instead, it is a demand which each Third World government will have
to assess and implement in coordination with other Third World nations. Second, it is a strategy whose implementation can only evolve
gradually and whose ultimate realization rests far in the future. The

call for self-reliance, therefore, is not likely to gain sustained high-level international attention, even though it represents a significant and radical departure in policy. This new strategy, however, should be of particular interest to those who examine the possibility of an evolving steady state. The manifestation of increasing self-reliance will be a persistent, if not sensational, theme throughout the coming decades and as such will have considerable relevance to the formation of a global equilibrium. It will be useful now to highlight the nature of the call for self-reliance and to illustrate its relevance to limited growth futures.

The concept of self-reliance is supported in virtually all of the resolutions and documents associated with the new international economic order. The Cocoyoc Declaration which emanated from a jointly sponsored--UNCTAD and the United Nations Environment Program (UNEP)--symposium held in the fall of 1974 emphasized the necessity of national self-reliance while also giving approval to collective Third World self-reliance. The declaration states: "Self-reliance at national levels may also imply a temporary detachment from the present economic system; it is impossible to develop self-reliance through full participation in a system that perpetuates economic dependence."[26] The Program of Action on the Establishment of a New International Economic Order, drawn up at the Sixth Special Session of the United Nations, calls for the promotion of cooperation among Third World nations and urges the establishment and strengthening of economic integration at the "regional, subregional, and interregional levels."[27] In the resolution adopted at the Seventh Special Session of the United Nations, regional and subregional joint efforts were again emphasized and the UN secretary-general was urged to commission studies on suitable and effective methods of promoting scientific, economic, and technical cooperation among Third World nations.[28]

There may appear to be serious contradictions in the new international economic order because of the mixture of both new and old elements and strategies within it. This is true only if one neglects the various time frames and perspectives involved. Since Third World nations are so intimately connected and dependent upon the existing economic order, it would be folly for them to reject a "better deal" now that they possess the political clout to achieve it. Clearly, however, most Third World governments now perceive inhibiting limits to the extent of the gains they can make through the existing economic order. There is no commodity possessed by Third World nations, other than oil and natural gas, which can bring great wealth--regardless of new and favorable trade or commodity arrangements. In addition, exceedingly high and burdensome debt levels, as well as distorted economic growth patterns and inequities,

are seen as primary manifestations of continued devotion to the
1960s development strategy. The implementation of self-reliance
policies, therefore, is viewed as a means of gradually superseding
dependence upon the global international system and a way of providing the impetus toward self-sustaining growth. Though some
Third World nations can still make gains by "stacking the deck" of
the old game, long-term development for most nations requires
greater emphasis upon self-reliance. At least of equal importance,
self-reliant development would produce important psychic benefits.
This was emphasized in an article by I. G. Patel, deputy adminis-
trator of the United Nations Development Program: "While the developing countries proclaim the rhetoric of one world and advocate
the language of international cooperation, they want to develop primarily on their own steam and would not accept a position of prolonged dependence on others no matter what the cost in economic
terms."[29]

The growing acceptance of national and collective self-reliance
as a development strategy represents a victory for scholars who,
during the 1960s and 1970s, have championed what is termed "dependency" theory.[30] The dependency theory, originally propounded
by Latin American theorists, has always been popular in Third
World academic circles, but only recently has it gained adherents
within the governments of the Third World. In short, dependency
theorists posit that the international system is a dichotomy made up
of dominant or dynamic nations (the industrial nations) and subordinate or dependent nations (the Third World). Dependent nations
fail to develop through the functioning of the existing international
system, it is said, because their economies are structured to fulfill
only those roles and functions necessary for the perpetuation of
dominant-nation economies and their commercial enterprises. As
such, the dependent nations forego the opportunity to develop indigenous economic capacities. The consequences of this relationship
have been described by T. Dos Santos:

> The relation of interdependence between two or
> more economies, and between these and world
> trade, assumes the form of dependence when
> some countries (the dominant) can expand and
> give impulse to their own development, while
> other countries (the dependent) can only develop
> as a reflection of this expansion. This can have
> positive and/or negative effects on their immedi-
> ate development. In all cases, the basic situation
> of dependence leads to a global situation in depen-
> dent countries that situates them in backwardness
> and under the exploitation of the dominant countries.[31]

According to dependency theory, therefore, concessions to Third World nations on trade, aid, and commodity arrangements, while having beneficial short-term effects, will only postpone the necessary policies and programs to eliminate the primary cause of economic stagnation, which is dependence.

Rejection of dependence is based upon perceived political consequences as well as economic. The ability of leaders from highly dependent nations to pursue independent or autonomous policies is severely inhibited or circumscribed by the dependency relationship. Since breaking a highly dependent relationship means paying immediate economic costs, policy circumscription is a price that must often be paid to retain economic benefits. In other words, as a nation builds a stronger dependency relationship in order to capture greater economic rewards, the discretionary powers of that nation's leaders diminish. A dependent nation, therefore, in contrast to an independent nation, places itself very much under the control and influence of political forces beyond its borders. As one dependency theorist has noted, "the capacity to negotiate of a country thus penetrated becomes qualitatively different from that of the dominant country; that is the nub of dependency."[32]

Patel has written that the goal of Third World nations is not economic equality with the industrial nations but "psychological parity."[33] It is doubtful that under a continued dependency relationship Third World nations could achieve economic equality and is certain that they would never achieve psychological parity. A successful demonstration of national or collective self-reliance, on the other hand, could at least provide the desired psychic gains.

The goal of national self-reliance, no matter how much desired, probably is an unattainable target for nearly all Third World countries. Undoubtedly the most successful implementation of the self-reliance strategy today is demonstrated by China. Though China's self-help methods and philosophy have been admired and carefully examined by numerous Third World leaders, it is questionable whether these leaders can or desire to implement the sometimes harsh means necessary to achieve the coveted end. Even more fundamentally, Third World countries do not possess the vast resource base of China, which allows it to be independent of the world economy. A strategy of national self-reliance, therefore, would require a radical change in resource consumption patterns from traditional development models.

Prospects for a collective self-reliance system, based at regional and subregional levels, appear brighter though the ambitiousness of this task should also not be underestimated. It cannot occur overnight because the current economic relationship among Third World nations is relatively weak. Though total trade between Third

World countries has doubled between 1955 and 1971 (and manufac-
tured exports have tripled), trade with the industrial nations has
expanded at a faster pace.[34] Table 15.2 illustrates the level of
trade between Third World countries for a number of commodities.

The new development strategy, therefore, embodied in the
call for a new international economic order, represents a clear departure from traditional practices and will require persistent, long-
term devotion. The basic institutional framework for a long-term
endeavor already exists in regional trading blocs, regional economic banks, and UN economic commissions. Undoubtedly, new
regional and functional organizations will arise to facilitate collective efforts. What is ultimately required, however, is the formation of a carefully structured and specific program, setting targets
and dates, for the expanded utilization of incipient and future institutions. Political will to implement such a program must be demonstrated early if the program is to have future success. International
forums bringing Third World nations together thus far have not dealt
in great depth with the specifics of a collective self-reliance effort.
It is probable that within five years time a program with an appropriate timetable will be collectively developed and featured. It is
impossible to predict the exact nature of such a program, but some
of the general and major features of it can be foreseen with some
certainty. There will of course be an increasing amount of trade
between Third World nations, facilitated by preferential trade agreements. There are more fundamental measures which will be taken,
however, which deserve brief review:

A gradual and persistent shift to agricultural self-sufficiency
is likely to occur. Whereas many Third World nations now produce
one-crop agricultural commodities for export on rich agricultural
land, a diversification of agricultural crops will take place in the
future with a consequent deemphasis placed upon exportation. The
effort toward agricultural self-sufficiency will be undertaken in conjunction with a broader program of rural life enhancement, designed
to stem the population flow to the already overcrowded cities.

There will still be a strong movement toward industrialization,
but the role of the foreign-based MNC will diminish proportionately
to indigenous industrial development. In the Lima Declaration of
1975, Third World nations set the goal of manufacturing 25 percent
of the world's industrial product by the year 2000. This goal has
been repeated in subsequent forums. It is probable that industrialization in the Third World will not simply mirror the industrial processes currently utilized in the industrial nations. Important differences might include a smaller scale of plant operations, utilizing
labor-intensive technology, and an emphasis again upon producing for
one's own domestic consumption.

TABLE 15.2

Third World Exports and Inter-Third World Trade According to Commodity Group, 1955 and 1971

Commodity Group	Third World Exports (millions of U.S. $)		Percent Share of Third World Exports in Total World Exports		Third World Exports to Third World (millions of U.S. $)		Percent Share of Third World Exports to Third World in Total Third World Exports	
	1955	1971	1955	1971	1955	1971	1955	1971
Food, beverages, tobacco	7,720	13,120	42.0	29.0	1,460	2,150	18.9	16.4
Crude materials, excluding fuels; oils and fats	6,970	9,800	33.9	29.4	1,150	1,410	16.5	14.4
Mineral fuels and related materials	5,990	23,320	58.3	65.2	2,160	4,630	36.1	19.9
Chemicals	240	940	5.1	3.9	80	460	33.3	48.9
Machinery and transport equipment	125	1,440	0.7	1.6	92	640	73.6	44.4
Other manufactured goods	2,700	10,020	11.2	10.2	810	2,320	30.0	23.2
Total manufactures	3,065	12,400	6.7	5.8	982	3,420	32.0	27.6
Total	23,730	59,280	25.4	17.0	5,790	11,710	24.4	19.8
Percent of manufactures in total	12.9	20.9	--	--	17.0	29.2	--	--

Source: H. Jon Rosenbaum and William G. Tyler, "South-South Relations: The Economic and Political Content of Interactions among Developing Countries," International Organization, Winter 1975, p. 264.

In conjunction with the above, there will be increasing efforts to locate mineral processing facilities in Third World nations. The Dakar Declaration and Action Program of the Conference of Developing Countries on Raw Materials called for an end to the "triangular system of trade" whereby industrial nations serve as processing intermediaries in Third World mineral flows.[35] Control over the initial stages of mineral production can be less than fully satisfying if downstream activities are still controlled by MNCs.[36] Industrial and Third World nations may eventually perceive a congruence of interests on this matter as the environmental costs of locating processing facilities in industrial nations become increasingly intolerable.

There will be an expansion of joint or multilateral financing of development projects supported primarily by OPEC nations and other relatively well-off Third World nations. This financing could take place through existing institutions and organizations, or it might be part of new financial institutions which would be geared specifically to meet Third World needs. Multinational plans have already been developed for wholly owned Latin American MNCs to play an increasing role in regional development.

CONCLUSION

Global limited-growth advocates need not be blind to the conditions and needs of the Third World as they have in the past. There appears not to be a fundamental conflict of interest between slowed-growth advocates and Third World representatives, but a significant coincidence of interest when viewed over the long term and within a new international economic order. The focus of attention among advocates of limited growth should remain with the industrial nations since they are the prime source of environmental degradation and overconsumption of resources. There is no sufficient reason to believe, however, that a solution to the ills of industrial society today should also fit the ills afflicting the Third World.

The Third World movement toward national and collective self-reliance deserves support and further analysis regarding implementation. Ultimately, the disentanglement of the Third World from the global economic system would allow all nations to pursue more independent economic policies than they now do. This would have positive consequences for at least two reasons: (1) should policy makers in the industrial countries wish to place limits upon growth levels in their own societies, they would not be inhibited from doing so by concerns for Third World welfare; and the corollary being, (2) Third World nations would be able to develop independently and not as a reflection of industrial-nation growth rates. In sum, limited-growth advocates should recognize, as has Aurelio Peccei, that a responsible and stable world order is produced not only by living with resource means, but by producing a more satisfactory distribution of resources. These two factors are inseparable for world peace.

NOTES

1. Donella H. Meadows et al., The Limits to Growth (New York: Universe Books, 1972).

2. Galtung correctly forecasted that subsequent analyses would be disaggregated upon a regional basis, witness the Club of Rome-sponsored study by Mihajlo Mesarovic and Eduard Pestel, Mankind at the Turning Point (New York: E. P. Dutton, 1974). Galtung was justly critical of such attempts, stating: "The objection [to The Limits of Growth] is not in terms of horizontal variations from one region to another. . . . The real problem lies in the vertical differences between rich and poor." Johan Galtung, "The 'Limits to Growth' and Class Politics," Journal of Peace Research 1-2 (1973): 106.

3. Jay W. Forrester, World Dynamics (Cambridge, Mass.: Wright-Allen, 1971), p. 12.

4. Preston E. Cloud, Jr., as cited in Nazli Choucri and James P. Bennett, "Population, Resources, and Technology: Political Implications of the Environmental Crisis," International Organization, Spring 1972, p. 190.

5. Kenneth Boulding, "Fun and Games with the Gross National Product: The Role of Misleading Indicators in Social Policy," in The Environmental Crisis: Man's Struggle to Live with Himself, ed. Harold Helfrich (New Haven, Conn.: Yale University Press, 1970), p. 166.

6. Forrester, op. cit., pp. 12-13.

7. Meadows, op. cit., p. 179.

8. Geoffrey Barraclough, "The Haves and the Have Nots," New York Review of Books, May 13, 1976, p. 32.

9. Report of the Ad Hoc Committee of the Seventh Special Session, "Development and International Economic Cooperation," A/10232, September 24, 1975.

10. Garrett Hardin, "Lifeboat Ethics: The Case Against Helping the Poor," Psychology Today, September 1974, pp. 38 ff.

11. Wade Green, "Triage," New York Times Magazine, January 5, 1975, pp. 9 ff.

12. Galtung gives a review of such reaction in his article, op. cit.

13. Michael S. Teitelbaum, "Population and Development: Is a Consensus Possible?" Foreign Affairs, July 1974, p. 748.

14. Quoted in Galtung, op. cit., pp. 104-05.

15. Joao Augustro de Araujo Castro, "Environment and Development: The Cast of the Developing Countries," in World Eco-Crisis: International Organizations in Response, ed. David A. Kay and Eugene B. Skolnikoff (Madison: University of Wisconsin Press, 1972), p. 240.

16. Cited by Herman E. Daly, "Introduction," Toward a Steady-State Economy, ed. Herman E. Daly (San Francisco: W. H. Freeman, 1973), p. 13.

17. Ibid., pp. 11-12.

18. Robert O. Keohane and Joseph S. Nye, "World Politics and the International Economic System," in The Future of the International Economic Order: An Agenda for Research, ed. C. Fred Bergsten (Lexington, Mass.: Lexington Books, 1973), p. 155.

19. Johan Galtung, "A Structural Theory of Imperialism," Journal of Peace Research, no. 2 (1971), pp. 81-118.

20. Chile's Minister of Finance claims that each cent decline in the price of copper on the London Metal Exchange means an $18 million loss in Chile's earnings. Wall Street Journal, October 30, 1974, p. 40.

21. Barraclough, op. cit., p. 33, quotes an American commentator as saying: "The most important single thing the OECD countries can do for the Fourth World is to continue to prosper."

22. UN General Assembly Resolutions 3201 (S-VI) and 3202 (S-VI), May 1, 1974.

23. See, in particular, the Charter of Economic Rights and Duties of States (UN General Assembly Resolution 3281, December 12, 1974); The Dakar Declaration and Action Programme of the Conference of Developing Countries on Raw Materials (UN Doc. E/AC.62/6, April 15, 1975); The Cocoyoc Declaration (October 1974). All can be found in the volume Beyond Dependency, ed. Guy F. Erb and Valeriana Kallab (Washington, D.C.: Overseas Development Council, 1975).

24. Article 2, Chapter 2 reprinted in ibid., pp. 205-06.

25. Declaration on the Establishment of a New International Economic Order, reprinted in ibid., p. 187.

26. Reprinted in ibid., p. 174.

27. Ibid., pp. 195-96.

28. UN General Assembly Resolution 3362 (S-VII), document No. A/RES/3362, September 19, 1975, p. 14.

29. I. G. Patel, "What Do the Developing Countries Really Want?" United Nations Development Forum, September-October 1975, p. 11.

30. See Osvaldo Sunkel, "The Pattern of Latin American Dependence," in Latin America in the International Economy, ed. Victor L. Urquidi and Rosemary Thorp (New York: Halsted Press, 1973), pp. 3-34; Theotenio Dos Santos, "The Structure of Dependence," American Economic Review, May 1970, pp. 225-40; Galtung, "A Structural Theory of Imperialism," op. cit.

31. Quoted in Dale L. Johnson, "Dependence and the International System," in Dependence and Underdevelopment, ed. James D. Cockcroft et al. (New York: Anchor Books, 1972), pp. 71-72.

32. Sunkel, op. cit., p. 34.

33. Patel, op. cit., p. 11.

34. H. Jon Rosenbaum and William G. Tyler, "South-South Relations: The Economic and Political Content of Interactions among Developing Countries," International Organization, Winter 1975, p. 252.

35. Action Program, principle 1 (f), reprinted in Beyond Dependency, op. cit., p. 220.

36. Theodore H. Moran, "New Deal or Raw Deal in Raw Materials," Foreign Policy, Winter 1971-72, pp. 119-34.

16

SOCIALIST CONSTRUCTION
AND THE STEADY STATE:
SOME DIALECTICS IN
THE DEBATE
James A. Kuhlman

Debates about limits to growth realism and steady-state idealism in the international arena become more heated and more complicated as the model which one employs for economic analysis becomes more and more disaggregated. Put succinctly, different regions of the world have different opinions on the subject of growth.
Further, within each region potential for disagreement increases as
levels of development are more and more differentiated. The sponsorship of a selective growth policy, in accordance with the disaggregated, multiregional model of Mesarovic and Pestel, at the
fourth Club of Rome meeting in Philadelphia during the summer of
1976, was an objective acknowledgment of the political as well as
economic realities determining growth policy globally today.[1]
Without leaving the so-called developed world context itself,
a broad range of responses on growth issues may be discerned.
Comparisons both within and between the regions of Western and
Eastern Europe clearly illustrate some dilemmas. At the levels at
which policy-relevant economic issues must be met in the contemporary world--the global where the two Europes represent a considerable intrusive economic actor vis-a-vis almost every other region
on earth, the regional where the two regions represent significantly
distinctive and competitive types of socioeconomic systems, and the
national where the components of each respective community are
arrayed across a developed/developing continuum at a distance comparable to that found in the world at large--these two regions offer
relevant examples. Eastern Europe (including the Soviet Union, a
theoretical and substantive necessity in the opinion of this author) is
a region economically distinct from Western Europe. National units
within the former area are noticeably more differentiated on key economic indicators than are those systems in Western Europe.[2] Though

this particular point is an argumentative one in the eyes of many
East European economic analysts, the political cohesiveness of the
Eastern socialist community must be viewed in the perspective of
vast economic disparity, especially in terms of natural resources,
between the core of that region and the peripheral states.[3] Tables
16.1 and 16.2 serve to demonstrate some obvious dimensions of
these problems.

TABLE 16.1

EEC/CMEA Relative Development

EEC	CMEA	Level of GNP*
Ireland		4.5
	Bulgaria	7.0
	Hungary	12.4
	Rumania	15.2
Denmark		17.0
Belgium- Luxembourg		29.8
	Czechoslovakia	30.8
Netherlands		34.6
	East Germany	34.9
	Poland	44.2
Italy		100.4
United Kingdom		135.9
France		172.4
West Germany		196.9
	USSR	343.4

*In billions of dollars at 1971 world market prices. Socialist
countries' GNPs are figured by means of Material Product Balances
with allowance made for missing data on public and private service
sectors.
    Source: 1973 World Bank Atlas (Washington, D.C.: World
Bank, 1974).

    The purpose of this chapter is to outline some significant is-
sues in the consideration given to the growth debate by socialist systems. Socialist construction and capitalist profit motives suggest
generalized ideological dichotomies which have had differing consequences for the ecological crisis globally experienced today, which

are having unique considerations for planning under each national system type, and which will have distinct implications for regions within which one ideological orientation is predominant over the other. The focus here is upon East European countries in contrast to Western systems, in relation to each other as socialist coordinates, and with respect to the power typology found not only globally but in microcosm within Eastern Europe itself (superpower, middle power, small power). Regionally identified these rankings may appear as "core" and "periphery," namely the Soviet Union vis-a-vis the entire array of actors in the Soviet sphere of influence.[4]

TABLE 16.2

EEC/CMEA Relative Standard of Living

EEC	CMEA	Per Capita GNP*
	Rumania	740
	Bulgaria	820
	Hungary	1,200
	East Germany	1,350
	USSR	1,400
Ireland		1,510
Italy		1,860
	Czechoslovakia	2,120
	Poland	2,190
United Kingdom		2,430
Netherlands		2,620
Belgium		2,960
Luxembourg		3,130
West Germany		3,210
France		3,360
Denmark		3,430

*In U.S. dollars.
Source: 1973 World Bank Atlas (Washington, D.C.: World Bank, 1974).

One initial clue to the dynamics of the growth debate both between East and West and within the East is found in figures on productivity over the postwar years. During the period 1950-65 market-oriented economies generally outranked the command-oriented

systems in the East on indexes of growth in labor productivity (see
Table 16.3). Japan, Yugoslavia, and Italy appear at opposite ends
of a continuum with Czechoslovakia, Poland, and Hungary at the opposite extreme. Further, those East European economies which
rank near the top of the development ladder in their region, such as
Czechoslovakia, East Germany, and Poland, find themselves out-
distanced in growth of labor productivity by lesser developed systems such as Rumania and Bulgaria. It is specifically this dichotomy
(here one might begin to use the term dialectic instead) of development levels versus rates that complicates the normal assumptions
about who is on what side of the growth debate. For instance Poland,
which ranks highest in per capita GNP and second in GNP within the
socialist community, comes in last in the indicators on recent increases in labor productivity (see Figure 16.1).

TABLE 16.3

Productivity of Selected Eastern and Western Systems

Country	Gross Domestic Product per Unit of Labor*
Japan	6.6
Yugoslavia	5.4
Italy	5.2
Rumania	5.0
West Germany	4.4
Austria	4.1
East Germany	4.0
Hungary	3.2
Poland	2.6
Czechoslovakia	2.5

*Figures in average annual percent increase, 1950-65.
Source: "The Background to East-West Trade," European
Trends, Annual Reference Supplement (London: The Economist In-
telligence Unit, 1974).

The East European socialist view of the historical development and contemporary structure of the world economy sets the
framework within which attitudes toward the specific issue of a
steady state may be seen in their logical, or perhaps more accurately

FIGURE 16.1

Growth of Labor Productivity for CMEA Countries, 1966-72

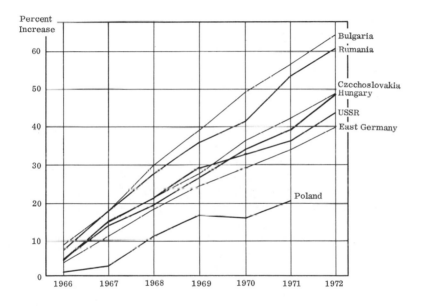

Source: "The Background to East-West Trade," European Trends, Annual Reference Supplement (London: The Economist Intelligence Unit, 1974).

rational, formulation. The Hungarian economic theorist Ferenc Kozma has devised a diagrammatic depiction of the development of the world economy through several "eras of advance": from backwardness, through structural revolution, to the scientific-technological revolution.[5] During the first era there is an absence of any form of mass production, no agroindustrial base capable of its own development, and not even early forms of accumulation. This scheme begins the stages in the development of the forces of production. During the backwardness era, countries may experience "archaic" and "handicraft" stages.

The era of structural revolution sees subsequent developments in forces of production from the "manufacture" stage, through the stage of "fundamental mechanization," to the stage of "complete mechanization." Research and development activities during this period, though the modernization process overall is still piecemeal, are characterized by sector-by-sector progression. The stage of complete mechanization provides a bridge into the final era, and with the stage of automation, systems enter the scientific-technological revolution.

Interestingly enough this developmental scheme accommodates the significantly accelerated advance of the forces of production since Marx, and therefore it incorporates theoretical stages beyond those accounted for in the original Marxist categorizations. Whereas the era of structural revolution is characterized by the rapid growth of vertical branches which produce the tools of labor, the scientific-technological era distinguishes itself by the process in which one country takes over existing technologies from another country. This distinction between structural revolution and the scientific-technological revolution serves to point out crucial aspects of the contemporary world economy. Spatial location in the contemporary world economic structure, as opposed to the traditional historical delineation of developmental types, differing levels of development, or differing stages of growth, may be more highly correlated with the outcomes on the current growth debate.

Through an international division of labor, countries at different stages of development affect the growth of each other. Some divergence between Soviet and East European conceptions of global economic developments are possible to discern within this framework (see Figure 16.2). The traditional categories of developed, developing, and socialist countries, generally adhered to in Soviet, Western, and even UN literature, are reformulated into more specific groupings. Developed countries are divided further into three entities: the United States which has experienced structural revolution, developed capitalist countries which have not completed that process, and certain Latin American and other systems which are well along the path to and through structural revolution.

FIGURE 16.2

Scheme of the Development of the World Economy, 1910-70

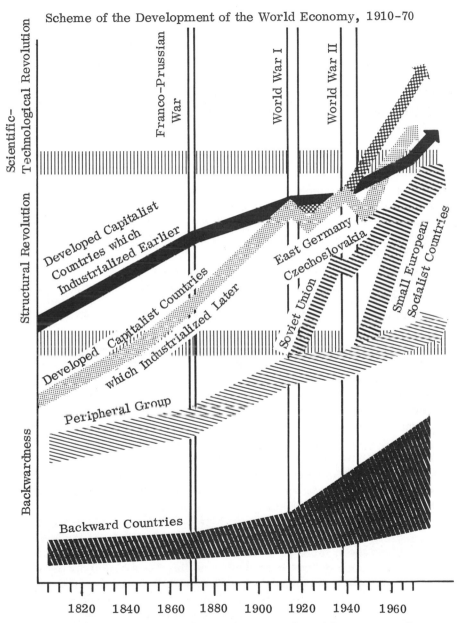

Source: F. Kozma, Some Theoretical Problems Regarding
Socialist Integration and the Levelling of Economic Development
(Budapest: Hungarian Scientific Council for World Economy, Trends
in World Economy No. 6, 1971), p. 29.

331

Socialist categories derived from this scheme fall into groups identified as nonindustrialized, the small but industrialized, and the Soviet Union. Many of the Cold War classifications built upon East-West ideological criteria must be rethought in the context of the present world economic system. Political logic might indicate that the Soviet-East European regional subsystem would be an economically identifiable unit of analysis for purposes of approaching the issue of growth spirals. But portions of that region politically circumscribed might better be put into a different economic context. Some of the small, nonindustrialized Eastern economies share motivations for modernization in much the same fashion as certain areas of the Third World.

Thus, several East European systems are caught in the development paradox plaguing nonsocialist, Third World systems. This is that in economic interaction between a developed and a nonindustrialized type of economy, the development of the former is quantitatively and qualitatively enhanced to a greater extent than is the case for the latter system. The historical advantages of the development process increase for the already developed country. [6]

Though the Hungarian thesis referred to above goes on to imply that the CMEA economies are developing within an integration context that is markedly less differentiated in development levels than is the case with its Western counterpart, and therefore is more likely to avoid the polarization projected by many pessimists in international economic forecasting, it does set the scene for a greater degree of differentiation in socialist economic policy according to national criteria. [7] If the implication for the Western developed countries is that diffusion of wealth and power is a necessary condition for the reversal of the continued and increasing development gap between have and have-not nations, then an equally pressing need is justified within the socialist community for raising itself by whatever means to the development levels of the Western, industrialized countries. Trade and technology flows from West to East are important means to this end.

At this point the popularized tenets of Marxism currently consigning the West and the United States in particular to decay and doom give way to more pragmatic concerns about the state of the domestic economies in the East. From the Eastern standpoint at least, the debate on detente in the West and in particular in the U.S. election forum evidences a political and economic ignorance of global realities (that is, necessities). There can be little doubt about the need for trade and technology transfer from West to East. As Table 16.4 below vividly demonstrates, even at grave political risk CMEA economies are indebted to Western sources. Attention must also be directed to the fact that these figures do not indicate the additional indebtedness of all CMEA members to the Soviet Union itself. One can easily see the point perplexing to East European decision makers: Countries such as Poland, even relatively well-off in resources and development within the socialist context, are bound by pressures for imports of goods in an international system within which they rarely operate at parity with quantity or quality of their own products on the one hand, and yet also find domestic constraints against raising prices and productivity on the other hand.

TABLE 16.4

Current CMEA Economic and Trade Indicators

	GNP	Trade Balance with West	Western Indebtedness
Bulgaria	13.0	−672	1.5
Czechoslovakia	37.4	−168	1.1
East Germany	40.4	−460	2.4
Hungary	19.5	−812	2.0
Poland	60.8	−2173	4.5
Rumania	34.6	−657	2.5

Note: GNP is figured in billions of dollars at 1974 world market prices. Trade balance with the West is given in millions of dollars at 1975 world market prices. Indebtedness to the West is given in billions of dollars at 1974 exchange rates.

Source: U.S. Trade Status with Socialist Countries, U.S. Department of Commerce, Bureau of East-West Trade, Office of East-West Policy and Planning, monthly reports, 1974/76.

Productivity is one obvious answer to the problem, but it is only one such corrective measure and a traditionally vexing one at that for socialist labor. Even the Soviet Union has balked at paying the increasingly expensive development bill for its East European partners, considerably altering the price structure for exportation of energy resources to CMEA members.

Systems that do not enjoy any measurable degree of resource independence, meaning all but Poland (with coal) and Rumania (with oil), feel the full impact of such a situation. The political and economic consequences of being underdeveloped and dependent within a natural (real) environment of regionalism are for the most part negative. Neither the Soviet Union nor its East European neighbors can afford the necessary technology for advanced development (services) or for access to natural resources (energy) without a commitment to increased productivity.

The global disadvantages faced by developing East European systems are openly acknowledged by their own theorists. Competitiveness in world markets is a goal of every socialist system, and because of the economic liability factor in Soviet-East European relations, increased exportation to the West is an objective shared by all concerned. While the usual protestations are voiced against the unstable influences of "fluctuations on the capitalist market" and calls for "qualitatively new and deeper processes of integration among the socialist countries" are invoked as an antidote, the conclusions are clear:

> However, since we have to sell a sizable propor-
> tion of our exports on capitalist markets, we must
> in the future attain a world standard of modern-
> ness to be able to take flexible advantage of their
> swings and to switch part of domestic output to the
> export trade. This will require a thorough moderni-
> zation of existing capacities.[8]

Both ideologically and economically the socialist approach to growth is preordained by population and productivity figures for the globe as a whole. If the global economic goal were to take from each region according to its population abilities and to give to each region according to its population needs, then the imbalances evidenced in the statistics found in the literature on growth problems would be even more glaring. The general Marxian formulation of taking from each according to his abilities and giving to each according to his needs must be ideologically embarrassing to the socialist world, in particular in the global context. Accountability in the international system gives poor marks to the socialist systems, as evidenced in Table 16.5.

The economic necessities and ideological motivation for rapid growth in socialist economies may be seen, as this chapter argued at the outset, increasingly evident as one lowers the level of analysis employed. What remains true in a political and economic sense when one views the socialist community as a unit of analysis in the global body politic becomes near doctrine when one sees the situations confronted by each socialist system, especially in relation to the Soviet core of the region (see Table 16.6).[9]

The resource dependence of East European countries upon the Soviet Union, Soviet interest in shifting some of the development

TABLE 16.5

Shares of Global Population and Production

	Percent Population	Percent Production
United States	5.4	25.8
Other developed noncommunist	12.4	38.5
USSR	6.3	12.5
Other developed communist	2.7	4.6
India	14.6	2.1
Other developing noncommunist	34.0	12.1
China	22.9	3.6
Other developing communist	1.7	.8
	100.0	100.0

Notes: 1973 population totalled 3,933 million. 1973 GNP totalled $4,998 billion.
Source: Department of State data.

TABLE 16.6

Soviet/East European Shares of Regional Population
and Production

	Soviet Union	Other Eastern Europe[a]
Population (1972, millions)	248	107
GNP[b]	549	206
Production:		
Coal (million metric tons)	544	366
Crude steel (million metric tons)	126	45
Electric power (billion KWH)	858	284
Crude petroleum (million metric tons)	394	19
Primary aluminum (thousand metric tons)	1,800	390
Motor vehicles (thousands)	1,379	610
Passenger cars	730	420
Commercial vehicles	649	190

[a]Includes Albania, Bulgaria, Czechoslovakia, East Germany, Hungary, Poland, and Rumania.
[b]1972 GNP in billions of dollars at 1972 rates according to Gilbert-Kravis method. See "The Planetary Product in 1972: Systems in Disarray," RESS-46, September 20, 1973, unclassified, for methodology.
Source: Department of State data.

burden of Eastern Europe onto Western systems, the Soviets' own technology deficiencies, East European objectives of sovereignty, and the Soviet insistence on continuing hegemony (sovereignty balanced by international duties of socialist countries, as outlined in the so-called Brezhnev doctrine) in East European affairs all point to a complicated and inconsistent pattern for socialist policy on metaissues such as socialist construction and the steady state. The disarray represented by nations skewed across a distribution of resources, development, and population, with the array different on each dimension, may be discerned again regionally in such areas as Eastern Europe. The result is an inevitable display of ideological acrobatics: accusations of capitalist doom along with acceptance (dependence?) of technology transfer, protestations of trade bloc discrimination from the West along with announcements of comprehensive programs for socialist integration in the East, and formulations for redistribution of wealth within countries alongside of implementation of only selective support for developing, even communist developing, countries in the global arena.

Where one finds congruence between ideology and behavior in policy is on the question of socialist construction. The hard reality of global, regional, and national economics for socialist systems determines that productivity is the number-one problem, number-one necessity, and number-one objective. While the socialist ethic within each East European country may evidence progress on issues such as equitable distribution of wealth and regional (subnational) equality, the growth debate outside that framework dictates that growth be the principal policy. East European countries must pursue it, economically and politically, in relation to the Soviet Union. The USSR in turn must continue to pursue growth in the context of its external political and economic relations in the role of superpower and bloc member.

Perhaps at best one might view the discrepancies between socialist construction realism and the growth-related idealism as at least possibilities for breaking down barriers between ideologically opposed systems. Continued growth and productivity seem to be putting demands on both market and command economies to interact. Innovation on the part of each type of system would seem to be logical and inevitable.[10]

NOTES

1. See the "Second Report to the Club of Rome" or Mihajlo Mesarovic and Eduard Pestel, Mankind at the Turning Point (New York: E. P. Dutton, 1974). In addition to the report's major

revision of the global model put forth by The Limits to Growth author
Jay Forrester, in which ten regions replaced a single system approach, Mesarovic and Pestel stressed that notions of self-reliance
(such as those recently espoused under the guise of "Project Independence" by several U.S. politicians) are economically infeasible.

2. See James A. Kuhlman, "Eastern Europe," in World Politics: An Introduction, ed. James N. Rosenau, Kenneth W. Thompson,
and Gavin Boyd (New York: The Free Press, 1976), especially pages
450-53.

3. See especially the essays by Thad P. Alton, "Economic
Structure and Growth in Eastern Europe," J. G. Polach, "The De-
velopment of Energy in East Europe," Laszlo Czirjak, "Industrial
Structure, Growth, and Productivity in Eastern Europe," and Gregor
Lazarcik, "Growth of Output, Expenses, and Gross and Net Product
in East European Agriculture," found in Economic Developments in
Countries of Eastern Europe (Washington, D.C.: Subcommittee on
Foreign Economic Policy, Joint Economic Committee, 91st Con-
gress, U.S. Government Printing Office, 1970).

4. For further explication of these regional concepts, see
Louis J. Cantori and Steven L. Spiegel, The International Politics
of Regions: A Comparative Approach (Englewood Cliffs, N.J.:
Prentice-Hall, 1970).

5. See Ferenc Kozma, "Some Theoretical Problems Regarding
Socialist Integration and the Levelling of Economic Development,"
Trends in World Economy, no. 6 (1971) (Budapest: Hungarian Scien-
tific Council for World Economy).

6. See Bela Kadar, "Recent Trends in the Industrialization of
the Developing Countries and the Global Strategy of the Leading Capitalist Countries," Trends in World Economy, no. 14 (1974) (Budapest:
Hungarian Scientific Council for World Economy).

7. See Mihaly Simai, "Economic Growth and The Development
Level," Trends in World Economy, no. 7 (1972) (Budapest: Hungarian Scientific Council for World Economy).

8. Mieczyslaw Nasilowski, "Development Options Till 2000,"
Polish Perspectives 18, no. 1 (January 1975): 11-21; see p. 17.

9. For an interesting and objective treatment of the problems
faced by "underdeveloped" members of regional economic associa-
tions, see Sandor Ausch, Theory and Practice of CMEA Cooperation
(Budapest: Akademiai Kiado, 1972).

10. Since steady-state objectives, irrespective of ecological
conscience, seem to be a secondary concern to developed/developing
and East/West groups alike, whatever may be achieved in the area
of technology transfer could well be the means by which real economic objectives of all parties (East-West, North-South) could be

satisfied without overt political objections. For an interesting inventory of research possibilities on this subject, see Robert W. Campbell and Paul Marer, eds., East-West Trade & Technology Transfer: An Agenda of Research Needs (Bloomington: International Development Research Center, Indiana University, 1974).

ABOUT THE EDITOR AND CONTRIBUTORS

DENNIS CLARK PIRAGES is Associate Professor of Government and Politics and Director of the Program in Technology, Resources, and Sustainable Growth at the University of Maryland. He is a futurist with interdisciplinary training in the social and natural sciences. He is editor or author of six books and many chapters and articles in scholarly journals and collections. His most recent books include Ark II: Social Response to Environmental Imperatives (with Paul Ehrlich), Managing Political Conflict, and Global Ecopolitics. He is presently doing research on sustainable modernization in less developed countries.

EARL COOK is Professor of Geography and Geology, and Dean of Geosciences, Texas A&M University. He has published articles on energy flow through industrial society, ionizing radiation, and limits to exploitation of nonrenewable resources. He is the author of Man, Energy, Society.

JOHN P. HOLDREN is Associate Professor in the Energy and Resources Program at the University of California, Berkeley, holding the first campus-wide interdisciplinary professorship at that institution. An engineer and plasma physicist by training, he is a consultant to the Magnetic Fusion Energy Division of the Lawrence Livermore Laboratory, the Energy and Environment Division of the Lawrence Berkeley Laboratory, and the Energy Project of the International Institute for Applied Systems Analysis. He has coauthored three books on energy and environmental science, has co-edited three others, and has published some 60 papers, articles, and chapters on energy technology and policy, global environmental problems, and human population.

NAZLI CHOUCRI is Associate Professor of Political Science at the Massachusetts Institute of Technology. She has written extensively on resource issues in international relations. She is co-author of Nations in Conflict: National Growth and International Violence, and author of Population Dynamics and International Relations: Propositions, Insights and Evidence, and has recently completed a book on energy problems entitled International Politics of Energy Interdependence: The Case of Petroleum.

HERMAN E. DALY is currently Professor of Economics at Louisiana State University. In addition to L.S.U., Dr. Daly has taught at Vanderbilt University, and was Ford Foundation Visiting Professor at the University of Ceará in Brazil during 1967-68. In 1970 he was a Research Associate at Yale University. He is interested in economic development, demographic economics, and environmental questions. He is editor of a recent volume on environmental economics entitled Toward a Steady-State Economy.

EDWARD F. RENSHAW is a Professor of Economics at the State University of New York at Albany. He is the author of numerous books and articles including The End of Progress which was published by the Duxbury Press in 1976 and a paper on "Productivity," which was published in 1976 by the U.S. Joint Economic Committee in their compendium, U.S. Economic Growth from 1976 to 1986: Prospects, Problems and Patterns.

WILLIAM OPHULS is a writer and lecturer. He received his doctorate in political science from Yale University in 1973. He has been a Foreign Service Officer with the Department of State serving in Abidjan, the Ivory Coast, and Japan. He is the author of Ecology and the Politics of Scarcity.

MICHAEL E. KRAFT is a political scientist currently affiliated with the Center for Demography and Ecology at the University of Wisconsin-Madison. He received his Ph.D. from Yale University in 1973 and for a number of years taught in the Department of Political Science at Vassar College. He has published numerous articles on environmental politics, and is coediting a symposium on population policy for the Policy Studies Journal.

DAVIS B. BOBROW is Professor and Chairman of the Department of Government and Politics at the University of Maryland. His major fields of interest are in international affairs, the design of public institutions, and the evaluation of public policy. In addition to numerous books and articles, he has served as a member of the National Academy of Sciences - National Research Council Committee on Energy and the Environment.

PETER G. STILLMAN is at present an Assistant Professor at Vassar College, where he teaches political philosophy and modern political thought. He has written extensively about environmental issues, including a paper on ecological political theory, co-authored with Michael E. Kraft, delivered at the 1973 Annual Meeting of the American Political Science Association and a review essay, also co-authored with Kraft, on recent books in environmental politics, in Polity (Spring 1976). In addition, he has published articles in books and journals including Polity and The American Political Science Review.

DAVID VOGEL is Assistant Professor of Business Administration, University of California, Berkeley. He is the author of Ethics and Profits: The Crisis of Confidence in American Business (with Leonard Silk) and of a forthcoming study of nongovernmental political pressures on business corporations in the United States. He has served as a consultant to the Council on Foreign Relations and has published articles on aspects of business-society relations in several academic and popular periodicals.

LEE RAINWATER is Professor of Sociology at Harvard University and Faculty Associate of The Joint Center of Urban Studies of MIT and Harvard. His research interests center on social stratification and family behavior in the United States and Europe. He is the author of What Money Buys: Inequality and the Social Meanings of Income and Behind Ghetto Walls: Black Family Life in a Federal Slum.

JOHN PLATT is a research scientist at the Mental Health Research Institute of the University of Michigan. His collections of essays on the interactions of science and society include The Excitement of Science, The Step to Man, and Perception and Change. He is currently completing a book, On Social Transformation, on future global prospects and strategies for change.

KOICHI HAMADA is Assistant Professor of Economics, University of Tokyo. He has published widely in the fields of economic theory, mathematical economics, international economic relations and law and economics in the American Economic Review and other leading journals.

VICTOR D. LIPPIT is Assistant Professor of Economics, University of California, Riverside. His published articles include essays on economic planning in Japan and the steady-state economy, as well as numerous essays on Chinese economic development. He is the author of Land Reform and Economic Development in China: A Study of Institutional Change and Development Finance.

JACK N. BARKENBUS is a Political Scientist with the Institute for Energy Analysis, Oak Ridge Associated Universities, Oak Ridge, Tennessee. He has authored several articles on the politics of deep

341

seabed resource allocation and is working on a book, entitled <u>Deep Seabed Resources: Politics and Technology</u>, to be published by the Free Press. He is currently conducting research on the expansion of the global nuclear energy system and its implications for nuclear weapons proliferation.

JAMES A. KUHLMAN is an Associate Professor of Government and International Studies at the University of South Carolina. He has edited and contributed essays to <u>The Future of Inter-Block Relations in Europe</u>, <u>Changing European Relations</u>, <u>America and European Security</u>, and <u>The Foreign Policies of Eastern Europe</u> among other volumes.

THE EFFECTS OF URBAN GROWTH: A Population
Impact Analysis
>Richard P. Appelbaum,
>Jennifer Bigelow, Henry P.
>Kramer, Harvey L. Molotch,
>and Paul M. Relis

INNOVATIONS FOR FUTURE CITIES
>edited by Gideon Golany

PERSPECTIVES ON U.S. ENERGY POLICY:
A Critique of Regulation
>edited by Edward J. Mitchell

*PLANNING ALTERNATIVE WORLD FUTURES:
Values, Methods, and Models
>edited by Louis Rene Beres
>and Harry R. Targ

QUALITY OF LIFE INDICATORS IN U.S. METROPOLITAN
AREAS: A Statistical Analysis
>Ben-Chieh Liu

URBAN NONGROWTH: City Planning for People
>Earl Finkler, William J. Toner,
>and Frank J. Popper

*THE UNITED STATES AND WORLD DEVELOPMENT:
Agenda for Action, 1975
>James W. Howe and the Staff
>of the Overseas Development
>Council

* Also available in paperback as a PSS Student Edition.